GLOBAL HISTORY, GLOBALLY

GLOBAL HISTORY, GLOBALLY

RESEARCH AND PRACTICE AROUND THE WORLD

Edited by Sven Beckert and Dominic Sachsenmaier

Bloomsbury Academic
An imprint of Bloomsbury Publishing Plc

BLOOMSBURY
LONDON · OXFORD · NEW YORK · NEW DELHI · SYDNEY

Bloomsbury Academic
An imprint of Bloomsbury Publishing Plc

50 Bedford Square
London
WC1B 3DP
UK

1385 Broadway
New York
NY 10018
USA

www.bloomsbury.com

BLOOMSBURY and the Diana logo are trademarks of Bloomsbury Publishing Plc

First published 2018

© Sven Beckert, Dominic Sachsenmaier and Contributors, 2018

All rights reserved. No part of this publication may be reproduced or transmitted in any form or by any means, electronic or mechanical, including photocopying, recording, or any information storage or retrieval system, without prior permission in writing from the publishers.

No responsibility for loss caused to any individual or organization acting on or refraining from action as a result of the material in this publication can be accepted by Bloomsbury or the author.

British Library Cataloguing-in-Publication Data
A catalogue record for this book is available from the British Library.

ISBN: HB: 978-1-3500-3635-2
PB: 978-1-3500-3634-5
ePDF: 978-1-3500-3637-6
eBook: 978-1-3500-3636-9

Library of Congress Cataloging-in-Publication Data
A catalog record for this book is available from the Library of Congress.

Cover design by Holly Bell
Cover image © Ralph Morse / Getty Images

Typeset by Integra Software Services Pvt. Ltd.

To find out more about our authors and books visit www.bloomsbury.com. Here you will find extracts, author interviews, details of forthcoming events and the option to sign up for our newsletters.

CONTENTS

Acknowledgments   vii

Notes on Contributors   ix

Introduction
Sven Beckert and Dominic Sachsenmaier   1

Part I: Regions   19

1   Global History in (Northwestern) Europe: Explorations and Debates
Gareth Austin   21

2   Re-presenting Asia on the Global Stage: The Rise of Global History in East Asia
Q. Edward Wang   45

3   Latin America and the Caribbean: Traditions of Global History
Rafael Marquese and João Paulo Pimenta   67

4   African History and Global History: Revisiting Paradigms
Omar Gueye   83

5   Deconstructing Imperial and National Narratives in Turkey and the Arab Middle East
Selçuk Esenbel and Meltem Toksöz   109

6   The World History Project: Global History in the North American Context
Jerry H. Bentley   127

Part II: Central Themes in Global History   143

7   New Perspectives on Workers and the History of Work: Global Labor History
Andreas Eckert and Marcel van der Linden   145

Contents

8 Scale, Scope and Scholarship: Regional Practices and Global Economic Histories
   Kenneth Pomeranz   163

9 Global Histories of Migration(s)
   Amit Kumar Mishra   195

10 The Challenge of the Global in Intellectual History
   Dominic Sachsenmaier and Andrew Sartori   215

Part III: Problems in the Practice of Global History   233

11 Writing World History in Africa: Opportunities, Constraints and Challenges
   David Simo   235

12 World History, Nationally: How Has the National Appropriated the Transnational in East Asian Historiography?
   Jie-Hyun Lim   251

13 Writing the Globe from the Edges: Approaches to the Making of Global History in Australia
   Marnie Hughes-Warrington   269

14 Japanese Efforts to Overcome Eurocentric Paradigms in the Study of Global History
   Shigeru Akita   283

   Index   295

ACKNOWLEDGMENTS
Sven Beckert and Dominic Sachsenmaier

This book collects the writings of authors from around the world on global history, authors who connect to local debates as much as to global ones. It is driven by the idea that if global history is to flourish and deliver on its promises, global debates about its methods, questions and theoretical considerations are urgent. In that sense, it is an exercise in global intellectual history.

Global History, Globally draws on discussions that emerged from conferences and workshops bringing together scholars from all continents. The purpose of these meetings was to provide a forum for leading global historians to consider the state of the field. During these gatherings, we discussed the recent rise of global history as a space for academic innovation and the multifaceted research landscape that emerged from it—a research landscape that had never before been properly assessed on a global level. We debated developments in various world regions and reflected upon how local particularities and transnational methodologies intersected with one another. The conferences also considered the impact of politics and cultural identities on the practices of global history.

This collection of essays grew out of these conversations, and we want to thank all scholars who participated in these meetings.

Without the support of many institutions and people we could not have embarked upon this project. The inaugural conference, "Global History, Globally" was held in 2008 at Harvard University, cosponsored by the Harvard's Weatherhead Center for International Affairs and the Duke Center for International Studies. In 2010, a conference focusing on "Global History in East Asia" took place at Duke University, where it was supported by the Duke Asian Pacific Studies Institute and the Duke Transcultural Humanities Committee. "Global Dialogues on Global History" was the title of the next meeting; it convened at the Freiburg Institute of Advanced Studies and was chiefly funded by the Volkswagen Foundation. A year later, the international research center *re:work. Work and Human Life Cycle in Global History* hosted the conference "Global History in a Worldwide Dialogue," financed by the German National Research Foundation. We thank these institutions for their generosity and their courage in supporting a project that broke with many conventions within our discipline.

Without a group of exceptionally dedicated authors this volume could not have come into being, and we want to thank you for all the time, passion and energy that you invested in this project. When the book went into production, a remarkable group of people helped move the project along, especially our editor at Bloomsbury, Emma Goode, and Manikandan Kuppan, who produced the volume. A big thank you also

Acknowledgments

to Martha Schulman for working through these essays. Along the way we also enjoyed the dedicated support from many of our students, especially Joane Chaker and Holger Droessler in Cambridge, who coordinated many of our efforts, Laura Wollenweber in Berlin, and Nastassja Salewski, Li Can and Christoph Zimmer in Göttingen. Aaron Bekemeyer ably translated one of the volume's essays, while he, along with Rachel Steely, Samantha Payne, and Joane Chaker, provided important support to some of its authors. Thank you also to the Weatherhead Initiative on Global History (WIGH) and Jessica Barnard, as well as to the University of Göttingen, for their support.

At a moment when nationalism is ascendant in many countries, we offer this volume as a contribution to the history—and politics—of our times.

NOTES ON CONTRIBUTORS

Shigeru Akita is Professor of Global History in the Department of World History and the Director of Division of Global History Studies, Open and Transdisciplinary Research Initiative (OTRI), at Osaka University, Japan. He is an expert on the British Empire, the history of international relations in Asia and global history. He is currently the President of Asian Association of World Historians (AAWH), an international research association for the promotion of Global/World History Studies in the Asia-Pacific region. His main publications include *International Order of Asia and the British Empire* (in Japanese, 2003), *The History of the British Empire from Asian Perspectives* (in Japanese, 2012) and *From Empires to Development Aid* (in Japanese, 2017). He edited several books with international scholars, including *Gentlemanly Capitalism, Imperialism and Global History* (2002) and (with Gerold Krozewski and Shoich Watanabe) *The Transformation of the International Order of Asia: Cold War, Decolonization and the Colombo Plan* (2014).

Gareth Austin is Professor of Economic History at Cambridge University. His publications include *Labour, Land and Capital in Ghana: From Slavery to Free Labour in Asante, 1807–1956* (2005), *Labour-Intensive Industrialization in Global History* (ed. with K. Sugihara, 2013) and *Economic Development and Environmental History in the Anthropocene: Perspectives on Asia and Africa* (2017). His work has appeared in many journals, including *Business History Review*, *Economic History Review* and the *Journal of African History*. After teaching at a *harambee* school in Kenya, he took a BA at Cambridge and PhD at Birmingham. A former president of the European Network in Universal and Global History (ENIUGH), his past employers include the University of Ghana, the London School of Economics and the Graduate Institute of International and Development Studies, Geneva.

Sven Beckert is Laird Bell Professor of American History at Harvard University. Beckert's research and teaching focus on the history of the United States in the nineteenth century, with a particular emphasis on the history of capitalism, including its economic, social, political and transnational dimensions. His publications have concentrated on the nineteenth-century American bourgeoisie, on labor, on democracy and, in recent years, on the global history of capitalism. His latest book, *Empire of Cotton: A Global History*, won the Bancroft Prize, the Premio Cherasco and was a finalist for the Pulitzer. The *New York Times* chose it as one of the ten best books of 2015. Beckert was a Guggenheim Fellow, a fellow of the ACLS and won the Bessel Prize of the Alexander von Humboldt Foundation. He cochairs the Weatherhead Initiative on Global History at Harvard University and coedits a series of books at Princeton University Press on "America in the World."

Notes on Contributors

Jerry H. Bentley† was Professor of History at the University of Hawai'i at Manoa and editor of the *Journal of World History*. He wrote extensively on the cultural history of early-modern Europe and on cross-cultural interactions and exchanges in world history. His research on the religious, moral and political writings of the Renaissance led to the publication of *Humanists and Holy Writ: New Testament Scholarship in the Renaissance* (1983) and *Politics and Culture in Renaissance Naples* (1987). His book *Old World Encounters: Cross-Cultural Contact and Exchange in Pre-Modern Times* (1993) studies processes of cultural exchange and religious conversion before modern times. He also wrote on the periodization of world history and on historiographical issues relating to world history. Dr. Bentley taught courses in world history, early-modern history and the expansion of Europe.

Andreas Eckert is Professor of African History at Humboldt University in Berlin, Germany. Since 2009 he is also Director of the International Research Center "Work and Human Life Course in Global History," funded by the German Federal Ministry for Education and Research. He widely published on nineteenth- and twentieth-century African history, colonialism, labor and global history and served for many years as editor of the *Journal of African History*. Eckert also regularly publishes for German newspapers like the *Frankfurter Allgemeine Zeitung* and *Die Zeit*. His most recent book is *Global Histories of Work*, (ed.), 2016. He is currently working on A *Short History of Colonialism*, to be published by Princeton University Press.

Selçuk Esenbel is Professor (emeritus) of History at Bogazici University's Department of History in Istanbul. She is the founding director and presently the academic coordinator of the Asian Studies Center and the Master of Arts in Asian Studies. Her recent publications include *Japan on the Silk Road: Encounters and Perspectives of Politics and Culture in Eurasia*, Brill, forthcoming 2018; *Japan, Turkey, and the World of Islam*, Brill, 2011; and "Japan's Global Claim to Asia and the World of Islam: Transnational Nationalism and World Power 1900-1945," *The American Historical Review* (October 2004). Her publications in Turkish include *Turkiye'de Cin'i Duşunmek* (*Thinking of China in Turkey*), 2013, and *Turkiye'de Japonya Calişmalari II* (*Japanese Studies in Turkey*), 2015, by Bogazici University Press. Major awards include: Alexander von Humboldt Foundation Georg Forster Research Award, 2013; Order of the Rising Sun; Special Prize of the Japanese Minister of Foreign Affairs; and Special Award for Japanese Studies of the Japan Foundation, 2007.

Omar Gueye, Professor of History at Cheikh Anta Diop University, Dakar, works on Labor and Social History. He holds a PhD in Social History from the University of Amsterdam, a PhD in Modern and Contemporary History from Cheikh Anta Diop University and an MBA in Management of Cultural Heritage from the Université Internationale Francophone Léopold Sédar Senghor in Alexandria. Besides other work experiences and various organizational memberships, he was a Fulbright Scholar at the University of Michigan, a fellow at WIGH-Harvard and a fellow at IEA-Paris. He dedicated almost all his works to African labor and social history. Omar Gueye is a contributor to many jointly authored books, and he has recently published three books: *Sénégal: Histoire du mouvement syndical, la marche vers le Code du Travail*, 2012; *Sanokho ou le métier du rire*, 2013; and *Mai 1968 au Sénégal. Senghor face aux étudiants et au mouvement syndical*, 2017.

Marnie Hughes-Warrington is Deputy Vice-Chancellor (Academic) at the Australian National University in Canberra. Prior to taking up this position in 2012, she was Pro-Vice Chancellor (Learning and Teaching) at Monash University. She is the author of six books, including *Fifty Key Thinkers on History* (now in its third edition); *"How Good an Historian Shall I Be?": R. G. Collingwood, the Historical Imagination and Education* (2003); History *Goes to the Movies* (2007); and *Revisionist Histories* (2013). Her newest book project is on the role that Aristotle's metaphysics has played in shaping the discipline of history through time.

Jie Hyun Lim is Professor of Transnational History and founding director of the Critical Global Studies Institute at Sogang University in Seoul. In 2010, he initiated the "Flying University of Transnational Humanities" as a transnational academic venture and serves as the president of the "Network of Global and World History Organizations," as a board member of CISH and as a trustee of the Toynbee Prize Foundation. He held visiting appointments at Cracow Pedagogical University, Warsaw University, the Harvard-Yenching Institute, Nichibunken, EHESS, Paris II University and Wissenschaftskolleg zu Berlin. Most recently, he published five volumes of the Palgrave series of *Mass Dictatorship in the 20th Century* (as the series editor). Relevant publications in the field of global history include "Historicizing the World in East Asia," "Second World War in the Global Memory Space," "A Postcolonial reading of German Sonderweg" and "Mass Dictatorship as a Transnational Formation of Modernity." He presently does research on a transnational history of "victimhood nationalism," covering post–Second World War Korea, Japan, Poland, Israel and Germany.

Marcel van der Linden is Senior Fellow and former Research Director of the International Institute of Social History, Professor of Social Movement History at the University of Amsterdam and President of the International Social History Association. He has published extensively on labor and working-class history and on the history of ideas. His books include *Workers of the World. Essays Toward a Global Labor History* (Leiden and Boston: Brill, 2008; paperback edition Chicago: Haymarket, 2010; Brazilian, German and Turkish translations); *Western Marxism and the Soviet Union. A Survey of Critical Theories and Debates* (Leiden and Boston: Brill, 2007; Chinese and Korean translations); and *Capitalism. The Reemergence of a Historical Concept* (London: Bloomsbury Academic, 2016), edited with Jürgen Kocka.

Rafael Marquese, PhD in History (University of São Paulo, 2001), is Professor in the Department of History at the University of São Paulo. With João Paulo Pimenta, he coordinates the Laboratório de Estudos Sobre o Brasil e o Sistema Mundial (LabMundi). He is the author of *Administração & Escravidão: Ideias sobre a gestão da agricultura* *escravista brasileira* (1999); *Feitores do Corpo, Missionários da Mente: Senhores, letrados e o controle dos escravos nas Américas, 1660–1860* (2004); *Slavery and Politics: Brazil and Cuba, 1790–1850* (coauthored with Tâmis Parron and Márcia Berbel, 2016); and *Escravidão e Capitalismo Histórico no Século XIX: Brasil, Cuba, Estados Unidos* (coedited with Ricardo Salles, 2016). He is currently working on a book project on the history of slavery and the global coffee economy between 1760 and 1930.

Amit Kumar Mishra teaches at the Centre for Study of Indian Diaspora, University of Hyderabad, India. His research and publications engage with Indian labor diaspora, causes and consequences of labor mobility, histories of labor intermediation and migration from the perspectives of state–society relations. More recently he is trying to reread the movement of Indian indentured laborers during the age of empire from the perspectives of global history. He has held fellowships at National University of Singapore and Weatherhead Initiative on Global History, Harvard University. He has also served as consultant to the Trust and Justice Commission, Mauritius.

João Paulo Pimenta holds a PhD in History (Universidade de São Paulo, 2004). He is "Livre-Docente" Professor in History of Colonial Brazil (2012) and Professor at the History Department of Universidade de São Paulo. He was a visiting professor at El Colégio de México (2008, 2016), Universitat Jaume I, Spain (2010), Pontifícia Universidad Católica de Chile (2013), Universidad de la República, Uruguay (2015) and Universidad Andina Simón Bolívar, Ecuador (2015, 2016). He mainly works on the history of eighteenth and nineteenth centuries, with a focus on Brazil and its relationships with Spanish America. He is particularly interested in the national question and collective identities, and the history of historical times in Brazil and the Western World. He is the author of *Brasil y las independências de Hispanoamerica* (Castelón: Universitat Jaume I, 2007) and *Estado y nación hacia el final de los imperios ibéricos* (Buenos Aires: Sudamericana, 2011), among others. With Rafael Marquese, he coordinates the Laboratório de Estudos Sobre o Brasil e o Sistema Mundial (LabMundi).

Kenneth Pomeranz is University Professor in History and East Asian Languages and Civilizations at the University of Chicago. He was president of the American Historical Association in 2013 and a fellow of the British Academy. He has written, edited, coauthored or coedited ten books, over sixty scholarly articles and many other writings. They include *The Great Divergence: China, Europe, and the Making of the Modern World Economy* and *The Making of a Hinterland: State, Society and Economy in Inland North China*, 1853, 1937, both winners of the AHA's award for best book in East Asian history. His current projects include a book called *Why Is China So Big?* as well as a coauthored college world history textbook. He also writes on contemporary topics, mostly connected to Chinese environmental issues and economic affairs.

Dominic Sachsenmaier is Professor of "Modern China with a Special Emphasis on Global Historical Perspectives" at Georg-August-University Göttingen. In the past, he held faculty positions at Jacobs University Bremen, Duke University, as well as the University of California, Santa Barbara. Professor Sachsenmaier's main current research interests are Chinese and Western approaches to global history, transnational connections of Chinese intellectual cultures and seventeenth-century Sino-Western cultural relations. Professor Sachsenmaier is an elected member of the European Academy of Sciences and Arts, and he is the president of the Boston-based Toynbee Prize Foundation (Global History). Among other works, he is the author of *Global Entanglements of a Man Who Never Traveled* (Columbia University Press). He is also among the three editors of the book series *Columbia Studies in International and Global History* (Columbia University Press).

Andrew Sartori is Professor of History at New York University. He is the author of *Liberalism in Empire: An Alternative History* (University of California Press, 2014) and *Bengal in Global Concept History: Culturalism in the Age of Capital* (University of Chicago Press, 2008), as well as coeditor, with Samuel Moyn, of *Global Intellectual History* (Columbia University Press, 2013), and, with Prasenjit Duara and Viren Murthy, of *Companion to Global Historical Thought* (Wiley-Blackwell, 2014). He is also an editor of the journal *Critical Historical Studies*.

David Simo is Professor of German and Comparative Literature and Culture. He teaches at the University of Yaoundé in Cameroon but has also been a visiting professor in various German, French and American universities. He is a specialist of postcolonial cultural studies and publishes on postcolonial criticism and theory as well as intercultural epistemology. He is the director of the German African Center for scientific cooperation and coordinates the postgraduate school in arts, cultures and civilization in his university.

Meltem Toksöz is Associate Professor of History at Boğaziçi University, Istanbul, Turkey. Besides her work *Nomads, Migrants and Cotton in the Eastern Mediterranean: The Making of the Adana-Mersin Region in the Ottoman Empire, 1850–1908* (The Netherlands: Ottoman Social and Economic History Series, E. J. Brill Publications, 2010), she has coedited *Cities of the Mediterranean: From the Ottoman Times to the Present* (London: I.B.Tauris, 2011). She has also published on the Eastern Mediterranean cotton agriculture and trade, on the regional history of Cilicia as well as on Turkish and Ottoman historiography. Her research interests include historiography, intellectual history, economic history and the modernization of state and society in late Ottoman history.

Q. Edward Wang is Professor of History and Coordinator of Asian Studies at Rowan University, the United States, and Changjiang Professor at Peking University, China. He serves on the board of the International Commission for the History and Theory of Historiography and is the editor of *Chinese Studies in History*. His research interests are global history, comparative historiography and cultural history in East Asia. His recent publications include *Chopsticks: A Cultural and Culinary History* (2015), *A Global History of Modern Historiography* (coauthored; 2008 and 2017 revised edition) and *Mirroring the Past: The Writing and Use of History in Imperial China* (coauthored; 2005).

INTRODUCTION
Sven Beckert and Dominic Sachsenmaier

Global history seems to be everywhere. Wherever you look—the course offerings of history departments, the catalogues of publishers, the programs of history conferences—the words "global history" appear. You can sign up for a lecture course on global social history at the Vrije Universiteit Amsterdam, pursue an MA in global history at Capital Normal University (CNU) in Beijing, study the global history of capitalism at the University of Capetown, read a global history of 1968 published in Dakar and attend a conference on the global history of slavery at the University of São Paulo. The Harvard University libraries contain 437 books with "global history" in their title. Thirty of these books were published between 1962 and 1990, twenty-six in the 1990s, 115 in the 2000s and in the past five years alone the libraries acquired 266 more books on global history.[1] Further testifying to the enormous popularity of global history, the 2014 European Congress on Global History attracted more than 800 participants—an astounding number considering that the first such Congress was convened less than a decade ago. And by 2017, centers for the study of global history had been established at universities in Shanghai and Osaka, Oxford and Berlin, São Paulo and Dakar as well as places in between.[2]

No matter whether you call it "world history," "global history," "transnational history" or the "new global history," historical scholarship that operates on larger scales is growing rapidly and is increasingly focused on the creation of archive-based studies. Many doctoral dissertations are now being written in the field. Perhaps most importantly, scholars with different regional expertise have discovered global history as a common ground for scholarly exchange and even collaborative work.

The emergence of global history is one of the most significant developments in the discipline of history since the social history revolution of the 1970s. It is a remarkable shift that challenges the institutional logics of history writing as if we have known since the mid-nineteenth century. For more than a century and a half, most history writing and teaching has been focused on national or regional histories. There have long been experts on French, Chinese or Argentinean history, and on world regions ranging from South Asia to Eastern Europe and from Latin America to sub-Saharan Africa. Yet only few scholars were able to draw connections across these regions. To put it in a different way, there was very little institutional encouragement to think globally.

Starting from the nineteenth century, most scholars were trained as experts in a particular nation's history—of Italy, or Japan or the United States and many other countries. They joined associations dedicated to the study of these national histories, published in journals with a national focus and occupied chairs defined by particular national histories. To be sure, national boundaries did not demarcate the horizons of all researchers: ancient and medieval historians, for example, dealt with eras before the rise of the nation-state, while intellectual and economic historians have long paid attention to the crossing of borders. In the study of modern history, however, the boundaries of the nation-state loomed large, perhaps larger than in any other discipline. Such framing was hardly surprising, considering that history as an academic discipline emerged in the nineteenth century not just chronically hand in hand with the nation-state but ideologically and foundationally as well. As statesmen and ideologues created nation-states, they needed a useful—that is to say, national—past. Many historians were only too happy to oblige.

Of course, histories written from regional or national parameters have provided us with a rich view of the past. In quite a few areas of the world, a focus on national histories enabled the rise of a history profession, mobilized funds dedicated to history education in schools and universities, created intellectual communities among scholars and allowed for the rise of broad audiences. In the best cases, by helping to forge national communities, these histories allowed citizens to use a shared history to make demands on the state, claim new rights or mobilize against colonial powers. In the worst cases, such national histories fostered exclusionary nationalisms that seemed to justify the exclusion, expulsion or even extermination of those deemed not to be part of the national community.

Along with accomplishments, the hegemony of national and regional histories has had certain shortcomings. By privileging connections and processes unfolding within particular nation-states, historians often overlooked developments that crossed boundaries. Such constrained views had significant interpretive consequences. Just take one example: the Industrial Revolution. Huge numbers of books have been written on the British economy in the eighteenth and nineteenth centuries as if this history could be understood from a purely national perspective, as if the history could be complete if it only featured the tinkerers of Lancashire, the merchants of Liverpool and the statesmen of London. An almost equal number of publications treated the beginnings of industrialization as a wholly Western European phenomenon. Such histories left out hugely consequential events that took place beyond Britain's or Europe's boundaries: the importance of technology transfers from India, the opening of markets in Africa and the slave-produced commodities of the Americas, among others.[3]

This example also points to another limit of much of modern historiography: a strongly Eurocentric perspective. Developments in Western history were often defined as a universal norm. This has left many historians unable to understand how processes unfolding in one part of the world fit into developments elsewhere. Take for example the question of labor under capitalism. Hundreds of historians writing in Europe and the United States have taken wage labor as the quintessential modern form and assumed the urban factory as the location of such labor. They then universalized that model and wrote a history of labor that charted the transition from bonded agricultural labor to wage labor and, then, depicted the formalization of these labor relations. Because this story was often cast as the universal norm, Europe's past was assumed to foreshadow the future for the rest of the world. A global perspective that is sensitive to local conditions, however, immediately recognizes that the forms of labor under capitalism vary widely—from slavery to wage work, from peasant production to informal peddling—and thus radically revises the allegedly universal story that we have told for all too many years.[4]

Global history thus breaks with both an exclusively national, respectively regional, focus and Eurocentric perspectives.[5] It breaks with them not because it wants to marginalize the historical importance of the nation-state or the era of Western dominance during parts of the modern era. To the contrary, the analysis of nation-states is a central project of much of global history, as is the study of Western hegemony. Instead, it breaks with them because it sees that vast swaths of human history are not best understood within these frameworks, and that a global perspective allows for a wealth of themes to come into focus. Studying nationalism and state-building programs as transnational ideologies, for example, can help us recognize individual national experiences as part of wider, interconnected patterns. New research on transnational institutions ranging from the Catholic Church to Standard Oil to intergovernmental organizations such as the United Nations has granted us new insights into the complex interplay between global and local power systems. Alternative approaches to the history of colonialism and slavery have accentuated the agency of those who found themselves at the bottom of these systems of power.

As a whole, the field of global history has begun to challenge many "common wisdoms" manufactured in (and by) a Eurocentric age. Consider the history of the Enlightenment: from this new global perspective, the Enlightenment, once seen as a singularly European event, appears as part of a more global and diversified pattern. Some scholars have shown how the eighteenth-century Chinese Kaozheng School shared much with contemporary European movements. Other scholars, by pointing out that in societies like Meiji Japan the concept of "Enlightenment" carried rather different attributes, have shown the utility of comparing the European Enlightenment with those occurring in other countries, while also illuminating links between them.[6] In a similar vein, global human rights discourses can no longer be understood as European export; instead they are now recognized as multidirectional, moving between places and times, as when, for example, Haitian slaves appropriate concepts of the French Revolution globalizing them in the process.[7] Other branches of global history have come to rethink global migration during the nineteenth century, challenging the myth of the exceptional scope of trans-atlantic migration, showing that movements of similar magnitude occurred in East and Southeast Asia during the same time period.[8]

Beyond its revisionist character, global history is both connected history and comparative history. On the most basic level, it is the search to understand how human societies have developed as an interactive community across the world. Searching for alternative modes of conceptualizing the past, global history examines processes, networks, identities and events that cross boundaries of modern states, regions and landmasses. Interested in circulation, global history focuses on the connections between people, ideas, fashions and commodities across borders. It also considers shared transformations (from technological innovations to political ideologies) and changes to distributions of power that have affected people all over the world. Global history does not necessarily assume that such transformations have made the world more homogenous or just, and thus it pays particular attention to the highly specific ways in which local communities have been and are affected by global change and how local changes transformed global connections.[9]

Studying global transformations with attention to local specifics implies comparative and connective perspectives. This is a general principle for most global historical work. One useful example is the history of racism.[10] There are many instances of racism across the world that can be usefully compared allowing us to understand each instance better. But true global history also considers that racisms are connected, as the global circulation of ideas and ideologies about difference did have a powerful impact on each and every local instance, and as each and every local instance of racism can impact global ideas and ideologies.

Using global history to critically rethink the history of a particular society or world region thus does not abolish differentiation. In fact, it allows the distinctions that persist in diverse human communities to be put into a framework that illuminates the continuing tension between the shared and the specific, between the similar and the different. It allows historians to compare with more refinement and to communicate more effectively with other social sciences such as anthropology, sociology, political science and economics, while keeping history's disciplinary uniqueness, its ability to pay so much heed to local specificities.

By connecting and comparing developments unfolding in distant parts of the world, global history has also put greater emphasis on the more sustained, drawn-out patterns of history. While the cultural turn during the 1980s and 1990s has often emphasized the indeterminate nature of history and the impossibility of "knowing," global history has returned historians' attention to making causal arguments, often linking factors such as environmental change, demography, the violence of state making and the importance of economic change.

This is not to say that global history returns to the teleological determinism that framed much of the 1960s social science scholarship when modernization theory was en vogue within Western academia. In contrast to scholars such as Talcott Parsons, today's global historians usually do not assume that societies around the world are becoming more similar as they develop economically. Recent scholarship, instead, has focused on local particularities and regional specificities. The decisive difference between global and local history, however, is that the former tries to understand the local while at the same time paying attention to its global entanglements. It is indebted neither to approaches that conceptualize the global as a delocalized universal nor to epistemic traditions of digging into the local while ignoring the global. Global history explores the complex and fascinating ways that the global and the local entwine and entangle, and it sees in these entanglements the constitutive elements of both the global and the local.

Privileging border-crossing connections and at the same time partaking in the spatial turn, global history does not take the nation or the region as the natural container for social processes. The field critiques Eurocentrism and tends toward a relational history that sees developments in various parts of the world as affecting one another, rather than assuming a one-way street of influence. It is this history—its methods, themes and debates—that this volume focuses on. It shows that global history in itself is a global undertaking and aims to further a project that embeds the production of historical knowledge in new global communities of scholars.

The trajectories of global history

Of course, as historians will be the first to point out, everything has its antecedents, and thus border-crossing history has its own distinguished history. This book will provide some insights into that long history. Already in ancient Greece, China and the Arab world, some scholars endeavored to write the history of the known world.[11] In the eighteenth century, Immanuel Kant proposed to write history with a cosmopolitan intent, and so did Kang Youwei around the beginning of the twentieth century. Such ideas have flourished now and again through time. Most such writings took a civilizational approach, defining the writers' own cultural realms as the norm and portraying outsiders as the "Other." Particularly during the nineteenth century, it became common among historians to divide the world's people into a number of nations and civilizations, a move that obstructed many possibilities for alternative approaches to human history.

The belief in civilizations and, later, nations, as basic, almost natural units of human order also shaped the field of world history. Even though it clearly remained in the shadow of national history, world history became significant during and after the nineteenth century. Many famed historians, including Leopold von Ranke—often regarded as the founder of academic history writing—attempted world historical reflections.[12] But more often, he and other scholars preferred to line up their histories of single cultures and nations as quasi-autochthonous units—taking little interest in their entanglements, transfers and connections.

In essence, world history was often understood as the triumphant rise of Europe as it progressed via its own civilizational forces. Consequently, many works in the field confined their visions to European history, perhaps adding some brief chapters on the early Chinese, Indian, Egyptian or Mesopotamian pasts. The main epochs of world history were defined by changes in Europe—the advent of Greek philosophy, the Reformation or the Enlightenment.[13] Many non-Western authors accepted the basic visions of this interpretation of the courses of human history. Perhaps less surprisingly, much scholarship in the communist world also builds upon these Eurocentric narratives.[14]

Starting from the 1960s, the field of world history began to change in many parts of the globe.[15] In India and China (prior to the advent of the Cultural Revolution), an increasing number of scholars tried to view the history of our planet at least partly through categories and concepts not solely derived from the European experience.[16]

And in the United States, world historians became far more critical of Eurocentric perspectives. Despite these departures, however, world history retained many of its earlier characteristics. As a teaching field, it was usually represented by one person in a given history department—and that person was supposed to cover the entire world outside the West. As a research field, world history long remained a domain whose main focus seemed to be the production of textbooks covering vast stretches of time and space.[17]

Compare that with the situation today: the number of global historical publications has risen sharply, while their character and scope has changed. The body of academic literature in global history today mainly consists of specialized studies that deal with single themes and almost always focus on well-defined time periods considerably smaller than the entire sway of human history. The scope of these publications is usually not "global" in the sense of covering the entire world equally; instead they typically focus on a selection of world regions relevant to a particular problem, and do so with appropriate local sensitivity. The transformation into a research field is evidence that global history has arrived.

Let us pause to consider why that reorientation occurred. Some reasons are applicable to large areas of the world; some are unique to particular regions. This should not surprise us since, as they say, all history is contemporary history, and since, as historians know, each locality experiences contemporary events in its own way and through its own lens. The first wave of more global approaches to history emerged during the 1990s, a decade characterized by widespread discussion of globalization and a sense that the world had suddenly become much more interconnected. Unsurprisingly, this discourse influenced historians, who then tried to shape it by arguing that globalization itself had a history that went much before the 1970s. But this happened in specific ways: in parts of the global North, for instance, it was the need to explain the apparent destabilizing of nation-states that led historians to take a more sustained look at the longer histories of global connections.

Global challenges also drove the embrace of global history. Throughout the world, environmental issues have encouraged thinking in increasingly global terms, with climate change, for example, affecting the planet and humanity as a whole. Moreover, we are entering a new historical moment when the global realities of yesterday no longer hold. The seers predicting the end of the nation-state may have exaggerated, but it is beyond doubt that the nation-state's power as a container of human activity is shifting. It has become much easier for people, goods and ideas to transcend national boundaries, and the power of state institutions to regulate these flows has declined. In fact, we are witnessing a redistribution of economic wealth and political influence on a global scale. We are not on our way to a world of equal distribution of wealth and power, but we are moving toward one that is no longer centered on the North Atlantic Rim. Together, all these developments make Eurocentric assumptions increasingly problematic, thus opening up large-scale narratives of human history to reinterpretation by incorporating new regions of the world into them.

Historians themselves, moreover, began to circulate in a much more international community. Certainly, prior generations of historians read one another's books even if they were separated by oceans, but the advent of cheap air travel and new modes of communication made international contacts much easier and more frequent. Living in this interconnected world showed historians in a very real and personal way the connections and comparisons that increasingly have come to characterize their scholarship.

Last but not least, there is the logic of historical research itself. Once historians started looking for connections across vast geographic distances, they kept finding them. In the United States, for example, once scholars began to treat the French, Spanish and English settlements in North America as more than the prehistory of the United States, it became ever more obvious that every aspect of North American history was linked to developments in Europe, Africa, Latin America and Asia. All the major institutions of North America then needed to be compared to those of other colonial societies; colonial America was now connected back to the world, influencing and influenced by larger global shifts that contained within them many different paths and possibilities.[18] Similar developments occurred in histories of other regions of the world as well.

Global History, Globally

The title of this book, *Global History, Globally*, does not refer to its subject matter only but also to its global scope. To put it in a different way, this collection of essays introduces the burgeoning field of global history while tracing it in its global settings. It is based on an effort to create a forum for global historians from all corners of the world. In a series of conferences, leading scholars based on all continents debated the past, present and future of global history in a critical and collegial spirit.[19] Participants in these meetings reviewed the state of the field in different parts of the world, discussed the debates on core themes in global history and considered—not without controversy—some of the problems global history raises intellectually and institutionally. These conversations were not easy, given the variety of standpoints, academic traditions and modes of arguing involved, but it was precisely that breadth that made the meetings so productive. This book makes these debates available to a broader public, giving readers a comprehensive and global view of one of the most significant developments in the field.

Beyond charting the enormous diversity and vibrant nature of global history, these chapters allow for some general observations. For one, it becomes clear that local conditions matter greatly to the ways global history is conceived and practiced. The directions of global historical scholarship in Brazil or Argentina, for example, have differed from those in, say, the United States or France. For global history, as for other areas of history, the local conditions the global: the world of global history is not flat.

Yet the global also conditions the local. The chapters show how global collaborations—and the related flows of people and ideas—influence research agendas and interpretive strategies all around the world. The rather simultaneous rise of global history in different parts of a world is a perfect example of the global entanglements of historical scholarship in today's world. However, the question of how exactly global and local patterns are enmeshed with one another remains a complex one, and is discussed at length in many of the chapters here.

One of the key assumptions underlying our project has been the idea that global history must establish global dialogues and global intellectual exchanges. The times when only Western scholars had the stature to develop perspectives of a global magnitude are definitely over. More often than not, historians writing on North American and European history are familiar with the history of these regions but rarely have an understanding of Latin American, Indian or African historical experiences. Yet the opposite is not true. Historians in East Asia or the Middle East are far from ignorant about the West's historical heritage. Chinese historians of China, or Egyptian historians of Egypt, may only focus on their national histories in their own research and teaching, but the parameters of their thinking usually encompass the history of Europe and North America, or at least key parts thereof. The imprint of colonialism on the non-Western world has meant that historians working outside the West often have had to take a transcontinental, or even global, approach.

An earlier and more sustained attention to global history in regions like East Asia or Latin America, however, did not translate into a greater presence in the global marketplace of ideas. Indeed, *Global History, Globally* shows that just the opposite was frequently the case, as the vibrant research emanating from other parts of the world was often completely ignored in the halls of North Atlantic academia. It is common for a Chinese historian of China or an Indian historian of India to take notice of British, US or other Western publications relevant to his or her own field. Yet the same is not necessarily the case in the opposite direction. As one of the chapters illustrates, it is almost unacceptable for a Japanese historian of the world economy to be unfamiliar with the works of Immanuel Wallerstein, but it is perfectly acceptable for historians in Europe and North America to ignore the works of Japanese scholars of the "world system." The power to interpret the world has been and continues to be distributed in radically uneven ways.

The chapters also deliberate on the commonalities and differences between the rise of global historical perspectives within subfields of historiography such as social and environmental history. The spread of global history into most corners of the historians' guildhall should not lead us to assume that its contours look the same everywhere. The "global turn" may mean something quite different to an economic historian than to a cultural historian. Simultaneously, a particular phrase will not necessarily mean the same thing to cultural historians in France as it will to those working in India.

As mentioned, our historical thinking ought to change along with these new global realities. This is easier said than done, not least because sustained hierarchies still characterize the field of history. The global academic system, which is both nation- and Western-centric, thwarts many of global history's possibilities. Certainly, in their own work, global historians have begun to leave historiographical nationalism and Eurocentrism behind. But how can this field unfold if the current structures of historiography remain unchanged? How powerful can historians' arguments be, if the field's practitioners in the West continue to ignore scholarship produced in other parts of the world?

The answer to these questions is obvious: the community of global historians needs to make sustained efforts to change both historical thinking and its underlying patterns of interaction. Most importantly, the field's debates and exchanges need to move past the West-Rest axis, which has characterized it up to the present day. It needs to become more multilateral and create more opportunities for scholars to engage in critical global dialogues with one another. If it does, the possibilities of global history will be enormous.

* * *

This book is divided into three parts: the practices of global history in various regions of the world, central themes in global history and key problems of global history. Rather than covering all possible regions, themes and key problems, each of these sections provides a sample of some of the most important traditions, debates and complications within the field.

The first part underlines one of global history's key messages: the global historical turn emerged in many parts of the world, but it is not a globally homogenous approach. Local academic communities producing global historical scholarship have shaped the field. In other words, it makes a difference whether global historians are located in the United States, Chile, Italy, India or Singapore. And these differences are not necessarily rooted in the size of libraries, history departments, or the availability of funding. While these factors are important, it is local academic structures, public discourses, historiographical traditions and the forms of historical memory that shape global history as it is practiced. The landscapes of global historical research around the world are not simply extensions of the field as it has been shaped in the global North. On the other hand, the chapters in this part also prove that we must refrain from resorting to cultural stereotypes. We should not assume that scholars in places like China or the Arab World approach global history through iron-clad traditions, frozen in time.

These chapters discuss the trajectories of the field in East Asia, Western Europe, Africa, Latin America and the United States. Far from homogenizing these large areas, they show the diversity of traditions and approaches within each of them. They deal with the question of how much the nation-state shapes historiography—for example, through targeted funding measures and the creation of academic and departmental structures. Some of the authors also discuss whether and how older national or regional imaginations relate to new global forms of historical scholarship. In a number of cases, these chapters can draw upon an already richly developed meta-discourse on global history; in other cases, the authors are trailblazers in trying to understand the configurations of global history in a particular part of the world.

Focusing primarily on Western Europe, Gareth Austin reviews the emergence of global history in this part of the world. He charts the development of the field since the 1990s, tracing its origins to dissatisfaction with increasing specialization, the contemporary experience of intensifying global interactions and the challenges to Eurocentric thinking. According to Austin, global history emerged first in Britain and the Netherlands, from where it spread to Germany, Switzerland, France and, eventually, the rest of Europe. At first the conversation was largely between historians with expertise in regions outside Europe; it was still unclear how much global history would turn into a wider research movement. In recent years, however, global history has increasingly thrived as an archive-based project; or, as Austin puts it, global historians in Europe now largely focus on "how to get on with it." At the same time, global history has been increasingly institutionalized, with centers in the UK, the Netherlands, France, Germany, Austria and other countries. Central to that emerging research agenda has been the desire to "provincialize Europe"; the goal of overcoming the "Eurocentrism of agency" has, Austin says, largely succeeded, but "conceptual Eurocentrism" has proven much more difficult to overcome. Austin emphasizes that the increasing interconnections between global history scholars around the world make it difficult to distinguish between "national" or "continent wide" approaches to the field.

In his chapter "Re-presenting Asia on the Global Stage," Edward Wang focuses primarily on Japan, Korea and China. He argues that historiographical developments in this region are characterized by some remarkable parallels, despite all the national, linguistic, political and ideological divides. For example, from the nineteenth century onward, nation-centered perspectives thoroughly transformed the earlier historiographical traditions of East Asia. Then, after the Second World War, world history became more prominent (primarily as a teaching field), despite the thoroughly different ideological contexts in East Asian countries. Wang points out that these forms of world history were typically based upon Eurocentric perspectives and remained centered on individual national histories.

Wang uses these perspectives to discuss the origins of more recent forms of global historical scholarship in East Asia. Among other themes, he illuminates the rise of "relational histories" in Japan during the second half of the Cold War: works that operated on a transcontinental scale. In China, he observes a mounting interest in the history of transnational connections and global transformations at around the same time, particularly after the end of the Mao Period. Closer to the present, Wang depicts the growing presence of global historical perspectives since the 1990s in much of East Asia. He presents an overview of the wide variety of scholarship in this field and takes up the way it has been institutionalized in different East Asian societies. At the same time, Wang cautions us against taking a naive view of the development of global history in East Asia. He stresses that throughout the region, national historical outlooks remain dominant in historical research and education. No matter whether in Korea, mainland China or Taiwan, global history is surprisingly often written from a decidedly nationalist perspective.

Like East Asia, Latin America has a distinguished tradition of global history, and indeed Latin American scholars have written some of the most influential studies in this field. Rafael Marquese and João Paulo Pimenta review relevant academic developments over the past 150 years, showing how from the very beginning historians of Latin America embedded their histories in transcontinental narratives. This is perhaps not surprising, considering the central importance of European colonialism in the continent's modern history. In much of Latin America it was almost impossible to write history in a purely national mode, and one could say that a transcontinental perspective was the water in which historians had to swim if they wanted to make sense of the continent's history. The authors cite three examples to show how transcontinental and global perspectives taken by historians in Latin America had an impact on scholarship elsewhere. First, they review a group of Caribbean historians, C.L.R James and Eric Williams most prominently among them, whose efforts to connect the history of Caribbean slavery to European economic ascendancy were widely ignored when their studies came out, but their books are now considered a foundational perspective on Atlantic history. Marquese and Pimenta show how Fernand Braudel's thinking about global capitalism was greatly influenced by his encounter with Brazilian historians when he taught at the University of São Paulo, and how, in turn, his global perspective influenced generations of historians in Latin America who, like Braudel, saw that capitalism could only be understood as a world system. Their final example is the dependency school, which was forged by Latin American economists and sociologists such as Raul Prebisch and Fernando Henrique Cardoso. This school introduced the notions of "center" and "periphery" into global debates, ideas that have had a profound influence on what historians and others have called the "world system."

Omar Gueye's chapter on the history of global perspectives in Africa confirms this general point: it would be nearly impossible to write the history of Africa in the modern era without references to places, people and processes on different continents, and very few African historians did so. As a consequence, African historians almost always took on a wider, if not yet global, perspective. They wrote the history of the continent or of substantial parts of it; they wrote pan-African history that included the African diaspora in the Americas or they wrote global economic history centered on Africa, as in the pioneering work of Abdoulaye Ly. Yet history was as central to the forging of African nation-states as it was elsewhere: in the twentieth century, history became a prime ideological battleground, as African historians asserted their versions of history against European-dominated narratives that saw Africa as a continent "without history." Gueye describes the early and central role historians played in the struggle for national liberation and the ways that the global orientation weakened as newly forged nation-states sought to establish their legitimacy. Historians wrote national histories that became central to the project of nation making, but still these histories remained connected to events outside the continent. It was only later that the transnational perspective became less prominent, as African historians increasingly focused their work on subnational groups. Today, Gueye says, the wealth of research accumulated over the past decades has encouraged African historians to step back out into the world and connect aspects of the continent's past, including local histories, to that of the globe.

Following this chapter, Selçuk Esenbel and Meltem Toksöz analyze the trajectories of historiography in Turkey and the Arab Middle East. From the beginnings of modern academic historiography in Turkey, conceptions of both the local and the global past changed continuously along with the politics of identities and other political realities.

Most notable was the significant historiographical transition between the multiethnic polity of the Ottoman Empire and the Republic of Turkey during the 1920s. Esenbel and Toksöz point to the diversity of late Ottoman historiography and the globality of parts of it. During the late nineteenth century, world histories were being written that operated on conceptual grounds and narrative traditions that were significantly different from their Western counterparts.

Esenbel and Toksöz next describe the rise of nationalist historiographies in both Turkey and the Ottoman Empire's Arab successor states. In addition, they pay attention to the influence of European imperial powers and their impact on history writing and education. Western influence remained strong during the Cold War, when there was a debate between Turkish historians over modernization theory versus World Systems theory. Since the 1980s, paradigms such as alternative or shared modernities have grown more influential. At the same time, there has been a resurgence of interest in the Ottoman Empire, which has given rise to a wealth of studies operating beyond contemporary national boundaries and returning to different—regional and other—visions of the past. In their concluding thoughts, Esenbel and Toksöz remind us of the importance of considering sociologies of knowledge when we reflect upon historiographical developments. The authors remind us that internationally mobile scholars from Turkey, Palestine and other regions were a crucial social group behind the rise of transnational approaches to history in Turkey and the Arab Middle East.

The concluding chapter of Part I takes up developments of global history in North America. It was authored by the late Jerry Bentley, shortly before his untimely death in the summer of 2012. Bentley emphasizes the continuities between global history and world history in the American context; in fact he is opposed to drawing a distinction between these two field designations. According to Bentley, world history has long been a field whose main protagonists have sought to overcome both Eurocentric and nation-centered perspectives. World historians problematized these pillars of modern academic historiography while at the same time remaining loyal to their main field's key conceptual and methodological principles.

Bentley discusses new forms of world historical scholarship that started in the 1960s and situates these developments within the wider intellectual and social transformations in the United States. At the same time, Bentley does not neglect the important role of individuals who had a major impact on the development of world history in North America. He also touches upon key institutions, associations and journals that were major sites of activity and carried significance for the wider community of world historians. He contends that world—or global—history has increasingly acquired the character of a vibrant research field. The scholars active in that field have not articulated a clearly discernible political or ideological position, but they usually belong to the liberal camp, which might connect to their shared critique of Western-centric perspectives. For that reason, a number of world or global historical projects have become the targets of right-wing critics who blame the field for undermining national identities.

Introduction

The second part of this collection centers on significant themes of and debates within global history. More specifically, the authors focus on the ways that global history has transformed the fields of labor, economic, immigration and intellectual history. Setting the agenda, Andreas Eckert and Marcel van der Linden investigate the history of labor from a global perspective and find that such a viewpoint significantly alters our understanding of core themes within the field. The widened focus—moving past workers in the West to look at those in Asia, Latin America and Africa—has shown that North-Atlantic-focused labor history, with its emphasis on wage workers, industry and cities, has provided a radically incomplete picture of labor, one that ignores the vast amount of labor done in the countryside, outside of wage relations and in agriculture. Global labor history thus puts the subsistence laborer, the slave and the sharecropper next to the wageworker and explores the complex entanglements between them. This understanding of the global scope of labor history undermines a core narrative of the emergence of the modern world that emphasizes the development of labor toward contract, freedom and formalization—a narrative that turns out to be wrong when the entire world is kept in mind.

The next chapter, by Kenneth Pomeranz, charts the way the global turn has influenced the field of economic history. Although deeply rooted in national histories, economic history has now morphed into a core area of research in global history, and in fact, the rise of global history has given new impetus to economic history. Pomeranz introduces us to a number of research projects in the United States, Europe and Japan engaged in writing connected and comparative histories of the world economy. An important part of this research agenda is measurement—the generation of data that allows comparison of wages, growth rates and economic structures over very long time periods and large parts of the globe. Pomeranz also discusses economic historians who explicate connections between different regions of the world; he moves from Immanuel Wallerstein to Fernand Braudel to more recent historians who look at the history of particular commodities such as sugar and cotton. Comparative questions have also become important, for instance, studies that explore a crucial moment such as the so-called great divergence, the point when some parts of the world suddenly became much wealthier than others. Himself a central participant in these debates, Pomeranz shows how global perspectives are overthrowing old Eurocentric certainties, replacing them with a story that is much more contingent, much more global and much more persuasive.

Human migrations transcend single regions and nation-states, yet, as Amit Mishra shows in his chapter, their study does not always reflect that obvious fact. All too often, the histories of significant migration movements have been written in isolation from one another and without considering the global constellations that channeled the flow of particular people to particular places. Migration history for all too long has been surprisingly North-Atlantic-centric, ignoring Pacific and Indian Ocean migrations even though these movements of people were, in numerical terms, just as important. A global approach, says Mishra, brings all human migrations into focus, reveals their connections to each other, compares them and sees how developments in one part of the world have an impact on developments elsewhere, as when the end of the transatlantic slave trade caused the migrations in the Indian Ocean world to intensify. Global migration historians, Mishra says, have increasingly acknowledged these connections and made these comparisons, which has deepened our view of migration history. Yet all too often these historians still write from a Eurocentric perspective: they universalize arguments about global migrations based on North Atlantic cases, which leads them to underemphasize the importance of coercion, imperialism, exploitation, racism and violence in the movement of peoples. He concludes that the "history of global migration is critical for studying the history of the world and therefore global migration history is a crucial subset of writing global history."

In the last chapter of Part II, Dominic Sachsenmaier and Andrew Sartori reflect on patterns of global intellectual history. For too long, they argue, intellectual historians were slow to react to the global turn. Discussing recent developments toward global intellectual history, Sachsenmaier and Sartori focus chiefly on Anglo-American and Chinese universities. They argue that in the United States, more intellectual historians began to do work who crossed the Western/non-Western divide. Among other developments, experts on South Asian history were becoming more influential in the field, which triggered new debates and paradigm shifts. Many concepts that one or two generations ago had been widely accepted were now challenged, including the idea of a quasi-hermetic "Western civilization" with its allegedly unique intellectual traditions.

Sachsenmaier and Sartori point out that in recent years far more complex—global and local—patterns of thinking have replaced these kinds of assumptions. Furthermore, they demonstrate that Chinese intellectual historians have also been seeking to decenter intellectual history traditions. Already a century ago, intellectual history in China put a strong emphasis on comparative perspectives and the history of transfers between China and societies like Japan and other "advanced" Western societies. The challenge for global intellectual history in China is now to move beyond this binary focus on China and the "developed world" by including world regions outside of the West in their comparisons.

The third part of this volume looks at specific problems in the growing field of global history. As a movement that challenges earlier historiographical traditions, global history faces many epistemological and methodological tests, and also political pushback. For instance, in some parts of the world, global historical critiques of nation-centered perspectives evoke counterreactions from nationalist forces, both inside and outside of academia. In an age of heightened nationalism, global history can and should be read as a critique of a history too closely aligned with the nation-state—a critique that is less than welcome in many quarters. As the chapters show, sometimes such concerns make the practice of global history difficult; sometimes they encourage a global history from a nationalist perspective. These conflicts emerge in many places with each case characterized by locally specific dynamics.

For this reason, contributions to this part of the book focus on specific parts of the world while also discussing more general challenges to global historical scholarship. In the first chapter, David Simo deals with the question of finding a voice when writing world history from an African vantage point. Concentrating on sub-Saharan Africa, his chapter starts with reflections on the general conditions of historiography in this part of the world. Scholarship in Africa, Simo maintains, cannot be understood without considering the effect of Western, particularly North American, universities' domination of African academia. In Simo's eyes, the growing presence of intellectuals from the Global South at universities in the Global North has not only granted them access to resources and sites of academic production but has given them a voice that will come to challenge dominant narratives and concepts.

When reflecting upon the possibility of an African voice in global history, Simo cautions against merely constructing an African "Other." He is also wary of mobilizing allegedly pristine African epistemological traditions. If African historians want to create alternative global historical perspectives, they need, Simo says, to develop them through critical dialogues with the currently dominant disciplinary cultures, which, of course, were shaped by and under Western hegemony. Simo points out that starting from the 1980s, an increasingly visible group of African intellectuals have spoken against national and linear modes of thinking about the past. In the meantime, quite a few influential scholars in Africa have grown convinced that the rewriting of African history must involve the critical reconsideration of dominant global historical master narratives.

In the next chapter, Lim Jie-Hyun reflects upon the danger of national interests instrumentalizing global historical viewpoints for their own purposes. He does so in the context of intellectual and academic landscapes in East Asia, particularly Korea and Japan. Revisiting the history of modern historiography in these societies, Lim cautions us against understanding world history and national history as antithetical. Starting from the nineteenth century, he argues, both fields developed simultaneously and complemented one another. While national history was supposed to support state-building efforts, world history long had the primary mission of describing the paths traced by industrialized countries. Eurocentric perspectives dominated both national history and world history, including various Marxist schools (before and after the Second World War), which did not deviate from this pattern, as they too had a linear reading of modernization. The main opposition to identifying Western historical developments as role models for East Asia, Lim holds, emerged from Pan-Asianist circles, who articulated their visions for new Asia-centered world histories mainly within the context of Japanese imperialism.

With an eye on today's situation, Lim shows that nationalist camps in East Asia share an "antagonistic complicity" in their rejection of transnational and global historical approaches. Border-crossing scholarship is often seen as unpatriotic because it runs counter to national interests. Nevertheless, East Asia has recently witnessed efforts such as the production of transnational history textbooks and the establishment of international historians' commissions. In both cases global historical approaches play important roles.

Next comes Marnie Hughes-Warrington's discussion of the challenges global historical scholarship faces in a postcolonial settler society. Choosing Australia as her focal point, Hughes-Warrington argues that the trajectory of global history as a research and teaching field has been closely entangled with the development of Aboriginal history. The Aboriginal dimensions of Australia's past have long been neglected, even silenced, by the majority of historians. More recently, Aboriginal history has been granted a more visible space within national public memory and history education. In this context, Hughes-Warrington discusses scholars who draw on Aboriginal understandings of time and space to develop alternative visions of global history. In her eyes, a historiography that takes these Aboriginal visions seriously would have the possibility of breaking with the Western narratives that still dominate historical scholarship in Australia.

Hughes-Warrington demonstrates that also in other branches of historiography, Australian academia has witnessed a surging interest in scholarship that transcends national boundaries. Some projects are comparative; others deal with transfers and connections. Hughes-Warrington subsequently outlines possibilities of further developing global historical scholarship in Australia.

Last but not least, Shigeru Akita's chapter focuses on efforts to develop alternatives to Eurocentrism in global history by detailing the Japanese contributions to global economic history. Emphasizing the long and distinguished traditions of writing global history in Japan, and the diverse perspectives in which it was embedded, he presents an Asia-centered research agenda on the history of global economic change. That agenda seeks to overcome both of the Eurocentrisms that Gareth Austin speaks of—the Eurocentrism of agency and the Eurocentrism of concepts. In his view, some renowned Japanese global historians have written the actions, interest and beliefs of Asians into the emergence of the global economy, while at the same time emphasizing specifically Asian paths toward industrialization. Both perspectives question the universalism of the European model and the idea of the West as the sole shaper of the world economy.

As should by now be clear, this book introduces not just the field of global history but also the global conversations that have arisen around it. The result of several years of intense debate among historians on all continents, *Global History, Globally* is a collaborative effort to rethink both the work of historians and the ways historians work. It is a beginning of what we hope will be an exciting journey to develop the tools that allow us all to rethink human history beyond the confines of particular cultures or the nation-state.

Notes

1. Hollis, https://hollis.harvard.edu/primo_library/libweb/action/search.do?vid=HVD, (accessed August 30, 2017).
2. The examples mentioned above refer to: East China Normal University in Shanghai, the research institute "re:work. IGK Work and Human Life Cycle in Global History" at Humboldt-University Berlin, Lab Mund at USP in Sao Paulo, the Center for Global History Studies at the Institute for Academic Initiatives, Osaka University, and Oxford University.
3. Joseph Inikori, *Africans and the Industrial Revolution in England: A Study in International Trade and Economic Development* (New York: Cambridge University Press, 2002); Eric Williams, *Capitalism and Slavery* (Chapel Hill: University of North Carolina Press, 1994); Sven Beckert, *Empire of Cotton: A Global History* (New York: Alfred A. Knopf, 2014).
4. See Marcel van der Linden, *Workers of the World: Essays towards a Global Labor History* (Leiden: Brill, 2008).
5. Our book's cover page displays a young Caucasian man investigating a variety of globes (see http://www.bloomsbury.com). On one side, it symbolizes the spirit of multiperspectivity and the willingness to operate on a wide variety of scales, characterizing much of recent global historical scholarship. On the other side, as a historic photo, it is meant as a critique of earlier forms of world historical scholarship that had often been written chiefly from the perspective of white males.
6. On-cho Ng and Q. Edward Wang, *Mirroring the Past: The Writing and Use of History in Imperial China* (Honolulu: University of Hawai'i Press, 2005); Sebastian Conrad, "Enlightenment in Global History: A Historiographical Critique," *American Historical Review* 117:4 (2012), 999–1027.
7. Laurent Dubois, "An Enslaved Enlightenment: Re-thinking the Intellectual History of the French Atlantic," *Social History* 3 (2006), 1–14.
8. Adam McKeown, "Global Migration, 1846–1940," *Journal of World History* 15 (2004), 155–89.
9. For very similar wording, see the Weatherhead Initiative on Global History, https://wigh.wcfia.harvard.edu/, (accessed February 10, 2015).
10. See for example Marilyn Lake and Henry Reynolds, *Drawing the Global Colour Line White Men's Countries and the International Challenge of Racial Equality* (New York: Cambridge University Press, 2008).
11. Dominic Sachsenmaier, "The Evolution of World History," in David Christian and Marnie Hughes-Warrington (eds.), *Introducing World History* (= Cambridge History of the World, vol. 1) (Cambridge: Cambridge University Press, 2015), 56–83.
12. Ernst Schulin "Universalgeschichte und Nationalgeschichte bei Leopold von Ranke" in Wolfgang J. Mommsen (ed.), *Leopold von Ranke und die Moderne Geschichtswissenschaft* (Stuttgart: Klett-Cotta, 1988), 37–71.
13. See for example Jerry H. Bentley, *Shapes of World History in Twentieth-Century Scholarship*, Vol. 14 of *Essays on Global and Comparative History* (Washington, DC: American Historical Association, 1996).
14. See for example Denis Kozlov, "Athens and Apocalypse: Writing History in Soviet Russia," in Axel Schneider and Daniel Woolf (eds.), *The Oxford History of Historical Writing*, vol. 5 (Oxford: Oxford University Press, 2011), 375–98.

15. See for example Jürgen Osterhammel, "World History," in Axel Schneider and Daniel Woolf (eds.), *The Oxford History of Historical Writing*, vol. 5 (Oxford University Press, 2011), 93–112.
16. Wang, Q. Edward. "Encountering the World: China and Its Other(s) in Historical Narratives, 1949–89," *Journal of World History* 14:3 (2003), 327–58.
17. Patrick Manning, *Navigating World History: Historians Create a Global Past* (New York: Palgrave Macmillan, 2003), ch. 1.
18. See for example Rosemarie Zagarri, "The Significance of the 'Global Turn' for the Early American Republic: Globalization in the Age of Nation-building," *Journal of the Early Republic* 31:1 (Spring 2011), 1–37; Nicholas Canny, "Atlantic History and Global History," in Jack P. Greene and Philip D. Morgan (eds.), *Atlantic History: A Critical Appraisal* (Oxford: Oxford University Press 2009), 317–36.
19. These conferences were held twice in the United States and twice in Germany. The hosting institutions were the Harvard Weatherhead Center for International Affairs, the Duke Asian Pacific Studies Institute, the Freiburg Institute of Advanced Studies and the research center "Work and Lifecycle in Human History" at Humboldt University Berlin. Funding for the latter two conferences was provided by Volkswagen Foundation and by the German National Research Foundation.

PART I
REGIONS

CHAPTER 1
GLOBAL HISTORY IN (NORTHWESTERN) EUROPE: EXPLORATIONS AND DEBATES
Gareth Austin

My brief is to discuss the study of global history in Europe. This presents two major difficulties. The first is the impossibility of doing justice to all strands of this varied literature in different languages from diverse places within the continent (even allowing for the much-commented-upon predominance of English in the global/world history literature).[1] It is generally accepted that the resurgence of world/global history began earlier and is still much more marked in the west than in the east of Europe. While scholars on both sides of the Elbe have tried to transcend the national frameworks that have partitioned historiography in Europe,[2] in Eastern Europe this has mainly been done through transnational history, whereas in Western Europe, transnational and global/world history have both been on the rise—and the distinction between the two is now less frequently drawn. Even so, it is likely that the following pages represent in exaggerated form the differences of emphasis between the ways historians in Western and Eastern Europe have sought to achieve their common aim of transcending national historiographies. It is also admitted that works available in English (especially) and French unduly predominate, and that I have probably overlooked contributions in southern European languages. On the positive side, the following pages also reflect numerous conversations and panels that have brought together historians from around (and beyond) Europe, notably the triennial European congresses in world and global history.

The second difficulty arises from intellectual "globalization" itself: how to distinguish (there is no intention or even possibility of isolating) individual and collective initiatives taken in Europe from those taken elsewhere, when all are profoundly interconnected. The academic profession is asymmetrically but deeply "globalized," especially in English-speaking universities. Hence the study of any sort of history in any one space is both entangled with work going on elsewhere and carried out partly by workers from elsewhere. For example, this volume is the outcome of an extended conversation initiated by two German scholars (the editors) while they were both based in the United States. The growth of global history owes much to European scholars at North American universities and to the Asian academic diaspora in both Europe and North America. It is thus necessary to balance a recognition of some continuing national, subregional and regional patterns with an emphasis on the—perhaps dominant—extent to which global historiography in any one place is an intercontinental product.

The discussion is organized in two parts. The first tries to trace the adventures in global history in which European-based scholars have participated, from tentative conversations to publications and institution-building. The second introduces and comments upon some of the main debates in which they have engaged, and some of the ways in which global history has altered historians' understandings of West European history.

Explorations

In the inaugural issue of the *Journal of World History* (JWH), Gilbert Allardyce observed, "As the practice of history become professional, the practice of world history became identified with amateurism."[3] Though, over many centuries and from different cultures, there have been numerous ventures into some sort of world or universal history,[4] the emergence and practice of history as an organized profession was characterized by an affirmation of spatial boundaries: a focus on the history of specific "civilizations," "nations" or parts of nations. In Europe as well as the United States, from the late nineteenth century until late in the twentieth, world history was left to (the more enlightened) secondary schools and popular publishers.[5] Most academic historians treated world history as "sociological" speculation at worst and as scene-setting at best: no more than a way into the serious business of specialized research. This section begins by considering what scholars based in Europe have come to mean by "global" and/or "world" history. It then describes the impulses behind the resurgence of global history in the continent and comments on the phases through which its study has moved.

Definitions

If participants in the project of "global history" in Europe in the later 1990s and early 2000s distinguished between it and "world history," the former meant the study of "connections and comparisons" across and between world regions,[6] whereas the latter was more encompassing, closer to the history of humanity. From this perspective, global history was an approach; world history was a subject. This distinction partly reflected awareness that (for better and worse) the interest in global history in Europe—initially, mainly in Britain and very soon also in the Netherlands—was not driven by a concern to offer grandly synthesizing first-year undergraduate courses in the subject, which was one of the drivers of world history in the United States.

Increasingly, however, the distinction gave way to the straightforward conviction that the terms were interchangeable. In the early years Patrick O'Brien, who more than anyone, inspired the development of global history in Britain and indeed (especially through the Global Economic History Network [GEHN]) in multiple universities within Europe and beyond, used to combine the "connections and comparisons" definition of global history with a propensity to quote with approval William McNeill's dictum that the art of writing world history is "knowing what to leave out." By the time he wrote the first article for the new *Journal of Global History*, in 2006, O'Brien presented connections and comparisons as different strategies for practicing the subject, rather than as its formal definition. Indeed, he is emphatic that "world" and "global" history are interchangeable: a view generally shared among practitioners in Europe today.[7]

Three clarifications should be added. First, as far as I am aware, no practitioner of global history in Europe has accepted Bruce Mazlish's proposal that it should be confined to the study of globalization.[8] On the contrary, the focus of global historiography in Europe has been the period 1500–1900,[9] and historians here (as elsewhere) have emphasized the longevity and discontinuity of "globalization" in its various senses.[10] Again, Frederick Cooper's skepticism about the value of the concept of "globalization" as an analytical tool for historians of Africa is shared by a high proportion of global historians, whether particularly focused on Africa or not.[11] The understandable tendency to equate global history with the history of globalization has been confusing and misleading.[12]

Second, as far as I am aware, no practitioner of global/world history in Europe (or elsewhere) shares the assumption of some colleagues (outside the field) and administrators that global/world history is to be equated with "non-European" history. A village in Bohemia may well have been as globally entangled as a village in China.[13] Thus the global history perspective is illustrated by the title of an article by Jan Lucassen and Leo Lucassen: "The mobility transition revisited, 1500–1900: what the case of Europe can offer to global history."[14] The global history approach implies that the study of Europe or its components is just as much "Area Studies" as is the study of anywhere else.

Third, it might be suggested that global history differs from transnational history in that the latter is exclusively concerned with connections, whereas the former is also concerned with comparisons. Relatedly, global historians are concerned to offer causal explanations, whereas on the narrower definitions of transnational history, description might be sufficient. Overall, however, the two styles of history not only complement each other and share the aim of transcending nation-state historiographies, they overlap.[15] So it is no surprise that the *Journal of Global History* has published articles that are explicitly transnational in approach, such as the special "cluster" of articles on "The transnational history of international institutions" published in July 2011.[16]

Impulses

From outside the field, it is easy to reduce the growth of global historiography to a direct response to global history itself: the economic resurgence of East and South Asia, and the period of increasing integration in capital and goods (though not necessarily labor) markets around the planet during the generation preceding the world (especially Western) economic crisis of 2008. From within, it is apparent that the intellectual, professional and indeed personal roots of the resurgence of global history in Europe go back further. I detect three lines of thought whose pursuit brought scholars together to explore the global dimension of history.

One was a reaction against the increasing fragmentation of the study of history that was the downside of the expansion of the history profession and, especially, of its increasing specialization. Certainly, the proliferation of doctoral theses, published monographs and journals devoted to subfields was a massive advance in making evidence accessible, in analyzing it and in critically reviewing both the evidence and its interpretations. The problem, however, was that both the production and reception of historical knowledge became to a great extent segmented into discrete compartments, whether defined by subdiscipline, period or geography. Already by the 1980s, the historiographical consequences of the monograph, or, more precisely, of the fact that periodic production of specialized monographs and articles had been institutionalized as the basic requirement of academic employment, were beginning to be regarded as a mixed blessing. Scholarship was not uncommonly seen as increasingly fragmented into tiny communities of experts, each operating in increasingly narrowly defined subfields. Rare indeed was the polymath who could master more than one such area. This was being said both of long-established and voluminous national historiographies and of the expansion of research on the history of the "Third World."[17]

My impression (and personal recollection, in the case of London) is that a major reason for the growth of global history was (and is) precisely that it has the temerity to tackle issues that are big or, more specifically, that connect the fragments: in logical reaction against the way the profession had been evolving. The growth of global history in London, for example, began in 1996 with the convening of a regular seminar on that theme at the Institute of Historical Research. I think it is fair to say that all the regular participants were attracted primarily by the sense that these conversations between specialists in different periods and places permitted engagement with what the seminar convener, O'Brien, called "meta questions."[18] In the words of the editorial statement that prefaced the first issue of the *Journal of Global History* a decade later, "A deluge of monographs is obscuring the landscapes of historical knowledge, even in relatively neglected parts of the globe."[19]

A second impulse behind the (re-)emergence of global history in the European academy was a reaction against what may be called Eurocentrism of agency (the assumption that it has been mostly Europeans—or at least Westerners—who have changed the world) and Eurocentrism of concept (the dominance in history and social science of models derived from perceptions of European/Western experience, even when the object of analysis is experience elsewhere). While the former exaggerates European exceptionalism, the latter entails the opposite: the long-standing tendency to "naturalize" European history by treating it as the norm, such that it is the departures from that supposed template which are thought to need explanation. The reaction against Eurocentric tendencies in scholarship goes back to the 1950s (and even before), notably in the challenges to Eurocentric understandings of the history of science, and of history much more generally, by such scholars as Joseph Needham (in Cambridge) and Marshall Hodgson (in Chicago).[20]

Indeed, the most fundamental intellectual requirement for the development of global history as a field or approach was the massive growth of historical research on the non-Western world that has occurred since 1945 and, especially, since 1960. Needham and Hodgson have already been mentioned. To give a more extended example, research on the economic history of various parts of Asia and Africa before European colonization and gunboat diplomacy increasingly pointed to general conclusions that (though naturally debatable in detail) basically contradicted the Eurocentric assumptions of Marxists, modernization theorists and a multitude of historians. The evidence suggested that market behavior (of kinds familiar to economic theorists) and even economic growth were far from being European innovations. It is reasonable to identify a tradition of such historical work going back to Thomas Smith on Tokugawa Japan (1959, 1992) and Irfan Habib on Mughal India (1967).[21] That tradition was extended by A. G. Hopkins on precolonial West Africa (1973), and by John Richards (1993) going beyond Habib in arguing that the markets of Mughal India were strongly rooted in local societies rather than resulting from the partly unintended consequences of ultimately self-limiting fiscal policies and practices.[22] Eric Jones (1988) brought together part of this revisionist economic historiography of non-Western societies with the results of new work on early-modern Europe,[23] which pushed the roots of industrialization deeper into the early-modern period.[24]

Thus it was no coincidence that specialists on Africa and Asia were disproportionately represented among the participants in early seminars and other initiatives in global history. In Britain this applied, for example, to the South Asia specialists B. R. (Tom) Tomlinson (School of Oriental and African Studies [SOAS]) and David Washbrook (Cambridge)—joined by Tirthankar Roy when he moved from Pune to the London School of Economics (LSE). Before leaving Cambridge, England, for Austin, Texas, Hopkins orchestrated a pioneering volume on *Globalization in World History* (2002), one of whose major themes was that globalization has both non-Western and Western roots.[25] At Cambridge, Christopher Bayly, a leading historian of South Asia, went on to write a history of the period 1780–1914 that highlighted the importance of the historical agency of Asians and Africans even in the period of greatest European power.[26] A further example is the first chief editor of the *Journal of Global History*, William Gervase Clarence-Smith (SOAS), an Africanist who had also become a Southeast Asianist and has worked increasingly on themes spanning continental as well as national boundaries.[27] Meanwhile in Germany, Jürgen Osterhammel (Konstanz) started from a non-Western specialization, in his case modern Chinese history, and came to write about the history of empires and colonialism, and globalization, before writing a world history.[28] He himself maintains that in Germany "an area specialization within Non-western history … has been by far the most important avenue towards" global history in the sense used here.[29] This applied, for example, to the Africanist Andreas Eckert, who has gone on to become the founder and director of the international research center on Work and Human Life Cycle in Global History at the Humboldt University in Berlin.

A third source of the new global historiography was less an impulse than a context: awareness of the rising importance of China and South Korea in the world economy, contemporary (turn of century) economic and cultural globalization and, perhaps even more important, intellectual globalization. The material reality of contemporary globalization, or more precisely its human and cyber-spatial dimensions, may also have made it easier for historians to think in global terms. We have already touched on a major example: the long-distance migration of scholars. This phenomenon, much older than the nation-state, reached a new level when the two world wars and the Nazi "final solution" generated a massive exodus of—especially Jewish—intellectuals from Germany, Poland, Russia and some of their neighbors. This supplied British and American universities with new talent and new perspectives, which were to be reflected in the historical writing that the émigrés produced in their adopted countries.[30] Yet there has not been a period of academic globalization to match the last thirty-five years or so, in the expansion of international flows of academic labor, and the increasingly cosmopolitan composition of university departments. As with other forms of globalization, these flows have been far from equal in every direction: academic migration has been overwhelmingly from poor to rich countries and, among the latter, in the early twentieth century most markedly from Germany to Britain, North America and Switzerland, though the pattern continues to evolve.[31] Despite the asymmetry, the overall point remains. When we review the origins of global history in different national historical communities, we find that such communities are often much less "national" than they used to be.

Improvements in the speed and cost of intercontinental exchanges of information have also contributed directly to changing the conditions of academic production in ways that facilitated international cooperation. As early as the 1990s, the leading journal in African history, the *Journal of African History*, moved from locating its editorial team only in Britain to having editors on three continents. It thus became a pioneer of a new tendency in scholarly publishing: for "international" journals to become exactly that, in editing as well as in their lists of contributors and the composition of their readerships. None of this guaranteed that the intellectual content of scholarship would become more globally minded, but it surely helped to inspire and facilitate the trend.

Variations and phases

Scholars who devote part of their writing to global history (under either of the definitions given above) can now be found in all but the tiniest of countries in Western Europe, from north to south. By 2011, if the 500 attendees of the Third European Congress in World and Global History in London that year are any guide, the European country with the greatest density of scholars working in the field relative to the size of its population was Switzerland.

Yet within Western Europe, the growth of the new global history was initially uneven. In the later 1990s and early 2000s it was most evident in Britain, especially in the Economic History Department of the LSE,[32] and then also in the Netherlands, at Leiden and Utrecht. This was never a discrete development: individuals based in several other countries in the subregion were involved almost from the start, and in interaction with colleagues based in the United States and Japan, in particular. According to Osterhammel, global history expanded somewhat later and more slowly in Germany, which was ironic considering the prominence of German scholars in the earlier history of world history. One reason, he suggests, was the priority given by much of the historical profession in Germany in the 1970s and 1980s, when most of those who held chairs in the 1990s and

2000s were trained, to explaining the origins of Nazism.[33] In any case, the University of Leipzig became a pioneer of global as well as transnational history in Germany, and it went on to become, in organizational and networking terms, the leading center for the promotion of transnational and global history in Europe.[34]

Both partisans and critics of global/world history generally agree that there was initially less interest in it, and more suspicion of it, in France than in Britain or Germany,[35] despite the precedent of the Annales school's explorations in world history, especially Fernand Braudel's magisterial trilogy, *Civilisation materielle, economie et capitalisme, XVe-XVIIIe siècle* (1979). Braudel's successor, Emmanuel Le Roy Ladurie, produced the pioneering *L'Histoire humaine et comparée du climat* (volume I, 2004 and volume II, 2009).[36] The very fact that the Annales school had engaged in world history was seen by some as a reason for being unenthusiastic about the new global history, as it felt that the rest of the world was—at best—merely catching up. And in some quarters of the French academy, the fact that so much of the new literature was in English and that the world history movement was associated with the United States were also grounds for suspicion.[37] Moreover, during the 1990s, the proportion of scholars in France researching the history of other countries actually fell, perhaps reflecting the influence of the micro-history approach.[38]

During the last decade, however, the situation regarding world or global history in France has been transformed. In the years 2007–2009, besides an edited volume of translations of essays by major Anglophone contributors to global history,[39] other collections, whether published as special issues of journals or as books, presented (mostly) French scholars' reflections on *histoire globale*: in one case with the particularly apt subtitle *un autre regard sur le monde*.[40] Among single-authored books, already in 2004, a major (and much-debated) study by Olivier Pétré-Grenouilleau situated the history of slave trading firmly in the context of world history, a book now followed by the same author's similarly global *Qu'est-ce que l'esclavage* (2014).[41] Alessandro Stanziani, an Italian scholar who is currently professor of global history at l'École des hautes études en sciences sociales, extended his research on the comparative history of labor coercion from Eurasia to the Indian Ocean.[42] Besides the history of forced labor of various kinds, recent global historiography in France has continued the Annales tradition of researching the history of relations between humans and the physical environment. To Christian Grataloup's extended and illuminating geographical commentaries on world history can be added the first critical and extended historical dissection of the concept of the present geological era as the Anthropocene, by Christophe Bonneuil and Jean-Baptiste Fressoz.[43] Meanwhile the 2014 European Congress on World and Global History was hosted by the École normale supérieure in Paris, attracting a record number of papers and participants.

These national variations complicate any idea that the precocity of the growth of global historiography in any one country correlates to an imperial past.[44] If that was the decisive influence, Belgium should have been as pioneering as the Netherlands in this context, and France as pioneering as Britain.[45] But Belgian public and scholarly opinion was apparently less willing than the Dutch to consider the colonial past; while in France, as we have noted, there were other influences and precedents. Again, a colonial legacy hardly accounts for the leading role of the University of Leipzig. Rather, the long history of overseas empire in Atlantic Europe contributed to the initiation of global history in a different sense: cumulative investment in the academic study of Asia, Africa and Latin America provided the principal former colonial powers with the libraries and specialists required to take the lead in the study of what used to be called the "Third World"—should the scholars wish to avail themselves of this opportunity. In fact, the presence of a deep imperial past surely contributed to the emergence in the same countries of both writers and readers determined to reject Eurocentrism, and therefore ready to either initiate or respond positively to the challenge "global history" posed to Eurocentrism.

My impression, inadequately documented as it may be, is that the development of global history followed a similar dynamic in several countries, with variations of timing and content. Roughly, two phases may be distinguished. There was an initial phase of discussions about whether a meaningful and useful global history was possible, and, if so, whether it was simply a "conversation"—the term O'Brien used at the beginning of the Global History seminar in London—between specialists on different parts of the world or whether there was a research agenda as well. This preliminary phase also involved discussion about the definition of global history, whether it was different from world history, and how it related to other approaches that crossed national historiographical borders, such as transnational history and *l'histoire croisée*.[46] This initial phase can also be seen in the development of subfields of global history, such as global labor history. Thus in the early 2000s, a series of international workshops at the Wissenschaftszentrum Berlin (organized by Jürgen Kocka and Andreas Eckert) explored whether it was possible in any serious sense to study labor history globally, and if so, what problems and opportunities it would involve.

The next phase involved "getting on with it" through institution-building, research, teaching and writing. New fora were and are being created through the launch of journals and book series. The *Journal of Global History* (originally owned by the LSE, published by Cambridge University Press) appeared in 2006. In recent years the journal *Comparativ*, from the University of Leipzig, founded in 1991, has become increasingly important as a channel for world as well as transnational history.[47] The first French journal dedicated to global and related forms of history, *Monde(s): histoire, espaces, relations*, started in 2012.[48] Meanwhile, new book series include Brill's "Global Economic History" series (Leiden), Routledge's "Themes in Global History" (London) and two series published in German in Vienna.[49]

Meanwhile the European Network in Universal and Global History (ENIUGH) was founded in 2007 at a congress at Leipzig, which became its headquarters. Since then, in conjunction with partner hosts in different countries, it has organized the now-triennial European congresses on world and global history, attracting (so far) successively larger numbers of participants.[50] ENIUGH is now one of several regionally based associations of world and global historians, which since 2007 have themselves been formally linked.[51] During the last few years, research centers have also been founded in several major

European universities. For example, the labor workshops in Berlin paved the way for a successful application for funding to establish the above-mentioned research center on the Work and Human Life Cycle in Global History at Humbolt University. In Britain, the Global History and Culture Centre has been running since 2007 at Warwick University (initially directed by Maxine Berg), and in 2011 Oxford opened a Centre for Global History (directed by John Darwin and then James Bellich).[52] In France, a major multidisciplinary research and teaching program has been established at the Ecole normale supérieure in Paris, directed by Michel Espagne. Meanwhile, other older institutions that do not have "global" or "world" or even "transnational" in their titles have nurtured global history. The International Institute of Social History in Amsterdam and the journal edited there—the *International Review of Social History*—have respectively provided leadership and a forum for the emergence of a self-conscious global labor history. All these initiatives have been part of a wave of decisions about resource allocation, big and small, in various European countries, which over recent years have resulted in the establishment of individual positions in global and transnational history at a range of universities and institutes.

They have also involved the initiation of undergraduate and graduate teaching in the field, from individual courses to—at graduate level—whole degree programs. The first master's degree program in global history offered in Europe was started in 2000 by the Economic History department at the LSE. This has recently been subsumed into perhaps the most notable teaching initiative so far, the Erasmus Mundus MA in global studies, supported by the European Union, in which students spend a year each in two of several partner universities (Leipzig, LSE, Vienna, Wroclaw and now also Roskilde).

Perhaps above all, "getting on with" global history has increasingly involved new research. In the case of global economic history, the Leverhulme-funded GEHN of 2003–2006 provided a bridge between the phase of conversation between specialists and the subsequent development of research initiatives. Typical of global history, GEHN was anything but a purely regional initiative: it involved a consortium of universities on three continents, a series of small conferences leading to publications and nearly fifty individual scholars from twenty-nine universities in eleven countries.[53] Over the last several years, many individual and a few collective research projects have been launched or even completed. These include a five-person quantitative study of real wages in cities across Eurasia, from the eighteenth to the early twentieth century.[54] Again, Jan Lucassen, Karin Hofmeester, Marcel Van der Linden and their colleagues at the International Institute of Social History in Amsterdam have taken the lead in orchestrating an intercontinental effort to produce a database about the size and composition of the workforce in each world region at certain benchmark dates over the last several centuries. Finally, Linda Colley's *The Ordeal of Elizabeth Marsh: A Woman in World History* (2007), which traces the intercontinental travels of an eighteenth-century Englishwoman, demonstrates how imperial and global themes can be illuminated through the biography of an individual of humble origin and no real power.[55] Thus the practice of historians has answered the earlier question about whether global history was purely an exercise in synthesis.

Debates

Scholars based in Europe have contributed far too much to the emerging world historiography for me to mention all strands. Conversely, since these debates are mostly not specifically European, it would be contrived to try to isolate European contributions. It is, however, appropriate to comment on how far global historians based in Europe have tackled the problems of Eurocentrism. I will then consider different responses in Europe to the question of at which level of abstraction, and in what forms, analysis and theory are best deployed and developed in global history. Finally, we will ask whether global history has influenced historians working on geographically smaller scales.

Tackling Eurocentrism

I emphasized above that the struggle against Eurocentrism—both the Eurocentrism of agency and the Eurocentrism of concept—was and is one of the major motives for the global history project in Europe as elsewhere. Yet there is always the danger that the language of "world" and "globe" may be used to re-dress, rather than redress, the traditional narratives of Western exceptionalism. This issue continues to provoke debate.

On the Eurocentrism of agency, Peer Vries has averred that "History is 'provincializing' Europe: it does not need historians to do so": the decline of Western dominance deprives such thinking "of most of its material base and in any case makes it much less convincing and acceptable…. Amongst global historians, anti-Eurocentrists already far outnumber Eurocentrists."[56] Indeed, the new global historiography tends to emphasize very strongly non-Western contributions to the making of events and processes. At the level not just of monographs but of broad and sophisticated synthesis, the tendency to overlook elements of non-Western agency has been severely reduced, as was mentioned above in the context of the work of Bayly and Hopkins. Further, John Darwin's overview of "global empires" since 1400 fully absorbs the implications of recent global economic historiography of the early-modern era, which shows the economic world before the Industrial Revolution as very much polycentric.[57] Darwin complements this with his thesis that the period of European imperial hegemony arrived much later than has usually been thought.[58] And in reply to very influential papers by growth economists reasserting the view that, for better and worse, the choices of colonial rulers determined the relative economic prosperity of the relevant territory for centuries to come,[59] historians have insisted upon the importance of Asian and African agency—even under colonial rule.[60] Other scholars with a different but not unrelated approach have employed the notion of "multiple modernities" to dispute the unthinking equation of modernization with Westernization.[61] Finally, a nice example of the tendency for recent global history to present a more multisided view of historical agency is Felipe Fernández-Armesto's history of exploration, which underlines the role of non-Westerners as well as Westerners in this fundamental process of world history.[62]

Conceptual Eurocentrism is more resilient and has been much less comprehensively challenged.[63] To be clear, the problem is not that a concept happened to originate in reflections on some part of Western historical experience: that does make it necessarily unhelpful for the analysis of experiences elsewhere. Rather, the objection is that up to now the flow of concepts is predominantly one way, from the study of the West to the study of other parts of the world. This unidirectionality surely hinders our understanding of the history of both "the Rest" *and* the West. E. A. Wrigley, the historical demographer of Britain, noted that "ironically, it may be that the understanding of European history has suffered the more."[64]

The problem of conceptual Eurocentrism has begun to be ameliorated. The tool kit of social science has been enriched in recent decades by models derived outside the West. Starting with the Nobel Prize–winning Amartya Sen, Indian economists have become extremely influential within development economics. This in turn has led historians of famine to experiment critically with Sen's "entitlement" approach—inspired by the case of colonial India—as a framework to study famines elsewhere.[65] Again, historians concerned with the cultural and political dimensions of modernity and globalization need no reminding of the work of the Indian anthropologist Arjun Appadurai, and social historians of Europe and North America are well aware of the Subaltern Studies approach to South Asian history.[66] But while the trend is encouraging, it still has a long way to go: the tools we think with are still mainly of European origin. Thus we are very far from an intellectually decentered world. It is also true that the main diversification of the toolbox has been from South Asia, with other regions still neglected as sources of theoretical inspiration.

Methodologically, the general solution is surely the systematic adoption of the principle of "reciprocal comparison," defined by Kenneth Pomeranz as "viewing both sides of the comparison as 'deviations' when seen through the expectations of the other, rather than leaving one as always the norm."[67] Pomeranz and Bin Wong have attempted this for China and Europe in the context of economic history. Their example should be followed for other regions and in other fields. In the historiography involving Africa, for example, there have been pitifully few examples of reciprocal comparison so far, though there are signs that this is changing.[68] Part of the answer is for Africanists (in this case) to follow the example set by some Sinologists by thinking more about what specialists on other parts of the world might learn from their work.[69]

If they do, it may turn out that in some respects there are stronger similarities between certain societies in different periods on different continents than between societies during the same period on the same continent. For example, patterns of witchcraft accusation in colonial southern Ghana seem to resemble those of sixteenth- and seventeenth-century England more closely than they do those of twentieth-century Central or South Africa.[70] As we welcome the decline of the historiographical preoccupation with national frameworks, we must be careful to avoid substituting an essentialist insistence on regional ones.

The onus is not simply on specialists on regions outside the West. The method of reciprocal comparison requires Europeanists, too, to read beyond their own "Area Studies," with its familiar historiographies and conceptual templates. Dipesh Chakrabarty remarked in 2000 that "Third-world historians feel a need to refer to works in European history; historians of Europe do not feel any need to reciprocate."[71] That is significantly less true today, as is illustrated by some of the Europeanists participating in global history projects, but it still often applies. The same can be said within Europe itself: historians of Scandinavia are much more likely to refer to works on Britain or France than the other way around, and not only because of the demographic disparity. Economic historians of Scandinavia are familiar with the contesting models of British economic development, but it is rare for economic historians in Britain to consider whether they could draw ideas from work on Scandinavia.[72]

But to end this section on a historiographical advance that has already occurred, Van der Linden has provided a framework within which a genuinely global labor history can be written, one that precisely avoids naturalizing European experience and that facilitates reciprocal comparison. The crucial move is defining the "subaltern class" of capitalist societies as comprising all workers whose labor is commodified, whatever form that commodification takes.[73] This starting point should free us from any lingering tendency to regard the male proletarian as the quintessential worker, rather than as one among a number of categories, each of which needs to be carefully distinguished in its historical setting(s).

Levels and forms of analysis and theory

There has been considerable discussion about the most useful ways to study history across national borders. The core issue, perhaps, is how to join the dots: how best and at what level of generality to link specific lives, relationships and events. Up to the present, cultural historians have been probably the most reluctant to compare, preferring instead to focus, along with Espagne (1994, though reiterated in his keynote at the 2011 Third European Congress on World and Global History), on specific "cultural transfers."[74] Shalini Randeria, the historically minded anthropologist and sociologist, called for a focus on the "entangled histories" of different sides, including their mutual influence on their images of each other.[75] Such approaches surely work well in the study of connections across both national and cultural borders, and their emphasis on the frequently asymmetric character of connections ensures that the importance of politics is not neglected. Social and economic historians, and all those global historians who pursue causal explanation, however, would agree with Kocka that a focus on entangled, crossed and connected histories can be combined with comparative analysis—and may need to be, depending on the question that animates the inquiry concerned.

> Certainly, the act of comparison presupposes the analytical separation of the cases to be compared. But that does not mean ignoring or neglecting the interrelations between these cases (if and to the extent that they existed). Rather, such interrelations should become part of the comparative framework by analyzing them as factors that have led to similarities or differences, convergence or divergence between the cases one compares.[76]

Comparison is indeed far from unknown in global cultural history, if the latter includes the cross-continental comparative and historical sociology of Jack Goody, in a pioneering stream of much-cited books from the 1970s to the 2000s.[77] Goody particularly used comparison to try to distinguish possible explanations that were contradicted by comparative evidence from those that were not.

Scholars pursuing the overlapping ventures of transnational and global history have adopted a range of specific ways of conceptualizing connections and comparisons. Those seeking to build systematically on an analysis of connections have advocated a focus on "global moments" or "critical junctures of globalization."[78] Sebastian Conrad and Dominic Sachsenmaier define "global moments" as "events of a popular significance that appealed to people in discrete and distant locations," shaping and intensifying "global consciousness."[79] For example, the Ethiopian defeat of Italy in 1898 and the Japanese defeat of Russia in 1904, which ran against the grain of recent military encounters between Western and non-Western forces, changing the sense of what was possible in future. Matthias Middell and Katja Naumann, introducing "the spatial turn" to global historians, define "critical junctures of globalization" as "periods and arenas in which new spatial relationships are established."[80]

At a much more ambitious level of abstraction, World Systems theory is used by some global historians, such as Eric Vanhaute, as a framework within which to integrate both comparisons and connections.[81] World Systems theory predated the new global history. Originating as a variation on dependency theory, it was heir to much of the latter's amalgam of Eurocentrism of agency with radical pessimism (as in *How Europe Underdeveloped Africa*, the title of Walter Rodney's 1972 book).[82] But from the 1990s on, World Systems theory became more encompassing, reorienting itself toward a longer-term view that went back not centuries, but millennia. In the process, it was able to give more attention to the multicenteredness of the preindustrial world, in economic and political terms.[83]

Between a focus on global moments or conjunctures and World Systems theory is the traditional kind of historians' analysis of causes and consequences, in which a detailed study of a single or a few cases in their contexts is often set, however briefly and sometimes only implicitly, within wider comparisons. This is the method employed in most global history that goes beyond the purely descriptive, albeit often for a range of geographically and chronologically defined cases rather than for a very few.

Offering the possibility of integrating all these levels of abstraction is Marxism, which—in more eclectic forms than ever—has continued to be one of the sources of some of the most imaginative thinking in global history.[84] Vastly more influential in social science today, however, are the rational-choice models offered by economists and political scientists. Among global (and other) historians, it is economic historians who most often and most explicitly draw on theories from this tradition. On many issues its analytical power is great, and it is flexible enough to generate conflicting arguments: it is a paradigm, not a specific theory. Yet in economic history, and even more so in the work of growth economists, there is a strong tendency for "new institutionalism" to celebrate the Anglo-American liberal myth of origin (in the sense of ideological foundation charter), in which private property and representative (strong but limited) government become *the* route to long-term national prosperity.[85] Global historians interested in this approach would be wise to be cautious. The late S. R. Epstein's comparative analysis of early-modern states in Europe falsified the claim of Douglass North and Barry Weingast that the establishment of secure private property rights in England following the "Glorious Revolution" of 1688 gave the country uniquely low interest rates (which could in turn help to account for the Industrial Revolution).[86] The wider comparative claims made in the same tradition are equally questionable, as is suggested by both historians[87] and current history (the thirty-plus years of express economic growth in China from 1978 hardly fit the "new institutionalist" model).[88]

Global perspectives and other histories

Historians based wholly or partly in Europe—not least in Italy, Spain and Switzerland—have made important contributions on global themes ranging (to take just some examples) from migration[89] to conceptions of humanity,[90] the history of the international monetary system,[91] histories of science and energy use[92] and the historical interaction of culture and economy.[93] Equally valuably, global perspectives have begun to alter understandings of European history.

Four examples of the latter will be given, if only briefly. First, it is appropriate to ask what difference a global history perspective makes to imperial historians. Before or independently of the resurgence of global history, the new cultural history of British imperialism had already done much to achieve a reciprocal integration of the histories of colony and metropole, bringing out the centrality of empire for the contemporary sense of British national identity.[94] Second, in the framework of transnational and global history, Conrad offered a global perspective on Germany in the late nineteenth and early twentieth centuries by arguing that migration and immigration contributed in several ways to the form, content and practice of nationalism in Willhelmine Germany, including "the racialization of the nation."[95] Third, with particular reference to Russian serfdom, Alessandro Stanziani has done much to advance the argument that the transition from forced to free labor came much later than previously supposed.[96] The general implication of his work and that of others on nineteenth-century Britain and the United States, and on the decline of slavery in colonial Africa, is that the notion of what I would call the self-possessing individual was rarely adopted before the late nineteenth or early twentieth century.

Finally, in economic history, the reinterpretations of the Industrial Revolution by specialists on China and India have produced an impressive reaction from economic historians of Britain and the Netherlands in the form of new research projects. In 1998, Prasannan Parthasarathi moved from a revisionist comparison of wages in cotton textile production in India and Britain to an argument about connections, emphasizing that Britain resorted to protectionism to permit the emergence of its mechanized products.[97] His severest critics, Stephen Broadberry and Bishnu Gupta, themselves now also argue that the British Industrial Revolution was in part an exercise in import substitution, taking markets from Indians.⁹⁸ Kenneth Pomeranz's argument that the Yangzi Delta was at least as advanced economically as Britain until it ran into resource buffers, from which Britain was saved by the fortuitous combination of coal at home and the "ghost acres" of the Americas—tilled to large extent by enslaved Africans—abroad, inspired Robert Allen, a Canadian economic historian then at Oxford, to undertake more detailed study of the quantitative side of the comparison.⁹⁹ It also moved Jan-Luiten van Zanden, in Utrecht, to do further comparative research. Both Allen and Van Zanden proceeded to write important books on the Industrial Revolution—in global perspective.¹⁰⁰ Most striking of all, it led to them collaborating with others to undertake the above-mentioned comparison of real wages in cities across Eurasia, over nearly three centuries.¹⁰¹ Such a project would have been inconceivable before the publication of Pomeranz's *The Great Divergence* (2000).¹⁰²

Reflections

This chapter has reflected on the European parts of the much wider transition from the treatment of the study of world history as a mere aperitif before the serious courses arrive, to the present status of global history as, increasingly, a stimulus to research and the framework used in some of the most sophisticated historical syntheses written today. In reviewing the origins of this shift, the main point that emerges is that, while historiographical trends almost always respond at least in part to contemporary political shifts, this is by no means the whole story. To be sure, the impetus came partly from the perception of contemporary globalization. In particular, there was a much greater receptivity toward evidence of non-Western historical agency. Yet there is more to the origins of global history than this. In particular, I emphasize the importance of the accumulation of evidence, and the progressive logic of debate and further research, in the histories of various parts of Asia and Africa. Those decades of dedicated scholarship mattered. Again, in the history profession generally, roughly a century of production of specialist articles and monographs eventually led increasing numbers of those professionals to search for bigger questions on which they could mobilize their learning.

Global history raises such bigger questions. At the same time, one thing on which I think historians participating in the project of global history agree is that researching, writing and teaching global history involve frequent movement between spatial scales—and that there should be no hierarchy of scales. The proof of the seriousness of this conviction is the fact that the production of global historiography, at least in Europe, has been almost entirely the work of scholars who started as and remain practicing specialists on much smaller geographical areas. Many are reluctant to call themselves global historians, both because of their other lines of work and because they are too modest to make any claim to such broad expertise.¹⁰³

But personal modesty should not cramp analytical ambitions. Global and transnational history shares a common interest in connections and entanglements across national and other borders. In the view of most practitioners, it is important to combine the study of connections with the study of comparisons. Scholars surely have a duty to summarize and explain, rather than to try (necessarily in vain) to reproduce or mimic the full complexity of reality. Simplification has a bad name in scholarship, but we should try to simplify in the best heuristic sense, that is, by striving to identify causes without omitting evidence. Hence the most informative response to the problem of *Provincializing Europe*, in Chakrabarty's well-known phrase,[104] is not to forswear meta-narratives on principle, but instead to work toward better—more genuinely general—ones. As Van der Linden says, "What we probably need are multiple 'large narratives' that may or may not coexist harmoniously."[105]

An indispensable part of this must be the displacement of the Eurocentrism of both agency and concept. As Vanhaute observed, "Much of the drive for a 'new' global history started with the aim to surpass or delegitimize the 'old' Eurocentric stories of the rise of a unified world."[106] We have made progress but have a long way to go. Further progress becomes all the more urgent if the political atmosphere in Europe becomes more inward-looking and nationalistic.[107]

Acknowledgment

I am grateful for feedback and stimulus from fellow participants in the three conferences in the "Global History, Globally" series, especially the final one in Berlin in October 2011, where I presented a draft of this chapter. I received further valuable comments on it at the "Globalizing Economic History" conference in honor of Patrick O'Brien, in Oxford, December 2012. I am grateful to Martha Schulman for a close reading and detailed suggestions. I also much appreciate the generosity of Blaise Wilfert-Portal (ENS, Paris) and Martina Winkler (Münster) in sharing with me the texts of their presentations to the closing roundtable of the Third European Congress in World and Global History, organized by the ENIUGH and hosted at the LSE, April 2011. I have now taken the opportunity, presented by Bloomsbury and the editors, to update this chapter at the very beginning of 2017.

Notes

1. And despite the education in developments in the former Soviet bloc that I have received from Matthias Middell, Steffi Marung and Katja Naumann (University of Leipzig) and from Attila Melegh (Corvinus University, Budapest).
2. I believe it may have been Jürgen Osterhammel who coined the phrase "History beyond the nation state": Jürgen Osterhammel, *Geschichtswissenschaft jenseits des Nationalstaats: Studien zu Beziehungsgeschichte und Zvilisationsvergleich* (Göttingen, 2001).
3. Gilbert Allardyce, "Toward World History: American Historians and the Coming of the World History Course," *Journal of World History* 1:1 (1990), 23–27.

4. Evoked in Patrick Manning, *Navigating World History: Historians Create a Global Past* (New York: Palgrave Macmillan, 2003), 17–54; Patrick O'Brien, "Historiographic Traditions and Modern Imperatives for the Restoration of Global History," *Journal of Global History* 1:1 (2006), 3–39.

5. If I may take a personal example, and if I remember correctly, the history syllabus that I studied in Britain in the early 1970s at age 14–16 was titled "World History since 1918." A few years later I found myself charged with teaching "World History" to first-year secondary school students in Kenya. (I began with a few minutes on the Big Bang, followed by a few minutes on the African origins of humanity.) Outside the classroom, world history has long been a staple of popular history. For example, the British novelist H. G. Wells, best remembered for his science fiction novel *The War of the Worlds*, confined himself to the domestic affairs of our planet in *A Short History of the World* (1922; revised editions 1946 and, posthumously, 1965 [Harmondsworth, UK: Penguin]).

6. This was the definition used, for example, in the pioneering Global History seminar run by Patrick O'Brien at the Institute of Historical Research in London from 1996.

7. Cf. Jerry Bentley (in this volume) on North American usage. For an emphatic illustration of the synonymity of the terms in the work of the leading Belgian global/world historian, see Eric Vanhaute, "Who Is Afraid of Global History? Ambitions, Pitfalls and Limits of Learning Global History," *Österreichische Zeitschrift für Geschichtswissenschaften* 20:2 (2009), 22–39. Vanhaute has also written a short introduction to world history, giving attention to concepts and methods, from what might otherwise be called a "global history" perspective: Eric Vanhaute, *World History: An Introduction* (London: Routledge, 2013).

8. Bruce Mazlish suggested the term "Global History" for works focused on one theme: the precursors of, and, for some, teleological progression toward, contemporary globalization. He also proposed "New Global History" for the study of the latter. See Bruce Mazlish, *The New Global History* (New York: Routledge, 2006), 2, 103–07.

9. Cf. Peer Vries's declaration that "The early modern period undoubtedly is the period that is covered best in global historical writing" (Vries, "Editorial: Global History," in special issue of *Österreichische Zeitschrift für Geschichtswissenschaften* 20:2 [2009], 5–21, especially 10), though readers of Bayly and Osterhammel's masterly global histories of the "long" nineteenth century (cited below) may think this is no longer the case.

10. See especially A. G. Hopkins (ed.), *Globalization in World History* (London: Pimlico, 2002).

11. Frederick Cooper, "What Is the Concept of Globalization Good For? An African Historian's Perspective," *African Affairs* 100:399 (2001), 189–214; reprinted as ch. 4, "Globalization," in Frederick Cooper, *Colonialism in Question: Theory, Knowledge, History* (Berkeley: University of California Press, 2005).

12. In particular, it has led to criticisms aimed at "global history" as a project, which in my view should be directed elsewhere: Chloé Maurel, "La World/Global history: questions et débats," *Vingtième siècle* 4:104 (2009), 164–66; G. Balachandran, "Writing Global History: Claiming Histories beyond Nations," *Working Papers in International History and Politics* 7 (2011), Graduate Institute of International and Development Studies (Geneva).

13. As noted by Martina Winkler, untitled paper for Concluding Roundtable, Third European Congress in World and Global History, organized by the European Network in Universal and Global History (ENIUGH) and hosted by the London School of Economics, April 2011.

14. Jan Lucassen and Leo Lucassen, "The mobility transition revisited, 1500–1900: what the case of Europe can offer to Global History," *Journal of Global History* 4:3 (2009), 347–77. For a nuanced discussion of the usage of "global history" in relation to related—and, as it turns out, allied—terms, see Dominic Sachsenmaier, "The Necessary Impossibility of

Defining Global History," *Global Perspectives on Global History: Theories and Approaches in a Connected World* (New York: Cambridge University Press, 2011), 70–78.

15. For an incisive discussion of different varieties of transnational history in relation to global history, see Jürgen Osterhammel, "Global History in a National Context: The Case of Germany," *Österreichische Zeitschrift für Geschichtswissenschaften* 20:2 (2009), 44–58, especially on 43–44, 53–54.

16. The cluster was edited by Glenda Sluga: *Journal of Global History* 6:2 (2011).

17. E.g. David Cannadine, "British History: Past, Present—and Future?," *Past & Present* 116 (1987), 169–91, especially 176–79. Even in 1987, Cannadine commented that "global history seemed more glamorous and important than the parochialism of the national past" (ibid., 176). For a US perspective, and a positive response, see Steve J. Stern, "Africa, Latin America, and the Splintering of Historical Knowledge: From Fragmentation to Reverberation," in Frederick Cooper et al. (eds.), *Confronting Historical Paradigms: Peasants, Labor, and the Capitalist World System in Africa and Latin America* (Madison: University of Wisconsin Press, 1993), 3–20.

18. Gareth Austin, "Global History and Economic History: A View of the L.S.E. Experience in Research and Graduate Teaching," in Patrick Manning (ed.), *Global Practice in World History* (Princeton: Markus Weiner, 2008), 99–111.

19. In the interest of transparency, I admit I quote myself, as I (as one of the proposers—though not editors—of the journal) drafted this phrase for inclusion in the statement. *Journal of Global History* 1:1 (2006).

20. Joseph Needham (initiator), *Science and Civilization in China* (Cambridge: Cambridge University Press, 7 vols, 1954–2008). For a relatively early and accessible critical survey, see Mark Elvin, U. J. Libbrecht, Willard J. Peterson and Christopher Cullen, "Symposium: The Work of Joseph Needham," *Past & Present* 87 (1980), 17–53. On Marshall G. S. Hodgson, see the posthumous collection of his essays edited by Edmund Burke III, *Rethinking World History: Essays on Europe, Islam, and World History* (Cambridge: Cambridge University Press, 1993).

21. Thomas C. Smith, *The Agrarian Origins of Modern Japan* (Stanford: Stanford University Press, 1959); Thomas C. Smith, *Native Sources of Japanese Industrialization, 1750–1920* (Berkeley: University of California Press, 1988); Irfan Habib, "Potentialities of Capitalistic Development in the Economy of Mughal India," *Journal of Economic History* 29:1 (1969), 13–31.

22. Antony G. Hopkins, *An Economic History of West Africa* (London: Longman, 1973); John F. Richards, *The Mughal Empire* (Cambridge: Cambridge University Press, 1993).

23. What Jan de Vries called "The Revolt of the Early Modernists," because of which "It is now sometimes conceded that substantial economic growth occurred before the technological breakthroughs of the Industrial Revolution" (de Vries, *The Industrious Revolution: Consumer Behavior and the Household Economy, 1650 to the Present* [New York: Cambridge University Press, 2008], 7).

24. Eric L. Jones, *Growth Recurring: Economic Change in World History* (Oxford: Oxford University Press, 1988).

25. Hopkins, *Globalization in World History*.

26. C. A. Bayly, *The Birth of the Modern World 1780–1914* (Oxford: Blackwell, 2004). Jürgen Osterhammel explicitly takes a more traditional view of this issue and, in a vast and generally exceedingly impressive book, devotes surprisingly little space to African polities before colonization. Jürgen Osterhammel, *The Transformation of the World: A Global History of the Nineteenth Century*, trans. Patrick Camiller (Princeton: Princeton University Press, 2014; German original 2009).

27. Among his many other such works, see William Gervase Clarence-Smith, *Cocoa and Chocolate, 1765–1914* (London: Routledge, 2000) and *Islam and the Abolition of Slavery* (London: Hurst, 2005), and his work on trading diasporas and on horses in world history.
28. Jürgen Osterhammel and Niels P. Petersson, *Globalization: A Short History*, transl. by Dona Geyer (Princeton: Princeton University Press, 2005; German original 2003); Osterhammel, *The Transformation of the World*.
29. Osterhammel, "Global History in a National Context: the Case of Germany," 44–45.
30. The prominence of émigrés in British scholarly life in the post-1945 decades was emphasized by Perry Anderson, "Components of the National Culture," *New Left Review* 50 (1968), 3–57.
31. The net outflow from Germany has been checked by internal changes within the university system, while Britain's status as a major net importer of talent is now in question because of issues created by the country's 2016 referendum decision to withdraw from the European Union.
32. Austin, "Global History and Economic History."
33. Osterhammel, "Global History in a National Context: The Case of Germany." See, further, the detailed account of global and transnational historiography in Dominic Sachsenmaier, Global Perspectives on Global History. *Theories and Approaches in a Connected World*, Cambridge: Cambridge University Press, 2011, 110–71.
34. See Matthias Middell and Katja Naumann, "World History and Global Studies at the University of Leipzig," in Patrick Manning (ed.), *Global Practice in World History: Advances Worldwide* (Princeton: Markus Weiner, 2008), 81–97.
35. See Caroline Douki and Philippe Minard, "Histoire globale, histoire connectées: un changement d'échelle historiographique? Introduction," *Revue d'histoire moderne et contemporaine* 54–55 (2007), 7–21; Maurel, "La World/Global history: questions et débats," in Philippe Beaujard, Laurent Berger and Philippe Norel (eds.), *Histoire globale, mondialisations et capitalisme* (Paris: La Découverte, 2009).
36. Indeed, the recent world/global historiography has partial precedents in a number of historiographical traditions. Among these *les Annales* stand out in the intellectual substance of their contributions over several decades, their involvement (led by Lucien Febvre) in the UNESCO-supported creation of *Cahiers d'histoire mondiale*, in 1953; and their direct influence on later pioneers writing in English. See Krzysztof Pomian, "*World History*: histoire mondiale, histoire universelle," *Le Débat* 154 (2009), 14–40.
37. Maurel, "La World/Global History: questions et débats." A paranoid version of this is Maurel's suggestion, linking Jarod Diamond's geographical determinism and Mazlish's equation of global history with the study of globalization, that global history is a form of US "soft power" that seeks to free the world's remaining superpower from responsibility for taking action on climate change and to provide an apologia for "une mondialisation fondée sur l'extension du système ulta-libéral (libre-échange, dérégulations) à toute la planète" (ibid. 164–66, quotation at p. 166). This misreads the relation between global history and the study of globalization, and misses the anti-Eurocentric, antihegemonic inspiration of much of the new global historiography (see elsewhere in this chapter).
38. Douki and Minard, "Histoire globale, histoire connectées," 14–16.
39. Beaujard and Norel (eds.), *Histoire globale*. Cf., for German-speaking readers, *Globalgeschicte: Theorien, Ansätze, Themen* (Frankfurt a.M., 2007) (cited by Vries, "Editorial: Global History," 5, 18n). "Anglophone" here refers to the language of original publication; as usual in this era of (asymmetric) "intellectual globalization," not all of the authors whose work was translated are native English-speakers.

40. Actually, the volume has two subtitles: "autre" on the cover, and "nouveau" inside. Laurent Testot (ed.), *Histoire globale: un nouveau regard sur le monde* (Paris: Éditions Sciences Humaines, 2008). See also the special issues of *Revue d'histoire moderne et contemporaine* 54–55 (2007), *Le Débat* 154 (2009), and *Vingtième siècle* 4:104 (2009).

41. Olivier Pétré-Grenouilleau, *Les traites négrières: essai d'histoire globale* (Paris: Gallimard, 2004); Grenouilleau, *Qu'est-ce que l'esclavage?* (Paris: Gallimard, 2014).

42. Alessandro Stanziani, *Bondage: Labor and Rights in Eurasia from the Sixteenth to the Early Twentieth Centuries* (New York and Oxford: Berghahn, 2014); Stanziani, *Sailors, Slaves, and Immigrants: Bondage in the Indian Ocean World, 1750–1914* (New York: Palgrave Macmillan, 2014).

43. Christian Grataloup, *Géohistoire de la mondialisation: le temps long du monde* (Paris: Armand Colin, 2010) and *Faut-il penser autrement l'histoire du monde?* (Paris: Armand Colin, 2011), following his *L'invention des continents: Comment l'Europe a découpé le monde* (Paris: Larousse, 2009); Bonneuil and Fressoz, *L'Événement anthropocène: la terre, l'histoire et nous* (Paris: Seuil, 2013); now translated by David Fernbach as *The Shock of the Anthropocene* (London: Verso, 2016). The latter can be read alongside John L. Brooke, *Climate Change and the Course of Global History* (New York: Cambridge University Press, 2014).

44. Still more difficult to explain in these terms is why the world history movement originated in Chicago (Bentley's chapter in this volume) rather than, at least, in an ocean-facing city of the United States.

45. Not to mention Portugal and Spain, on whose indigenous-language publications I do not presume to comment.

46. On the latter see, e.g., Michael Werner and Bénédicte Zimmerman (eds.), *De la comparaison à l'histoire croisée* (Paris: Seuil, 2004). An important example for this literature is the *histoire croisée* of Germany and France in the nineteenth century.

47. The online newsletter *geshichte.transnational*, founded in 2004, is also an important forum for global history.

48. It is intended to provide a forum for "des tendances neuves de l'histoire internationale: histoire transnationale, histoire connectée, histoire globale, histoire impériale" (Robert Frank, cover letter enclosed with the first issue, May 2012). See, further, Frank, "Avant propos: pourquoi une nouvelle revue?," *Monde(s)* 1 (2012), 7–10.

49. Promedia's Edition Weltregionen, and Mandelbaum Verlag's Globalgeschichte—Die Welt 1000–2000 (Vries, "Editorial: Global History," 5, 18).

50. The 2017 Congress will be in Budapest, being held for the first time in Eastern Europe.

51. Under the umbrella of the Network of Global and World Historical Organizations (NOGWHISTO), administratively based in Leipzig.

52. Some of the agenda of these centers may perhaps be seen in two wide-ranging conference volumes inspired by their respective founders: Maxine Berg (ed.), *Writing the History of the Global: Challenges for the Twenty-First Century* (Oxford: Oxford University Press, 2013); James Belich, John Darwin, Margret Frenz and Chris Wickham (eds.), *The Prospect of Global History* (Oxford: Oxford University Press, 2016).

53. The consortium comprised the LSE (the base), Leiden, Osaka, and the University of California at Irvine. The published fruits include Giorgio Riello and Tirthankar Roy (eds.), *How India Clothed the World: The World of South Asian Textiles, 1500–1850* (Leiden: Brill, 2009) and (in large part) Gareth Austin and Kaoru Sugihara (eds.), *Labour-Intensive Industrialization in Global History* (London: Routledge, 2013).

54. Robert C. Allen, Jean-Pascal Bassino, Debin Ma, Christine Moll-Murata and Jan Luiten van Zanden, "Wages, Prices, and Living Standards in China, 1738–1925: In Comparison with Europe, Japan and India," *Economic History Review*, special issue on "Asia in the Great Divergence," 64:S1 (2011), 8–38.

55. Linda Colley, *The Ordeal of Elizabeth Marsh: A Woman in World History* (New York: Harper Press, 2007).

56. Vries, "Editorial: Global History," 16.

57. The most influential contribution to this economic historiography is Kenneth Pomeranz, *The Great Divergence: China, Europe, and the Making of the Modern World Economy* (Princeton: Princeton University Press, 2000).

58. John Darwin, *After Tamerlane: The Rise and Fall of Global Empires, 1400–2000* (London: Penguin, 2007).

59. Daron Acemoglu, Simon Johnson, and James A. Robinson, "The Colonial Origins of Comparative Development: An Empirical Investigation," *American Economic Review* 91 (2001), 1369–401; Acemoglu, Johnson and Robinson, "Reversal of Fortune: Geography and Institutions in the Making of the Modern World Income Distribution," *Quarterly Journal of Economics* 118 (2002), 1231–79; for a more accessible summary, see Acemoglu, Johnson, and Robinson, "Institutions as the Fundamental Cause of Long-Run Growth," in Philippe Aghion and Steven N. Dulauf (eds.), *Handbook of Economic Growth* (Amsterdam: Elsevier, 2005), vol. Ia, 387–470.

60. C. A. Bayly, "Indigenous and Colonial Origins of Comparative Economic Development: The Case of Colonial India and Africa," *Policy Research Working Paper No. 4474* (Washington, DC: World Bank), 2008; Gareth Austin, "The 'Reversal of Fortune' Thesis and the Compression of History: Perspectives from African and Comparative Economic History," *Journal of International Development* 20:8 (2008), 996–1027.

61. Dominic Sachsenmaier and Jens Riedel with Shmuel N. Eisenstadt (eds.), *Reflections on Multiple Modernities: European, Chinese and Other Interpretations* (Leiden: Brill, 2002).

62. Felipe Fernández-Armesto, *Pathfinders: A Global History of Exploration* (Oxford: Oxford University Press, 2006).

63. Jack Goody, however, assailed both kinds of Eurocentrism in *The Theft of History* (2006), after his *The East in the West* (1996), and followed by *Renaissances: The One or the Many?* (2009) and *Metals, Culture and Capitalism: An Essay on the Origins of the Modern World* (2012). All Cambridge: Cambridge University Press.

64. Edward A. Wrigley, "The Process of Modernization and the Industrial Revolution in England," in Wrigley (ed.), *People, Cities and Wealth: The Transformation of Traditional Society*, (Oxford: Blackwell, 1987 [1972]), 46–74, especially 48.

65. Megan Vaughan, *The Story of an African Famine: Gender and Famine in Twentieth-Century Malawi* (Cambridge: Cambridge University Press, 1987); Cormac Ó'Gráda, *Famine: A Short History* (Princeton: Princeton University Press, 2004).

66. E.g. Arjun Appadurai (ed.), *The Social Life of Things: Commodities in Cultural Perspective* (New York: Cambridge University Press, 1986); Appadurai, *Modernity at Large: Cultural Dimensions of Globalization* (Minneapolis: University of Minnesota Press, 1996); forum on Subaltern Studies in *American Historical Review* 99:5 (1994); David Ludden (ed.), *Reading Subaltern Studies: Critical History, Contested Meaning and the Globalization of South Asia* (London: Anthem Press, 2001).

67. Pomeranz, *The Great Divergence*, 8. See also R. Bin Wong, *China Transformed: Historical Change and the Limits of European Experience* (Ithaca: Cornell University Press, 1997).

68. See the examples of Stefano Fenoaltea, "Europe in the African Mirror: The Slave Trade and the Rise of Feudalism," *Rivista di Storia Economica* 15:2 (1999) 123–65; Dylan C. Penningroth, "The Claims of Slaves and Ex-Slaves to Family and Property: A Transatlantic Comparison," *American Historical Review* 112:4 (2007), 1039–69.
69. Some specific suggestions are offered in Gareth Austin, "Reciprocal Comparison and African History: Tackling Conceptual Euro-Centrism in the Study of Africa's Economic Past," *African Studies Review* 50:3 (2007), 1–28.
70. Austin, "Reciprocal Comparison and African History," 13–14.
71. Dipesh Chakrabarty, *Provincializing Europe: Postcolonial Thought and Historical Difference* (Princeton: Princeton University Press, 2000), 28. Goody made a related though not identical point: "My argument is that while most historians aim to avoid ethnocentricity (like teleology), they rarely succeed in doing so because of their limited knowledge of the other (including their own beginnings). That limitation often leads them to make unsustainable claims, implicitly or explicitly, about the uniqueness of the west." Goody, *The Theft of History*, 4.
72. I owe this point to Göran Rydén (Uppsala).
73. Marcel Van der Linden, "Who Are the Workers?" 17–37 in his *Workers of the World: Essays toward a Global Labor History* (Leiden: Brill, 2008), 32.
74. Michel Espagne, "Sur les limites du comparatisme en histoire culturelle," *Genèses* 17 (1994), 112–21.
75. Shailini Randeria, "Geteilte Geschichte und verwobene Moderne," in Jörn Rüsen, Hanna Leitgeb and Norbert Jegelka (eds.), *Zukunftsentwürfe: Ideen für eine Kultur der Veränderung* (Frankfurt a.M.: Campus Verlag, 1999), 87–96; Shalini Randeria, "Entangled Histories of Uneven Modernities: Civil Society, Caste Solidarities and Legal Pluralism in Post-Colonial India," in Yehuda Elkana, Ivan Krastev, Elisio Macamo and Shalini Randeria (eds.), *Unraveling Ties: From Social Cohesion to New Practices of Connectedness* (Frankfurt a.M.: Campus Verlag, 2002), 284–311. See also Werner and Zimmerman (eds.), *De la comparaison à l'histoire croisée*.
76. Jürgen Kocka, "Comparison and Beyond," *History and Theory* 42:1 (2003), 39–44, especially 44.
77. In addition to his more recent books cited above, see Jack Goody, *Production and Reproduction: A Comparative Study of the Domestic Domain* (Cambridge: Cambridge University Press, 1976) and *Cooking, Cuisine and Class: A Study in Comparative Sociology* (Cambridge: Cambridge University Press, 1982).
78. Noted by Martina Winkler in her untitled paper for the concluding round table for the Third European Congress on World and Global History, April 2011.
79. Sebastian Conrad and Dominic Sachsenmaier, "Introduction" to their (eds.), *Competing Visions of World Order: Global Moments and Movements, 1880s–1930s* (New York: Palgrave Macmillan, 2007), 1–16, quotes at 13, 15.
80. Matthias Middell and Katja Naumann, "Global History and the Spatial Turn: From the Impact of Area Studies to the Study of Critical Junctures of Globalization," *Journal of Global History* 5:1 (2010), 149–70. For an excellent general discussion of "Space in global history," see Sebastian Conrad, *What Is Global History?* (Princeton: Princeton University Press, 2016), 115–40, 260–67.
81. Vanhaute, "Who Is Afraid of Global History?," 25, 31, 34–35.
82. Walter Rodney, *How Europe Underdeveloped Africa* (London: Bogle L'Ouverture Publications, 1972).

83. Andre Gunder Frank and Barry K. Gills, "The Five Thousand Year World System in Theory and Praxis," in Robert A. Denemark, Jonathan Friedman, Barry K. Gills and George Modelski (eds.), *World System History: The Social Science of Long Term Change* (London: Routledge, 2000), 3–23.

84. E.g. the late Giovanni Arrighi's *Adam Smith in Beijing: Lineages of the Twenty-First Century* (London: Verso, 2007).

85. I refer to the stream of long-term historical interpretations that runs from Douglass C. North and Robert Paul Thomas, *The Rise of the Western World: A New Economic History* (Cambridge: Cambridge University Press, 1973) to Daron Acemoglu and James R. Robinson, *Why Nations Fail: The Origins of Power, Prosperity, and Poverty* (New York: Crown Business, 2012).

86. Douglass C. North and Barry Weingast, "Constitutions and Commitments: Evolution of Institutions Governing Public Choice in Seventeenth-Century England," *Journal of Economic History* 49:4 (1989), 803–32; S. R. Epstein, *Freedom and Growth: the Rise of States and Markets in Europe, 1300–1750* (London: Routledge, 2000), 12–37.

87. The critiques of Acemoglu, Johnson and Robinson noted above.

88. See for instance Donald Clarke, Peter Murrell and Susan Whiting, "The Role of Law in China's Economic Development," in Loren Brandt and Thomas G. Rawski (eds.), *China's Great Economic Transformation* (Cambridge: Cambridge University Press, 2008), 375–428.

89. E.g. Giovanni Gozzini, "The Global System of International Migration, 1900 and 2000: A Comparative Approach," *Journal of Global History* 1:3 (2006), 321–44; three of the contributions to the section "Discussion—Global Migration," *Journal of Global History* 6:2 (2011).

90. Felipe Fernández-Armesto, *So You Think You're Human? A Brief History of Humankind* (Oxford: Oxford University Press, 2004).

91. E.g. C. L. Holtfrerich and Harold James, *International Financial History in The Twentieth Century: System and Anarchy* (Cambridge: Cambridge University Press, 2003); Marc Flandreau, *The Glitter of Gold: France, Bimetallism and the Emergence of the International Gold Standard, 1848–1873* (Oxford: Oxford University Press, 2004); G. Balachandran, "Power and Markets in Global Finance: The Gold Standard, 1890–1926," *Journal of Global History* 3:3 (2008), 313–35.

92. Karel Davids, "River Control and the Evolution of Knowledge: A Comparison between Regions in China and Europe, c.1400–1850," *Journal of Global History* 1:1 (2006), 59–79; Paolo Malanima, "Energy Crisis and Growth 1650–1850: The European Deviation in a Comparative Perspective," *Journal of Global History* 1:1 (2006), 101–21; Vaclav Smil, "The Two Prime Movers of Globalization: History and the Impact of Diesel Engines and Gas Turbines," *Journal of Global History* 2:3 (2007), 373–94; Tirthankar Roy, "Knowledge and Divergence from the Perspective of Early Modern India," *Journal of Global History* 3:3 (2008), 361–87; Patrick O'Brien, "Historical Foundations for a Global Perspective on the Emergence of a Western European Regime for the Discovery, Development, and Diffusion of Useful and Reliable Knowledge," *Journal of Global History* 8:1 (2013), 1–24.

93. E.g. Giorgio Riello, *A Foot in the Past: Consumers, Producers and Footwear in the Long Eighteenth Century* (Oxford: Oxford University Press, 2006); Carlo Marco Belfanti, "Was Fashion a European Invention?," *Journal of Global History* 3:3 (2008), 419–43.

94. Catherine Hall, *Civilising Subjects: Metropole and Colony in the English Imagination 1830–1867* (Chicago: Chicago University Press, 2002); Linda Colley, *Britons: Forging the Nation 1707–1837* (New Haven: Yale University Press, 1992).

95. E.g. Sebastian Conrad, "Globalization Effects: Mobility and Nation in Imperial Germany, 1880–1914," *Journal of Global History* 3:1 (2008), 43–66. See, further, Conrad, *German Colonialism: A Short History* (Cambridge: Cambridge University Press, 2012; translated by Sorcha O'Hagan from German original, 2008).
96. Alessandro Stanziani, "Serfs, Slaves, or Wage Earners? The Legal Status of Labour in Russia from a Comparative Perspective, from the Sixteenth to the Nineteenth Century," *Journal of Global History* 3:2 (2008), 183–202.
97. Prasannan Parthasarathi, "Rethinking Wages and Competitiveness in the Eighteenth Century: Britain and South Asia," *Past & Present* 158 (1998), 79–109.
98. Stephen Broadberry and Bishnupriya Gupta, "Lancashire, India and Shifting Competitive Advantage in Cotton Textiles, 1700–1850: The Neglected Role of Factor Prices," *Economic History Review* 62:2 (2009), 279–305. Their critique of Parthasarathi is summarized at 13–18 in their "Early Modern Great Divergence: Wages, Prices and Economic Development in Europe and Asia, 1500–1800," *Economic History Review* 59 (2006), 2–31. Parthasarathi has reasserted his optimistic view of Indian workers' incomes in *Why Europe Grew Rich and Asia Did Not: Global Economic Divergence, 1600–1850* (Cambridge: Cambridge University Press, 2011), 37–46.
99. Pomeranz, *The Great Divergence*; Robert C. Allen, "Agricultural Productivity and Rural Incomes in England and the Yangstze Delta, c.1620–1820," *Economic History Review* 62:3 (2009), 525–50.
100. Jan Luiten van Zanden, *The Long Road to the Industrial Revolution: The European Economy in a Global Perspective, 1000–1800* (Leiden: Brill, 2009); Robert C. Allen, *The British Industrial Revolution in Global Perspective* (Cambridge: Cambridge University Press, 2009).
101. Allen et al., "Wages, Prices, and Living Standards."
102. Another project hard to imagine before *The Great Divergence* is Akinobu Kuroda's far-reaching Sinocentric reinterpretation of the history of silver currencies in Europe. Kuroda, "The Eurasian Silver Century, 1276–1359: Commensurability and Multiplicity," *Journal of Global History* 4:2 (2009), 245–69.
103. E.g. Binu M. John, "I Am Not Going to Call Myself a Global Historian: An Interview with C. A. Bayly," *Itinerario: International Journal on the History of European Expansion and Global Interaction* 31:1 (2007), 7–14.
104. Chakrabarty, *Provincializing Europe*.
105. Marcel van der Linden, "Preface," *ISHA Newsletter* (International Social History Association), 1:1 (2011).
106. Vanhaute, "Who Is Afraid of Global History?"
107. A trend which emerged while this volume was in preparation.

CHAPTER 2
RE-PRESENTING ASIA ON THE GLOBAL STAGE: THE RISE OF GLOBAL HISTORY IN EAST ASIA
Q. Edward Wang

History writing has a long tradition in East Asia. From the mid-nineteenth century on, while the region faced the incursion of Western powers, this tradition underwent a significant transformation. As they struggled to cope with the Western presence, East Asians hoped to build strong nation-states. This desire turned them to nationalism, which played a key role in transforming the study of history in the region. Specifically, nationalist concerns caused Asian historians to reconsider the idea, style and content of history writing. For example, Fukuzawa Yukichi (1834–1901), a Japanese Enlightenment thinker and an advocate of a new approach to historiography, argued that history should be written to educate the entire nation by delineating national progress. Liang Qichao (1873–1929), a Chinese historian-cum-reformer, and Shin Ch'aeho (1880–1936), a Korean nationalist thinker, echoed and espoused Fukuzawa's ideas. In his 1902 series of essays, "New Historiography," Liang stressed that it was time for Asian historians to eschew dynastic historiography, the mainstream history writing tradition in Asia, and to experiment instead with nationalist historiography.

To this day, nationalist historiography remains the main current in East Asian history writing, chiefly because the search for a strong nation-state has followed a treacherous and zigzag course in the region. Indeed, the effort of national construction that began in the nineteenth century yielded successes and failures, victories and defeats, exuberances and frustrations, and unifications and separations. Before the Second World War, Japan was a successful model in modernizing itself into a rising nation-state, and later also a mighty empire. By contrast, Korea and China were examples of utter failures—the former lost its national sovereignty in 1910, whereas the latter, despite establishing a republic in 1912, remained prey to the aggressions of imperialism and colonialism. Beginning in the late 1920s and continuing through the Second World War, Communism gathered considerable strength in China. Chinese Communists established the People's Republic of China (PRC) in 1949, an event that led to the dominance of Marxist historiography. In contrast with nationalist ideology, Marxism is known for its cosmopolitan interest and ecumenical interpretation of a presumed social progress in human history.

Japan's defeat in the Second World War reoriented the direction of its history writing. As in China, it gave rise to Marxist historiography, which remains influential in the Japanese historical community to this day. For postwar Japanese historians, Marxist historiography was attractive because it provided a much-needed weapon and analytical tool to explain the rise and fall of militarism in the country since the mid-nineteenth century. The once-celebrated Meiji era (1868–1912), the formative period in Japan's modernization, for example, was critically reevaluated. Marxist historians such as Tōyama Shigeki (1914–) and Inoue Kiyoshi (1913–2001) saw the Meiji Restoration as incomplete in modernizing Japan. They held the restoration and preservation of Japan's imperial system accountable for the upsurge of militarism in subsequent eras.[1] It was not only Marxist historians who questioned the completeness, or thoroughness, of Japan's modernization: the Modernists, or liberal historians, including Ōtsuka Hisao (1907–96), the exponent of the Modernist school, did as well. Though their foci were different, in their attempts to reinterpret the route of Japan's modernization against the Western model, both schools helped broaden historical study in postwar Japan, paving the way for the study of world history. Their efforts were joined by the government. In 1949 the Japanese Ministry of Education, then under the aegis of the Supreme Commander of the Allied Powers (SCAP), instituted the teaching of "world history" as a subject in senior high schools throughout the country. At the college level, "world history" also replaced the institution of "Western history" of the prewar years to become one of the three major subfields (in addition to Asian history and Japanese history) in the historical discipline.

Thus in postwar China, Japan and, to some extent, also the Korean Peninsula, the interest in history became diversified and the study of world history, or histories of foreign countries, was established as a viable subfield in the discipline and as a subject in school curricula at the middle, high school and college levels. Almost immediately after the Second World War, "world history" became introduced to the school curriculum in South Korea and Japan.[2] A number of "world historians" specializing in histories outside those of their own nation were trained throughout East Asia. For China, for example, one estimate puts the number of "world historians" in colleges at about 40 percent of the total history faculty in the 1970s and the 1980s.[3] It should be said, however, that the postwar spike of interest in world history among East Asian historians built on earlier practices of the prewar years. As a school of historiography, Marxism had appealed to Asian historians as early as the 1920s. In Japan, for example, the Historical Science Society of Japan (HSS), a major center of Marxist historiography, was founded in 1932. Likewise, Chinese Marxist historians were already engaged in the "Discussion of Chinese Social History" during 1928–32, a discussion that has been called "the most dynamic and stimulating current in Chinese historiography,"[4] and one that gave Marxist historians a nationwide presence in China.

From comparison to the study of connections

For Asian historians, world history study means a subject matter that deals with all histories outside the domain of national history. From the postwar years to the present, East Asian historians, Marxist or otherwise, have produced many meaningful works in world history and the histories of various foreign countries. In fact, some important works actually appeared earlier than better-known works by their Western counterparts. As alluded to above, "world history" as a course was developed for the history curriculum from the early postwar years across East Asia, also earlier than was it incorporated in schools and colleges in Euro-America.[5] Coming from a region that has experienced Western colonialism and imperialism since the mid-nineteenth century, East Asians have shown a genuine interest in seeking alternatives to Eurocentric interpretations of world historical movements. At some level, of course, their interest was motivated by nationalist aspirations such as making their nation more noticeable on the world stage. At the same time, however, these works expanded the scope of historical study as their authors circumvented, challenged and transcended the practice of nationalist historiography, one of the hallmarks of historiographical accomplishment in the modern West. Especially in recent years, the study of world/global history has altered and modified the seemingly more deep-rooted national history practice in modern East Asia.

In postwar Japan, from different perspectives, the Marxist and Modernist Schools both questioned the nature and success of Japan's modernity. The early Marxist historians in Japan were more or less associated with the Japanese Communist Party founded in 1922. Drawing on Marxist doctrines on historical development, Japanese Marxists in prewar times had already delivered much criticism of Japan's modernization. In postwar times, having resumed their voice, they offered even harsher criticism of Japan's modernization; to them, its "incompleteness" was responsible for the country's military aggression in the Second World War, as well as for its final defeat. Tôyama Shigeki, Inoue Kiyoshi and Eguchi Bokurō (1911–1989), a world history professor at the University of Tokyo, played a key role in reviving the HSS after the war. In order to gain a better understanding of modern Japan, they stressed the need to obtain a broad view of historical developments in the world. Eguchi's works seemed particularly important; not only did he urge his compatriots to critically reflect upon the teaching of "Western history," but he also helped spark an interest in the histories of the Middle East, Africa and other parts of Asia. Moreover, Eguchi called attention to important changes in contemporary history, such as the victory of the Chinese Communist Revolution. For him, these events in China and other transformations marked an end of Western imperialism and offered Japan new possibilities to join major developments in world history.[6]

Ōtsuka Hisao, who represented the influential Modernist School, was also convinced that Japan needed a critical overhaul of its modern past. As a noted historian of Europe at Tokyo University, Ōtsuka offered some in-depth studies on the rise of capitalism in early-modern Western Europe. Influenced by Karl Marx but more by Max Weber, he hoped to examine the reasons why Western Europe took the leap forward in developing capitalism. Like Weber, Ōtsuka did not believe that trade profit helped modern capitalism, for it had long existed. Instead, he argued that the rise of the middle class, or the yeoman farmers as its prototype, was more important. By contrast, having suffered from "patriarchal dominance," Japan and other Asian countries fell behind in the genesis of individualism and entrepreneurial spirit.[7] Without question, Ōtsuka and his supporters' views were more Eurocentric than the world historical outlooks of the Marxist School. Yet both schools had two elements in common. One was their world-historical, or comparative, approach and the other their focus on nations as the basic units for comparison. While clearly broader in his perception of world history, Eguchi Bokurō, author of *Imperialism and Nations* (Teikoku shugi to minzoku, 1954), also invariably regarded nation-states as a useful category of historical study.

All the same, Ōtsuka and Eguchi were no exceptions of their time. The publication of a 31-volume world history series by Iwanami-shoten, a prominent academic publisher in Japan in the early 1970s, was a case in point. Its editors and contributors arranged the series' volumes chronologically and geographically. Prior to the medieval period, the world was divided into four zones of civilization: Europe (the Mediterranean), South Asia, East Asia and Central Asia, whereas from the modern times on, historical development in the world was narrated by following the rise and fall of major nation-states. To some extent, the world history series was a culmination of the growing interest in world history in postwar Japan. From 1945 to 1970, nearly 1,000 books were published whose titles contain the term "world history."[8]

Indeed, there occurred a boom of world history study in postwar Japan. This growth was conducive to new approaches and experiments, especially among economic historians. Geographically speaking, the Kansai region produced some innovative projects. Since its founding in 1897, the University of Kyoto has been a strong rival of the University of Tokyo, which had been established about two decades before. With regard to world historical studies, as discussed by Shigeru Akita in his contribution to this volume and elsewhere, meaningful research on the history of capitalism at the University of Kyoto and other colleges in the Kansai region began in the 1960s. They aimed to challenge the domineering influence of Ōtsuka Hisao and his disciples at the University of Tokyo. According to Akita, Kawano Kenji (1916–1996) and Tsunoyama Sakae (1920–2014) were two leading figures; the former then taught at the Institute for Research in Humanities (IRH) of the University of Kyoto and the latter at Wakayama University. Trained as a French historian, Kawano drew attention to other models of capitalist development in Europe than that of England. Sharing Kawano's concern, Tsunoyama delivered relentless criticisms of Ōtsuka's thesis that England served as an absolute model of modern capitalism. They and their associates launched numerous projects to examine aspects of the development of "world capitalism."[9]

To a certain extent, the effort made by the Japanese historians from the Kansai region to look at worldwide capitalist developments bore an important and interesting resemblance to the works of André Gunder Frank (1929–2005) and Immanuel Wallerstein. The Japanese also conducted their research around the same period, if not earlier, as did their Western counterparts. The similarity lay in that like the early Western world historians, the Japanese economic historians hoped to present the heterogeneity of modern capitalism. At the same time, they recognized that due to capitalist development, the modern world was turned into one comprehensive unit, into which various national economies had been absorbed. As such, the Japanese historians looked for "connections," "linkages" and "relationships" among many regions, with a focus on parts of Asia and changes in the nineteenth century. For example, Tsunoyama Sakae and Kawakita Minoru saw that by the nineteenth century, modern capitalism had reached and, indeed, encompassed many corners of the world. While industrial products spread from Euro-America to non-Western regions, agricultural goods also spread from Asia to the West. That is, trading activities in the worldwide network were multidirectional rather than unidirectional.

Like their counterparts in Japan, Chinese Marxist historians, who became the dominant group after 1949, were inspired by the comparative and ecumenical interests of Marxist historical theory. Some of the early Chinese Marxists such as Guo Moruo (1892–1978) came to Marxism through the works and translations of Japanese historians. Over time, Chinese Marxists became aware of the limits of Marxist historiography: Marx knew little about non-European histories and thus his extrapolation of universal development of history was based essentially on Europe's development. Still, in the early PRC era, after Marxism was established as the official ideology, historians felt a great urgency to use Marxist historical theory, or historical materialism, to guide their research. For that purpose, they turned to Soviet historiography for guidance. Not only did the Chinese invite Soviet historians, whom they dubbed "foreign experts," to serve as advisers at their universities and research institutions, they also rendered, religiously, Soviet historians' works into Chinese, together with the works of Marx, Engels, Lenin and Stalin. In the 1950s, the Chinese translated the ten-volume world history series by Russian historians into Chinese as soon as it appeared in the Soviet Union. Following the Marxist theory of social progress, this Soviet world history offered a periodization framework, highlighting the transitions from primitive society and slavery to feudalism, followed by the rise of capitalism and its nemeses—socialism and communism—in human history.[10]

But even with its ecumenical scope and perspective, this Soviet world history was Europe-centered, as well as Russia-centered. The ten volumes were devoted mostly to the history of Europe, including of course Russia, whereas their coverage of Africa, Asia and Latin America was inadequate and insignificant. Moreover, in describing the evolution (e.g., from slavery through to socialism) of history, the Soviet authors used, without exception, events in European history (the fall of the Roman Empire, the English Civil War, the French Revolution, etc.) as essential markers to delineate the course of social progress. Under the influence of Soviet historiography, some Chinese historians produced similar studies of world history. The four-volume world history published in 1962 and edited by Zhou Yiliang (1913–2001) and Wu Yujin (1913–93), two Harvard-educated historians, is an illuminating example. It devotes over two-thirds of its pages to covering Euro-America, whereas the histories of Africa, Asia and Latin America altogether only constitute the remaining one-third. To some extent, this Euro-American bias still grips the minds of Chinese historians and the educated public in today's PRC.[11]

Concurrently, however, other Chinese historians became concerned about the Europe/Western focus in modern historiography in general and in Marxist historiography particularly. During the 1950s, the heyday of the Chinese borrowing from the Soviets, these historians openly voiced their objections to the Eurocentric focus of the histories produced by their Russian colleagues. Zhou Gucheng (1898–1997), for example, an acclaimed historian who had authored a world history text in the 1940s, criticized the aforementioned ten-volume Soviet world history. He expressed his disappointment that the book failed to qualify as a "true world history" because it overlooked many aspects of the non-Western world.[12] Moreover, the Soviet world history, as well as Soviet works on Chinese history, failed to provide much help in the task of reinterpreting the course of Chinese history. Indeed, Chinese historians had to tackle the task of comparing their country's history and assessing its importance against the broad framework of worldwide historical development. Like their Japanese counterparts, they generally adopted a critical stance toward the evolution of Chinese history, as it seemed to have failed to fit with the Marxist model of social progress. As such, Chinese Marxist historians searched for explanations in their country's past. The so-called Five Golden Flowers in the garden of history, which preoccupied the attention of Chinese historians in the 1950s and 1960s, was one approach. Heatedly debated in historical communities as well as in public, these "Golden Flowers" were (1) the transition from slavery to feudalism, (2) the changes in feudal landownership, (3) the role of peasant rebellions in history, (4) the emergence of the capitalist "sprouts" in late imperial China and (5) the formation of the Han Chinese nation. The underlying issues in those studies were questions about how and why Chinese society did not follow the "standard" course of development illustrated by Marx. Opinions expressed in the studies were diverse, making some of the debates rather intense. While some blamed Chinese peasants for their inability to successfully create a new, alternative society, others drew attention to Marx's Eurocentric bias. But regardless of opinion, all participants acquired a comparative framework; they all compared and contrasted the vicissitudes of Chinese history with those of other countries, Western and otherwise.

The debates on these issues made these "Golden Flowers" blossom, enabling Chinese historians to gain a comparative perspective, and the debate on the so-called Asiatic mode of production seems most significant. This debate, launched during the same period, raged with the same intensity and extensity as other debates in the historical community of China. In his *Contribution to the Critique of Political Economy* (1859), Marx had introduced the notion of the "Asiatic mode of production" as an umbrella term to describe the status (and stagnation) of Asia in his scheme of human evolution. Historiographically, the significance of the debate on the Asiatic mode of production is twofold. One is that it underscored, perhaps more clearly than the studies of the "Golden Flowers," the Eurocentric characteristic of Marxist historical theory. The other is that it further broadened the vista of Chinese historians: to fully understand the so-called Asiatic mode of production and the characteristics associated with the "Orient," they now needed to study the histories of other non-Western countries and regions more closely. In so doing, Chinese historians extended their interest from the history of the West to that of the world. Thanks to the debate, therefore, world history study received unprecedented attention among all historians in China.[13]

Indeed, after they embarked on the study of world history and acquired a comparative perspective, Asian historians quickly noticed how Asia was (mis)represented in writings by Western historians, including those by Western and Russian Marxists. Karl Marx himself fared no better. In his observation of the Taiping Rebellion, which occurred during his lifetime in 1850s China, Marx condemned the role of Western imperialists. But he also agreed with the prevalent Western view that China, or Oriental society in general, was socially stagnant, awaiting the West to pull it up and into modern development.[14] The task of correcting this bias and re-presenting Asia thus became the paramount task for world historians across Asia.

Discovering Asia in the global network

During the 1970s while China was in the midst of the Cultural Revolution, Japan stunned the world by its miraculous economic expansion, one that also withstood the oil crises of 1971 and 1979. In the field of history, especially in world history, Japanese historians in the period also produced interesting and meaningful research from the 1960s through the 1980s. As its name suggests, The Institute for Research in Humanities (IRH) at the University of Kyoto is a multidisciplinary research center that consists of experts from various fields. It provides a useful venue for the scholars on the campus and in the region to conduct collaborative research. These collaborations helped raise the status of the University of Kyoto. Indeed, already in the early twentieth century, there had emerged a "Kyoto School," led first by such philosophers as Nishida Kitarô (1870–1945) and Tanabe Hajime (1885–1962). Then the school was not confined to philosophy. In the study of Asian history, or *tôyôshi*, Kyoto scholars like Naitô Konan (1866–1934), Kano Naoki (1868–1947) and Kuwabara Jitsuzô (1871–1931) also garnered a superb reputation in the field. Those prewar accomplishments by Kyoto scholars left their visible imprints in the works and careers of postwar scholars from that same region. In the postwar period, Kyoto scholars continued, and expanded, on a fundament of collaborative and interdisciplinary scholarly traditions. Kuwabara Takeo (1904–1988), son of Kuwabara Jitsuzô and a colleague of Kawano Kenji at the IRH, for instance, played a leading part in bridging over different fields in the humanities and social sciences. That is, besides the economic studies of "world capitalism" led by Kawano and his associates mentioned above, other Kyoto scholars also produced works that came to reshape the field of world history in Japan, on both theoretical and methodological levels.

One key theoretical concern addressed by the "Kyoto School" was how to regard Japan's relationship with the modern West. During the 1930s, Nishida Kitarô and other philosophers had proposed the "overcoming modernity" (*kindai no chôkoku*) thesis. In light of Japan's rise, they sought to overcome the dominance of European civilization and establish a new world order. From a new perspective, Umesao Tadao (1920–2010), a Kyoto anthropologist, developed his ecological view of the history of civilizations. According to Umesao's theory, which was first published in an essay form in 1957 and later in a book in 1967, civilizations in Eurasia belonged to two ecological zones. The first zone consists of Western Europe and Japan, whose ecological environments are identical but markedly different from those in the second zone. Several splendid civilizations had emerged in the second zone from the past, such as the worlds of China, Russia, India and Islam, whose successes had influenced the civilizations in the first zone. However, while on the periphery and backward in the development of civilizations, Western Europe and Japan also grew unscathed from the repeated nomadic invasions that occurred frequently in the second zone. Furthermore, thanks to their geographical and ecological advantages, Western Europe and Japan were able to obtain a quicker pace of development for their civilizations in modern times.

Formulated at the early stage of Japan's impressive postwar economic recovery and expansion, Umesao's theory was received exceedingly well, not only in academic communities but also by the general public. A chief message delivered by Umesao Tadao, which became very influential among historians, was that Japan was on a par with Western Europe. Without the latter's influence, Japan would have developed its civilization on its own as successfully as did its counterpart in the same zone. In other words, Japan's modernization did not imitate (nor need to) the Western model, as suggested by Ōtsuka Hisao and his followers at the Tokyo University.[15]

In order to substantiate Umesao Tadao's thesis that Japan was an equal partner in the historical progress of the modern world, one needed in-depth analyses of the origins and development of modern capitalism. This in turn required profound knowledge of the history of many societies outside of Japan as well as the history of transregional connections. World historians in Japan, such as Kawano Kenji, first took on the task, even though they were more customarily referred to as "scholars of Western history" (*seyôshi gakusha*). In 1967, for example, Kawano published *The Formation of World Capitalism*, coedited with Iinuma Jirô (1918–2005), his colleague at Kyoto University and a noted expert on the history of agriculture. Three years later, the two coedited another anthology, entitled *The Historical Development of World Capitalism*. Both books present detailed research conducted at IRH, with a focus on examining how the worldwide trade network developed.

To foreground the multidirectional exchange in the global trade network, Japanese historians emphasized that while industrialized products moved from Europe to Asia, certain commodities—agricultural and later also manufactured goods—from Asia also reached Europe, changing the lives of modern Europeans. Tsunoyama Sakae's work on the history of tea, published in 1980, was an early example of such research, and in 1984 it was followed by a social history of clocks by the same author. During the same period, Kawakita Minoru published important studies investigating themes like the rise of consumerism and its impact on the shaping of capitalist societies, such as that in the metropolitan center of nineteenth-century London. Kawakita's *The Historical Premise of Industrialization: British Empire and the Gentleman* (1983) is particularly interesting in that a few years later, British economic historians P. J. Cain and A. G. Hopkins coined the term "gentlemanly capitalism" in their well-noted British Imperialism. While their research interests were different, Kawakita, Cain and Hopkins all drew attention to non-industrial factors in the rise of the British Empire, especially in its imperial expansion during the nineteenth century.[16] Historiographically speaking, their work converged economic history with new trends in historical study such as social, cultural and gender history. The fruit of this approach is that the historians are able to present "complementary" trading activities among many regions, including Europe, East and Southeast Asia and/or the Middle East.

From the 1970s onward, a new generation of Japanese historians who were not only based in the Kansai region but also in Kantô where the University of Tokyo is located, produced innovative research that later gained them a high reputation inside and outside Japan. Three names among them deserve our special attention. The first is Hamashita Takeshi who, after receiving his education at the University of Tokyo, has taught at both his alma mater and the University of Kyoto, among other places. Trained in Chinese history, Hamashita has devoted his research to examining China-centered tribute trading networks in both East and Southeast Asia between the sixteenth and nineteenth centuries. As such, his research interest goes beyond Chinese history per se. Hamashita has shown that Asia played important roles in world historical development, not only in the nineteenth century as Kawakita Minoru and others have revealed in their writings, but also during the preceding centuries when European powers first entered Asia. His findings problematize the notion that thanks to Western incursion, traditional models in Asia were transformed and replaced. Instead, he shows that in order to establish trade relations in Asia, Western powers had actually worked with the existent intra-Asian tribute networks. Even after treaties with Western powers were signed, many intra-Asian exchange relations remained largely intact throughout the nineteenth century, and so did their ideational bases. In Hamashita's own words, "The concept of East and West did not spatially overwrite one another, but rather it can be said that the tribute concept, that is the concept of hierarchical order, remained primary, with the treaty relationship subordinated to it."[17]

Hamashita Takeshi therefore argues that a "maritime Asia" had exerted a lasting impact on shaping the course of world history—in both premodern and modern times. Kawakatsu Heita is another historian who shares this interest in exploring the importance of maritime Asia. Educated at both Waseda University and Oxford University, Kawakatsu also taught at Waseda for many years before assuming other posts. A well-known cultural critic and a politician at both local and national levels, Kawakatsu has published extensively on the significance of seas and oceans in human history. A critic of Umesao Tadao yet also indebted to Umesao's macroscopic view of history, Kawakatsu published his well-received *History of Civilization: An Oceanic View* in 1997, in which he contends that the modern world actually originated in maritime Asia. More specifically, observes Kawakatsu, an ecological crisis occurred across Eurasia during the fourteenth century, which prompted some island nations like Spain, Portugal, England and Japan to turn to the seas and oceans for new resources. At that time—and in the centuries after—maritime Asia was the center of trading activities around the world, which resulted in a series of changes that eventually gave shape to the European world system.[18]

The third historian is Sugihara Kaoru who received his education at both Kyoto and Tokyo Universities and taught at SOAS, University of London, for over a decade before returning to teaching in Japan during the mid-1990s. Like Hamashita Takeshi, Sugihara focuses his research on intra-Asian trading networks. Besides working on East and Southeast Asia, his interest in the development of the modern cotton industry also takes his research to South Asia and the Middle East. In his many publications in both Japanese and English, Sugihara argues forcefully that intra-Asian trade, and multi-regional economic exchanges in general, was an integral part in forging the expansion of world capitalism. In addition, he observes that by the early twentieth century, while world capitalism seemed to have become an integrated and comprehensive system, regional economies such as the one in Asia remained "autonomous" in many regards. Sugihara has also been quite vocal in arguing that in contrast to the industrial revolution in the West, there was an "industrious revolution" in Asia from the early-modern period onward, which had a long-lasting impact. He shares the interest of Kenneth Pomeranz and other Western historians in exploring the divergent paths of economic developments between Asia and Europe.[19]

The new trends in world historical scholarship were also somewhat reflected in a new series of world history published, in ten volumes, by Iwanami-shoten between 1989 and 1991. The series adopted a thematic approach that was quite different from the chronological structure of its predecessor in the 1960s. The new series stressed three aspects of the study of world history: (a) the relationship between the natural environment and human beings; (b) various kinds of social affiliations or integration processes and reactions against them; and (c) the role of "regions" in contrast to the nation-state framework. These aspects were reflected clearly in the ten volumes in the series: (1) nature and history; (2) skills of ordinary life and technology for production; (3) migration and exchange; (4) social cohesion; (5) norm and integration; (6) popular culture; (7) authority and power; (8) regions in history; (9) a structured world and (10) state and revolutions.

If a new trend in world/global history occurred in the mid-1980s Japan, some Chinese world historians in the 1980s made a comparable effort to explore "relations" and "connections." After Mao Zedong's death in 1976, the Cultural Revolution that had paralyzed the whole country for a decade came to an end. In 1978, under Deng Xiaoping's leadership, China entered the "Reform and Open-up" (*gaige kaifang*) period. Chinese historians resumed and revived their research and writing. Between 1983 and 1993, Wu Yujin, the coeditor of the aforementioned 1962 world history, published four influential articles exploring from a macro-history perspective the emergence of capitalism and its impact in integrating world history.[20] Wu argued that prior to the fifteenth and the sixteenth centuries, or before the rise of capitalism, there had existed two competing worlds: agriculture and husbandry. Starting in the fifteenth and sixteenth centuries, these two worlds began to converge, resulting in an integrated world history. By proposing this grand-narrative thesis, Wu acknowledged, perhaps out of political necessity, that he was inspired by Marx's observation that "World history has not always existed; history as world history [is] a result."[21] But if one looks more closely at his writings, one can also detect traces of Wu's early training in economic history in China and at Harvard. At first look, to be sure, his thesis emphasizes that the fifteenth and sixteenth centuries were the mark of a new historic era, which reminds one of the persistent interests among Marxist historians in periodizing history according to the Marxist scheme of social development. But Wu's real interest, it seems, is to stress and analyze what he called the "horizontal movement of history" during and after the period, to explore and reveal how various regions were connected to one another in the early-modern and modern world. To this purpose, Wu, who was then vice president of Wuhan University, established a research center for the study of fifteenth- and sixteenth-century world history, which produced several volumes of publications and trained new generations of scholars in the field of world history. Thanks to Wu, Wuhan University remains one of the premiere institutions in world history in today's PRC, along with other well-known Chinese institutions such as Peking University, Nankai University and the World History Institute at the Chinese Academy of Social Sciences.

In 1990, Wu Yujin edited the "world history" volume in *Encyclopedia Sinica* and wrote a general introduction that summarized the task of the world historian in China. He acknowledged the importance of the work of Oswald Spengler, Arnold Toynbee, Geoffrey Barraclough and L. S. Stavrianos in exploring alternative ways of viewing and interpreting world historical development. At the same time, he stated that much remains to be done in overcoming Eurocentrism in historiography, for world history study requires "examining comprehensively the history of every area, every country, and every nation in the light of the world as a totality." It is in its horizontal and vertical development, he maintained that history "has more and more become world history." Therefore, "to study world history, we must see the world as an overall situation and investigate the whole process of how it develops from mutual disconnection to intimate connection, from separation to integration. This entire process is world history."[22] In short, like his Japanese counterparts, Wu Yujin and his colleagues and students hope to explore, investigate and analyze the global nexus in shaping the history of the modern world.

Global history as opportunity and challenge

From the 1990s on, thanks to the robust advance of globalization, global history has become one of the most eye-catching developments in historical communities across East Asia. In Japan, after the initial spike in world history publications in the immediate postwar years, the trend became rather steady from the 1970s through the 1990s. Then, from the 1990s to the present, a new and heightened interest has appeared: not only have more books bearing the title "world history" (*sekaishi*) been published in the period, but many them are also titled "global history," or "gurobaru hisutori" in Japanese transliteration.[23] In the Chinese-speaking world, since the mid-1990s, scholars across many disciplines have paid significant attention to globalization.[24] A similarly high level of interest in globalization is also observable in Taiwan and Hong Kong, where scholars examine and analyze the impact of globalization from many angles. In the case of Taiwan, studies of globalization have touched upon a wide array of topics, ranging from the preservation of indigenous culture and customs, religious studies and the teaching of Chinese and foreign languages to architectural design, agricultural development and the tourist industry.[25]

Since the mid-1990s, historians in the PRC have demonstrated great enthusiasm for studies of global history and the history of globalization. They have published thousands of academic articles, in addition to editing dozens of world history textbooks as well as monographic studies like *Introduction to Global History* (2012) by Zhang Yiping, *Theories of Global History and the Study of Civilizational Interactions* by Liu Wenming (2015) and such important anthologies as *Globalization and Global History* (2007) by the World History Institute, Chinese Academy of Social Sciences (CASS), *New Orientations in Historiography: Regional History and Global History* (2011) by East China Normal University and *Global History, Regional History and National History* (2016) by Fudan University.[26] But academic historians are not the only ones interested in global history. The Chinese translation of "global history" is "全球史" (*quanqiushi*), but there is also a more popular phrase: "全球史观" (*quanqiu shiguan*), or "global view of history." A survey was conducted in March 2017 on Baidu, China's most popular web search site, using both phrases as search terms; the first yielded over one and half million and the second over two and half million hits![27] That there are two Chinese phrases referring to "global history" is also significant, suggesting that many Chinese historians and readers are quite interested in seeking new ways to expand and alter their view of history.

To both academic historians and the educated public in China, global history is of great interest because it offers an alternative to the Eurocentric matrix that has hitherto circumscribed their understanding of history. As shown in a recent forum in the *Lishi yanjiu* (Historical Research), a main organ of historical publication in the PRC, Chinese scholars think that global history is significant because it (re)introduces the notion of "civilization" to historical study, transcending the confines of national historiography and because of their interest in seeking out interconnections and cross-cultural communications among civilizations. These two features, they believe, have distinguished the recent works in global history from the tradition of world history inside and outside China, for earlier versions of world history expanded the scope of historical study but retained nation-states as the basic unit. As such, these studies were unable to overcome Eurocentrism.[28]

The work of Asian historians on global history has attracted global attention. One example is the 20th annual convention of the World History Association (WHA), which was hosted by the Capital Normal University (CNU) in Beijing in July 2011 and attended by several hundred historians from around the world. In 2004, CNU established the Research Center of Global History, which publishes a journal and a book series. In South Korea, Ewha Women's University established the Institute of World and Global History (IWGH) in 2008, led by Cho Ji-Hyung. In addition, the Research Institute of Comparative History and Culture (RICH) at Hanyang University, directed by Lim Jie-Hyun till 2015, promotes the study of comparative and transnational history. In Japan, Osaka University plays a leading role in the study of global/world history. In 2009, Osaka University hosted a meeting that led to the founding of the Asian Association of World Historians (AAWH).[29] At the University of Tokyo, Haneda Masashi, director of the Research Institute of Asian History, and his team of researchers have made important attempts at promoting global history. In his most recent book on the need for global history—*Toward a New World History: Reflections on the Making of Global Citizens*—Haneda offers a brief survey of world history education in modern and contemporary Japan, followed by a strong thesis that in order to nurture "global citizens," historians must transcend Eurocentrism and look at the world from multicentered perspectives.[30]

In promoting global history study, Asian historians have collaborated closely with their counterparts elsewhere. For example, between 2006 and 2012, Jerry Bentley, editor of the JWH and coauthor of the acclaimed textbook on global history, *Traditions and Encounters: A Global Perspective on the Past* (2003), was an endowed visiting professor at CNU for several years, and there he regularly taught seminars and supervised students. David Christian, another noted global historian and author of *Maps of Time: An Introduction to Big History* (2004), was a guest professor at Ewha Women's University, where he worked with Cho Ji-Hyung in advocating for a global view in historical study and education. Associated with Christian's visit, the IWGH introduced a new undergraduate course: "A History of Everything after the Big Bang," which treats the earth as a unit of historical analysis and touches on phenomena such as the Big Bang, the birth of the earth, the appearance of human beings and the nature of today's world. Drawing on the idea of Big History, the course suggests new ways to address crucial issues for transcending Eurocentrism in world history education in South Korea.

To many East Asian historians, global history is attractive because it enables them to see historical movements beyond the nation-state framework. Thus in South Korea as we illustrated above, as well as elsewhere in Asia, "transnational history" is almost a synonym of "global history." Promoting "transnational history" is another way to challenge the hegemonic influence of the West in historiography, for not only did nation-states first appear in Europe but nationalistic historiography was also a product of the West. "Transnational history," which emphasizes connections—relations—not only between the West and the non-West but also among various regions outside of the West, thus offers a way for Asian historians to see beyond the dominant Western historical view and to critique—or challenge—the entrenched practice of nationalist historiography.

Due to the same desire to transcend Western models of historiography, Haneda Masashi, a professor at Tokyo University and a major proponent of global history in Japan, has gone as far as to state that "global history" (*gurobaru hisutori*) is not the best choice to convey the efforts of Japanese historians to pursue a new understanding of worldwide historical developments. Haneda believes that the term "new world history" (*atarashii sekaishi*) is a better choice, in that it not only distinguishes recent works from earlier studies in the field but also suggests that the new trend has not necessarily been a mere reflection of Western influence in Japanese historiography.[31] In one of his most recent books on the need for global historical or world historical perspectives—*Toward a New World History: Reflections on the Making of Global Citizens*—Haneda offers a brief survey of world history education in modern and contemporary Japan, followed by the strong thesis that in order to nurture "global citizens," historians must transcend Eurocentrism and look at the world from multicentered perspectives.[32]

57

In addition to the Kansai region, it seems that scholars at Tokyo University and Waseda University have caught up with the rise of global history in recent years. Haneda Masashi is a professor of Middle Eastern history and director of the Institute for the Study of East Asian Culture at Tokyo University. He has played a leading role, together with Akita Shigeru and Momoki Shirō, a historian of Southeast Asia and Akita's colleague at Osaka University, in researching and promoting global history in Japan. Having collaborated with Akita Shigeru and others, Haneda Masashi has coedited the book *World History in World History Perspective* (2016). He also authored *Regional History and World History* (2016) and *Global History and East Asian History* (2016). Through Haneda's research institute, Tokyo University has also formed working relations with Princeton University in the United States, Humboldt University in Germany and the École des Hautes Études en Sciences Sociales in France, to explore new and collaborative studies in global history.

In promoting global historical studies, therefore, Asian historians have collaborated closely with their counterparts elsewhere. A notable example is the 20th annual convention of the WHA, which was hosted by CNU in Beijing in July 2011 and attended by several hundred historians from around the world. Since its establishment in 2004, the Research Center of Global History at CNU in Beijing has pursued several research agendas, including the study of global history theories, comparisons of medieval Europe and the Mediterranean, globalization and the early-modern and modern West, international conflicts in the twentieth century, cross-cultural exchanges in world history, and China's relationship with the rest of the world. Since 2007, the College of History at CNU, which houses the center, has trained graduate students in global history at both master's and doctoral levels.[33] Some of them, together with the center's faculty members, made interesting presentations at the WHA convention in Beijing. And since 2008, the Research Center has edited the *Global History Review*, which comes out annually and from 2015 biannually. The 2011 WHA convention might be seen as a showcase of the progress made by Chinese scholars in global history study in the years before. In addition to overseas participants, a good number of Chinese world/global historians presented papers. One of the topics of interest is the study of cross-cultural exchanges among civilizations in Eurasia, which includes China's relations with its neighbors, near and far, ancient and modern.

In his keynote speech, Liu Xincheng, CNU's then president and founder of the Center of Global History, offered an overview of the status of global history study in the PRC. Liu stated that on the one hand global history, or the global view of history, has met some enthusiastic response from the Chinese historical community. On the other, Liu acknowledged, Chinese scholars have voiced criticism and caution about this enthusiasm. In his words, "The Chinese acceptance of global history has been a rather natural process." What he means is that the Chinese naturally welcomed the attempt by overseas global historians to de-emphasize the role of the West in shaping modern world history. The reasons, he stated, are both political/nationalistic and academic, as many Chinese historians are interested in new developments in worldwide historiography.[34] Indeed, many Chinese historians see global history's emphasis on cross-regional and cross-cultural exchanges as a good opportunity to re-envisage and re-present China's relations with the rest of the world. Like their Japanese and Korean counterparts (some of whom, notably Momoki Shirō, also presented papers), the Chinese show a great interest in studying, for example, "maritime Asia" and the spread of tea and opium, and in introducing transregional and/or intraregional perspectives into the studies of global history.[35]

In more recent years, more research centers of global history study have emerged in mainland China, including the Research Institute for Global History at Beijing Foreign Studies University, the Research Institute for Global History and Transnational History at Shandong University, and the Research Center of Transregional Civilizations at East China Normal University. Have these attempts at finding inter-regional and intra-regional connections succeeded in downplaying the nation-state focus in history writing? It is too early to tell. To be sure, transnational studies open up the historian's view, enabling him or her to see changes in history beyond a national framework. At the same time, this interest in global history has also, perhaps inadvertently, as well as invariably, registered nationalist concerns. The study of globalization in Taiwan is a good illustration. As mentioned above, globalization has become a hot subject there, providing, *inter alia*, a new angle from which Taiwanese historians can view their island's history. Instead of focusing on Taiwan's relation with mainland China, both past and present, Taiwanese historians have been increasingly interested in finding the island's links with its other Asian neighbors. They hope to resituate Taiwan, economically, culturally and historically, in the intra-Asian network in order to transcend the Taiwan-China binary that once dominated their view of history. In articulating whether and how Taiwan should seek its political independence, a touchy issue for most islanders, Taiwanese scholars have searched for alternative ways to address this nationalist aspiration. Some have argued that due to globalization, a nation-state, in its current full-fledged form, is no longer the most suitable option for the Taiwanese.[36] Although their ideas vary, many Taiwanese historians are doing history with an eye to Taiwan's national future.

Inspired by global history, historians in the PRC have also attempted to modify the dominance of nationalist and Marxist historiography. In particular, they have criticized the residual influence of Soviet historiography and argued for downplaying revolution (nationalist and Communist alike) as the chief, if not only, driving force in Chinese history in particular, and world history in general. Qian Chengdan, a historian at Peking University, who was one of the earliest PRC scholars interested in global history, has advocated that modernization should replace the class struggle as the lens through which Chinese historians delineate historical development from the sixteenth century onward. Instead of the social change, or revolutions, lionized by Marxist historians, he suggests seeing economic development and its transformative impact around the world as the central theme in understanding the movement of history.[37]

One may, perhaps, detect visible traces of Eurocentrism in Qian's articulation of the important role modernization played in world history. Since modernization first began in Euro-America, using modernization as a way to outline and interpret historical movement would invariably lead to the belief that the West is the model for the rest of the world.[38] Qian's thesis might also be tinged with a political overtone. Over the past several decades, China has experienced an explosive economic modernization. Emphasizing the role of modernization in history thus lends support to the government policy initiated by Deng Xiaoping in the Reform and Open-up era from 1978 to the present. China's rapid modernization, first and foremost, is for returning the country to the world-power status it once held, an overtly nationalist goal. In a word, global history seems to be a double-edged sword vis-à-vis the practice of nationalist historiography. It definitely has offered new, fresh perspectives on historical study. If in China the global view of history has helped moderate the emphasis on revolution and class struggle in history writing, in South Korea and Taiwan, the interest in global history has encouraged scholars to seek new alternatives to nationalist thinking. And in Japan, associated with the advances in Asian economic history, it has occasioned important research on maritime Asia in premodern times and its connections with the growth of capitalism in Britain, and in Europe in general. For the general public, William McNeill's and Jared Diamond's works on world/global history have also aroused great interest. And this public interest in global history is not confined to Japan, but seen elsewhere too.[39]

But global history can be, and at times has been, co-opted into existing nationalist agendas. There are supporters and critics of global history in China today and both those who favor it and those who oppose it can be motivated by nationalist sentiment. For their advocates, global historical studies are of value because they create room for them to inject China and Asia into the course of world history. Thus many Chinese scholars praise the works of André Gunder Frank, Kenneth Pomeranz, R. Bin Wong, William McNeill and Jerry Bentley for their sharp critique of Eurocentric historiography. Yet critics of global history remain suspicious of the efficacy of global history in eradicating the residue of Eurocentrism. They worry that global historians' emphasis on developing an integrated view of history might allow them to impose Western values as the universal onto the non-Western world.[40] Indeed, as China today is seeking to experiment with its own model of development—"peaceful rise" (和平崛起 *heping jueqi*)—different from Western and Japanese models, Chinese historians are increasingly interested in discovering and utilizing models from their own past. Some of them are thus doubtful about Western scholars (e.g., André Gunder Frank and Kenneth Pomeranz) interpreting the course of Chinese history.[41]

Ideally and ultimately, global history's de-emphasis of nation-states in historiography and its interest in transnational and inter-regional connections should help alleviate the tension among East Asian nations regarding their shared past. Over the past decade, interesting progress has been made toward developing a transnational framework in history writing, as historians of Japan, South Korea and China have worked together and produced valuable and promising works.[42] Yet whether these collaborative products can eventually bridge the gaps between the perceptions of history within the general public in each countries, history textbook writing remains, with a varying degree, under government control. And with few exceptions, the textbooks currently used in these countries are written according to the nation-state framework and, as such, tend to underscore national progress and accentuate the characteristics of national ethos.

Clearly then, there is a gap between historical research and history education—despite the valiant and valuable attempts made by many world history teachers and researchers at revamping the history curriculum in schools of all levels. After reviewing the teaching guidelines in Japanese schools in 2015, Haneda Masashi questioned and lamented that "Can East Asian history be understood simply by placing the three independent histories [of China, Korea and Japan] side-by-side? How should they be combined and integrated? In my view, the answer to this question still seems vague and unclear. In any case, I repeat that Japanese history is still taught separately from world history in high schools."[43] To close the gap, meaningful works of global history need to trickle down to schools and exert influence in modifying and changing the history curricula in both colleges and secondary schools. Until this happens, nationalist historiography will continuously exert a strong influence in shaping the historical mind of the young generation of East Asians.

Notes

1. Nagahara Keiji, *20 seiki Nihon no rekishigaku* (20th century Japanese historiography) (Tokyo, 2005), 124–45; Sebastian Conrad, *The Quest for the Lost Nation: Writing History in Germany and Japan in the American Century*, trans. Alan Nothnagle (Berkeley: University of California Press, 2010), 21–30; Curtis Anderson Gayle, *Marxism and Postwar Japanese Nationalism* (London: Routledge, 2003); and "The Importance and Legacy of Marxist History in Japan," in Q. Edward Wang and Georg Iggers (eds.), *Marxist Historiographies: A Global Perspective* (London: Routledge, 2016), 174–90.
2. See Lim, (Jie)-hyun, "Historicizing the World in Northeast Asia," Douglas Northrop (ed.) *A Companion to World History* (Malden, MA: Wiley-Blackwell, 2012), 418–432.
3. Ralph Croizier, "World History in the People's Republic of China," *Journal of World History* 1:2 (1990), 145–60.
4. Arif Dirlik, *Revolution and History: Origins of Marxist Historiography in China* (Berkeley: University of California Press, 1978), 2.
5. See Croizier's article in footnote 2 and Haneda Masashi, "Japanese Perspectives on 'Global History,'" *Asian Review of World Histories*, 3:2 (July 2015), 219–234, especially 225–226 and note 12. Also Kenneth Pomeranz & Daniel A. Segal, "World History: Departures and Variations," *A Companion to World History*, 418–432.
6. See for example Eguchi Bokuro, *Rekishi no Gendankai* [The present stage of history] (Tokyo: Tokyo daigaku shuppansha, 1958) and *Sekaishi no Gendankai to Nihon* [*The Present Stage of World History and Japan*] (Tokyo: Iwanami-shoten, 1986). Also Curtis Anderson Gayle, "Progressive Representations of the Nation: Early Post-War Japan and Beyond," *Social Science Japan Journal*, 4:1 (Apr. 2001), 1–19, especially 10–11.
7. Ōtsuka Hisao, *The Spirit of Capitalism: The Max Weber Thesis in an Economic and Historical Perspective*, trans. Masaomi Kondo (Tokyo: Iwanami Shoten, 1982) and *Kindai Ōshū*

Keizaishi Jyosetsu (*An Introduction to Modern European Economic History*) (Tokyo: Iwanami-shoten, 1944). Also Conrad, *Quest for the Lost Nation*, 178ff.

8. This author finds that National Diet Library in Japan holds 934 books published between 1945 and 1970 which have "sekaishi" in their titles.

9. See Tsunoyama Sakae, *Seikatsushi no hakken: firudo wâku de miro sekai* (*In Discovery of the "History of Life": The World Seen in Fieldworks*) (Tokyo: chûô kôron shinsha, 2001), 9–126. And Akita Shigeru, "World History and the Emergence of Global History in Japan," *Chinese Studies in History*, 43–3 (Spring 2010), 86–87.

10. Xu Luo, "Reconstructing World History in the People's Republic of China since the 1980s," *Journal of World History* 18:3 (2007), 325–50. For the Soviet influence in Chinese historiography, see Q. Edward Wang, "Between Marxism and Nationalism: Chinese Historiography and the Soviet Influence, 1949–1963," *Journal of Contemporary China* 9:23 (2000), 95–111.

11. Xu, "Reconstructing World History in the People's Republic of China since the 1980s."

12. Zhou Gucheng, *Zhou Gucheng shixue lunwen xuanji* [Selected essays of Zhou Gucheng on history] (Beijing: Renmin chubanshe, 1983). See also Li Yong, "Ping Zhou Gucheng shijie tongshi bianzhuan sixiang ji shijian yu dangdai 'zhengtishi' guan he 'quanqiushi' guan de xiangguanxing" [On Zhou Gucheng's Idea and Practice of World History and Their Relevance to the Global View of History and Total History of Our Times], *Xueshu tansuo* (Scholarly explorations), 6 (2004).

13. The debate on the Asiatic mode of production did not occur for the first time in the 1950s or only in China—it occurred in Russia and Japan in the 1920s and the 1930s. But in the 1950s and the 1960s, Chinese historians vigorously revived the debate just as world-history study, which included the study of Asian history, entered a period of rapid development in the PRC. For a comparative study of the debate in English in the earlier period, see Joshua A. Fogel, "The Debate over the Asiatic Mode of Production in Soviet Russia, China, and Japan," *American Historical Review* 93:1 (February 1988), 56–79.

14. Karl Marx, "Articles on China, 1853–1860," in Marx-Engles Archives, http://www.marxists.org/archive/marx/works/1853/china/index.htm (accessed November 28, 2017). Relevant studies on the subject include Keith B. Anderson, *Marx at the Margins: On Nationalism, Ethnicity and Non-Western Societies* (Chicago: University of Chicago Press, 2011).

15. Tsunoyama Sakae, for example, recalled that in his early career, he drew inspirations from the writings of Umesao and Imanishi Kinji (1902–1992), Umesao's predecessor, also a Kyoto University anthropologist. See Tsunoyama, *Seikatsushi no hakken: firudo wâku de miro sekai*, 33–37.

16. Kawakita Minoru, *Kôgyoka no rekishi teki zentei: teikoku to gentleman* (Tokyo: Iwanami-shoten, 1983); Peter J. Cain & Anthony G. Hopkins, *British Imperialism* (London: Longman, 1993); Raymond Dumett (ed.), *Gentlemanly Capitalism and British Imperialism: the new debate on Empire;* and *Gentlemanly Capitalism, Imperialism and Global History*, (ed.) Shigeru Akita (Houndmills: Palgrave Macmillan, 2002).

17. Hamashita Takeshi, "Tribute and Treaties: Maritime Asia and Treaty Port Networks in the Era of Negotiation, 1800–1900," see, Giovanni Arrighi, Takeshi Hamashita and Mark Selden (eds.), *The Resurgence of East Asia: 500, 150 and 50 Years Perspective*, (London: Routledge/Curzon, 2003), 17–50, 24. Also, Hamashita Takeshi, *Kindai Chugoku no Kokusaiteki Keiki: Choko Boeki Shisutemu to Kindai Ajia* [*International Factors Affecting Modern China: Tributary Trade System and Modern Asia*] (Tokyo: Tokyo daigaku shuppansha, 1990), *Choko Shisutemu to Kindai Ajia* [*Tributary Trade System and Modern*

18. Kawakatsu Heita, *Bunmei no kaiyō shikan* (Tokyo: Chûô kôronsha, 1997). Kawakatsu's other publications include *Ajia kōekiken to Nihon kōgyōka, 1500–1900* (Asian trading network and Japanese industrialization) (Tokyo: Riburo Pûto, 1991), which he coedited with Hamashita Takeshi and *Japanese Industrialization and Asian Economy* (London: Routledge, 1994) and *Asian Pacific Dynamism, 1550-2000* (London: Routledge, 2000), both of which he coedited with A. J. H. Latham.
19. See for instance Sugihara Kaoru, *Ajia-kan Boeki no Keisei to Kozo* [*Patterns and Development of Intra-Asian Trade*] (Kyoto: Mineruva-Shobo, 1996) and Kaoru Sugihara (ed.) *Japan, China and the Growth of Asian International Economy* (Oxford: Oxford University Press, 2005), introduction; Kaoru Sugihara, "British Imperialism, the City of London and Global Industrialization," in *Gentlemanly Capitalism, Imperialism and Global History*, 185–206 and, more succinctly, "East Asia Path," *Economic and Political Weekly*, 39:34 (August 2004), 3855–3858. In his "Is There an East Asian Development Path? Long-term Comparisons, Constraints and Continuities," Kenneth Pomeranz offers his comments on Sugihara's thesis, *Journal of the Economic and Social History of the Orient* 44:3 (2001), 322–362.
20. Wu Yujin, "The Nomadic World and Nomadic Peoples in World History," *Yunnan Social Sciences* 1 (1983), 47–57; "Physiocratism and Mercantilism in World History," *Historical Research* 1 (1984), 3–24; "The Incubation of Agrarian Civilization to the Industrial World," *World History* 2 (1987), 1–18; and "The Responses of Various Countries in the Traditional Agrarian World to the Impact of the Newly Rising Industrial World," *World History* 1 (1993), 3–22.
21. Karl Marx, "Outline of the Critique of Political Economy (*Grundrisse*)," Marx-Engles Archives, http://www.marxists.org/archive/marx/works/1857/grundrisse/ch01.htm (accessed November 28, 2017).
22. Wu Yujin, "World History," *Zhongguo dabaike quanshu* (*Encyclopedia Sinica*), foreign history volume (Beijing: Zhongguo dabaike quanshu chubanshe, 1990), 1, 5, 15.
23. A search, using "sekaishi" (world history) as a title word, in the National Diet Library finds that between 1991 and 2017, an impressive total number of 2720 books were published, whereas between 1971 and 1990, the number of the same titled books was merely 727. The Library also holds 38 books that are entitled "global history," with the first one published in 1996.
24. Having used "globalization" as the keyword to search in the Chinese Academic Journal Database (CNKI), which contains journal articles between 1979 and 2017, we have found 34,896 articles that address globalization's various impacts in a broad range of areas: from fine arts, architecture, tourism and linguistics to international finance, business and educational administration, political economy and geopolitics, urban development and religious studies. More important, an overwhelming majority of the articles (34,887) were published after 1994.
25. An academic journal database in Taiwan showed that between 1999 and 2017, 2,279 articles were published that discuss the impact of globalization. The journal database at Chinese University of Hong Kong also revealed that between 1980 and 2017, 571 articles were published on a wide array of topics regarding the influence of globalization. See Q. Edward Wang, "Globalization, Global History and Local Identity in 'Greater China,'" *The Asia-Pacific Journal* Vol. 8-4-09, February 17, 2009 (http://www.japanfocus.org/-Q__Edward-Wang/3055) (accessed November 28, 2017).

26. Zhang Yiping, *Quanqiushi daolun* (Beijing: Renmin chubanshe, 2012); Liu Wenming, *Quanqiushi lilun yu wenming hudong yanjiu* (Beijing: Zhongguo shehui kexue chubanshe, 2015). Yu Pei (ed.), *Quanqiuhua he quanqiushi* (Beijing: Shehui kexue wenxian chubanshe, 2007); Zhu Zhenghui and Hu Fengxiang (eds.), *Quanqiu shiye xiade shixue: quyuxing yu guojixing* (Shanghai: Shanghai cishu chubanshe, 2011); Fudan daxue wenshi yanjiuyuan (ed.), *Quanqiushi, quyushi yu guobieshi: Fudan, Dongda, Pulinsidun sanxiao hezuo lunwenji* (Beijing: Zhonghua shuju, 2016).
27. Liu Xincheng, "The Global View of History in China," keynote speech delivered at the 20th convention of the World History Association at Capital Normal University, Beijing, China, on July 8, 2011. For a critical review of the rise of world/global history in China, see Dominic Sachsenmaier, *Global Perspectives on Global History: Theories and Approaches in a Connected World* (Cambridge: Cambridge University Press, 2011), ch. 4.
28. See the essays by Liu Xincheng, Jiang Zhushan, Zhang Xupeng, and Wang Yongping in the "Global History Forum," *Lishi yanjiu* 1 (2013), 4–31. It is worth noting that Dominic Sachsenmaier has also published an essay in the forum titled "Global History and Its Potentials," 31–37.
29. Cf. Akita, "World History and the Emergence of Global History in Japan," 91–94.
30. Haneda Masashi, *Atarashii sekaishi he: Chikyu shimin no tame no koso* [*Towards a New World History: An Idea for Global Citizens*] (Tokyo: Kabushiki Kaisha Iwanami Shoten, 2011).
31. Haneda, "Japanese Perspectives on 'Global History'."
32. Haneda Masashi, *Atarashii sekaishi e: chikyū shimin no tameno kōsō* (Tokyo: Iwanami-shoten, 2011). Also, his "Japanese Perspectives on 'Global History'."
33. http://www.global-history.org/.
34. Liu, "The Global View of History in China."
35. Zhong Weimin, *Chaye yu yapian: shijiu shiji jingji quanqiuhua zhongde Zhongguo* (Tea and Opium: China in the Nineteenth-Century Economic Globalization) (Beijing: Sanlian shudian, 2010). At the World History Association convention in Beijing, there were panels devoted to the studies of "maritime Asia" and intra-Asian trade. See the program of the convention.
36. Q. Edward Wang, "Globalization and Taiwan: Seeking an Alternative to Nationalist Aspiration," paper presented at the International conference, "Global History, Globally," University of Freiburg, Germany, May 24–26, 2010. For a general survey of the rise of global history in Taiwan's historical circle, see Chiang Chu-shan, *Dangdai shixue yanjiu de qushi, fangfa yu shijian: cong xin wenhua shi dao quanqiu shi* (*Trends, Methods and Practices in Contemporary Historiography: From New Cultural History to Global History*) (Taipei: Wunan tushu chuban gongsi, 2012).
37. Qian Chengdan, "Constructing a New Disciplinary Framework of Modern World History around the Theme of Modernization," *Chinese Studies in History* 42:3 (Spring 2009), 7–24.
38. Q. Edward Wang, "'Rise of the Great Powers'=Rise of China? Challenges of the Advancement of Global History in the People's Republic of China," *Journal of Contemporary China* 19:64 (March 2010), 273–89.
39. "World History Books Finding Popularity," *Yomiuri Shimbun*, March 18, 2012, which describes how Japanese readers turned to the translated works by William McNeill and Jared Diamond. Diamond's *Guns, Germs, and Steel: The Fates of Human Societies* also has Chinese translations and sold quite well in both China and Taiwan.

40. See for example Wu Xiaoqun, "Do We Really Need a 'Global View of History'?" *Chinese Studies in History* 42:3 (Spring 2009), 45–50.
41. See the different reactions from Chinese scholars to the works of Frank and Pomeranz in the "California School in China," *Chinese Studies in History* 45:1 (Fall 2011).
42. Cf. Q. Edward Wang, "Remembering the Past, Reconciling for the Future: A Critical Analysis of China-Japan Joint History Research Project (2006–2010)," *Chinese Historical Review* 17:2 (2010), 219–37.
43. Haneda, "Japanese Perspectives on 'Global History'," 229.

CHAPTER 3
LATIN AMERICA AND THE CARIBBEAN: TRADITIONS OF GLOBAL HISTORY
Rafael Marquese and João Paulo Pimenta

I

On February 24, 1821, Agustín de Iturbide, a key military commander for the New Spanish Viceroyalty, announced the Plan de Iguala, a peace treaty that would serve as the foundation for Mexican independence. Significantly, Iturbide's words were directed not at Mexicans, but at Americans: "*Americans! Under whose name I understand not only those born in America, but also to Europeans, Africans and Asians who live in it.*"[1]

In the early nineteenth century, the challenges to and the subsequent collapse of the Iberian empires of America were grounded in ideas, analyses, discourses, concepts and vocabularies that saw the era's major events—the result of which would be the creation of nearly two dozen independent and sovereign national states—as forming a crucial chapter in the history of human development. That history was conceived as one composed by Americans, Europeans, Africans and Asians within a broader global context. This concept of history, already commonplace in early-nineteenth-century discourse, can be studied in itself as a relevant dimension of the intellectual history of the era. This orientation also came to provide a foundation for those who would later devote themselves to the study of how the Iberian empires disappeared and how new societies and political bodies took their place.

Scholars of Latin American and Caribbean history, however, have not always seen the histories of their respective countries as part of a more general history. During the nineteenth century, the building of modern nation-states was followed by the emergence of historical narratives that emphasized the alleged singularity—and sometimes also the superiority—of each state and society. These narratives, frequently making political uses of the past, would become largely dominant everywhere, not only in Latin American and Caribbean nations, but worldwide. Their lasting effects are strong to this day. Yet the triumph of national history also gave rise to a different framing, especially the embrace of history's comparative dimension: the notion that each nation could be considered unique only *in relation to* other nations. Moreover, despite the wide prevalence of national and nationalist narratives, many scholars continued to push the spatial horizons of "Latin American history" to encompass multiple countries in the American hemisphere, the continent as a whole and even the continent integrated with the rest of the world.

In Latin America, global and comparative historical approaches—appreciating processes and phenomena as parts of larger realities and going far beyond discrete and nationally isolated times and spaces—are getting stronger day by day. Yet these approaches are perhaps less innovative than some current practitioners are willing to acknowledge. Often practiced as if *overcoming* previous forms of historical writing, they might better be seen as *renewing* them.

By examining some examples of Latin American and Caribbean history writing, our purpose is to recover scholarship that today can be seen as exercises in global history *avant la lettre*—past scholarly work that can support the practice of writing global history today, and serve as inspiration for scholars working on Latin America as well as other parts of the world. The historiography of Latin America and the Caribbean is full of such work.[2] For this reason, we will conduct an introductory rather than an exhaustive analysis. In selecting our examples, we have focused on thematic relevance, theoretical density and historiographical impact. These examples are not perfectly homogeneous or cohesive in analytical approach or authorial intentionality, but these rough groupings allow us to put in perspective the kind of self-praise that obscures the history of global history's practice and, in so doing, limits its potential for future innovation.

Selecting proper examples of such scholarship is complicated. Much of what has been written in the field we today consider "global history" was not recognized as such at the time. Not only did the scholars we discuss not identify as "global," their works were conceived and written in different contexts and with distinct goals. In a sense, however, this recognition only sheds further doubt on the claims made by some current global historians, as it reveals the almost natural way that past scholars saw the history of the New World as an assemblage of histories both national and transnational. Is this not, after all, the basic premise of global history today?

Let us quickly recall some early cases: take, for instance, Bartolomé Mitre, a central figure in the debates over the establishment of a canonical national historiography in Argentina. In the same year that he published the fourth and final edition of his *Historia de Belgrano y de la Independencia Argentina* (1887), he started another work centered on the founding fathers of the *"Rioplatenses:" the Historia de San Martín y de la Sudamericana Emancipation*.[3] Here a hero of national stature is taken as the protagonist of a history that transcends the national to become a truly continental history. Shortly thereafter, Brazilian publicist Joaquim Nabuco followed a comparable path. In *Balmaceda* (1895), Nabuco developed an analysis of the Chilean civil war four years earlier—and the role of Chile's president in that war—but with an eye on Brazil and the whole American continent. Still he complained:

> South America … has not had a historian; there is no complete critical sketch of its political existence; nobody has extracted yet from the vast materials buried in its distant capitals a framework of a history. Nothing has been written from the standpoint of a universal view.[4]

It is possible to agree with Nabuco on the absence of a universal historical perspective *of America*, but there is no doubt that in the late nineteenth century many of the New World's historians seemed to have embraced the necessity of analyzing the history of the continent and beyond.

Just half a century after Nabuco, that lesson was duly learned: the history of America was now firmly portrayed as part of world history. For example, Antonello Gerbi's *La Disputa del Nuovo Mundo* (1955) analyzed a set of intellectual elaborations whose multiple variations throughout history converged on the recognition that the Americas have always been integrated in a single historical entity. Or take Edmundo O'Gorman's *La Invención de América* (1958), in which the notion of a "discovery" of the continent—until then the consensus view of the vast majority of scholars—gave way to the notion of a process of the continent's incorporation into a European worldview—a major innovation. Even Sérgio Buarque de Holanda, in *Visão do Paraíso* (1959), analyzed the formation of a collective imaginary about the colonization of America in a truly global perspective, one that was at the same time both comparative and integrative.[5]

These are but a few examples of a much wider historiography. They open our view to the long and distinguished tradition of spatially expansive views of Latin American history. To better understand the range of analytical possibilities of such approaches, we focus on three core themes in Latin American history and show how analyses of each theme have been framed in global terms over the course of the twentieth century, thus shaping some of the historiographical traditions we can classify as global. These traditions were made not only by Latin American historians but also by Latin Americanists from outside the continent who worked in dialogue with their local counterparts. By putting them together, we begin to conceptualize the telling of Latin American global history globally.

II

The first tradition stems from the Marxist-inspired work on Caribbean slavery, pioneered by two historians and politicians born in Trinidad & Tobago: C.L.R. James and Eric Williams. Published in the late 1930s, their books on the French and British colonies in the West Indies inscribed New World slave systems into the broader historical processes of the Western Hemisphere, thus reshaping the field.

The Black Jacobins (1938) by C.L.R. James made its perspective clear right in the title. The author analyzed the history of the massive Saint-Domingue slave rebellion in its multiple intersections with European economic, social and political dynamics. As James explained, the systematic exploitation of Caribbean colonies during the eighteenth century gave rise to powerful merchant groups based in Nantes, Bordeaux and Marseille. Jealous over the colonial monopoly, such groups came into frequent clashes with resident Caribbean planters over the problem of smuggling and trade with rival British and the American merchants. At the local level, the position of the resident slaveholders was challenged by conflicts with the poor white settlers and the thriving community of free blacks and mulattos living in the colony. James also pointed out how these tensions were shaped by the structure of European colonialism in the Caribbean and the dynamics of inter-imperial competition: the growing rivalry between the French bourgeoisie and those in the British bourgeoisie who favored a new imperial project focusing on the East Indies (driven by criticism of black slavery) pushed the conflict to a global level. After the Seven Years' War (1756–63) and the American Revolution (1776–83), Saint-Domingue—the main plantation rival of the British West Indies—became the locus of the next and decisive round of contention between these two world powers. According to James, "these then were the forces which in the decade preceding the French Revolution linked San Domingo to the economic destiny of three continents and the social and political conflicts of that pregnant age."[6]

At the outbreak of the slave uprising of 1791, events in the Caribbean would prove crucial to the course of revolution in Europe itself, positioning the colonial question at the heart of the political destinies of the West.[7] More important, though, was the way that subaltern groups—the enslaved laborers of Saint-Domingue—emerged as a collective historical subject.[8] Even if the book's title, which evoked the association between the masses of Paris and the colonial black slaves, was inaccurate from a historical point of view, it clearly signaled James's new approach: a *global history from below*.

The work of Eric Williams was equally far-reaching. In his classic *Capitalism & Slavery*, Williams modeled his examination of black slavery in the British Caribbean on *The Black Jacobins*, a fact made evident by looking to the work's origins as an Oxford PhD dissertation completed the same year James's book was published. In the 1930s, the "British imperial school" dominated the writing of the history of colonialism and Caribbean slavery, and worked in many ways to legitimate the foundations of the British Empire.[9] For Williams and James, the writing of that history from an alternative set of assumptions formed part of the campaign for the empire's dissolution.

As Williams's dissertation focused on the economic factors leading to the abolition of the transatlantic slave trade and African slavery in the British Empire, it departed from the interpretation of the prevailing "imperial school." Nevertheless, it was a work that followed the established pattern of academic PhD dissertations in history, especially with regard to its strict chronological narrative and its exhaustive control of the evidence. Concentrating on the years between 1783 and 1838, the dissertation examined the declining economic importance of the West Indies to the British Empire after the American Revolution, the growth of the slave trade and slavery in Saint-Domingue, the British attempts to conquer the French colony during the slave rebellion, and the impact of the failure of this attempt on the abolition of the transatlantic slave trade in 1807. Williams also addressed the decline of the British Caribbean sugar production in the face of the other global competitors, the threat of slave rebellions in Barbados, Jamaica and Demerara; the impact of such rebellions on British public opinion; and the limitations imposed by the monopoly of the West Indies for the advancement of capitalist forces in the metropolis.

The failure to immediately publish the dissertation and Williams's subsequent difficulty in finding a job in the British university system led him to move to the United States. At Howard University, he found stimulating conditions for the revision of the original plan of his work. The most important element in reshaping the book project was the appearance of C.L.R. James's work in 1938.

In an interesting movement of global history from the margins into the mainstream of the profession, Williams's interpretation of the contradictory relationship between capitalism and slavery was directly taken from *The Black Jacobins*. Moreover, Williams would add to his book, eventually published in 1944, three axes absent from the 1938 dissertation: the understanding of black slavery as an economic phenomenon in the elaboration of racism as a functional aspect of class exploitation, the centrality of Atlantic slavery to the rise of industrial capitalism in England and the role of slave resistance in the overthrow of the slave system—a theme apparent but undeveloped in the dissertation. Williams was also inspired by the political tone of C.L.R. James and his direct, acidic and engaging writing, which conveyed James's belief that the practice of history should be regarded as a political activity.[10]

James and Williams were thus among the first historians to connect the building of global capitalism to the mass enslavement of Africans in the New World. Their scholarship placed black slavery at the genesis of the modern world, and, in so doing, they paved the way for a range of research on uneven development in the arena of the capitalist world economy. They were also the first to present an analytical model that viewed historical processes in different parts of the Atlantic area as constituting an organic unit, with events in the Old World and the New World shaping each other in multiple and reciprocal determinations.

III

The global perspective of C.L.R. James and Eric Williams inspired historians and social scientists in the 1960s and 1970s as they grappled with Latin America's colonial past. Another source of inspiration came from a different strain, far from James and Williams's Marxism but also originating in the 1930s: the scholarship related to the so-called Second Generation of the Annales school, led by Fernand Braudel. It is well known that the collective project of this remarkable group of historians shared a concern for grasping the objects under investigation through a comprehensive and totalizing perspective of history, with a strong dialogue with geography, demography, sociology, anthropology and economics. Another hallmark of the group was the focus on the dialectics of historical times—in the Braudelian formulation, the perception of different temporal rhythms of "structures," "conjunctures" and "events."[11]

It is worth mentioning a more specific "Latin-American moment" in Braudel's elaborations. His pioneering formulation appeared in the first edition of *The Mediterranean*, presented as a PhD dissertation (*Doctorat d'État*) at the Sorbonne in 1947, in which the equation of the different rhythms of historical times occurred through a tripartite scheme of "geographic time," "social time" and "individual time."[12] This was not the definitive conceptualization that Braudel went on to offer in his 1958 essay on the *longue durée*, but it had in itself a research program that would motivate historians associated with the Annales for about a quarter of a century. How did Braudel come to this formulation? In the move from a dissertation conceived in the 1920s in the field of diplomatic history to a completely different result twenty years later—one that heralded a new understanding of the relationship between time and space in historical writing—two episodes were crucial. First there was the intellectual contact with the first generation of the Annales, especially Lucien Febvre, and second his experience, from 1935 and 1937, as a professor at the University of São Paulo. In his last years, Braudel said that he became "smart" going to Brazil. This statement should of course be read as a form of personal nostalgia, but experts in the work of Braudel have demonstrated that it also reflects the importance of the Brazilian experience—as a *global* experience—to the elaboration of his concepts on the plurality of historical time.[13]

While held captive by the Nazis during the Second World War, Braudel considered writing a secondary dissertation (then a requirement of the French university system for obtaining a PhD) about sixteenth-century Brazil, but did not. However, while at the Sorbonne between 1945 and 1946, he taught a course on Latin America at the beginning of the nineteenth century, attracting students such as Frédéric Mauro and Pierre Chaunu, who soon became engaged with his analytical perspective.[14] In the following decade, Chaunu and Mauro published crucial books on the Spanish and Portuguese empires in the Atlantic context, anchored in the geo-historical model originally proposed by Braudel for the Mediterranean. The analysis of Chaunu's multivolume work on the trade relations between Seville and Spanish America was devoted to furthering a comprehension of the invariance and inflections of structural time. Mauro examined a geographical area (the South Atlantic) that was commanded at its frontiers by a single European power. He called attention to the forms of production imposed by the Portuguese and to the structural role of black slavery in the operation of an imperial system that—as he knew well—had always been a global system.[15]

Braudel's perspective attracted the Portuguese historian Vitorino Magalhães Godinho, whose academic career began in Portugal in the early 1940s with an investigation of fifteenth-century Portuguese overseas expansion. Facing difficulties under the Salazarist regime, Godinho sought refuge in France, where he found shelter in the Annales group. From 1949, besides publishing considerable articles and essays and working as a visiting professor at the University of São Paulo (occupying the same position Braudel held in the 1930s), Godinho prepared his monumental work, *Os Descobrimentos e a Economia Mundial* (*The Overseas Discoveries and the World Economy*). Initially presented in France in 1969 as a dissertation for *Doctorat d'État*, the book appeared in Portuguese in the early 1980s. In an eloquent discussion of the global history of the era following European overseas expansion, Godinho eschews Eurocentrism to carefully evaluate the complex economic, social and cultural relations created by the expansion of Western capital through Asia, Africa and the Americas.[16] Of particular importance is Godinho's examination of the specific commodities at the core of Portuguese expansion, as well as his conceptualization of what he calls the "historical-geographical complexes" of the world economy between the twelfth and seventeenth centuries. This theoretical framework ultimately allowed him to assess the ways that New World history was produced by global history and the ways that New World history in turn shaped global history.[17]

We should also highlight a book based on the notes of a course taught at the Sorbonne University in the late 1960s by a well-known Marxist author and expert in the history of modern Catalonia. Pierre Vilar's *A History of Gold and Money, 1450–1920*, which initially appeared in Spanish in 1969, examines the place of Latin America in the global history of gold and silver exploration, as well as its economic implications in the modern world.[18] He examines the exploitation of silver in Potosí (looking at its implications for the organization of indigenous society and regional markets, ecology and labor forms) and its relationship with global economic expansion in the second half of the sixteenth century. He also analyzes transformations in global finance from the seventeenth to the early twentieth century. By integrating the large circuits of production and circulation of silver and gold, Vilar deals substantively with the long-term implications of the integration of America into the European economic space, anticipating many of the debates mobilizing current discussions of the role of New World precious metals in the consolidation of world capitalism.[19]

Finally, we must not forget the *magnus opus* of Fernand Braudel, which can be regarded as a synthesis of much of the collective research effort already summarized. In his three-part history of capitalism from the fifteenth to the eighteenth century, he gives Portuguese and Spanish America and the Caribbean a prominent role as privileged spaces of the action of European capital and therefore of the "decoupling" of the West from Asia.[20] Even those authors associated with the Annales school who abandoned the Braudelian concept of the "capitalist world-economy" (for instance, Ruggiero Romano in his book on the opposing conjunctures of seventeenth-century crisis in Europe and Spanish America[21]) kept the core of the school's theoretical and methodological perspective, that is to say the observation of the historical phenomena subjected to the analysis through its multiple spatial-temporal scales. Over the years, this perspective has maintained the prestige of global approaches to the history of Latin America.[22]

IV

A third strand of global study focused on the history of Latin America and the Caribbean emerges from the economic debates on the issue of regional development and underdevelopment. If some of its roots can be found among the authors and works already presented, this strand nonetheless developed as a direct response to the global political and economic context of the Great Depression. Indeed, it was as a public manager in Argentina in the 1920s and 1930s that Raúl Prebisch began a critical review of the assumptions of classical and neoclassical economics about international trade and comparative advantage. In studies written for a small audience when he was the general manager of the Central Bank of Argentina, inspired by Keynes, Prebisch suggested, perhaps for the first time, that hierarchies were crucial to international trade and categories such as *center* and *periphery* necessary for understanding the world economic system. After being appointed executive secretary of the Economic Commission for Latin America (ECLAC) in 1948, Prebisch not only elaborated on these concepts but developed related ones such as deteriorating terms of trade, the dualist structure of peripheral economies and inward development.[23] To be properly explored, such analytical tools required a deep dive into the history of Latin America and the Caribbean based on a truly global perspective.

Perhaps the ultimate expression of the employment of Prebisch's categories in the study of Latin American history is in the work of the Brazilian economist Celso Furtado, another prominent member of ECLAC. In *The Economic Growth of Brazil* (1959), Furtado examined the Iberian colonization of the New World within the broader context of European commercial expansion, emphasizing the asymmetries between what he called the New World's "exploitation colonies" (comprising tropical areas such as Northeastern Brazil, the West Indies, the colonial Chesapeake and South Carolina, and the Iberian mining zones in New Spain, Peru and Minas Gerais) and the "settler colonies" (the northern colonies in continental British America).[24] A systematic comparison of these two colonial experiences let Furtado explain the historical split between the economic development of the United States and the underdevelopment of Latin America and the Caribbean. Compulsory labor (African or indigenous) was a basic feature of "exploitation colonies," nearly all the production of which was destined for centers of global capitalism. Subsequent concentration of land ownership and income and the atrophy of sectors oriented to internal markets (also characterized by low capital formation and productivity) closed the road to self-sustaining economic growth based on industrialization, the true mark of development. The "settler colonies," in contrast, characterized by free labor, an economy attentive to local needs and a more balanced distribution of land and income, took the path of "inward development" based on strong internal markets.[25]

The so-called dependency theory, born in the universities of Latin America, emerged from a critique of the ECLAC model's ineffectiveness at either explaining historical change or overcoming underdevelopment. Although developed primarily by sociologists and economists not committed to the archival work of historians, two works from this school have particular relevance to a globally framed study of Latin American history. Fernando Henrique Cardoso and Enzo Falleto offered an analysis of class relations in the peripheries of the capitalist world system as a key element in understanding historically imposed barriers to development. Andre Gunder Frank emphasized that the main source of capital accumulation in metropolitan centers was the systematic exploitation of the satellite zones of the world capitalist system from the sixteenth to the twentieth century, highlighting such resource transfer as the real obstacle to development, regardless of the forms of production or labor existing in the periphery.[26]

The work of Cardoso, Falleto and Gunder Frank had a great impact on the community of historians—not only through their followers but through their detractors as well. In 1970 Stanley and Barbara Stein published a short study examining the distinctions between the historical process of Spanish and Portuguese colonization, whose metropolises were still characterized by feudal structures, and British and French colonization, whose metropolises were transitioning to industrial capitalism. With this book, the Steins began an ambitious research program on the relations between New Spain and global capitalism.[27] We can also mention the Argentine historian Tulio Halperin Donghi. In two books (1968 and 1985), he examined the historical trajectories of Portuguese and Spanish America, covering the colonial and the national periods and emphasizing connections between the material base and social and political dynamics in the *longue durée*.[28] In Brazilian historiography, Fernando Novais's (1979) work on the European exploration of Portugal and Brazil and how this history fit within the broader history of colonialism simultaneously incorporated Eric Williams's ideas about the contradictory relationship between capitalism and slavery, the Braudelian conception of the plurality of historical times, and the dependency school's formulations of the relation between center and periphery.[29]

Among the critical responses, Ernesto Laclau's and Ciro Flamarion Santana Cardoso's harsh censures of both the ECLAC and the dependency paradigms stand out. Laclau and Cardoso emphasized the analytical priority of the colonial relations of production: the history of America's relative autonomy in the world market. It is worth noting that this perspective, on the one hand, gives explanatory primacy to the colonial world's "inner" face (a framework rejected by globalists, for whom there is no "internality" or "externality," only their integration), and on the other hand, stresses the need for comprehensive comparisons between different historical formations in Latin America and the Caribbean, thus remaining open to global approaches. This is also true of Cardoso's concept of the "colonial slave mode of production," which is founded on a broad grasp of the different slave societies of the Americas and is in close dialogue with the historiographical traditions of Caribbean Marxists and the second generation of the Annales (Cardoso was trained in France by Frédéric Mauro).[30]

The critical debates around these three legacies (Caribbean Marxism, Annales school and dependency theory) provided the intellectual context for the development of world system analysis. Indeed, one can clearly identify the contributions of Eric Williams, Fernand Braudel, Raul Prebisch and Andre Gunder Frank in the influential *oeuvre* of Immanuel Wallerstein.[31] Following the steps of those authors but with a highly original theoretical and methodological proposal, Wallerstein presented strong arguments about how the incorporation of the Americas into the European capitalist world economy shaped the genesis and development of the "modern world system." Indeed, the conquest and colonial exploitation of the New World in the long sixteenth century were considered by him as decisive steps toward the crystallization of the international division of labor, which constituted one of the foundations of this world system. The exploitation of the natural resources of the Americas based on the compulsion of indigenous and African labor became a decisive factor in the dynamics of the conflicts between European metropolises and, therefore, in the hierarchy of the central and semi-peripheral powers of the capitalist world economy.

One of the harshest reactions to the model of global history proposed by Wallerstein, however, would come from a major Latin Americanist. Steve Stern, in critically evaluating the evidence Wallerstein offered to explain the adoption of compulsory labor in the silver and sugar industries, questioned the general validity of the world system model for the investigation of the history of Latin America and the Caribbean. According to him, the global perspective suggested by Wallerstein would have little relevance to understanding the local dynamics of Latin America and the Caribbean, which would be better analyzed by focusing on the examination of internal social relations of the colonial world. Stern's criticism eroded for a time the appeal of global analytical perspectives for historians of Latin America and the Caribbean. Indeed, the controversy between Steve Stern and Immanuel Wallerstein had the effect of privileging chronologically and locally restricted approaches to Latin American history over approaches that see history as an active element of world history.[32]

V

Histories of Latin America and the Caribbean from a global perspective never disappeared and generated vibrant, internationally influential strands of historiography. And the global approach continues to yield important results in the twenty-first century. We do not intend to fully evaluate this recent production, except to note that significant works of the last decade inscribe Latin American and Caribbean history into global history, resonating deeply with the traditions we have identified.

The historiography of black slavery, for example, continues to show great dynamism in asserting the economic, social and cultural connections between Africa and the New World through a growing number of publications inspired by distinct theoretical and methodological frameworks.[33] Nevertheless, truly global approaches to the complex mutual determinations between Latin American and Caribbean regions and the broader forces of colonialism and modern capitalism are still infrequent. Thus it is noteworthy that some of the most innovative recent scholarship placing slavery in the Americas in hemispheric perspective is directly inspired by Eric Williams and C.L.R. James.

In a book published in 1988, Robin Blackburn examined all the New World slavery zones to shed light on their individual trajectories in the context of the general crisis of slavery and European colonialism at the turn of the nineteenth century. Blackburn emphasized the relationship between the abolition process in the British Caribbean and the slave revolution in the French Caribbean—two subjects often treated in isolation. Later, Blackburn proposed the categories of *baroque* and *modern slavery* as keys to understanding the disjunction between Iberian and French/British slaveries, linking them to the different positions their respective metropolitan powers occupied in European state system. Finally, in his most recent volume, he calls attention to a general model of the three ages of slavery in the New World (baroque slavery, modern slavery and the "new American" slavery of the nineteenth century)—this model has great potential for understanding the historicity of the relationships between capitalism and slavery in the long run.³⁴ Also inspired by Williams and James, but in a strong dialogue with world system perspectives, Dale Tomich proposed in a 1988 essay the concept of "second slavery" to account for the profound connections between the slaveries found in Cuba, Brazil and the Southern United States within the structures of the industrial world economy.³⁵ Tomich taught in several Brazilian universities in the 1980s and 1990s, and the "second slavery" concept has stimulated a good number of publications in Brazil, Europe and the United States that have a global conception of nineteenth-century slavery in the Americas.³⁶

With regard to the Annales heritage, in 2004 Serge Gruzinski—a specialist in the history of colonial New Spain—published an ambitious book in which he conceptualizes the Iberian Union period (1580–1640) as the first genuine effort at globalization under the sign of Western values and practices. Here we see an attempt to unite the historiographical turn toward anthropological history, which deeply informed post-1970 historiography, with the totalizing problems that had motivated earlier Annales scholars such as Pierre Chaunu, Frederic Mauro, Vitorino Magalhães Godinho and, especially, Fernand Braudel.³⁷ On the other hand, the geo-historical perspective of the two first generations of Annales—not fully explored by later members—was used by Luiz Felipe de Alencastro to analyze the crucial role of the South Atlantic slave trade in Brazilian historical formation. More than Atlantic history, his book puts the economic and political transformations in Brazil and Africa into a framework of multiple and reciprocal determinations modulated by the broader context of the European colonial disputes.³⁸

In a critical dialogue with the World Systems perspective by employing its concept of commodity chains, Steven Topik, Carlos Marichal and Zephyr Frank edited an important volume on the role of Latin American commodities in the world economy from the early sixteenth century to the late twentieth century. Despite reiterating criticisms of the World Systems perspective, the authors' analysis of various commodity chains that bound Latin American to the world economy (silver, indigo, cochineal, tobacco, coffee, sugar, cocoa, bananas, guano, rubber, henequen, cocaine) seems compatible with the original postulates of the modern world system approach.³⁹ Either way, the fruitful agenda presented in this volume offers a wide range of possibilities for those wishing to explore the links between New World production and the gears of the global economy.

We can now return to our point of departure, to the moment when the multiplication of nation-states and societies that emerged with the end of the Iberian empires in America in the early nineteenth century imposed a coeval perception that the history of that time could best be understood via a global perspective. The historiography of the processes of independence in America has never entirely abandoned that premise, as evidenced by the state of the historiography today.⁴⁰ The concerns that more than fifty years ago motivated the French historian Jacques Godechot to propose a history of "Atlantic revolutions" in a pioneering effort to reconcile the perspective of historical agents with their historians are still strongly present today.⁴¹

Within this debate, dynamic and multifaceted themes of global history emerge. This can be seen in the creative and fruitful effort coordinated by the Spanish historian Javier

Fernández Sebastián that has brought together hundreds of experts who are investigating the history of languages and political concepts used in Latin America and the Iberian world between the final decades of the eighteenth century and the early nineteenth century.[42] Based on a specific reading of assumptions established by Reinhart Koselleck, this team has been undertaking a politico-intellectual history with great spatial and temporal opening that goes beyond the Ibero-American world and the period directly contemplated by it. The originality of this venture, as well as its eloquent results so far—seen now in many academic papers, articles and book chapters—suggests a research potential still little explored: the articulation of political-intellectual, discursive and symbolic dimensions alongside the material dimensions (economy, trade flows, etc.) of Latin American societies.

Such potential could be enhanced through a deeper engagement with some of the forms of global history outlined in this chapter. Latin American and Caribbean histories and historians cannot be arbitrarily adapted to the current academic canons, however beneficial they may be. In spite of their divergences and their obsolete points, the historiographical traditions that we have examined here strongly suggest that the history of Latin America and the Caribbean can only be truly understood in its global dimensions.

Notes

1. Agustín de Iturbide, "Proclama y Plan de Iguala (24 de febrero de 1821)." Romero & Romero (orgs.). *Pensamiento político de la emancipación (1790–1825)* (Caracas: Ayaucho, 1997), vol. 2, 283.

2. Our argument thus departs from Matthew Brown's, according to whom there is a persistent and negative separation between the Latin America historiography and the studies on global history. Brown rightly emphasizes how the most prominent strands currently in Anglo-Saxon global history systematically ignore Latin American history. Our point, however, is not this, but rather that Latin American and Caribbean historiographical traditions are no less global because they have not been written in English, that they have been formulated before and have been independent of the historiographical trends of the English-speaking academic world. See Matthew Brown, "The Global History of Latin America," *Journal of Global History* 10:3 (November 2015), 365–86.

3. Fabio Wasserman, *Entre Clio y la Polis: conocimiento histórico y representaciones del passado en el Río de la Plata (1830–1860)* (Buenos Aires: Teseo, 2008); see also Fernando Devoto and Nora Pagano, *Historia de la historiografia argentina* (Buenos Aires: Sudamericana, 2009).

4. Joaquim Nabuco, *Balmaceda* (4a.ed., São Paulo: Cosac Naify, 2008), 27. For a broader study of his political and intellectual career, see Ricardo Salles, *Joaquim Nabuco, um Pensador do Império* (Rio de Janeiro: Topbooks, 2002).

5. Antonello Gerbi, *O Novo Mundo. História de uma polêmica, 1750–1900* (trad.port., São Paulo: Companhia das Letras, 1996); Edmundo O'Gorman, *A invenção da América* (trad. port., São Paulo: Ed.Unesp, 1992); Sérgio Buarque de Holanda, *Visão do Paraíso. Os motivos edênicos no descobrimento e colonização do Brasil* (Ed.rev., São Paulo: Brasiliense, 1992). The comparative, global perspective of Sérgio Buarque de Holanda in fact appeared earlier,

in his classic *Raízes do Brasil* (1a ed: 1936, Rio de Janeiro: José Olympio, 1986). Gilberto Freyre's *corpus*, relatively well known to the English-speaking audience, belongs in the same movement. See, in particular, *Casa Grande & Senzala*, originally published in Portuguese in 1933. English translation: *The Master and the Slaves: A Study in the Development of Brazilian Civilization*. (Berkeley: The University of California Press, 1987), and *New World in the Tropics: The Culture of Modern Brazil* (New York: Alfred Knopf, 1959).

6. C. L. R. James, *The Black Jacobins: Toussaint L'Ouverture and the San Domingo Revolution*, 2nd edition (New York: Vintage, 1989), 55.

7. James suggests, for instance, that the failure of the French and British military interventions in Saint-Domingue and the victory of the former slaves led by L'Ouverture Touissant were crucial in preventing the British attack on the French mainland between 1793 and 1799.

8. In a now-famous passage, James argued that the slaves of the New World plantations were closer to the modern industrial proletariat than the traditional peasantry, a fact that would have favored a revolutionary organization:

> the slaves worked on the land, and, like revolutionary peasants everywhere, they aimed at the extermination of their oppressors. But working and living together in gangs of hundreds on the huge sugar-factories which covered the North Plain, they were closer to a modern proletarian than any group of workers in existence at the time, and the rising was, therefore, a thoroughly prepared and organized mass movement. (84–86)

9. W. Roger Louis, *The Oxford History of the British Empire* (Oxford: Oxford University Press, 1999), vol. 5, 1–42.

10. Eric Williams, *Capitalism and Slavery* (1st edition 1944, Chapel Hill: The University of North Carolina Press, 1994). For an evaluation of the differences between the dissertation and the book, see Howard Temperley, "Eric Williams and Abolition: The Birth of a New Orthodoxy," in Barbara Solow; Stanley Engerman (eds.), *British Capitalism and Caribbean Slavery: The Legacy of Eric Williams* (Cambridge: Cambridge University Press, 1987), 229–57, and William Darity Jr., "Eric Williams and Slavery: A West Indian Viewpoint?" *Callaloo* 20:4; in Sandra Pouchet Paquet (ed.) *Eric Williams and the Postcolonial Caribbean*: A Special Issue (Autumn 1997), 800–16. For an exploration of the historiographical and political convergences and divergences between Williams and James, see Humberto García Muñiz, "Eric Williams y C.R.L. James: simbiosis intelectual y contrapunteo ideológico," in Eric Williams (ed.), *El negro em el Caribe y otros textos* (La Habana: Editorial Casa de las Américas, 2011), 419–50. Dale Tomich and William Darity Jr. have just edited Eric Williams's dissertation: *The Economic Aspect of the Abolition of the West Indian Slave Trade and Slavery* (Boulder, CO: Rowman & Littlefield, 2014).

11. Fernand Braudel's programmatic essays were published in the volume *Écrits sur l'Histoire* (Paris: Flamarion, 1969). The piece on the *longue durée*, originally published in 1958, got a new English translation by Immanuel Wallerstein: Fernand Braudel, "History and the Social Sciences: The Long Durée," *Review. A Journal of the Fernand Braudel Center* XXXII:2 (2009), 171–204.

12. Fernand Braudel, *O Mediterrâneo e o Mundo Mediterrânico na Época de Felipe II*. (1a ed: 1949; trad.port., São Paulo: Martins Fontes, 1983), 2 vols., here vol. 1, 26.

13. See Carlos Antonio Aguirre Rojas, *Braudel, o mundo e o Brasil* (trad. port., São Paulo: Cortez Editora, 2003), 95–128, and Luís Corrêa Lima, *Fernand Braudel e o Brasil. Vivência e Brasilianismo (1935–1945)* (São Paulo: Edusp, 2009). During his stay at the University of São Paulo and in the aftermath of his return to France, Braudel was also important in training the Brazilian historian Alice Piffer Canabrava, who wrote two important books

with a global history approach. In the first, she analyzed the economic, social and politic connections between the Portuguese and the Spanish in the Rio da Prata zone at the turn of the seventeenth century (*O Comércio Português no Rio da Prata, 1580–1640*. 1st edition 1942, São Paulo: Edusp, 1984); in the second one, she presented a comparative approach of sugar economy in Brazil and the Caribbean during the eighteenth century (*O Açúcar nas Antilhas, 1697–1755*. 1st edition 1946, São Paulo: IPE-USP, 1981).

14. Pierre Daix, *Fernand Braudel: Uma biografia* (trad.port, Rio de Janeiro: Record, 1999), 259–61.
15. Pierre Pierre and Huguette Chaunu, *Seville et l'Atlantique (1504–1650)* (Paris: S.E.V.P.E.N., 1955–1959), 8 vols.; Frédéric Mauro, *Le Portugal, le Brésil et l'Atlantique au XVIIe siècle (1570–1670)* (Paris: S.E.V.P.E.N., 1960), 2 vols.
16. We should remember, from the same moment, the synthesis of another important historian that did not share the theoretical and methodological framework of the Annales, but that was as Godinho a truly global historian: Charles Boxer, *The Portuguese Seaborne Empire, 1415–1825* (London: Longman, 1969). Equally important, dealing with the history of Spain: John H. Elliott, *The Old World and the New, 1492–1650* (Cambridge: Cambridge University Press, 1970). From the next generation, following Elliott's steps, see Anthony Pagden, *The Fall of Natural Man: The American Indian and the Origins of Comparative Anthropology* (Cambridge: Cambridge University Press, 1982).
17. Vitorino Magalhães Godinho, *Os Descobrimentos e a economia mundial* (Lisboa: Editorial Presença, 1981–1983), 4 vols. For a good explanation of Godinho's *corpus*, see Dale Tomich, "Vitorino Magalhães Godinho. Atlantic History, World History," *Review. A Journal of the Fernand Braudel Center* XXVIII:4 (2005), 305–12.
18. We use the Portuguese version: Pierre Vilar, *Ouro e moeda na História (1450–1920)* (Rio de Janeiro: Paz & Terra, 1980). The first English edition was published in 1976 by New Left Books. In 2011, Verso published a new edition of the book.
19. In this sense, the innovative work of Dennis Flynn and Arturo Giraldez (see, among others, "China and the Spanish Empire," *Revista de História Económica* 14:2 (Verano 1996), 309–38, and "Born with a 'Silver Spoon': The Origin of World Trade in 1571," *Journal of World History* 6:2 (Fall 1995), 201–21) would gain much from closer engagement with the implications of Pierre Vilar's analytical perspective.
20. Fernand Braudel, *Civilização Material, Economia e Capitalismo, séculos XV–XVIII* (1a ed.fr: 1979; trad.port., São Paulo: Martins Fontes, 1996), 3 vols.
21. Ruggiero Romano, *Coyunturas Opuestas: La crisis del siglo XVII en Europa e Hispanoamérica* (México: Fondo de Cultura Económica, 1993).
22. For a similar evaluation, see Sandra Kuntz Ficker, « Mundial, trasnacional, global: Un ejercicio de clarificación conceptual de los estudios globales », *Nuevo Mundo Mundos Nuevos* [on line], Débats, mis en ligne le 27 mars 2014. URL: http://nuevomundo.revues.org/66524 (accessed November 28, 2017).
23. Edgar J. Dosman, *The Life and Times of Raúl Prebisch (1901–1986)* (Montreal: McGill-Queen's University Press, 2010).
24. Furtado did not create these terms. They were used by a wide variety of authors including Karl Kaustky. In his essay *Socialism and Colonial Policy* (1907), Kaustky proposed the categories "work colonies" and "exploitation colonies" in terms that closely resembled the later ideas of Latin American social scientists.
25. Celso Furtado, *Formação Econômica do Brasil* (1a ed: 1959, São Paulo: Companhia das Letras, 2009) (English Translation: *The Economic Growth of Brazil. A Survey from Colonial to Modern Times*. Berkeley: The University of California Press, 1965). See also *Economic*

Development of Latin America. Historical Background and Contemporary Problems (Cambridge: Cambridge University Press, 1970).

26. Fernando Henrique Cardoso and Enzo Faletto, *Dependencia y Desarollo en América Latina* (Mexico: Siglo XXI, 1969); Andre Gunder Frank, *Capitalism and Underdevelopment in Latin America* (New York: Monthly Review Press, 1967).

27. Stanley J. and Barbara H. Stein, *The Colonial Heritage of Latin America* (New York: Oxford University Press, 1970); *Silver, Trade, and War. Spain and America in the Making of Early Modern Europe* (Baltimore: The John Hopkins University Press, 2000); *Apogee of Empire. Spain and New Spain in the Age of Charles III, 1759-1789* (Baltimore: The John Hopkins University Press, 2003); *Edge of Crisis. War and Trade in the Spanish Atlantic, 1789-1808* (Baltimore: The John Hopkins University Press, 2009).

28. Tulio Halperín Donghi, *Storia dell'America Latina* (Torino: Einaudi, 1968); *Reforma y disolución de los imperios ibéricos, 1750-1850* (Madrid: Alianza Editorial, 1985).

29. Fernando A. Novais, *Portugal e Brasil na crise do Antigo Sistema Colonial (1777-1808)* (São Paulo: Hucitec, 1979). Regarding this breadth, Novais explicitly acknowledged his intellectual debt to Celso Furtado, and before him, Caio Prado Junior, *Formação do Brasil contemporâneo* (1a.ed: 1942, São Paulo: Brasiliense, 1989).

30. Ernesto Laclau, "Feudalism and Capitalism in Latin America," *New Left Review* 67 (1971), 19-38; Ciro Flamarion Santana Cardoso, "Sobre os modos de produção coloniais da América," "O modo de produção escravista colonial na América," in Theo Santiago (org.), *América Colonial* (Rio de Janeiro: Pallas, 1975), 61-132; Ciro Flamarion Santana Cardoso, *Agricultura, escravidão e capitalismo* (Petrópolis: Vozes, 1979); see also Jacob Gorender, *O escravismo colonial* (São Paulo: Ática, 1978).

31. Immanuel Wallerstein, *The Modern World System, vol I: Capitalist Agriculture and the Origins of the European World-Economy in the Sixteenth Century* (New York: Academic Press, 1974); *The Modern World-System, vol II: Mercantilism and the Consolidation of the European World-Economy, 1600-1750* (New York: Academic Press, 1980); *The Modern World-System, vol III: The Second Era of Great Expansion of the Capitalist World-Economy, 1730-1840s* (New York: Academic Press, 1989); *The Modern World-System, vol IV: Centrist Liberalism Triumphant, 1789-1914* (University of California Press, 2011).

32. Steve J. Stern, "Feudalism, Capitalism, and the World-System in the Perspective of Latin America and the Caribbean," *American Historical Review* 93:4 (October 1988), 829-72; Immanuel Wallerstein, "Feudalism, Capitalism, and the World-System in the Perspective of Latin America and the Caribbean: Comments on Stern's Critical Tests," *American Historical Review* 93:4 (October 1988), 873-85; Steve J. Stern, "Feudalism, Capitalism, and the World-System in the Perspective of Latin America and the Caribbean: 'Ever More Solitary,'" *American Historical Review* 93:4 (October 1988), 886-97.

33. This historiography highlights what can be called "global microhistories." For three recent examples that diverge in their final results, see João José Reis, Flávio dos Santos Gomes and Marcus J. M. de Carvalho, *O Alufá Rufino. Tráfico, escravidão e liberdade no Atlântico Negro (c.1822-1853)* (São Paulo: Companhia das Letras, 2010); Rebecca J. Scott and Jean M. Hébrard, *Freedom Papers: An Atlantic Odyssey in the Age of Emancipation* (Cambridge MA: Harvard University Press, 2012); James H. Sweet, *Domingos Alvares, African Healing, and the Intellectual History of the Atlantic World* (Chapel Hill: The University of North Carolina Press, 2013).

34. Robin Blackburn, *The Overthrow of Colonial Slavery, 1776-1848* (London: Verso, 1988); *The Making of the New World Slavery from the Baroque to the Modern, 1492-1800* (London:

Verso, 1997); *The American Crucible: Slavery, Emancipation and Human Rights* (London: Verso, 2011).

35. Dale W. Tomich, *Through the Prism of Slavery: Labor, Capital, and World Economy* (Boulder, CO: Rowman & Littlefield, 2004).
36. Rafael Marquese, Tâmis Parron and Márcia Berbel, *Slavery and Politics: Brazil and Cuba, 1790–1850* (Albuquerque: University of New Mexico Press, 2016); Tâmis Parron, *A política da escravidão no Império do Brasil, 1826–1865* (Rio de Janeiro: Civilização Brasileira, 2011); José Antonio Piqueras, *La Esclavitud en las Españas. Un Lazo Transatlántico* (Madrid: Catarata, 2011); Rafael Marquese and Ricardo Salles (Eds.), *Capitalismo Histórico e Escravidão no século XIX: Brasil, Cuba e Estados Unidos* (Rio de Janeiro: Civilização Brasileira, 2016); Christopher Schmidt-Nowara, *Slavery, Freedom, and Abolition in Latin America and the Atlantic World* (Albuquerque: University of New Mexico Press, 2011).
37. Serge Gruzinski, *Les Quatre Partes du Monde: Histoire d'une mondialisation* (Paris: Éditions de la Martinière, 2004). Sanjay Subrahmanyam, in his efforts to write the history of the Iberian expansion on a global scale, is a close interlocutor of Gruzinski: S. Subrahmanyam, *The Portuguese Empire in Asia, 1500–1700: A Political and Economic History* (London and New York: Longman, 1993), and the article "Holding the World in Balance: The Connected Histories of the Iberian Overseas Empires, 1500–1640," *The American Historical Review* 112:5 (December 2007), 1359–85. We should remember that beyond Magalhães Godinho the Portuguese historiography has always paid attention to the global implications of its old colonial empire. See, among others, Luiz Filipe Thomaz, *De Ceuta a Timor* (Lisboa: Difel, 1994).
38. Luiz Felipe de Alencastro, *O Trato dos Viventes: Formação do Brasil no Atlântico Sul* (São Paulo: Companhia das Letras, 2000). As Ciro Cardoso, Alencastro was a former student of Frédéric Mauro.
39. Steven Topik, Carlos Marichal and Zephir Frank (eds.), *Latin American Commodity Chains and the Building of the World Economy, 1500–2000* (Durham: Duke University Press, 2006).
40. This consensus can be seen in a collection of interviews with historians of Latin America: Manuel Chust (ed.), *Las independencias ibero-americanas en su laberinto: controversias, cuestiones, interpretaciones* (Valencia: PUV, 2010).
41. At first Godechot developed the idea in collaboration with the American historian Robert Palmer, resulting in a celebrated paper presented to the *International Congress of Historical Sciences* in Rome, 1955; however, unlike Palmer (whose *magnus opus* was *The Age of the Democratic Revolution: A Political History of Europe and America, 1760–1800*. Princeton: Princeton University Press, 1959–64), Godechot placed great emphasis on Iberian America and the Caribbean in his model (Jacques Godechot, *La Grande Nation*. Paris: Aubier, 1956). A critical take on Palmer and Godechot's elaborations resulted in the proposal of the "Age of Revolutions" by Eric Hobsbawm, who greatly emphasized the development of capitalism on a world scale (Eric J. Hobsbawm, *The Age of Revolutions, 1789–1848*. London: Weidenfeld and Nicolson, 1962). A paradigmatic example of current global history that does not engage with earlier traditions outlined here is that of David Armitage and Sanjay Subrahmanyam (eds.), *The Age of Revolutions in Global Context c.1760–1840* (London: Palgrave, 2010).
42. Javier Fernández S. (dir.), *Diccionario político y social del mundo iberoamericano* (Madrid: Fundación Carolina/Sociedad Estatal de Conmemoraciones Culturales/Centro de Estudios Políticos y Constitucionales, 2009).

CHAPTER 4
AFRICAN HISTORY AND GLOBAL HISTORY: REVISITING PARADIGMS
Omar Gueye

This chapter on global history and its relation to African history attempts to understand the epistemological link between these two fields.[1] The various "African histories" as they have been written over the past half century—local, regional or national in scope—have had a problematic relation to world history. This is partly due to the paucity of connections made by scholars between the subject of their study and global developments, and partly because these African histories, even when acknowledged at all, too often lacked scholarly legitimacy prior to the work of the first generation of "Africanists" who sought to synthesize them.

Before 1960, African history, barely recognized as a legitimate field of study, was the object of polemical attacks. However, after long ideological and methodological debates, both African and foreign Africanists have since secured a central place for Africa in the writing of world history. The guardians of tradition remained the conservators of African history, while various historical "schools" were its propagators. The earliest figures we might identify as African historians—ancient authors like Herodotus, Diodorus Siculus and Strabo—took an interest in Africa, though their works focused on its Mediterranean region and on maritime and terrestrial expeditions, whose impacts still divide historians.[2] Millennia later, pioneers like Leo Frobenius and Maurice Delafosse were among the first to attempt to move from fragmented local histories and present an image of the continent as a whole.[3] By the middle of the twentieth century, African writers like Cheikh Anta Diop attempted to resituate Africa, the cradle of humanity, within global history.[4] Excellent synthetic works followed in the 1960s and 1970s, in both French (Robert and Marianne Cornevin, Hubert Deschamps, Charles Julien and Joseph Ki-Zerbo) and English (Basil Davidson, E. W. Bovill, John Donnell Fage and Raymond Oliver).[5] In spite of methodological difficulties, mental frontiers and ideological barriers, the most important currents of African history were thus finally incorporated into the currents of global history. Increasingly, the view that knowledge, in all its plurality and universality, is impossible to silo has *de facto* integrated the civilizations of the entire world, whatever be their particular characteristics. *Longue-durée* investigations have studied not only the influence of the precolonial civilizations of the continent—interrupted by a long phase of dependence and colonial control—but also the postindependence period.[6] African historians have adopted an epistemological stance that has eventually enabled the emergence of the field of the global history of the continent into the legitimate domain of specialization.

Global History, Globally

This article examines (1) the trajectory of African history, long characterized by foreign control; (2) methodological questions and ideological disputes that punctuated this trajectory; (3) the pioneering role of specific historical schools of thought like the "Dakar school"; (4) the passage from "peripheral" to global histories of Africa and, finally, (5) through the events of May 1968, an example of what this global history with an African focus can look like. Though hardly exhaustive, the chapter reviews the literature broadly, from the first writings on Africa to the attempts to elaborate a general African history. In the context of the globalization of knowledge, the legitimacy of this approach is justified by the necessity of transcending the isolation to which African history seemed condemned for all too long and by breaking with understandings of Africa as a "periphery"[7] of the "developed" world.

My objective is not to rewrite African history—a goal yet to be achieved—but to reflect on global history. I address this issue from the perspective of a generation of historians who have not participated in the nationalist or narrow ideological battles of the 1950s and 1960s and are thus less ideologically committed. The first generation of African historians paired political and scholarly engagement, as their circumstances demanded, and an anticolonialist and nationalist agenda influenced the different phases of African historiography. I do not claim to analyze exhaustively all the historical perspectives already developed—long discussed (and disputed) by our predecessors—but to present several issues that allow us to propose a "re-problematization" of the writing of African history embedded within a contemporary world context and the currents shaping global history.

Re-problematizing African history

African history has long suffered from a deficit of legitimacy. The subjugation, indeed the marginalization, of the continent has had lasting repercussions on scholarly understandings of Africa, its history and its place in the world, downplaying its global importance. In part this is true because under colonization African history was written from a Eurocentric point of view, which, through the use of the Hamitic myth, diffusionism and other theories, claimed the inferiority of Africans.[8] However, Africans themselves also employed a number of approaches to writing the history of Africa, typically either national history or regional history or histories of localities, that lacked reference to other regions and approaches.[9] Moreover, all African histories were shaped by the education of their authors in the metropole, the site where almost all local elites were trained.[10] And alongside the fragmentation of these various "African histories," the deficit of legitimacy was also rooted in methodological questions, particularly the problem of sources and oral sources.[11] Each of these constraints worked against the writing of a global history, a state of affairs that lasted until significant transformations shook the status quo in the middle of the twentieth century.

Since their inception, attempts to understand Africa were undertaken in the name of scientific curiosity and of the European and Arab need to understand relevant peoples and spaces in imperial contexts.[12] This infiltration took place over centuries, from antiquity to the early-modern period, and continued through the colonial and neocolonial periods. The need to understand a conquered territory was the impetus for creating institutions like the French "Académie coloniale," conceived as a laboratory of study dedicated to the colonial empire.[13] This hierarchical knowledge system operated until Africans themselves seized control of their destiny and rearticulated their own politics through material culture and history. The moment in which young Africans rebelled, calling into question the founding principles of this authority, greatly resembled the student movement of May 1968, to which we will return.

Against the backdrop of this history, several generations of African historians framed their agenda in terms of "recognition," seeking to resituate the continent's historical significance during and in the wake of independence struggles. They succeeded impressively in this enormous undertaking and eventually secured the legitimacy they had long sought. Paradoxically, the sense of being allotted the "smallest portion" of the history of the world may have been a powerfully mobilizing force, accelerating debates on the historicity of the peoples of the continent.[14] In particular, like many of their colleagues throughout the world, African historians called into question the dominant ideology of Eurocentrism:

> The fashion of ethnocentrism in history was shaken more in North America than elsewhere. In many schools, the old "history of the world," which was in reality nothing but a history of "Western civilization," gave way throughout the 1960s to new and more authentic currents that situated history in a global perspective, where Africa was placed on equal footing with other large cultural zones like South Asia or the East.[15]

The work of writing African history has thus succeeded paradigms that place African peoples in the context of a "backward" continent, a "late arrival" in the forward march of the world at an economic, political, social and especially mental level, as the president of the French Republic suggested at a 2007 speech in Dakar.[16] A grasp of African history is thus essential to understanding global history and its various approaches, convictions and inevitable imperfections.[17]

Stereotypes continue to shape negative perceptions of the continent, of its men and women. Many writers have thus worked to discover the continent through an "invention of Africa."[18] But until recently, few in world history have conducted meticulous studies of Africa itself.[19]

Of course, difficulties remain. Some are methodological: admittedly, there is often a gap between extant sources and the goal of characterizing Africa's role in the history of the world. However, we should not see this gap as setting an upper bound on the achievements of African history, but rather as posing a challenge to African historians, allowing them to better understand and appreciate the perspectives offered by global history. Indeed, the success of global history is a positive development for African history. It makes possible a true epistemological interconnection between different regional and local histories. A bridge between the continent and the rest of the world has been reestablished: increasingly scholars bring Africa into the global histories they tell.

Other difficulties are material. For this portion of the "Third World" that still carries the full stigma of underdevelopment, the question of resources to support the work of historical scholarship is acute. Widespread poverty inhibits the development of scholarship and research, and even when undertaken, this research covers different portions of a country and different "cultural zones" of the continent unevenly. Typically, references to "Africa" tend to signify "black Africa," situated "south of the Sahara." This perception belonged not only to Europeans or foreigners but also to North and South Africans—the "white" portions of the continent.[20] It is this "black Africa" that research has neglected.

Finally, the persistence of colonial epistemologies that distort debates on the "historicity" of African peoples has reinforced these inequities.[21] Many works have diminished the significance of the Nilotic thesis, precursor of the medieval golden age of the great African empires, deeming it a mere flight of fancy.[22] Others have taken South Africa and North Africa, the two extremities of the continent with substantial revenues and sophisticated human resources, as the reality to which evocations of a "positive" Africa refer. It is often tempting to declare that only "white" Africa understood the role of research in participating at a high level in the writing of global history. Certainly, many of these trends have begun to stabilize or reverse themselves due to renewed interest in African studies that has developed in several institutes, but much work remains.

In spite of these difficulties, the question of the "historicity" or "marginality" of the continent seems to have been definitively answered: Africa is now considered part of global history and no longer an entirely separate entity, as it seemed to be for several centuries. This growing interest has led to a flourishing of research entities such as Departments of African History in universities across Africa and the world, as well as Centers for African Studies, especially in Europe and the United States.[23] To these we must add Africanist researchers, African and non-African, who understand other fields of research and global history along with an increasingly large, well-documented and meticulously detailed understanding of African history. We thus must recognize the numerous contributions, beginning as early as the nineteenth century, that have enriched debates and facilitated striking advances in African historical studies—contributions not only by historians but also by practitioners of anthropology, glottochronology, lexicostatistics, ethno-archaeology and other fields.[24] Thus, in the new context of world history, developing a global perspective allows us to clarify our understandings of the continent and to reconsider our paradigms of and interest in Africa.[25]

Which history for a new Africa?

During and after the anticolonial struggles of the mid-twentieth century, the most fundamental task African historians faced was to define what "Africa" meant, and to move beyond the racial qualification "black" and the corresponding geographical qualification "sub-Saharan." It was essential to agree on the space in question as the subject of historical inquiry, and on which other disciplines to engage. Shaped by dominant paradigms and preoccupations, several types of history, both "sectional" and general, emerged at national and African levels, universal and global levels and at the level of linguistic zones (Anglophone, Francophone, Lusophone, Hispanophone and Arabophone).

Consolidating a singular vision of Africa was thus difficult, even for African historians themselves. On the same continent and in the same geographical reality, several visions of Africa were juxtaposed, with multiple histories centered on a given country or geographical region. African historians continued to express themselves within the educational framework provided by their respective metropoles—Paris, London, Lisbon and so on. Only later, particularly from the 1970s onward, did African history become a credible field of academic specialization and a general history of the continent was written, notably in multivolume works from Cambridge University Press (*Cambridge History of Africa*) and UNESCO (*Histoire générale de l'Afrique*).[26] In the same spirit, Bogumil Jewsiewicki and David Newbury called for collective reflection on African historiography and posed an important question to orient research—namely, "which history" for "which Africa?"[27] All generations of African historians have responded in some way to this problematic question.[28]

Various "schools" played an overwhelming part in this process, which at first largely obeyed the logic of colonial paternalism before the work of correction and rewriting was undertaken by anticolonial historians. Writers oriented toward global (or globalizing) history were thus left to define appropriate contours and paradigms. With this in mind, it is easier to understand the militant perspective of the first generations of African historians, such as Abdoulaye Ly and especially Cheikh Anta Diop, who led scholarly debates in a highly fraught political context, often generating lively controversy.[29] Abdoulaye Ly initiated a dialogue on the theorizing of capitalist connections among continents, inspired by laws of capital accumulation that regulated the dialectical relation between an expansionist capitalist center and a periphery dominated and exploited by it.[30] Cheikh Anta Diop's principal thesis rested on the cultural unity of black Africa and the historicity of the continent running back to the earliest civilizations (with pharaonic Egypt taken to be "black"). It inspired many writings against widely held notions of Africa as static since the dawn of time.[31] The pioneers of this militant history saw themselves as the avant-garde of the opposition to colonial ideologies.

The pioneers often faced ostracism in response to their investigations. However, young writers like Joseph Ki-Zerbo, Djibril Tamsir Niane, Mbaye Guèye, Oumar Kane, Ibrahima Baba Kaké, Elikia M'Bokolo, Boubacar Barry, Pierre Kipré, Abdoulaye Bathily, Thierno Diallo, Sékéné Mody Cissoko and others followed their senior colleagues Abdoulaye Ly and Cheikh Anta Diop to solidify once and for all the legitimacy of "writing an African history by Africans."[32] Many followed them, including a wave of researchers from French universities who participated enthusiastically in the creation of the "Dakar school."[33] Today, a significant diaspora of African historians lives abroad, especially in the United States, which is also home to a large number of non-African Africanists.[34] Altogether, their work has helped to ensure the long-term insertion of the continent into global history.

Long-standing debates and lively disputes took place, often leading to extreme positions on either side, notably among African writers reacting vigorously against their opponents. An ideological approach, more political than scholarly, became commonplace, along with the danger such an approach entails—namely adopting extreme positions as revenge against many centuries of ostracism and obscurantism. After "emancipation," "by a sort of talionic law, some young African states seemed to eliminate anything resembling the histories of former colonizers from their curricula."[35] In the French case, for instance, new states sought to establish an African program in place of the old colonial program exemplified by the phrase "Our ancestors the Gauls" (see below for more).[36]

History thereby served as an ideological weapon, with the *decolonization of African history* increasingly tending toward *Afrocentrism*.[37] Indeed, in the effort to rehabilitate African civilizations, there was a great desire to replace an external account of the origins of African civilization, "granted" after centuries of foreign occupation, with an internal one. The field needed a scholarly approach to contain this tendency toward an extremism that ultimately threatened to harm the cause of African history that it claimed to defend.

African historians came to understand this need to free themselves from increasingly obsolete quarrels and from the trap of historical traditions that were more ideological than scholarly. As the political and institutional context changed from the 1970s onward, and the task at hand was to establish greater scholarly rigor without becoming mired in the guilt-inducing blame of the West, nostalgia for an idyllic past or simple self-aggrandizement.[38] In this quest for recognition and globality, historians were concerned to avoid trading one myth for another. To replace "Our ancestors the Gauls" with "Our ancestors the Egyptians" would indeed be inadequate!

"Our ancestors the Gauls"

Africa's centuries-long experience of domination was not only political and economic but also cultural and scholarly. The metropole subjected all dominated territories to its influence, symbolized at the highest level, in the case of French Africa, by the program of cultural assimilation that taught all children in French colonies the phrase "Our ancestors the Gauls."[39]

The minds of young African students were molded to a colonial ideology that sought the formation of a good "subject"—either "assimilated" by the colonizer or "alienated" by the colonists.[40] Indeed, "history as it was taught in African schools prior to decolonialization took Europe as its setting, the French, English, Germans, and others as its actors; and, occasionally, [inserted] the 'African kinglets,' Samory 'the bloody,' Behanzin, Elhadj Omar."[41] With African history moored to a European framework that made Africa either inferior or invisible, historian Ibrahima Baba Kaké argued that "we may wonder whether, through this 'metropolitan' history, a history of African communities exists. We barely see signs of it, in any case, at most glimpsing it in slave traders or princes, outlined over a handful of pages, anonymous and abstract."[42] African history was a story above all about the foreign, and especially colonial, presence in Africa. The colonial history school was a site of acculturation and of the legitimation of foreign domination, the laboratory for the testing of different colonial theories and practices. The avant-garde of the later political awakening were themselves conscious of being products of this colonial school, educated with the "colonial library" and "colonial textbooks" before coming to denounce them.

Beginning in the 1940s, Alioune Diop, Cheikh Anta Diop, Aimé Césaire and their contemporaries broke with dominant colonial paradigms, leading the fight for a black consciousness and an end to the inferiority complex African youth had internalized.[43] The *Négritude* movement of Léopold Sédar Senghor, Aimé Césaire and Léon Gontran Damas, though controversial, operated in this framework alongside Pan-Africanist movements seeking the rebirth or affirmation of a black cultural identity. These actions had numerous ramifications for Africa and its diaspora, expanding the field of struggle to affirm Africans' cultural identity on an ideological, nationalist and Pan-Africanist level. In the 1960s and early 1970s, Africa was the focal point for the millions of descendants of slaves who wished to remember in order to live or survive in a society where racism justified their poverty.[44] Not by accident did black Americans play such a large role in the fight to affirm a black and Pan-African cultural identity.[45]

It was in this political fight against colonialism and neocolonialism in Africa that history took on such an ideologically charged role. Africans had to reappropriate their historical conscience by breaking with borrowed ideologies. And beyond the production of knowledge, consciousness of history plays an essential role in envisioning the future of the peoples of the world:

> Knowledge of history is culturally liberating and contributes to the constructions of founding myths and national consciousness. It is in the name of their glorious past that the Indians of South America wished to throw off Iberian domination; it is in the Indian past that the intellectuals (*boubous*) of the nineteenth century sought their weapons; Japan drew supplementary force from the Samurai code to resist competition from their American rivals; and Africa sought a shattered unity in the memory of its empires deposed by the slave trade and especially by colonization; and thus, the former Gold Coast became Ghana.[46]

The concerns of history are thus strategic. The desire for self-awareness and affirmation was one of the primary motivations to produce "local," mostly national, histories that preceded the broader histories with more globalist approaches of the ensuing decades. Thus, a number of histories were written in the name of the peoples of the new nations that reflected instead the logics of more local identities. However, in many cases, an (often equivocal) official history was taken up by emerging nation-states, giving meaning to the territory and its future and anointing (often controversial) national heroes. As summarized by Renan, one of the great theorists of the problem of nationalities, "[t]he nation's foundations consist in the community of the past, otherwise known as history."[47] For the new African nation-states, as for most nation-states, history writing responded to the nationalist project.

While writing a *General History of Senegal*, for instance, proponents of different national schools of thought clashed tacitly in the committee that guided its construction,[48] each school seeking legitimacy by privileging its own sources and methods. Professional historians educated at the French school that created the modern state; the Arabizing elite, lettered Muslims educated in Arab countries; and traditional elites, *griots* who resisted foreign "sciences," all contended with one another.[49] This multiplicity of approaches, sources and methods immediately generated an internally global or even more parochial perspective, the result of a national scholarly compromise between as yet disconnected schools of thought.

But even as national histories were written, sentiments of belonging to one continent— with one destiny, forged by one history, one geography and common struggles— persisted. It was from the perspective of African unity that the newly independent countries elaborated a program of global history for the continent. In the early sixties, for example, the Institute for African and Madagascan Curricula (IPAM) developed a program of study and textbooks designed for young Madagascans and other Africans.[50]

In sum, the feeling of "victimization" and the will to rehabilitate a long-denied past were decisive in the African reawakening. This cause was for some time a central theme for African writers, motivating the writing (or rewriting) of the history of Africa and scornfully rejecting colonial paternalism. However, no historian can long ignore the fundamental contributions to understandings of self and society that inter-societal exchanges have wrought. As Kaké argued, "[a] number of features emerged from the colonial situation: schools, industrialization, rentier culture, transformation of the countryside, railroads, and so on—many subjects that the African historian cannot ignore in his description of African societies."[51] Thus, despite racial prejudices that have persisted on either side, the openings induced by globalization and long-term contact between peoples were the key to new understandings of the world and its history.

Pioneering role of foreign Africanists

The work of writing African history can only be fully understood by considering contributions from foreign historians. Indeed, "foreign Africanists," especially Arabs and Europeans, were decisive to conceiving and elaborating the history of the continent, notwithstanding the prejudices that shaped foreign thought and domination. These historians participated enormously in giving African history a global vision.

Arab writers and sources contributed significantly to understandings of African history. A number of written works, known as chronicles or *Tarikh*, prolonged the Arab economic, cultural and religious presence.[52] Outside of this presence, the Islamic faith spread by Arabs bore in itself a form of globality: it asked the faithful to "seek knowledge as far off as China," which suggests an openness to the most distant countries of the world.[53] In the African version of this advice, Muslims were educated with reference to the universal values embodied in the *Ummah*, the world community of believers who reunite each year in the pilgrimage to Mecca.[54] Islam was thus another form of globalization that suggested the possibility of a broad openness to Africans, African history and its writers, Arabs as well as Africans. But these historical forms of expression both were sidelined by the colonial conquest and simultaneously inspired resistance to it, as the most ferocious rebels of West Africa fought colonization under the auspices of Islam (Samori, El hadj Omar, Fodé Kaba, Maba Diakhou Bâ, Ahmadou Bamba and others).

Many Africanists in France and the UK also played a pioneering role in interdisciplinary research, increasingly investing in the field alongside their European and American counterparts. France and England were the primary "centers of African studies" due to their long presence on the continent, which included their participation in precapitalist and capitalist economies, the slave trade, the Industrial Revolution, colonization and the integration of Africa into their imperial systems.[55] While a monolithic understanding of Eurocentrism has long obscured scholarly and epistemological controversies and disputes among European historians, French Africanists were nonetheless particularly influential in the writing and education of Francophone elites.

> Yves Person, and later Catherine Coquery-Vidrovitch and Jean Devisse, offered both in Dakar and Paris a remarkable contribution to the education of generations of historians at the University of Dakar. Similarly important is the pioneering work of Jean Suret-Canale, researcher in African history who published many articles and reference works on the colonial history of the continent; the work of anthropologists like Claude Meillassoux who opened the historiography of the "Dakar school" to the other social sciences; the work of historians Jean Boulègue, Yves Saint-Martin, and Christian Roche; and that of Christian Coulon, Jean Schmitz, and Jean Copans in sociology and anthropology.[56]

The American and Anglo-Saxon school contributed much to the elaboration of African history. More recently, Fred Cooper and Jane Burbank have contributed significant work on empires, in a recent synthesis that adds to the significant research already done by John Donnell Fage, Lord Haley, Michael Crowder, David Robinson, Philip Curtin, Georges Brooks, Allen Howard, Winston McGowan, Walter Rodney, Paul Lovejoy, Immanuel Wallerstein, John Hopkins, Martin Klein, George Wesley-Johnson, Patrick Manning, Lucie Colvin and others.[57] Transatlantic historians have thus opened a number of perspectives on our knowledge of Africa and on African studies.

Revival of interest in African Studies

The late twentieth and early twenty-first centuries have seen a renewed interest in African studies and African history. Research programs have been most dynamic in the global "North" (especially in Anglophone countries) and are organized around specific objectives and problematics. While this configuration once again allots African researchers the "least share" in the study of the continent, this situation is less detrimental than it was previously. The increasing systematization of disciplines has permitted a comparison and relativizing of views on Africa that attenuates colonial epistemologies, thereby allowing the continent and its inhabitants to enter prominently into global history.

Alongside these scholarly networks of significant means, others on the continent have survived as well as they could, often sitting neglected (alongside other sectors of the economy). Worse still, former metropoles continue to tacitly (or almost tacitly) exercise the same influence they enjoyed before the "independence" of their ex-territories. The imperative to "decolonize" African history became an urgent goal for those who aspired to the foundational legitimacy of credible scholarship. This goal did not evade African writers who adopted a militant posture, at least in the beginning. They established schools of African history written in French, English, Arabic and other languages. Similarly, alongside oral tradition, historians drew on many African sources written in the Ge'ez, Vai, Bamum and Ajami languages.[58]

A related issue is that the priorities of the nationalist project often exclude these dimensions of scholarly "decolonization," in part due to many political regimes' neglect of scholarship and their minimal funding of historical work. The North thus maintains the upper hand in research on African history: it determines the central questions of the field and often even the flow of Africanist researchers, which raises the controversial issue of "brain drain."[59] The goal of "decolonizing" African history was not simply to shake off a colonial paternalism that served as a guarantee of scholarly rigor but also to place African history back at the center of global questions to better illustrate the politics of development.

A militant history

The militancy considered in this section was originally an alternative to the objective constraints African historians faced. Their posture of "revolt" presupposed a refusal of the marginality (or the process of marginalization) intrinsic to colonial ideology, whose legacy continued to weigh heavily on the cultural life of the newly "independent" states. Consequently, this refusal implied a central preoccupation, namely: how to find a place on a global scale despite remaining tied to the continent's subaltern position on the international chessboard? This is certainly an intellectual preoccupation, but one also deeply linked to the nationalist political fight to liberate the continent from all forms of control and domination. It was difficult for African historians to substitute the political and ideological challenges of their countries or the paradigms that guided the construction of the new nation-states and their development.

History contributed notably to the fight for national liberation, with African historians of many generations entering political action. Moreover, confident in their knowledge of their country and the world, many sought the high office of President of the Republic, with occasional success.[60] African historians engaged in both scholarly and political activity to influence the destiny of their country, their continent and even the world. Marxism was for most both their political philosophy and their model of historical writing, which produced some controversies among African historians who seemed to deny any form of "intellectual control" or "ideological colonization." At the same time, references to Marxist ideology signified a tendency to operate within global ideological currents. This militancy and juxtaposition of roles created numerous challenges that remained within the horizon of the paradigms that structured the ideologies of independence: the significant role of politics and the state in the historical processes. African historians still must free themselves from their double subordination—to the ideology of the postcolonial state, on the one hand, and, on the other hand, to the Marxist political opposition that threatens to become as dominant and alienating as the colonial ideology that was fought for centuries.

Although the anticolonial and nationalist project of African historians was largely justified, we must also push back against it and investigate its relevance. The question is whether we seek to deconstruct colonial texts and ideology or instead to write an authentic history that interrogates forms of knowledge and responds to methodological questions facing the discipline. It seems these tasks may be conducted together, with (often-fluctuating) stakes and in contexts characterized by conflict. The militancy was almost certainly justified, especially during a certain period, but the logic of the development of the human sciences recommends that African history be coherently integrated into global trends. Such an approach would understand the continent as an integral part of a global whole rather than as an entirely separate and subaltern region in the development of the world.

Scholarship and militancy: The "Dakar school" examined

The fight for scholarly militancy operated not only at the level of declared intentions but also at the level of structures or mechanisms that operationalized theories conceived for this very goal. It was thus that various "schools" took charge of historical reflections and undertook the work of writing the history of the continent, in part or as a whole. While the universities of Wisconsin (with Jan Vansina or Philip Curtin), Birmingham and SOAS (with John Fage and Roland Olivier) and Paris VII (with Catherine Coquery-Vidrovitch) all claimed paternity of the historical study of Africa, alternative homes for the conception of and writing of Africa history were established on the continent at Ibadan, Dar es Salam, Makerere and Dakar in the wake of the Second World War. Mohamed Sahli operated within this logic, writing a pamphlet (*Decolonizing History*) around 1965 to introduce another way of understanding the history of the Maghreb.[61] Kenneth Onwuka Dike was a pioneer of the schools of African history and one of the founders of the Ibadan school that influenced the writing of Nigerian history.[62] He was significant for the generation of African historians who sought to separate from the influence of metropolitan and/or Eurocentric schools. Alongside Kenneth Onwuka Dike and his colleague Jacob Ajayi of the Ibadan school, Terence Ranger, Arnold Temu and Walter Rodney of the Dar es Salam school and Bethwell Ogot of the Makerere school and Abdoulaye Ly and Cheikh Anta Diop of the "Dakar school" all actively participated in the work of decolonizing and rewriting African history.

The "Dakar school," to explore one example in greater detail, brought together a community of scholars from different generations. The expression "the Dakar school" designates one center among many in Africa—Makerere, Ibadan, Dar Es-Salam—where specialists from many disciplines developed scholarship on African societies broadly informed by the ascendance of the anticolonial movement following the Second World War. Like its African counterparts, the "Dakar school" was distinguished by its commitment to unveil the falsifications regarding African societies that were deliberately woven by colonial scholarship.[63]

Without prior coordination, African writers undertook the task of writing their history, most likely inspired or encouraged by their *marabouts* of the North, but always with the goal of removing the continent from its isolation (imposed or consented to) and restoring it to its rightful place in the development of humanity.[64] Alongside their foreign counterparts, the members of these "schools" produced remarkable studies and participated significantly in scholarly inquiry and in restoring the dignity of the historical discipline in Africa. Their theories and methodologies were controversial and often debated, but they were made in the heat of polemical disputes. The schools took a decisive step forward in terms of research, producing much important scholarly work. The task of their successors was to surpass their objective limits and to reformulate the central debates of the field. This took place through a deconstruction of the limiting myths and stereotypes of African history, as well as through a broad reconstruction of paradigms that offered new knowledge and new methodological approaches. Historians produced numerous regional histories in both African and metropolitan centers of excellence, creating a balance between continental and global perspectives.

For quite some time, the task was to surpass the first mission of the precursors of the "schools," to write—or rewrite—African history in order to investigate new questions. This approach offered a way to break with or avoid a cloistering that threatened to distance the discipline from global currents and to limit it to arbitrary subjects or geographical zones, and to militant and subjective perspectives. This was and remains an urgent goal insofar as, from a methodological perspective, such an objective is broadly justifiable and achievable. Fortunately, following independence the second generation of African historians set themselves to this task. They were better connected to the epistemological processes of globalization and to the new methods of intellectual production. Better integration of laboratories and research networks gave these scholars a broader point of view that allowed them to shatter the disciplinary isolation that had constrained their predecessors.

The work of generations

Each generation of African historians participated in its part of the "mission" of rewriting the history of the continent, inspired by the context in which they produced their scholarship, expressing dominant paradigms and methodological possibilities.

Just as the postwar generation of historians fought against the colonial project and the postindependence generation distinguished itself in the militancy of "national construction" and the rewriting of African history, following generations integrated themselves into more global currents and paradigms that surpassed national and neocolonial spaces. Less ideologically involved, this generation of historians has only a distant relationship to the colonial system. For the most part they did not experience it directly, even if its intellectual heritage was broadly present in the structures of their education. They work in a context of *globalization* that has followed a *crisis of nationalism*. The subjects of their work are distant from the studies of localities, and they are interested in more cross-disciplinary and interdisciplinary themes.[65] Their methodologies also appear more open, offering more possibilities for investigation and for the juxtaposition of studies. Polemics have increasingly given way to collaboration among researchers from all continents and all social scientific disciplines, in a manner that is less indebted to academic forms of control and nationalist ideologies.

The first few generations of African historians have thus laid the foundation of an authentic knowledge of the histories of different regions, which together give the continent a common identity. It is quite possible today to synthesize these works and to integrate them into more general chronologies, effectively breaking the marginalization of many centuries. This seems to be the path toward a global history of Africa, which gives meaning to the totality of national, regional and local histories.

African history and global history

Much of the writing on African history has considered links to other parts of the world, and it is these traditions that historians of Africa can build upon. During the past few decades, historians have emphasized three major events in particular to chart connections between Africa and the rest of the world: the penetration of the continent by Islam, the Atlantic slave trade and colonization. In this view, the slave trade signified a sustained opening of the continent to the Atlantic region and its integration into commercial networks and the "world economy"—in other words, its integration into world history, as even African historians sometimes suggest. As Abdoulaye Ly wrote of this trend,

> Indeed, once we left behind the colonial frameworks that had too long structured the teaching of history, we turned almost immediately to developments that linked Africa to other continents. Most immediately, we considered the commerce of seventeenth-century black Africa—including, necessarily, the slave trade—and we saw it as an essential connection between world history and African history, but also as the first relatively sure way to access this history through the use of sources written by the colonizer.[66]

This dominant thought, especially the idea that the Atlantic constitutes the space of exchange and culture, structured all African theories and "schools" that emerged after the colonial period. Yet the logic that sees the Sahara and the Atlantic as opposites reinforces the idea that the African continent, and all its regions, was entirely subject to external influences (economic, political and intellectual). But connecting to these external trends might be seen as a quest for a historical legitimacy granted by the colonial intellectual aristocracy. The grave danger of that way of thinking is that it sees the beginning of African history as simultaneous with the emergence of these external contributions. It does so especially at the level of methodology, via the integration of the continent into the national histories and periodization of the colonizers. It is abundantly clear that historians systematically privileged external sources in the writing and rewriting of this history. This approach thus often created an "underhistory" characteristic of a sub-Saharan Africa inhabited by indigenous blacks, "the lumpenproletariat of the peripheral centers of a world system whose hubs resided in the North hemisphere."[67] Such was the characterization of Africa: "black" and "sub-Saharan," truly subaltern and peripheral!

It seems important in the light of new debates on history to break with the fetishism of the slave trade and colonialism as the only way to study African history in global terms. This is the best route to legitimate knowledge produced according to established scholarly norms—not granted or legitimated according to the criteria of an intellectual authority (for the South) or of the "*marabouts* of the North."[68] While questions tied to the slave trade and colonization have been studied intensively due to the abundance of documentation and their connection to the history of other continents, it is clear that other periods, from the ancient to the postmodern, are just as interesting and important. The same goes for geographic zones other than the Atlantic that also evidence long-term contacts and the long-term evolution of African peoples such as the Sahara and Indian Ocean regions.

Eurocentric conceptions of history have long predominated, with their "pseudoscientific racism" and cultural chauvinism.[69] This conception has long weighed on African history, of which different versions could be nothing but regional. The study of all historical periods and all geographical regions of the continent is a major scholarly objective, and there is no question of handing it over to specialized groups or interested persons. There is likewise no question of making it the exclusive business of Africans. History, "the only sector in Africa that has not been nationalized," testifies to the living relationship between Africa and the world.[70]

Connection to the world

For as long as victimization was the mobilizing cause for African history, as it was beginning in the 1950s, the results of this history remained the antithesis of the ideal objective of such engagement, namely a balanced effort to establish historical truth. Thus, as long as it was imperative to destroy restrictive myths and stereotypes, there was always the risk of falling into the traps already condemned here: a nostalgic history of "commemoration" or "navel-gazing," or even self-aggrandizement and sectarianism, with no place in its schema for the "other." Complex, difficult situations within Africa arose from the abuse of history, namely an incompatibility between official national histories and local histories that emphasized various particularities meant that it was impossible to anticipate several rebellions and "tribal wars" on the continent. These disjunctions revealed the fragile equilibria of the young African nations and their nationalist projects: the secession of Katanga illustrates this, as does the Nigerian Civil War in the 1960s; the Rwandan Genocide; the ethnically inflected civil wars in Sierra Leon, Liberia and the Congo; and the religious massacres in the Central African Republic over the past three decades—to name only a few examples.[71]

Beyond these methodological questions (reasonably settled with respect to certain subjects), writing history raises as many questions as it answers, and the African historian has at times been entangled with extremely problematic ideologies. The so-called intellectuals aligned with the regimes of certain countries have theorized racist, exclusivist and sometimes genocidal ideologies of war. This was true with respect to the notion of "ethnic cleansing," popularized by the "Radio Mille Collines"[72] station in Rwanda in 1994, or of "ivoirité," a key concept during the war in Ivory Coast.[73] The identitarian mistrust at the root of the stigmatization of the "other" is characteristic of societies that lack what may be called a globally national imaginary. This undeclared quest for a "dangerous purity" has been at the origin of recurrent troubles in postindependence Africa.[74] In all these conflicts, the goal was to construct an "us" distinct from "them," a distinction that presupposed the definition of a conceptual and territorial border, as for the theorists of these new doctrines, "[t]he identification of a self naturally presupposes its differentiation from the other. ... It is not possible to be at once self and other."[75] The paradox lies in the fact that the valorization of the self and the exclusion of the other cannot take place without knowledge of this "other" and his or her difference. It is this need for knowledge and understanding that dictates an intellectual attitude synonymous with opening to others and the world.

If such a history—yet unwritten—is to be credible, this opening to the world and to other disciplines would be a fortunate outcome. As Kaké has argued, "the wish to reduce historical education only to the history of Africa would be a disagreeable position. The chauvinist historian does a disservice to his country just as the fanatic does a disservice to his religion."[76] History has always led to contact and opposition among peoples—often tragically—but in the modern world we can all agree that there are no longer isolated peoples.[77] Despite their turbulent history, African countries are increasingly associated with international life, now that the domain of politics is the entire universe.[78] Africans are aware of this; moreover, this recognition was the basis of the thought of Léopold Sédar Senghor and his theory of the "Civilization of the Universal."[79] In what he calls the "Meeting of Giving and Receiving," no people may be left out, and each must contribute its own values. Senghor prefigured globalization well before the fall of the Berlin wall and the end of the Cold War.[80]

Knowledge of the world requires knowledge of its history in all its aspects and components. This further supposes that the citizen of the world must not limit himself or herself to knowledge of one's own country or locality; rather, this "global citizen" has the duty to understand other peoples and all neighboring points of view in space and time.[81] The focus on the history of Africa was necessary for the first generation of African writers because of the need to take charge of the history of the continent. This also implied an understanding of a unified Africa, from the Maghreb through Africa south of the Sahara and to Southern Africa. At the same time, this in no way signified a "ghettoization of Africa history." [82] As Kaké has said,

> A general view of the history of world is essential to those who wish to know the contribution of each social group to the development of humanity, to consider in their full complexity the great contemporary questions, to return to their origins, to pull a few lessons from the past. In these conditions, African history must not be nostalgic, content to evoke ancestors and forerunners and to place the golden age at the beginning of time. The elements of this history must be selected because of their value, not their general interest; it must not tend toward particularism, toward insular and desiccating nationalism, but must develop an attachment to the specificities of localities.[83]

In sum, and considering the terrain of the African laboratory, global history may be understood as a link between facts and events that connect different regions of the globe. From this viewpoint, the relationship between Africa and the rest of the world is necessarily connected and dialectical, though certainly not without discussion, polemics and stereotypes.[84] The transnational phenomena studied by this approach are connected by local, national, continental and transcontinental dynamics and the various scholarly and epistemological confrontations among historians, historical schools and historiographies. The prerequisite of global history rests, then, on a *global historiography* in which theoretical, methodological and heuristic contributions—from Africa, India, China, Europe and the Americas—as well as contemporary dynamics and trends are fundamental. It is the decentered narrative of a social, political, economic, cultural or scientific phenomenon that may begin with the study of a local phenomenon whose characteristics relate to other regions of the globe. (This is the approach we take to May 1968 below.) In the end, global history is another response to the identitarian retirement of Africans, to the temptation to secede, to the de-territorialization begotten by colonization and postcolonial re-territorialization—all of which takes place, on the one hand, through the deconstruction of myths and, on the other, through the sense of belonging to a global whole that must be built or rebuilt.

An example of a global history approach: Africa and the events of May 1968

The distinction between "global history" and "world history" is not always clear, given the similarities in their object of study—that is, a space that transcends national territorial frameworks. Global history cannot be a history of all societies of the world; rather, it necessarily considers local and temporal specificities encompassing all fields of study and all regions of the world. It brings together the large-scale stages of these societies—even if they are not synchronized with each other—a task that presupposes a history of large global transitions, perturbations, common changes, encounters and clashes, revolutions, and so on.

Societies have developed along internal lines, each according to its own values and trajectory, unaware of or subsuming others. New worlds have emerged from the encounters among them, shaped by new balances of power that have, throughout history, defined for them all a form of "globalization" shaped by the eyes and goals of the strongest powers. Different imperialisms and systems of domination can thus be seen as attempts at globalization in which many parts of the globe emerged from isolation and were integrated—often by force—into the global currents of the period, whether Roman antiquity, the Atlantic slave trade, mercantile capitalism, colonization, the Cold War and so on. Africa was at the heart of this process of peripheralization and domination, of course, but it became part of the globalization that these processes undergirded. This process led finally to the erection of a "global village" with which everyone identifies despite various inequalities and dysfunctions.[85] In his definition of the "civilization of the Universal," Léopold Sédar Senghor speaks of the meeting of "all peoples" and all cultures, by which he signifies not confrontation but rather reciprocity.[86] Global history, too, seeks to study this enlarged transnational frame.

An approach focused on events but spanning these largest stages of the evolution of world societies allows us to begin writing a global history, which operates at a planetary scale but does not necessarily include all the world's countries. It may be accomplished, for instance, through the intersection of the histories of capitalism, religion, migrations and ideas, among others. This approach allows us to see the links that exist among different parts of the world—Africa, Europe, Asia and America—and allows us to discover the connections among these spaces by an investigation of any social movement, such as the worldwide "May 1968" movement, which we address in this study.

May 1968 in the world

Comprehending global history—and, as a result, the connections among the societies of the world—is possible, thanks to an approach that devotes specific attention to events. Its goal is the de-territorialization of events by connecting their common elements across time and space. Indeed, although the May 1968 movement, a world youth revolt, did not systematically affect every city in the world, it was widespread in world capitals—large cities like Prague, Paris, Cairo, Dakar, New York, Chicago, Berlin, Frankfurt and others where university students expressed their particular concerns. The similarity and simultaneity of these movements, which unfolded at the same time across varied and distant spaces, organized around the same motivations, makes a global study of this event possible.

An explosion of ideas influenced youth across the world in the 1960s, a process that reached its global acme in 1968, when student protests at Berkeley spread throughout the world. Consequently, it is possible to understand the connection among all these youth movements and the shared desire for freedom by ill-appreciated youth; the collusion among regimes who faced, individually and together, this wave of international contestation; and the extent of the repression with the entry of tanks in Czechoslovakia, the charge of the CRS in Paris or the police invasion of the Dakar campus. Thus, similarities existed not only among youth movements, as in Senegal and France, but also in the interactions between the respective presidents of these countries: Léopold Sédar Senghor and Charles de Gaulle. It was also an era of diffuse influences between centers of protest on a global level. Each protested in the name of group interests (university students), of ideologies (left-wing ideas), against domestic heroes (critiquing Négritude in Senegal) or by invoking the issue of Vietnam, which elicited various reactions depending on the country. At these demonstrations, it was essential to integrate various causes, such as the protests against communism in Prague and those against "spoiled children" in both the United States and Dakar.[87] Together, all these factors linked the rebellious global youth movements.

With ideas transcending borders, these movements established substantive connections with each other. The university was one point of departure, serving everywhere as the motor of the social movements that went on to shape forms of governance in the coming years. It is necessary to consider not only the Cold War context and the state of the world economy but also the psychological disposition of the young people who believed it necessary to seize life in the present moment. In this sense, the global social movement of 1968 had a revolutionary impact on the world. Following the example of their colleagues across the world, the youth of Dakar took part, protesting in the name of the Vietnamese people, laying claim to left-wing ideas and declaring their desire for societal change.[88]

The goal of studying this example is to search for the roots and interconnections in the events that took place on a global scale and that shared common ideas. This takes the form of an "aggregation of local histories" that gives meaning to a "global history" but does not negate local histories. This project presupposes that the authors of global histories do not limit their understanding of a locality but are up-to-date on what is taking place in other parts of the world. All parts of the world constitute thereby a global whole, thanks to the imbrication and mutual dependence across all ages and historical (and even prehistorical) periods. As a result, the study of transnational phenomena transcends spaces, whether physically or mentally territorialized, to privilege a global approach to all regions and civilizations of the world.

Global history is thus a history rooted locally in order to extend globally, taking account of links between different event-producing centers and of the interdisciplinarity that leads to an exhaustive understanding of related facts. It is this inclusive approach that places Africa at the heart of world history.

Conclusion

African history has seen numerous twists and turns, often tumultuous and tragic, but always moored to the history of the world, to which it never ceased to be connected.

However, it took several centuries of epic struggle to secure recognition of Africa's rightful place in this history. Several generations of Africanists, African and non-African, have led this fight. Beyond the construction of nationalist chronologies, which accompanied the birth of young African nations and which fought against stereotypes, the goal has been to address questions pertinent across the world in novel and relevant ways. One thing is clear: much remains to be done in constructing an African historical narrative that dominant paradigms have sought for centuries to distort or render invisible. Today, scholars are revisiting and re-problematizing these paradigms in the light of new sources and new methodological approaches. The work of the pioneers cleared the way for a pluridisciplinarity that testifies to the avowed intention of new generations of African researchers to address incisive subjects on a continent definitively connected to global history—one that strives to study the world through the diversity of its spaces, its peoples, their memories and their different practices.

Notes

1. The distinction between global history and world history is often unclear. In the present text, we attempt to explore the nuances of this distinction to see how we may place Africa at the heart of the problematics and currents of global history.
2. Herodotus, the Greek historian dubbed "the father of history," established connections between ancient Europe and Africa, especially with pharaonic Egypt. Cheikh Anta Diop used his writings to argue for his controversial thesis of a black pharaonic Egypt. See Cheikh Anta Diop, *Nations nègres et culture* (Paris: Présence Africaine, 1979). Herodotus's Greek compatriots, the historian Diodorus Siculus and the geographer Strabo contributed to knowledge of the Greek world and its relation to the rest of the world.
3. Leo Frobenius, "hero of the black cause," enjoyed much success among African historians and inspired the writings of Négritude theorists like Senghor.
4. In the valley of the Omo in East Africa, Professor Leakey's team discovered the skeletal remains of the oldest men, which allowed him to argue for Africa as the cradle of humanity. In other words, human history began in Africa.
5. Robert Cornevin and Marianne Cornevin, *Histoire de l'Afrique: des origines à la deuxième guerre mondiale* (Paris: Payot, 1970); Basil Davidson, *Africa, History of a Continent* (London: Weidenfeld & Nicolson, 1966); Hubert Deschamps (ed.), *Histoire générale de l'Afrique noire* (Paris: PUF, vol. I 1970 & vol. II 1971); Joseph Ki-Zerbo, *Histoire générale de l'Afrique, d'hier à demain* (Paris: Hatier, 1972); Roland Oliver and John Donnell Fage, *A Short History of Africa* (Baltimore, 1962).
6. Fernand Braudel, *Écrits sur l'histoire* (Paris: Flammarion, 1969).
7. M. Samir Amin, "Préface," in Boubacar Barry, *Le royaume du Waalo* (Paris: Maspero, 1972), 7–4.
8. See Jack Goody, *Le vol de l'histoire. Comment l'Europe a imposé le récit de son passé au reste du monde (The Theft of History)* (Paris: Gallimard, 2010), 496; Pekka Masonen, *The Negroland Revisited. Discovery and Invention of the Sudanese Middle Ages* (Helsinki: Finnish Academy of Science and Letters, 2000).
9. We must note that, increasingly, regional history and the history of localities are today increasingly neglected in favor of global history.

10. Philip Curtin, Steven Feierman, Leonard Thompson and Jan Vansina, *African History, from Earliest Times to Independence* (London and New York: Longman, 1995).

11. Questions surrounding oral sources and their credibility imply questions about the credibility of African history, reliant as it is on such sources. These questions hindered the progress of the field until the appearance of major works by Yves Person, Djibril Tamsir Niane, Dioudé Laya, Boubou Hama, Amadou Hampâté Bâ, Jan Vansina and others. Despite their issues, historians now recognize the value of oral sources, which have contributed to important work (even if most of these historians tend to conflate the categories of *history* and *oral sources*).

12. Catherine Coquery-Vidrovitch, *La découverte de l'Afrique, l'Afrique noire atlantique, des origines au xviiie siècle* (Paris: L´Harmattan, 2003).

13. The "Colonial Academy," created in 1922, was one of several institutions dedicated to understanding colonial societies. The same goal led to the establishment in Dakar of IFAN (*Institut Français d'Afrique Noire*, or French Institute of Black Africa, which later became the Cheikh Anta Diop Fundamental Institute of Black Africa), which contributed enormously to collecting information on societies and the environment in West Africa and beyond.

14. Catherine Coquery-Vidrovitch, "Réflexions comparées sur l'historiographie africaniste de langue française et anglais," *Politique africaine* 66 (1997), 91–100; I. Thioub "'L'École de Dakar' et' et la production d'une écriture académique de l'histoire," in Momar Coumba Diop (ed.), *Le Sénégal contemporain* (Paris, Karthala, 2002), 109–53. Patrick Manning, "African and World Historiography," *The Journal of African History* 54:3 (2013), 319–30.

15. P. D. Curtin, "Tendances récentes des recherches historiques africaines et contribution à l'histoire en général," *Histoire générale de l'Afrique* (Unesco-Jeune Afrique, 1980), 77–95.

16. In his controversial *Dakar* speech (July 26, 2007), the president of the French Republic, Nicolas Sarkozy, declared that "Africans have not fully entered into history," provoking outrage and recentering persistent racial stereotypes. See Jean-Paul Chrétien (dir.), *L'Afrique de Sarkozy: un déni d'histoire* (Paris: Karthala, 2008). (A number of books that provoked further outrage were published following this controversy.)

17. The African diaspora has played an especially important role in this process. In the decades that preceded independence, Africans and their diasporic kin throughout Europe, the Americas and the Caribbean engaged in a vigorous cultural revival, founded on a literary production that touched on the entire world of experience of Africans.

    > Indeed, a dynamic African diaspora in these regions set to work claiming specificity and unique values, most often drawing connections to their African origins. Likewise, the need for identitarian affirmation and the refusal of cultural and intellectual marginalization served as a basis for cultural movements such as *la Négritude* and for claims to their portion of the "global," such as that expressed through Léopold Sédar Senghor's conception of the Universal.

    P. D. Curtin, "Préface," *Histoire générale de l'Afrique* (Unesco-Jeune Afrique, 1980), 9–14. See also Omar Gueye, "Léopold Sédar Senghor, un universel fondamental," *Ethiopiques*, Dakar, Revue Négro-africaine de Littérature et de Philosophie no. 76, 1er (Semestre 2006), 249–57.

18. Valentin Y. Mudimbe, *The Invention of Africa: Gnosis, Philosophy, and the Order of Knowledge* (Bloomington: Indiana University Press, 1988). Masonen, *The Negroland Revisited*.

19. Manning, "African and World Historiography," 326.

20. The North and the South were influenced respectively by the dominant Arab and European cultures and have differentiated themselves from the "other" Africa, black and sub-Saharan, despite being part of regional and continental political and economic organizations. In certain books, journals and museum collections, North—and white—Africa, often extended south to Mauritania, is even removed from the African continent and gratuitously attached to the Near East or the Mediterranean. However, we must note the presence of economically and intellectual influential minorities, such as Indians and others, in Uganda, Kenya and other Anglophone countries.
21. See Pierre Legendre, *Tour du monde des concepts* (Paris: Fayard, 2014).
22. See François-Xavier Fauvelle-Aymar, *La mémoire aux enchères. L'idéologie afrocentriste à l'assaut de l'histoire* (Paris: Verdier, 2009); Cheikh Anta Diop, *Civilisation ou barbarie* (Paris: Présence Africaine, 1981).
23. Increasingly, Centers for African-American and African Studies (CAAS) have proliferated in American universities, where various disciplines—anthropology, sociology, history, and others—have taken an interest in African and diaspora studies. The world saw an expansion of the discipline with the creation of the African Studies Association (ASA) in the United States in 1960, the first World Congress of Africanists in Accra in 1962 and the granting of 300 doctorates in the field in American universities between 1970 and 1972 (Curtin, "Tendances récentes des recherches historiques africaines et contribution à l'histoire en general," 75–95).
24. We must note the contributions of major writers like Edward Wilmot Blyden (*African Life and Customs*. London: C. M. Phillips, 1908), William E. Dubois (*Africa in Battle against Colonialism, Racialism, Imperialism*, 1960) and George Padmore (*Africa: Britain's Third Empire*. London: Dennis Dobson, 1949) and the continuation of their work in journals like "SANKOFA."
25. Manning, "African and World Historiography."
26. *Cambridge History of Africa*, edited by Cambridge University Press, 8 volumes between 1975 and 1986; *Histoire générale de l'Afrique*, edited in 8 volumes by UNESCO in collaboration with *Jeune Afrique*, les Nouvelles Editions Africaines-NEA, Edicef et Présence Africaine.
27. Bogumil Jewsiewicki and David Newbury (eds.), *African Historiographies: What History for Which Africa*? (London: Sage, 1986).
28. Mamadou Diouf, "Historians and Histories: What For? African Historiography between the State and the Communities" (SEPHIS-CSSSC, 2003).
29. Abdoulaye Ly, *La compagnie du Sénégal* (Paris: Ifan-Karthala, 1993). Cheikh Anta Diop, *Nations nègres et culture* (Paris: Présence Africaine, 1979), 2 vols.
30. Boubacar Barry, *Sénégambie: plaidoyer pour une histoire régionale* (SEPHIS-CEEA, 2001), 50.
31. Ibid., 51.
32. See Joseph Ki-Zerbo, *Histoire générale de l'Afrique, d'hier à demain*. Djibril Tamsir Niane, *Soundiata ou l'épopée mandingue* (Paris: Présence Africaine, 1961). Ibrahima Baba Kaké, *Combats pour l'histoire africaine* (Paris: Présence Africaine, 1982). Sékéné-Mody Cissoko, *Histoire de l'Afrique Occidentale: Moyen-âge et temps modernes, VIIIe siècle-1850* (Paris: Présence Africaine, 1966). Elikia M'bokolo, *L'Afrique noire. Histoire et civilisation*, in collaboration with Sophie Le Callennec, Hatier (Paris, 1992), 2 vols. Boubacar Barry, *Le royaume du Waalo. Le Sénégal avant la conquête* (Paris: Karthala, 1985). The slogan was that of Patrice Lumumba, founder of the National Congolese Movement (MNC), toward the end of the 1950s and leader of the political struggle for the independence of his country and African unity.

33. A nonexhaustive list of those from Paris 7 and the Sorbonne: Théophile Obenga, Achille Mbembe, Mamadou Diouf, Mohamed Mbodj, Yoro Fall, Mamadou Fall, Babacar Fall, Aboubacry Moussa Lam, Babacar Sall, Rokhaya Fall, Ibrahima Thioub and Ndiouga Adrien Benga.
34. Lansiné Kaba, Mamadou Diouf, Mohamed Mbodj, Ousmane Kane, Cheikh Babou, Emmanuel Akyeampong, Philip Curtin, Patrick Manning, Martin Klein, Frederick Cooper, Aly Dramé and Ibra Sène were among the many African historians in American universities.
35. Kaké, *Combats pour l'histoire africaine,* 38.
36. "Our ancestors the Gauls" was the French assimilationist program taught to the young students of the colonies and from which they wished to free themselves. The exponents of the "black Egypt" thesis, such as Cheikh Anta Diop, have been accused of seeking at any price a black Egyptian origin of civilization in an attempt to respond to the long centuries of exclusion suffered by the African continent in general and blacks in particular.
37. Curtin, "Tendances récentes des recherches historiques africaines et contribution à l'histoire en général," 77–95, 91–92.
38. Rightly or wrongly, oral traditions have been accused of being nostalgic or navel-gazing, allegedly containing exaggerations or approximations that foreclose the possibility of any historical or scholarly value.
39. The literature is filled with works explicating these notions of racial difference and inequality—works that have been the object of numerous criticisms. Among them are Georg Wilhelm Friedrich Hegel, *Leçons de la philosophie de l'histoire*, transl. J. Gibelin (Paris: Vrin, 1979). Joseph Arthur de Gobineau, *Essai sur l'inégalité des races humaines* (Paris: Firmin-Didot, 1884); R. Placide Tempels, *La Philosophie bantoue* (Paris: Présence Africaine, 1959); and many others.
40. As soon as he became aware of them, Aimé Césaire defended the arguments developed by Cheikh Anta Diop in *Nations nègres et culture* and engaged fully to the avant-garde of the Négritude movement he launched with Lépold Sédar Senghor and Léon Gontran Damas. However, because of ideological and political disagreements, Senghor was less inclined to share or defend Cheikh Anta Diop's arguments.
41. Kaké, *Combats pour l'histoire africaine*, 27.
42. Ibid.
43. In 1947, Alioune Diop created the publishing house *Présence Africaine* and its journal of culture in the black world, promoting the voices of African authors who wished to make themselves heard and distribute their writings. Diop, *Nations nègres et culture*, 2 vols. (1st edition 1954). Aimé Césaire, *Cahier d'un retour au pays natal* (Paris: Présence Africaine, 1956), 94.
44. See also Barry, *Sénégambie: plaidoyer pour une histoire régionale*, 31.
45. This struggle was led by a number of writers and activists such as William E. Du Bois, Marcus Garvey, Price, Frantz Fanon, Langston Hughes, the "Black Renaissance" movement and others, just as the Négritude movement benefited from the meeting of Lépold Sédar Senghor with Aimé Césaire, Jean Price-Mars, Léon-Gontran Damas, René Maran and others from Africa, Haiti and New York (especially participants in the "Harlem Renaissance"). Thus across borders, the desire for unity operated on the continent and in the diaspora on a humanistic but racially conscious basis.
46. Kaké, *Combats pour l'histoire africaine*, 1982, 33.
47. Ernest Renan (1823–1892): « Qu'est-ce qu'une nation? », Sorbonne 1882.

48. Despite a long-standing historical tradition and a centuries-long foreign presence, the global history of Senegal has never been written. The government of Senegal finally decided (in 2014) to write a *General History of Senegal*. This history raises all the questions and methodological issues with which African historians have long grappled.

49. See also Barry, *Sénégambie: plaidoyer pour une histoire régionale*, 55.

50. This ideal of the "founding fathers" of the African nations has gone through several stages, indicative of the political development of the continent itself and its symbolic representation in the Organization for African Unity (OUA) founded in 1963 in Addis Ababa (and the precursor to the African Union). Ultimately, countries returned to their national programs, though without necessarily renouncing the Pan-Africanist ideal. Later on, African historians worked within the Association of African Historians—AHA—created in 1972 in Dakar. In the same spirit, the Council for the Development of Social Science Research in Africa (CODESRIA) was created in 1973 in Dakar, along with the annual journal *Afrika Zamani*. The same moment also saw the creation of the Organization for Social Science Research in Eastern and Southern Africa (OSSREA). The association's domination by Francophones meant that Anglophone historians like A. F. Ajayi, A. Boahen and B. A. Ogot tended to avoid it.

51. Kaké, *Combats pour l'histoire africaine*, 1982.

52. A number of authors are known for their histories and travel narratives. Some of the most famous include Ibn Battuta, Mahmud Kati, Ibn Khaldun, Al Bakri, Abderrahmane Saâdi.

53. This passage, found in the Quran, demonstrates that borders were not a barrier to the global spread of Islam, a religion with a global mission.

54. The *Ummah*, or world community of believers, is a fundamental notion of Islam that groups together all Muslims of the world, without concern for race, culture or origin. The pilgrimage to Mecca, where they reunite annually, is thus a great moment of communion and solidarity.

55. Curtin, "Tendances récentes des recherches historiques africaines et contribution à l'histoire en général," 92.

56. Thioub, "'L'École de Dakar' et la production d'une écriture académique de l'histoire."

57. Jane Burbank and Frederick Cooper, *Empires. De la Chine ancienne à nos jours* (Paris: Payot, 2011), 688. John Donnell Fage, *An Introduction to the History of West Africa* (Cambridge, 1955). Lord Hailey, *An African Survey. A Study of Problems Arising in Africa South of Sahara* (Oxford University Press, 1957). Authors such as Michael Crowder, John Donnell Fage, Lord Haley or Donald Cruis O'Brien, among others, have made an important contribution to the global history of Africa. Michael Crowder, editor of the *Journal of African History*, was one of the most prolific African historians.

58. Numerous sources in Ajami—African languages written with Arabic characters—have opened up knowledge of African societies, which used Arabic writing to transcribe their texts in the local languages. On this question, see David Robinson, "Fulfulde Literature in Arabic Script," *History in Africa*, no. 9 (1982), 251-61. Fallou Ngom, "Ajami Scripts in the Senegalese Speech Community," *Journal of Arabic and Islamic Studies* 10 (2010), 1-23; Oslo, edited by Alex Metcalfe.

59. African countries confront this issue in all areas that see waves of emigration to the countries of the North, particularly their universities. In the context of research on African history, the numerous facilities and fora regularly organized by these institutions offer opportunities for study and publication that would be difficult to reproduce in Africa now. This does, however, give meaning to the sharing of resources for research and researchers.

60. Pioneers like Abdoulaye Ly and Cheikh Anta Diop cleared the path first for anticolonial militancy and later for the radical opposition to postcolonial power. They were followed by their young colleagues—Joseph Ki-Zerbo, Ahmadou Makhtar Mbow, Assane Seck, Sékéné Mody Cissoko, Iba Der Thiam, Abdoulaye Bathily, Alpha Oumar Konaré, Laurent Bagbo, Henriette Diabaté, among others—some of whom led political parties and competed for the presidencies of their respective countries (Senegal, Burkina Faso, Mali, etc.). Laurent Bagbo, for instance, was president of Côte d'Ivoire, and Alpha Oumar Konaré was president of Mali.
61. Barry, *Sénégambie: plaidoyer pour une histoire régionale*, 36.
62. Kenneth Onwuka Dike, *Trade and Politics in the Niger Delta, 1830–1885: An Introduction to the Economic and Political History of Nigeria* (Oxford, 1956).
63. Thioub, "'L'École de Dakar' et la production d'une écriture académique de l'histoire."
64. Professor Boubacar Barry used the phrase "'marabouts' of the North" to designate the intellectual authorities found in European universities or the "North" in general that African writers looked to validate their scholarship. See Boubacar Barry, "Preface," in Babacar Fall (ed.), *Le travail forcé en Afrique Occidentale Française, 1900–1946* (Paris: Karthala, 1993).
65. We can nonetheless see revivals in theses defended at Dakar by Mamadou Fall ("Terroirs et territoires dans la formation de l'espace régional ouest-africain," Dakar, Université Cheikh Anta Diop, 2014) and Rokhaya Fall ("Le Saalum de la fin du XVIe siècle au milieu du XIXe siècle. Populations, espaces et histoire," Dakar, Université Cheikh Anta Diop, 2014, 601) and in the ongoing writing of a *General History of Senegal*, which raises many interesting questions regarding a locality-based approach.
66. Ly, *La Compagnie du Sénégal*, VII.
67. Sophie Dulucq, *Écrire l'histoire de l'Afrique à l'époque coloniale (XIXe-XXe siècles)* (Paris: Karthala, 2009), 191. Joseph Ki-Zerbo, "Introduction générale," in *Histoire générale de l'Afrique* (Unesco-Jeune Afrique, 1980), 34.
68. Barry, "Preface."
69. Curtin, "Tendances récentes des recherches historiques africaines et contribution à l'histoire en général," 77–95.
70. Kaké, *Combats pour l'histoire africaine*, 36.
71. Yves Benot, *L'idéologie des indépendances* (Paris: Maspero, 1964), 427.
72. The famous "Radio-Télévision libre des Mille collines" (RTLM) played a large role in the genocide in which, between April and June 1994, between 800,000 and one million Tutsis and moderate Hutus were massacred in Rwanda. With its propaganda calling on "true Rwandans"—Hutus—to massacre the "cockroaches"—the Tutsis—who were thus not part of the human species, the broadcasts became the symbol of the genocide.
73. "Ivoirité," a concept that aimed to define Ivorian nationality, appeared in 1945 in Dakar among Ivorian students. It reappeared with President Henri Konan Bédié in 1993, who reused the concept to push aside his opponent Alassane Ouattara. The new definition rested on ethnic, religious and geographical differences. A person would be Ivorian only if his four grandparents had been born in Côte d'Ivoire, which led to feelings of exclusion among populations with foreign-sounding names, who were suspected of being bad Ivorians. This opportunistic definition of "ivoirité" betrayed a term that had originally embodied a positive cultural concept, that is, the "Ivorian miracle," or the mixing, in Ivory Coast, of elements from many subregional populations, contributing to the creation of a melting pot that could serve as an example to many societies on the continent. This prior definition contributed enormously to the economic power of the country in terms of production and prosperity."

(See "L'ivoirité, ou les dérives d'un discours identitaire," interview of Soeuf Elbadawi with Sidiki Kaba, *Africultures*.)

74. Bernard Henri-Lévi, *La pureté dangereuse* (Paris: Grasset, 1994).
75. Curdiphe, "L'ivoirité, ou l'esprit du nouveau contrat social du Président H.K. Bédié," Actes du forum Curdiphe du 20 au 23 mars 1996, publiés sous la direction de Saliou Touré, in *Ethics*, revue de la Curdiphe, Presses universitaires d'Abidjan, 1996.
76. Kaké, *Combats pour l'histoire africaine*, 28–29.
77. Samuel P. Huntington, *Le choc des civilisations* (Paris: Odile Jacob, 1997), 5p. Samuel Huntington, a former Harvard professor, originated the idea of the "clash of civilizations" in an eponymous article published in *Foreign Affairs* in 1993. His controversial point of view puts the cultures of the world in perspective and outlines a global context that presupposes the existence of distinct civilizations that are in conflict with each other.
78. Ibid.
79. Léopold Sédar Senghor, *Liberté 3: Négritude et civilisation de l'Universel*, discours, conférences (Paris: Le Seuil, 1977).
80. The fall of the Berlin Wall, symbol of the bipolarization of the world into Eastern and Western blocs, announced the end of the Cold War. The date of November 9, 1989, theoretically marked the end of a conflict that came to an end through its own internationalization, caught between two conceptions of the world ("Weltanschauung"). The dismantling of the Soviet Union was the sign of a new globalization in the name of the globalization of capitalist/liberal concepts that had finally overcome socialism and communism. This new redistribution announced a new order and a new globalization that, like the others, carried its own set of certainties and contradictions at all levels—political, economic, cultural and so on.
81. *Nous sommes 7 milliards de voisins*, Radio France Internationale.
82. Ref. Philip Curtin, *The Chronicle of Higher Education*, March 3, 1995.
83. Kaké, *Combats pour l'histoire africaine*, 1986, 28–29.
84. At the time of writing, the spread of Ebola has provoked fears of an epidemic in Africa. Much like HIV, this virus without a cure demands a global solution but reinforces certain stereotypes and can isolate the continent once again.
85. "Global village" is an expression Marshall McLuhan used to describe the effects of globalization on the media, information technologies and communication. The possible unity of the entire world under one culture suggests the notion that the world is one and the same community, one and the same village. See Marshall McLuhan, *The Medium Is the Message* (London: Penguin Books, 1967).
86. Léopold Sédar Senghor, Liberté 5: *Le Dialogue des cultures* (Paris: Le Seuil, 1992).
87. In Senegal, President Senghor described the students protesting against neocolonialism as "spoiled children." He critiqued their mode of operation by attacking their ideological references, especially Maoism, which he critiqued at length in his "speech to the nation" on May 30, 1968.
88. Omar Gueye, *Mai 1968 au Sénégal: Senghor face aux étudiants et au mouvement syndical* (Paris: Karthala, 2017).

CHAPTER 5
DECONSTRUCTING IMPERIAL AND NATIONAL NARRATIVES IN TURKEY AND THE ARAB MIDDLE EAST
Selçuk Esenbel and Meltem Toksöz

Time and space

Even though the present determines how we understand the past, our conceptual understanding of time and place constitutes the apparatus with which we anchor our narratives and understand collective memory—and this applies especially, of course, to historians. For Turkey, all these terms are complicated, as the state of historiography in Turkey reveals, because of the ongoing question of which place constitutes the historic site of the nation and polity.[1] Place, as Edward S. Casey says, is the concrete setting of local culture, but it is also a matrix, the place or medium in which something is bred, produced or developed, a place of origin and growth.[2] Thus the key question in Turkish and Arabic historiography is which place constitutes the matrix of collective memory in the historical narratives of Turkey and the Arab Middle East. This geographic region experienced catastrophic changes in political boundaries after the First World War, including the shift of the physical environment for nation-states and the severe disruption of existing national, ethnic and religious historic homelands when new nations were constructed. In the transition between the Ottoman Empire (c. 1299–1922) and, the aftermath of the First World War, Turkey's Independence War, the former European provinces of the empire were absorbed into nation-states, the Armenians made a bid for independence and Arab nationalism emerged in the face of mandate regimes across the Middle East. Historical time and place thus shifted radically. Turkish and Arab historians' perception of the connections between the "local" and the "global" has also shifted, along with the politics and culture of the catalytic shift from the Ottoman state tradition—a half-millennia-old polity that governed a multiethnic/religious empire—to a secular, Republican nation-state whose developmentalist project faces critical issues of democratization.

These issues form the basis of the present discussion about global history, transnational history and the state of historiography in Turkey and the Arab Middle East. The discussion of historiography will focus on efforts to develop global history as it relates to the Ottoman period, which includes both early-modern and modern transitions and constitutes the foundation of the debate about nationalism and national identity not only in modern Turkey but also in the Arab Middle East.[3] In fact, both the early-modern and modern transformations of Ottoman history and the main debate around nationalism inevitably position Ottoman history writing in a global context. Hence one of our points in this chapter is to underscore the inherent globality of writing Ottoman history. Of course, what constitutes global is a salient problematic in history writing today, since doing global history does not mean readily overcoming or even reconciling with the forces of nationalism.

It is also true, however, that the seeming incongruity between nationalism and globalism did not always lead to two opposed modes of history writing: nineteenth-century universal history writings owed as much to Rankean nationalist frameworks as they did to larger imperial imaginings. An example is the nineteenth-century Ottoman world histories written *à la histoire universelle* by intellectuals and scholars working outside the state-generated genre of chronicling. Indeed, many Ottoman intellectuals, some of whom taught history at the newly founded universities, joined the trend of writing the history of "mankind and civilization"—thus perhaps helping to lay out the foundations of today's global history. These world histories (*tarih-i umumi*) entailed a new understanding of history as a social science discipline, and they connected the Ottomans to the world at large in terms of both their view of the rest of the world and their place in it. This global view of history in general and world history in particular amply attests to the global outlook of Ottoman history writing in the last years of the nineteenth century.[4]

These world histories also point to the Ottoman intellectual legacy as made up of competing streams of thought, and thus they are much more complex than what a crude polarization of Islamic and Western contexts suggests. That the Ottoman intellectual world neither followed a single path to modernity as identified with the West nor solely reflected a tension point through Islam is most evident in world histories that position the empire as both modern and Islamic. Undoubtedly in the age of European hegemony when it was predominantly believed that progress was European, the Ottoman order of the day—that of conjoined struggle and adjustment in the Hamidian era (1876–1908)—created multiple contingencies in histories that gave space to the analysis of Islamic history and the history of the Ottoman Empire.[5] Such narrative historiography transcended the West and non-West dichotomy. At the same time, the rise of modern global consciousness and a distinct notion of global space meant that Ottoman history writing was intended to position the empire in world society and history. It is in this self-positioning of the Ottomans that we can locate Ottoman globalism, with historians situating the empire not as simply responding to European ideas of history but as creating and narrating its own encounter with modernity.

Perhaps reminiscent of this fundamentally global orientation in the historical discourse of the Ottomans, not just as a matter of intellectual reflection but also as an active mode of political endeavor, historical work today is politicized by current nationalist, ethnic, religious and geopolitical issues in today's Turkey and the realms of the Arab Middle East. In line with contemporary global trends, today historians with liberal-leftist views are highlighting the authoritarian/assimilative character of Turkish nation-state building in order to question the nationalist narrative of the anti-imperialist Turkish Republic founded in 1923 by the Kemalist revolution. These historians focus on questions of ethnicity and religion, providing a historical contextualization of present debates about the politics of military coups, human-rights violations—both recent and older—and the hope of joining the European Union. But this strand of historical "de-nationalization" continues to face strong opposition from proponents of the nationalism ingrained in the literature for generations. Contemporary problems around ethnicity and religion are translated into debates over medieval history concerning the Seljukid Turks, the Kurds and the Armenians, or orthodox Sunni Islam versus Alewite heterodoxy.[6] In the Arab Middle East as well, grand narratives of Arab nationalism and the concomitant post-1914 efforts to deconstruct them have continued in the interaction of national and global history writings.[7]

The concept of civilization in global history experiments and the construction of national identity

Like many revolutions, the Republic of Turkey's historical vision rejected its past—the Ottoman past—as a backward, failed history made worse by its connection with Islam. This secular Turkish critique of the Ottomans can almost be characterized as Orientalist in the Saidean sense, and a stern secularist/Westernist worldview continues to this day to define one pole of a divided Turkish political debate. The Kemalists went so far as to ban the Arabic script in 1928, substituting the Latin one in its stead—possibly the most radical cultural revolution in the twentieth century, given the purposeful severing of the new generation from its "oriental" past. The official national historiography of Turkey is thus on ambivalent and ambiguous ground due to this initial rejection of the history of its precursor. Ottoman history began making a vigorous comeback at the end of the Second World War, but the controversy over what constituted the national historical legacy of the Turkish "nation" had already begun.

In the 1920s and early 1930s, amid the revolutionary ardor of the new Republic, two interconnected theses about the construction of national identity were put forward. One was the fantastic vision of a Pan-Turkish historical identity that overlooked Islam and the Ottomans by speeding backward through space and time to find a homeland in the plains of Central Asia. The other vision was that of Anatolian Civilizations, an idea that the Republican government, using ideas derived from Near Eastern and Classical archaeology, set up as a rigorous scientific field under German and Austrian tutelage. What the two theories had in common was a connection to the European racial studies that marked the late-nineteenth and early-twentieth-century discourse about Turks as Asian nomadic "Barbarians" who had no place in the territories of civilized Indo-Europeans.

It was in this context that two congresses in the 1930s looked for a new Turkish history with which to construct the new nation. A group of scholars prepared a booklet entitled "The Main Outline of Turkish History: An Introduction"[8] as the agenda of the first conference of 1932, and the conference featured vigorous debates between modern Ottomanists who were quietly skeptical of the Turkist thesis, Europeanist ethnologists and anthropologists and Russian Muslim Turkist intellectuals now settled in Turkey. The new Turkish thesis of history sprang from this congress and soon entered textbooks.

The thesis mimicked its European counterparts that located Central Asia as the cradle of humanity, with Indo-European people originating there, and then, as they migrated starting around 5000 BC, bringing civilization to a wider realm. The Turkish version replaced Indo-Europeans with Turkic people and pushed the date back to 10000 BC.

But by 1937, when the second congress met, the Anatolian civilizations view, bolstered by the pseudoscientific racist anthropological tracts of the time that presented all Anatolians as brachycephalic Turks from the beginning—rather than the inferior dolichocephalic asserted by Western views—had won. This view complemented the Turkish history thesis' claim of the beginning date of Turkic migrations as 10000 BC, introducing iron technology and hence civilization to Anatolia. Thus it proved that Turks were rooted in an antiquity that was part of a shared European legacy. The Indo-European Hittites, the Ionian Greeks and, for a while, even the Sumerians were all descendants of the earliest "Turks" of the ancient world, and, by implication, of the modern world as well. Proponents went as far as inventing a phantasmagoric linguistic theory, the Sun-Language theory, based on the archaic Turkic word "a" meaning "sun."[9] According to this theory, all languages derived from this Turkish archaic mother tongue via nomad migrations from Central Asia to the rest of the world—including Britain, Germany, Japan, India and the Americas.[10]

This Pan-Turkish vision of world history presented the Turks galloping in an East-West direction from Central Asia, the land of Turan, mostly toward the West; in this thesis nobody went back to East Asia, where the Ancient Turks were born. The Anatolian civilization's vision of world history, in contrast, claimed that the Turks were related to the ancient peoples buried below the ground in Paleolithic and Neolithic Anatolia. At the time, the ancient Hittites fossilized deep below the soil of Anatolia were being studied with avid interest by the European (read, German) archaeologists searching for the roots of Indo-European peoples in the middle of Turkish-speaking Anatolia. There was a moment when even Atatürk, a former Ottoman officer from Macedonia, and his cadres claimed that the Hittites were Turks. Neither world history thesis looked at the actual Turks living in the Republic, who were mostly a Euro-Near-Eastern-Asian mixture left over from a recently dismantled empire. Nor did either thesis connect logically to the constitutional construct of the Republic, which defined the concept of the Turkish nation around citizenship that was supposed to integrate all non-Turk minorities as well, a goal that did not completely succeed. The Ottoman history that these new citizens had shared was no longer connected to the present except as a straw man against which to battle in the making of modernity.[11]

Republican historiography in Turkey is also a transnational historical narrative that involves the story of the various diaspora intellectuals who served the Republic as identity builders. The nationalist narrative of the nomadic Turks was not actually constructed in Turkey, but was instead the discourse of an émigré culture of Russian Muslim Turkic intellectuals and historians. After the 1917 October revolution, eminent scholars from the Romanov Russian imperial academy such as Yusuf Akçura and Zeki Velidi Togan found a haven in Turkey. So did the European intellectual diaspora who fled the Nazis and ended up in Kemalist Turkey, where they helped reform the university system.

German/Austrian archaeologists who established their field in Turkish universities partnered with their Turkish counterparts to identify the Turk with Anatolian ancient roots. Wolfram Eberhard, the German liberal historical sociologist of Ancient China, was invited by President Atatürk to study the Turkic (Hsiung-nu, Tu-Ch'ueh, To-pa, etc.) origins of many Chinese dynasties: he founded the Chair of Sinology in Ankara University Faculty of Letters and propagated his anti-Sino-centric view of Chinese dynasties. The demystification of the Chinese national thesis thus served to construct the national thesis in Turkey.[12]

The problem with this avant-garde experiment of rejecting the Islamic Ottoman past and adopting Turkist or Anatolian roots for a national identity is that it did not offer a site or topos on which to build this identity. For this reason, the Anatolian civilizations thesis has remained quite meaningless for most Anatolians, offering at best an elitist vision of a cultural legacy. In the case of the Turkist argument, globalizing affairs that took place "beyond the foggy mists," as Herodotus described the land of the Scythians, remained a fantasy for most who had difficulty penetrating the linguistic and cultural complexity of Turanist Central Asia, a region that remained inaccessible until the end of the Soviet Union. At its worst, however, the thesis has fueled ultra-nationalist ideologues bent on bashing leftists.[13]

Arab historiography and the Ottomans: A world of its own?

In the last days of the Ottoman Empire, as the empire lost more and more territory to the newly independent Balkan nations, what remained were Turkish Anatolia and the larger Muslim-dominated Arab regions. In both the Turkish- and Arabic-speaking regions, it was the Muslim-dominated professional middle class that was dependent on the state for social status and material well-being. It is now commonplace to view the *ulema*, the Islamic intellectual elite, as part of the general intellectual life of Ottoman society—a fact that, although overlooked by the Turkish nationalist historical approach, played a crucial part in the formation of Arab historiography. Pan-Islamism, perhaps a prelude to a global understanding of history, was an important concern for the Arabic-speaking *ulema*. Although Pan-Islamism did not lead to the development of a global historical vision, it did bring the Muslim intellectual elites together and implied a global outlook that connected Muslims in Ottoman society to those from lands as disparate as Russia, Central Asia, India and the Far East.[14]

In the end, Pan-Islamism gave way to a kind of proto-nationalism, but this link was neither obvious nor predictable in the late nineteenth century. One explanation for Pan-Islamism not being able to espouse an international outlook was the fact that it was part of the "Ottoman mission civilisateur," as Deringil calls it, which limited it to the world of Ottoman imperialism.[15] For instance, an important Arabic text from the end of the nineteenth century put forth a vision of a history of Arabia from before Islam to contemporary Ottoman rule as an assertion of Ottoman authority in the name of Islam and civilization.[16]

After the empire collapsed and was divided in the aftermath of the First World War, nationalism replaced many intellectual currents within Arab historiography. Of course Pan-Islamism was only one approach that did not exclude Ottomanism. It is not even certain that the Arab intellectual elite were torn between Ottomanism and other proto-nationalist historical visions. Many nineteenth-century Arab elites—like other members of the new educated Ottoman elite—were Ottomanists first; consider the intellectuals Shakib Arslan and Butrus al-Bustani, whose thoughts led to an era considered to be an "awakening" of Eastern identity.[17] Indeed, this is one of the topics that Arabic-reading Turkish historians have only very recently begun to study in an effort to move beyond the sharp nationalistic separations in Ottoman history writing.[18] This is a very important step toward a global historical understanding, as regional broadening constitutes the first step toward a world conceptualization.

The end of the empire may be said to have brought forth a new energy. According to a recent analysis, this was a creative rupture that "involved both a dramatic break from each successor state's imperial past as well as a continual reference to it."[19] Indeed, not just governments but also the intellectual elites saw nationalism as the only modern source of identity and legitimacy. The words of a pioneering Egyptian academic clearly demonstrate the Orientalist tone of those seeking legitimacy in nationalism in a postimperial environment:

> The truth about the question of stagnation is that the Ottoman state ruled over degenerated peoples, and the Ottoman rule was incapable of altering this. This is because the Ottomans were a nation that takes and not one that gives, and their organization, belief, and culture testify to that. They organized whoever they ruled ... and made sure that no change or transformation would reach them.[20]

So it is not surprising that the most striking absence in the Ottoman historiography of the twentieth century—whether written in Arabic, Turkish or English—was a global conceptualization. Yet two qualifications are necessary, and they reveal glimpses of and hope for a larger framework, that if not global per se at least moves toward it. First, nationalist narratives themselves were rather multiple and selective in the sense that they were not totally disconnected from global processes. Second, the sheer diversity of the historiographies of the many newly born states showed the multiplicity embedded in the Ottoman Empire itself as well as the impasses associated with it, some of which were quite global. Even within nationalist paradigms, these narratives of the twentieth-century Ottoman experience revealed a multinational or non-national past.

The pivotal period for the historiography of the Arab Middle East was the beginning of the twentieth century, before the First World War ended the Ottoman Empire. New states were established from former Ottoman lands, including the colonial-mandate states of Iraq, Syria, Lebanon and Palestine and tribal states in the Arabian Peninsula. The Palestinian Mandate included the Balfour Declaration of 1917, which meant that there was at least the promise of a Jewish homeland, which in turn meant that nationalisms in the Middle East came with a variety of Arab nationalisms, either regional or Pan-

Arab, as well as Jewish nationalism, or Zionism. Clearly these nationalisms developed historiographical tools with respect to not only a past Ottoman imperialism but also contemporary imperialism, as much of the historiography was dominated by thinking about the intentions of the imperial states in the aftermath of the war.

Scholarship on the Middle East and the First World War that utilizes key narratives such as imperialism, Arab nationalism and Zionism owes much to a single work: *The Arab Awakening* by George Antonius (New York, 1936). Still today, Antonius's major arguments were that the 1916 Arab revolt led by Sharif Husayn of Mecca was the result of earlier nineteenth-century Arab nationalist movements and that the revolt depended on the British promises of Arab independence from the Ottomans. The heart of the issue, for Antonius, was the creation of Palestine and Israel and what he saw as British duplicity. Antonius's arguments regarding Arab nationalism have largely been discredited, but they still loom over claims around Zionism to legitimize its development as against extant Arab nationalist militancy as early as 1916 if not earlier; in addition, they are used to implicate Arabs generally in the creation of Israel by blaming them for having depended on British promises of independence.[21]

The impact of the Annales on Ottoman historical scholarship and the post-Annales approaches

One very important reason for the late global conceptualization of Ottoman history relates to the fact that the Ottomans were never directly colonized. Although colonial history, either through modernization theory or Marxist and neo-Marxist history, has been one route to global history, it is not a route that Ottoman studies could fit into, given the debate over whether its imperial power amounted to colonization and whether it was itself semicolonized. But beginning with Ömer Lütfi Barkan, who can be considered the founder of Ottoman economic history (and who knew Braudel personally), the Annales Ecole had an indelible mark. Barkan laid the groundwork for much social and economic history and its later variations, and through the 1950s his systematic and detailed study of the Ottoman archives made him a unique example of erudite scholarship. This work separated him from fellow Ottomanists like Köprülü and Uzunçarşılı, who followed the modernization paradigm more strictly; in contrast, Barkan's investigations of Ottoman institutions across the empire allowed him to bridge Ottoman and European histories. Building on Barkan's contribution, Halil İnalcık, until recently the doyen of Ottoman history, wrote his seminal history of the early empire, contextualizing its decline as the dissolution of the "classical" model of the imperial realm that he identified in the same work.[22] Many others have followed his model, attributing the decline of the empire to its inability either to revert to the golden age or to modernize.

But that was not the only model after the Annales-influenced-Barkan-and-İnalcık to affect scholarship of the Ottoman Empire.[23] A second route, in both Turkish and Arab historiography, was through Braudel and his analysis of the Mediterranean. This model approached the Ottoman epoch from the vantage point of economic and social history, and confidently deconstructed the *sui generis* arguments of Ottoman-cum-Turkish trajectories in mainstream historiography. Indeed, since the 1970s, two generations of studies written from Braudelian perspectives have incorporated Ottoman history into world history.

In the 1970s, the heyday of both the modernization paradigm and the world system approach, a crucial question was the extent and means of European economic penetration into the Ottoman Empire, a question that inherently put Ottoman history in a larger context. The 1977 İslamoğlu-Keyder article on the agenda of Ottoman history is still a classic text on the question of whether change in the empire stemmed from within or without.[24] Many others, however, criticized the modernization paradigm, espousing instead the Wallersteinian approach. Historians and social scientists such as Şevket Pamuk and Çağlar Keyder used the Wallersteinian center-periphery analysis to explain the Ottoman integration into global capitalism.[25] Others, like Donald Quataert, were critical of both modernization theory and the Wallersteinian model, which he viewed as a simplistic characterization of economic incorporation as one-sided and oblivious to internal dynamics. For him, the European-Ottoman encounter needed to be studied through the twin notions of resistance and disintegration.[26]

In step with world trends, classic Marxian interpretations have also given way to the idea of shared modernities as a globalizing explanation. Along with other historians, Huricihan İslamoğlu, who has looked in depth at the theoretical issues of property rights in the Ottoman empire, has used the Annales frameworks within this context of a shared modernity.[27] İslamoğlu's work on the state and the peasantry contests the Wallersteinian approach by emphasizing indigenous dynamics of state-peasant relations as well as property ownership.

But all these approaches use Europe as the main reference point from which to consider Ottoman economic and social developments. A case in point would be the question of European Absolutism as juxtaposed against Despotism, both in the early-modern and modern states. Suraiya Faroqhi, the leading scholar of early-modern Ottoman history, notes that recent research has cast doubt on the clear-cut opposition between a "European Absolutism" based on a class society and private property as the roots of European modernity and an "Ottoman Despotism" with patrimonialism and no private property or nobility.[28] In turn, a less Eurocentric and more global model of the transformation of the state from early-modern to modern has served as an explanatory method for Ottomanists in Turkey and overseas, including Halil Sahillioğlu, who has worked on the history of money in the Ottoman state, and Mehmet Genç, whose theoretical formulation of the Ottoman economy as a mode of provisioning the state pioneered part of the debate on state formation. These founding works constitute the fundamental bibliography for anyone venturing into comparative Ottoman history.[29] Ariel Salzmann's analysis of the "Tocqueville" in the Ottoman Empire is an example of the scholarship of the last three decades that takes Anderson, Tilly and other Europeanists as a comparative frame, thus blurring the typically sharper divide between the East/West state and society transitions.[30]

Since the 1980s, the movement in Ottoman historiography from a framework of imperial failure has situated the nineteenth-century empire as successfully integrating, at least at the cosmopolitan level, the Enlightenment and imperial transitions to modernity.³¹ Thus it is now possible to move past the 1970s' decline thesis and/or its rejection by Marxist class analysis to a "softer" approach that reappropriates the late Ottoman period as a modern legacy that was "lost as a possible trajectory" in the postempire nation-state quagmire.³² This critical distancing from a linear analysis of the emergence of secularist nation-states out of the ashes of an Islamic empire starts with Şerif Mardin's restudy of Ottoman intellectual and political movements. Mardin approaches Turkish modernization through the lens of a conflict between Republicanism and empire, a contestation between Islam and secularism. His research strikingly fits Samuel Moyn and Andrew Sartori's discussion of global history implicit in Joseph Levenson's 1969 examination of the crisis of China's classical claims to civilizational universality in the face of modern Europe's higher universalism. For Levenson, the Hegelian supersession of the Chinese by Western universalism forced Chinese intellectuals to choose between the radical embrace of modern universalism and a new traditionalism that valued tradition for its particularity rather than its universality.³³ Using Levenson's thesis to interpret Mardin's 1961 study of the *Genesis of Young Ottoman Thought*, which came out a few years before Levenson's work, on Turkish modernization as global intellectual history, helps us understand that Mardin's Ottoman intellectuals, whether they embraced Turkish nationalism and secular Westernism or the late Ottoman reformist venture of constructing a modernity suitable for Islam, were responding to European claims to universal modernity and "Islam" became tradition.³⁴

A similar take on the modernization of the empire is easily discernible in İlber Ortaylı, the historian of the nineteenth century whose short but seminal book on what he calls "the Ottoman Empire's Longest Century" compares Ottoman reforms to contemporary efforts in Austria and Russia. The book has been a best seller since it was published in 1990, attesting to the new public awareness that the late empire was a constructive modern force whose legacy was distorted by the abrupt Jacobin turn into a crude national state.³⁵ For Selim Deringil, the age of Abdülhamid II, the late-nineteenth-century autocrat called the "Red Sultan" by the leaders of the Young Turk and the Kemalist revolutions, saw the inception of a shared modernity comparable to the experience of other empires. Edhem Eldem prefers to seek modernist processes in the financial institution of the Ottoman Bank, once seen as the agency of European imperialism, and the bourgeois tendencies of the Istanbul once accused of being "half-baked failed moderns." Zafer Toprak makes the continuum argument with the Young Turk period after the 1908 constitutional revolution, which he sees as the repository of the institutions and ideology of the nation-state and national economy in the Republic.³⁶ In addition, in step with global scholarship, topics such as labor, rebellion, gender and consumption now have their place in the field.³⁷

Today's historiography: Beyond Arab and Turkish?

In terms of the Arab Middle East, Albert Hourani, now unequivocally the doyen of Arab history, followed up on Antonius and made an undeniable imprint on Arab scholarship.

Hourani's *The Emergence of the Modern Middle East* (London, 1981) can perhaps be considered the first step toward a broader view of Arab nationalism and hence a step toward a more regional outlook. In another way, his work can be considered as the first exploitation of the now-abundant literature on theories of nationalism published since the 1980s. Similarly Hisham Sharabi, whose 1966 book *Nationalism and Revolution in the Arab World the Middle East and North Africa* traced the history of Arab intellectuals in a nineteenth-century world that included conservative Muslims, reformist Muslims and secular nationalists, was one of the first to revisit Arab nationalism and enlarge its theoretical and geographic frames.[38] The 1970s also marked a beginning of reconsidering Arab nationalism. The Nahda, the Arab renaissance of the 1890s, once seen as literary, philosophical and cultural movement, was now studied as a political one. These studies asserted that while Pan-Islamism was part of the Arab intellectual legacy and Ottomanism was still viable, it was the *Nahda* that paved the way to proto-nationalism in Arab lands, not those movements.[39] From Benedict Anderson's imagined communities to Charles Tilly's elaboration of collective action, theories of nationalism have helped Arab historiography of both the Ottoman and post-Ottoman worlds move toward a postnationalist approach and a larger regional framework. This has had a similar impact to that of the development of postcolonial studies in ushering a new era in global historiography.

Undoubtedly, nationalism was a major obstacle in the development of a framework that put the Ottoman Empire into a world historical context. It is interesting that not even the Braudelian impact on Ottoman scholarship could create a Mediterranean context, given that the post–Braudelian World Systems approach revolved around port cities. Arguably, the initial interest that scholars of the World Systems perspective had in the Mediterranean was not for itself, but for the way it crystallized the processes of peripheralization. This agenda eventually gave way to research on port cities in the Mediterranean context, with the Eastern Mediterranean providing the foundation for studies on both Arab and Turkish port cities.[40]

This new mode has promise, as previously disparate nationalistic historiographies have begun to look at connections to the wider polity of the Ottoman Empire. Arguably, the study of Arab history as part of imperial Ottoman modernization as opposed to a nationalist and hence anti-imperial paradigmatic stance began with Engin Akarli's work on Lebanon.[41] Now identifiable as "bringing the state back in," the approach seems to have brought larger connections than those afforded by nationalisms in the twentieth century. The recognition of Ottoman modernity as part of Arab historiography has opened the way for research into how problematic historians found having to choose between the nation and the larger Ottoman Empire—whether Islamic, modern or both. Notable here are the writings of scholars of the Arab provinces who successfully moved beyond nationalist historiographies to tie the Arab nations of today back to their Ottoman past.[42] There are also important contributions that consider the elite and nonelite in the dynamic processes of change in the Ottoman Empire, and link nationalism, imperialism and globalization.[43] Today's scholarship on the Arab Middle East is thus unavoidably global in its language; the challenge now is to find a historiography in Beirut, in Aleppo, in Amman to chronicle a world that is under attack, or a society that must assert a self-definition in the face of existential challenges, or a world that has been lost, or a society whose hitherto prevailing national myths and norms now appear bankrupt, or challenges to identity and self-understanding posed by forces of internal migration and international globalization.[44]

Looking at the present historical debate positively, it is clear that all is out in the open, even the most controversial topic of all, that is, the 1915 deportation and subsequent death of a large population of Ottoman Armenians during the First World War. That said, this slaughter on the war's eastern front is still met with a fiercely defensive reaction from nationalists in government circles—and violence from virulent extremist nationalists outside it. As Deringil said, "the brutal murder of the Armenian journalist and human rights activist Hrant Dink is a tragic reminder that in the Turkey of the twenty-first century the past is not history."[45]

Concluding remarks: From local to global: International scholarship as a globalizer?

Turkish scholars constitute the major community of scholarship in Ottoman/Turkish historiography, and historians who have been internationally engaged since the 1970s have played a leading role in shaping the transformative debates in the field. However, a significant process since the 1970s has been the internationalization of Ottoman historical studies, as scholars outside Turkey, mainly from the United States, Israel, Lebanon, Europe and Japan, have entered the field, and as Turkish historians have begun teaching in Europe and the United States.[46] Given this international cast, it is hard to define who represents the international and who represents the local in this shared discourse, especially as the work of many non-Turkish historians is increasingly translated into Turkish and widely available. At the same time, Turkish historians now publish in English or French in addition to Turkish, which means they are immediately part of international academic debate. Scholars such as Feridun Emecen, Kemal Beydilli and Ali Akyıldız have been producing Ottoman historical studies in Turkish based on primary sources and archival materials on a wide range of topics.[47] International scholars who work on Ottoman history connect to their work as well; overall, the communication revolution has brought the academy closer together.

A new phenomenon is an inter-regionality reaching from the Near East to the Mediterranean, Central Asia to the Indian Ocean, Inner Asia and East Asia, that surfaces as a new political and cultural platform for constructing a transnational frame of historical analysis beyond Ottoman borders. Esenbel has ventured into global history by using this geopolitical and cultural frame by using materials in Japan and the United States on the transnational interaction between Japanese Pan-Asianists and Pan-Islamist actors in Russia, the Ottoman Empire and India to study Japanese interaction with the Islamic world, a subject that had not been much studied in either Japanese or Turkish historiography.[48] Thus a topic that began as *local* history was also *global*, as it connected modern Japanese or Chinese history to that of the Middle East/Central Asian/East Asian zone. Relatedly, this initially local production became more global via English-language publications and the resulting burgeoning of scholarship in Japan, Turkey and the United States.[49]

For Arab historiography as well, the impact of English education and publications in translation is undeniable. Another globalizing effect for Arab historiography is the fact that Palestinian diaspora intellectuals are scattered across Europe and the United States. These Palestinians, along with Arab-American academics (who are much more numerous than Turkish scholars in the United States), have worked to spread frameworks of Ottoman imperial modernization across regions and languages. Certainly, area studies paved the way, but as of the early 1990s, this Arabization (in both background and language) of the American academic scene could no longer be attributed to area studies, as they were out of fashion. Additionally, Israeli scholars of the Ottoman Empire have moved key discussions in Arab history and historiography forward. One recent development also merits attention: Islamist revisionism, notably active in Egypt, but present elsewhere in the Arab world and Turkey, is revaluing the Ottoman legacy. However, nationalism will likely remain on the scene, as it has multiple uses and side effects—from seeing the Ottomans as a bulwark against Western imperialism to strategically using the Ottoman policy of Pan-Islamism as a modern tool to unite all Muslims anew and safeguard the empire's legacy against foreign pressure.

The internationalization of Turkish and Arab historiography of the post-Annales generations since the 1970s is a complex and ongoing process that cannot be shoehorned into the global "abroad" and "local" dichotomy. In addition, any discussion of global historiography has to incorporate the reality of today's highly mobile people, ideas and information. While globalization appears to blur the distinction between production sites and patterns of dissemination, every site has distinct discursive environments that use history as a means of contestation and that come out of their own relationships to the global and the local.

Notes

1. Benedetto Croce, *History: Its Theory and Practice* (New York: Russell and Russell, original 1921) for history as the history of the present.

   For the present debate in Turkey and an evaluation of the state of historiography, we thank Selim Deringil and Zafer Toprak. The ideas they generously shared contributed to the preparation of this paper. While their perspectives differ on some of the salient issues in the current debate on national historiography, their work represents the few examples of distilled scholarly opinion in an environment rife with polemical argument. Selim Deringil, 2008, "Recent Trends in Turkish Historiography, The Use and Abuse of History," unpublished paper given in American University of Cairo for the quotation, henceforth as Deringil, 2008; Zafer Toprak, 2008, "Üçüncü Cumhuriyet Fransası, Aydınlanma ve Osmanlı da Tarihyazıcılığı"

(France of the Third Republic: The Enlightenment and Ottoman History Writing). Unpublished report to the Turkish Academy of Science (TÜBA), on the state of history writing in Turkey, henceforth as Toprak, 2008.

2. Edward Casey, *The Fate of Place: A Philosophical History* (Berkeley: University of California Press, 1997) "Beyond its strictly anatomical sense, matrix means 'a place or medium in which something is bred, produced, or developed,' 'a place or point of origin and growth.' In the matter of the matrix, place remains primary," 24.

3. For world history, Jeremy H. Bentley, *Old World Encounters: Cross-Cultural Contacts and Exchanges in Pre-Modern Times* (New York: Oxford University Press, 1993; for "interconnected" history, Joseph Fletcher, edited by Beatrice Forbes Manz, *Studies on Chinese and Islamic Inner Asia* (Aldershot and Brookfield, VT: Variorum, 1995); for international history, Akira Iriye, "The Internationalization of History," *The American Historical Review* 94:1 (February 1989), 1–10. Our approach to global history has benefited from the above.

4. For example, Mehmed Murad (also known as Mizancı Murad), *Muhtasar Tarih-i Umumi (Concise World History)* (Istanbul: Kitabci Karabet, 1891).

5. Meltem Toksöz, "The World of Mehmed Murad: Writing *Histoires Universelles* in Ottoman Turkish," *Journal of Ottoman Studies* 40 (Fall 2012), 121–42.

6. Ahmet Yaşar Ocak, "Türk ve Türkiye tarihinde İslam'ı çalışmak yahut 'arı kovanına çomak sokmak'" (Studying Islam in the history of the Turks and Turkey or "to insert a stick into a bee hive") *Toplum ve Bilim* (Winter 2001/2002), 100–14 for the hegemony of nationalist perspectives over the study of the medieval history of the Turks and Islam.

7. For example, Adeed Dawisha discusses the impact on Arab historiography of the transition of the early idea of the political unity of Arabic-speaking peoples to the singular nation-states as a transition from a regional to a national outlook, calling for conceptual distinctions between "Arab nationalism," "Arabism" and "Pan-Arabism." See his *Arab Nationalism in the 20th Century* (Princeton: Princeton University Press, 2003).

8. Afet Hanım, Samih Rıfat, Akçura Yusuf, et al., *Türk Tarihinin Ana Hatları: Methal Kısmı (The Main Outline of Turkish History: An Introduction)* (İstanbul: Devlet Matbaasi, 1931).

9. Hasan Reşit Tankut, *Güneş-Dil Teorisine Göre Toponomik Tetkikler* (Ankara: Devlet Basimevi, 1936) and *Prehistuvar'a Doğru Bir Dil İzlemesi ve Güneş-Dil Teorisinin İzahı* (Istanbul: TDK, 1937). For one of the first and most renowned books based on this approach, degrading Arabic as a simple derivative of Turkish language and culture, see Naim Hazım Onat, *Arapçanın Türk Diliyle Kuruluşu (On the Construction of Arabic as a Turkish Language)* (İstanbul: Maarif Matbaasi, 1944).

10. Büşra Ersanlı, *İktidar ve Tarih, Türkiye'de "Resmi Tarih" Tezinin Oluşumu (1929–1937)*, (Political Power & History, "Official History" Thesis in Turkey), Istanbul, AFA, 1992 (2nd expanded edition, 1996, 1998, 4th edition İletişim Yayınları 2002, 2006, and 2008), 139–230.

11. Ersanlı, in *passim*, and p. 216 for Anthony Smith, *Ethnic Origins of Nations* (Oxford: Basil Blackwell, 1986) discussion of central Anatolian Hittite identity to justify moving the capitol from Istanbul to Ankara, 162.

12. Ersanlı, 205–20; Wolfram Eberhard, *Çin: Sinolojiye Giris (China: Introduction to Sinology)* (Ankara Üniversitesi Yayınları, no. 6, 1946); idem., *Çin Tarihi (History of China)* (Ankara: Türk Tarih Kurumu, 1947); idem., *Conquerors and Rulers: Social Forces in Medieval China* (Leiden: E. J. Brill, 1970). The German Sinologist Eberhard's US publications made use of his work in Ankara to continue this transnational multiethnic approach to Chinese history. Zeki Velidi Togan, political activist of the revolution in Russia and a brilliant scholar of Turkish history in Eurasia from Russia, settled in Turkey after the Bolshevik Revolution.

He introduced the scholarly study of this ancient Turkish historiography to the few Turkish students here who might have been interested, but, lacking the necessary Russian and Chinese; they were mostly incapable of following in his tracks. It is hard to be proudly fascinated with one's ancient roots if they are inaccessible, as far away as Ulan Bator or the Silk Road terrain in Central Asia, which at the time was under harsh Stalinism.

13. Ersanlı, appendix on high school textbooks.
14. Adeeb Khalid, "Pan-Islamism in Practice: The Rhetoric of Muslim Unity and its Uses" in Elizabeth Özdalga (ed.), *Late Ottoman Society: The Intellectual Legacy* 201–24 (Milton Park: RoutledgeCurzon, 2005).
15. Selim Deringil, *The Well-Protected Domains: Ideology and the Legitimation of Power in the Ottoman Empire* (London: I. B. Taurus, 1999), 158.
16. This is the *Mer'at ül-Harameyn* of Eyub Sabri Pasha, Istanbul, 1898, 3 vols., as cited by Ussama Makdisi, "Ottoman Orientalism," *The American Historical Review* 107:3 (June 2002), 768–96, especially 788.
17. See the influential volume edited by Rashid Khalidi et al., *Origins of Arab Nationalism* (New York: Columbia University Press, 1991).
18. Hasan Kayalı, *Arabs and Young Turks: Ottomanism, Arabism, and Islamism in the Ottoman Empire, 1908–1918* (Berkeley: University of California Press, 1997).
19. Amy Mills, James A. Reilly and Christine Phillou, "The Ottoman Empire from Present to Past: Memory and Ideology in Turkey and the Arab World," *Comparative Studies of South Asia, Africa and the Middle East* 31:1 (2011) 133–36.
20. Shafiq Ghurbal cited in Gabriel Piterberg, "The Tropes of Stagnation and Awakening in Nationalist Historical Consciousness: The Egyptian Case," in James Jankowski and Israel Gershonş (eds.), *Rethinking Nationalism in the Arab Middle East* (New York: Columbia University Press, 1997), 56–57.
21. See Charles D. Smith, who studied Arab historiography from the vantage point of World War I in his "Historiographies of World War I and the Emergence of the Contemporary Middle East" in Amy Singer, Y. Hakan Erdem and Israel Gershoni (eds.), *Middle East Historiographies: Narrating the Twentieth Century* (Seattle: University of Washington Press, 2006) 39–69. According to Smith, the writings in English by non-Arab scholars on Anglo-French imperialism in the Arab lands during the war are by and large a defense of that imperialism, at odds with general colonial historiography. Examples are Elie Kedourie, *In the Anglo-Arab Labyrinth: The McMahon-Husayn Correspondence and Its Interpretations, 1914–1939* (Cambridge: Cambridge University Press, 1976), and Isaiah Friedman, *The Question of Palestine: British-Jewish-Arab Relations, 1914–1918* (London: Transaction Publishers, 1973). As for scholarship by Arab authors in English, two trends can be differentiated: Abd al-Latif Tibawi argued that Palestine was definitely included in the British promises, and Albert Hourani approached the issue more historically and argued that both Anglo and French imperialisms left the settlement of their imperial objectives for later.
22. Fuat Köprülü, *Osmanlı Devleti'nin Kuruluşu* (*The Foundation of the Ottoman State*) (Ankara: Türk Tarih Kurumu, 1959); idem., *Bizans Müesseselerinin Osmanlı Müesseselerine Tesiri* (*The Impact of Byzantian Institutions on Ottoman Institutions*) (Istanbul: Ötüken, 1981 reprint). Beginning in 1939, Barkan wrote numerous articles that formed the basis for debate over Ottoman land tenure and political economy. His first English publication is "The Price Revolutions of the Sixteenth Century: A Turning Point in the Economic History of the Near East" *IJMES* VI, 3–28; idem., *Süleymaniye Cami ve Imareti Inşaatı (The Construciton of the Süleymaniye Mosque Complex)(1550–1557)* (Ankara: Türk Tarih Kurumu, 1972). See also

Halil Inalcık, *The Ottoman Empire, the Classical Age, 1300–1600* (London: Widenfeld and Nicholson, 1972).

23. For a review of this post-Annales mood in Turkish economic history and historiography, see Oktay Özel and Gökhan Çetinsaya,"Türkiye'de Osmanlı Tarihçiliğinin Son Çeyrek Yüzyılı: Bir Bilanço Denemesi," *Toplum ve Bilim* 91:Kış (2001), 8–38.

24. Huri Islamoglu and Çaglar Keyder, "Agenda for Ottoman History," *Review* (Summer 1977) 31–55; reprinted in Anne Bailey and Josep Llobera (eds.), *The Asiatic Mode of Production* (London: Macmillan, 1981) 301–24, and in Huri İslamoğlu (ed.), *The Ottoman Empire and the World Economy* (Cambridge: Cambridge University Press, 1987) 42–62; also published in German, Hungarian and Serbo-Croatian.

25. Şevket Pamuk, *The Ottoman Empire and European Capitalism, 1820–1913, Trade, Investment and Production* (Cambridge: Cambridge University Press, 1987); Çağlar Keyder, *State and Class in Turkey, a Study in Capitalist Development* (London: New York: Verso, 1987); Resat Kasaba, *The Ottoman Empire and the World Economy: The Nineteenth Century* (Albany: State University of New York Press, 1988). For an assessment of the new approaches to global capitalism, see Meltem Toksöz, "Reform ve Yönetim: Devletten Topluma, Merkezden Bölgeye Osmanlı Modernizasyonu," in Halil İnalcık, Mehmet Seyitdanlıoğlu (eds.), *Tanzimat: Değişim Sürecinde Osmanlı İmparatorluğu* (İstanbul: İş Bankası Kültür Yayınları, 2011).

26. Donald Quataert, *Social Disintegration and Popular Resistance* (New York: New York University Press, 1983). Earlier dissatisfaction with the Wallersteinian approach can be found in his articles, one example of which is "Limited Revolution: The Impact of the Anatolian Railway on Turkish Transportation and the Provisioning of Istanbul," *The Business History Review* 51:2 (1977), 139–60.

27. Suraiya Faroqhi, *Approaching Ottoman History: An Introduction to the Sources* (Cambridge: Cambridge University Press, 1999), as excellent entry into the state of Ottoman historiography today; Suraiya Faroqhi, *Pilgrims and Sultans* (Cambridge: Cambridge University Press, 1994); idem., *Towns and Townsmen of Ottoman Anatolia, Trade, Crafts, and Food Production in an Urban Setting* (Cambridge: Cambridge University Press, 1984); idem., *Men of Modest Substance, House Owners and House Property in Seventeenth Century Ankara and Kayseri* (Cambridge: Cambridge University Press, 1987); Huricihan İslamoğlu, *State and Peasant in the Ottoman Empire* (Leiden: E. J. Brill, 1994); Huricihan İslamoğlu (ed.), *Ottoman Empire and the World Economy* (Leiden: E. J. Brill, 1994).

28. Suraiya Faroqhi, Contribution to Halil Inalcik with Donald Quartaert, *An Economic and Social History of the Ottoman Empire, 1300–1914* (Cambridge: Cambridge University Press, 1994).

29. Mehmet Genç, *Osmanlı İmparatorluğu'nda Devlet ve Ekonomi* (İstanbul: Ötüken Yayınları, 2000); Halil Sahillioğlu, *Studies on Ottoman Economic and Social History* (İstanbul: IRCICA, 1999).

30. See Ariel Salzmann, *Tocqueville in the Ottoman Empire Rival Paths to the Modern State* (Leiden: Brill, 2004); This trend in comparative frameworks with a critique of Eurocentrism has however not meant a new direction in European/western historical research and/or teaching in Turkey. That is to say, scholarship in Turkey has not moved beyond its own geography, former and present, as there are very few historians who do primary research into European history. Exceptions are few: Halil Berktay, *Kabileden Feodalizme* (İstanbul: Kaynak Yayınları, 1983) which discusses the transition from tribal society to feudalism in Europe and compares the Ottoman transition. İslamoğlu voiced for the first time the necessity of not just reading European histories (Ottoman Turks were already doing this in the late eighteenth century) but conducting original research on European history. Marshall G. S. Hodgson and William McNeill can be recognized as salient threads in the Ottomanists' critique of Euro-centered world-history narratives.

31. Contested Ottoman history is not just the nation-state-engendered history of Turkey and the Middle East; there is also the contested historical platform of other Balkan countries founded upon former Ottoman provinces and territories, either by nationalist independence movements or as European imperialist projects. As Maria Todorova, the eminent historian of the Ottoman Balkans, has said, "It is ludicrous to talk about the Ottoman legacy in the Balkans. The Balkans are the Ottoman legacy." The national/local historical discourse today in Greece and Bulgaria, for example, has developed an integrative view of the Ottoman phase of their respective societies. Hence the challenge of global history in the region is to come up with a de-nationalized explanatory narrative that explains the shared historical process of populations now divided among different nation-states whose grand narratives of independence and nationalism need to be deconstructed. The issue is particularly relevant in view of the prospective integration of Turkey into a Europe with an Eastern Europe that includes the Ottoman Balkan legacy. Since the 1990s, Turkish, Greek historians and Balkan historians have begun to discuss the historical process of the Ottoman world as a shared experience, thus contributing to the deconstruction of the methodological boundaries of Area Studies.

32. For the transition narrative, see Erik J. Zürcher, *Turkey a Modern History* (London, New York; I. B. Tauris). For a favorable account of the Republican revolution, see Bernard Lewis, *The Emergence of Modern Turkey* (New York: Oxford University Press, 2002) revised edition of 1961 original.

33. Samuel Moyn and Andrew Sartori, *Global Intellectual History* (New York: Columbia University Press, 2013); Joseph R. Levenson, *Confucian China and Its Modern Fate: A Trilogy* (Berkeley: University of California Press, 1968).

34. Şerif Mardin, *The Genesis of Young Ottoman Thought* (Princeton: Princeton University Press, 1961). Other leading names are Şükrü Hanioğlu, *The Young Turks in Opposition* (New York: Oxford University Press 1995), and Selim Deringil, *The Well-Protected Domains: Ideology and the Legitimation of Power in the Ottoman Empire* (London: I. B. Taurus, 1999).

35. İlber Ortaylı, *İmparatorluğun En Uzun Yüzyılı* (İstanbul: Timaş Yayınları, 1983); Ortaylı's concept of the Long Nineteenth Century is in line with the discussion in Jürgen Osterhammel, "In Search of a Nineteenth Century," *GHI Bulletin* 32 (2003), 28.

36. Selim Deringil, *The Well-Protected Domains*, in Edhem Eldem (ed.), *A History of the Ottoman Bank* (Istanbul: Osmanlı Bankası, 1999); idem., *French Trade in Istanbul in the Eighteenth Century* (Leiden: Brill, 1999); Zafer Toprak, *Türkiye'de Milli Iktisat 1908–1918* (*National Economy in Turkey 1908–1918*) (Ankara: Yurt Yayınları, 1982).

37. As example of internationalization, Halil Inalcık with Donald Quataert, *An Economic and Social History of the Ottoman Empire, 1300–1914* (Cambridge: Cambridge University Press, 1994); Suraiya Faroqhi, Bruce McGowan, Donald Quataert and Sevket Pamuk, *An Economic and Social History of the Ottoman Empire 1600–1914* (Cambridge: Cambridge University Press, 1994).

38. Hisham Sharabi, *Arab Intellectuals and the West: The Formative Years, 1875–1914* (Baltimore: The Johns Hopkins University Press, 1970).

39. See the articles in Marwan R. Buheiry (ed.), *Intellectual Life in the Arab East, 1890–1939* (Beirut: American University in Beirut Press, 1981).

40. Meltem Toksöz, *Nomads, Migrants and Cotton in the Eastern Mediterranean: The Making of the Adana-Mersin Region in the Ottoman Empire 1850–1908* (Leiden: Brill, 2010).

41. Engin Akarlı, *The Long Peace: Ottoman Lebanon, 1861–1920* (London: Centre for Lebanese Studies and I. B. Tauris, 1993); Kamal Salibi, *Crossroads to Civil War: Lebanon, 1958–76*

(London, 1976). Abdul Rahim Abu-Husayn and Engin Akarlı, "The Subordination of the Hawran Druzes in 1910, the Ottoman Perspective," in Kamal Salibi (ed.), *Druze Realities and Perceptions* (London: Druze Heritage Foundation, 2005), 115–28.

42. Ussama Makdisi, *The Culture of Sectarianism: Community, History, and Violence in Nineteenth-Century Ottoman Lebanon* (Berkeley: University of California Press, 2000); Jens Hanssen, Thomas Philipp, Stefan Weber (eds.), *The Empire in the City: Arab Provincial Capitals in the Late Ottoman Empire* (Würzburg: Ergon in Kommission, 2002); Malek Sharif, *Imperial Norms and Local Realities: The Ottoman Municipal Laws and The Municipality of Beirut (1860–1908)* (Würzburg: Ergon, 2014).

43. Timothy Mitchell, *Colonizing Egypt* (Berkeley: University of California Press, 1988).

44. Amy Mills, James A. Reilly and Christine Phillou, "The Ottoman Empire from Present to Past: Memory and Ideology in Turkey and the Arab World," *Comparative Studies of South Asia, Africa and the Middle East* 31:1 (2011), 135.

45. Deringil continues: "We are at least able to discuss the Armenian issue, even if we risk rowdy nationalists throwing rotten tomatoes and eggs at us. Murat Belge actually called this progress because, he declared, before, in the 1970s it used to be the bullets" (2008).

46. In this sense, it is difficult to define a clear-cut divide between "national historiography" and international scholarship in today's global academic world. One can, however, still distinguish between divergent discourses that circulate among historians working at home or abroad. Cemal Kafadar of Harvard and Sükrü Hanioğlu of Princeton are examples of Turkish historians in the States.

47. Examples of Turkish language publications are Feridun Emecen's monographic studies of Black Sea communities and the Ottoman classical period. Emecen's recent work is on the religious and political controversies concerning the biography of Selim I, known as Selim the Grim, who defeated the Safavid Dynasty in the sixteenth century. Feridun Emecen, *Yavuz Sultan Selim* (İstanbul: Kapı Yayınları, 2016). On modernization in the Ottoman Empire, one should mention at least one classic work: Mehmet Seyitdanlıoğlu, *Tanzimat Devrinde Meclis-i Vâlâ, 1838–1868* (Ankara: TTK, 1994). Seyitdanlıoğlu also edited a volume with Halil İnalcık on the perception of Tanzimat reforms that now includes recent works on Ottoman modernization as a global affair; see his *Tanzimat—Değişim Sürecinde Osmanlı İmparatorluğu* (revised edition, İstanbul: İş Bankası Kültür Yayınları, 2011). Another recently reprinted classic is from Halil İnalcık, *Rönesans Avrupası—Türkiye'nin Batı Medeniyetiyle Özdeşleşme Süreci* (Istanbul: İş Bankası Kültür Yayınları, 2011). But also see Ali Akyıldız, *Osmanlı Bürokrasisi ve Modernleşme* (Istanbul: İletişim, 2004) on Ottoman bureaucracy and modernization and *Osmanlı Arap Coğrafyası ve Avrupa Emperyalizmi* (İstanbul: İş Bankası Kultur Yayınları, 2015) on Ottoman Arab Geography and European Imperialism.

48. See Selçuk Esenbel, *Japan, Turkey, and the World of Islam* (Leiden: Brill, Global Oriental, 2011); "Japan's Global Claim to Asia and the World of Islam: Transnational Nationalism and World Power 1900–1945," *The American Historical Review* (October 2004), 1140–70. The roots of the above research began in Istanbul back in the 1990s with "İslam Dünyasında Japonya İmgesi: Abdürresid İbrahim ve Geç Meiji Dönemi Japonları" I, II (The Image of Japan in the World of Islam: Abdurresid Ibrahim and the Late Meiji Japanese) *Toplumsal Tarih* (Journal of Social History) Temmuz (July) 1995, (August), 18–26.

49. Renee Worringer's work on the Islamic Middle East and Japan and Cemil Aydin on comparative Pan-Asianism and Pan-Islam as intellectual history are examples in the United States; Sakamoto Tsutomu, Misawa Nobuo and others in Japan; Selçuk Esenbel, Nadir Özbek, Merthan Dündar and Erdal Küçükyalçin in Turkey. They represent the global nature of the scholars who are tracing the connections between Japan and the Muslim world. Turan

Kayaoglu on Extraterritoriality in Japan, the Ottoman Empire, and China is a recent effort to place the Ottoman experience into a global comparative frame. Renee Worringer (ed.), *The Islamic Middle East and Japan* (Princeton: Wiener Markus Publishing, 2006); Cemil Aydin, *The Politics of Anti-Westernism in Asia: Visions of World Order in Pan-Islamic and Pan-Asian Thought* (New York: Columbia University, 2007); Turan Kayaoglu, *Legal Imperialism: Sovereignty and Extraterritoriality in Japan, the Ottoman Empire, and China* (Cambridge: Cambridge University Press, 2014).

CHAPTER 6
THE WORLD HISTORY PROJECT: GLOBAL HISTORY IN THE NORTH AMERICAN CONTEXT
Jerry H. Bentley

North America was not the birthplace of global approaches to the past, but it has offered a fertile environment for global historical approaches of several distinctive species. Indeed, since the 1960s and especially since the 1980s, North America has nourished a remarkable development that I refer to here as "the world history project." By this term I mean to imply that world history has not simply represented one among many alternative analytical approaches to the past—political history, economic history, art history and the like. Rather, more like women's history, gender history, labor history and environmental history, the North American version of world history has served a recognizable intellectual agenda.

First, though, what's in a name? The rubric most commonly used in North America for global approaches to the past is "world history." Most North American practitioners recognize no significant distinction between "world history" and "global history," but use the two terms interchangeably. This usage differs from practice in some other parts of the world. In China, for example, "world history" (*shijie shi*) usually refers either to a broad survey of all the world's societies or else to expertise in foreign (non-Chinese) history, while "global history" (*quanqiu lishi*) refers to analysis of historical problems and developments from global perspectives. For the most part, North American historians have not found this kind of distinction to be particularly useful. Their reluctance to adopt such a terminology perhaps stems from the fact that in North America, "world history" had become the default term for global historical analysis at least as early as the 1950s. As a result, "world history" referred both to a general survey of world societies and to the analysis of historical problems and processes from global perspectives. North American historians have manifested much less interest in matters of terminology—"world history" or "global history" or some other label—than in the kinds of analyses and studies historians have offered under whatever rubric they have chosen to characterize their work.

The intellectual agenda of the world history project in North America has involved three general concerns. First, with respect to scholarship, world historians have sought to develop alternatives to Eurocentric analyses of the global past and to identify alternatives to nation-states as frameworks of historical analysis. Eurocentric assumptions and a fixation on nation-states have long been deeply engrained features of professional historical scholarship—ideological associations that the discipline of history acquired as it became a professional field of knowledge in the nineteenth century. In dealing with these issues and the analytical problems they created, historians in North America created a new world history dramatically different from earlier versions that approached the global past in ways that were more philosophical or speculative than empirical. The new world history employs the methods and techniques of professional historical scholarship as they have developed since the nineteenth century, while at the same time striving to overcome the problems of Eurocentric and nation-centric history.[1] Second, while pursuing these general scholarly goals in basic research as well as analytical and synthetic works, world historians in North America have also devoted serious attention to educational programs in world history. Scholarship in the new world history has deeply influenced the development of North American educational programs, especially in secondary, higher and postgraduate education. In North America more than in most other regions, educational programs in their turn have had significant implications for the development of the new world history as a distinctive approach to the global past. Third, many if not all world historians in North America have viewed their work as harboring important implications for their larger society. While they do not view the new world history as an overtly political or ideological expression, most of the new world historians have held political and social views that, in the North American context, are liberal or progressive. They fully understand that every history reflects the historian's own perspective, but they reject efforts to make world history into a vehicle promoting political, partisan, patriotic, religious or other ideologies. And they believe that a global perspective is crucial for a realistic understanding of world history, which in turn is a matter of deep importance for any democratic society.[2]

This chapter will proceed by considering the origins of the new world history in North America in the 1960s and 1970s, the emergence of several different kinds of institutions that have directly supported the new world history and the scholarship that has defined the new world history since the 1980s. The three main concerns on the intellectual agenda of the new world historians will appear as themes threading their way through the chapter, and they will serve to justify the claim that the new world history is not simply one among many possible approaches to the past, but the foundation of the world history movement in North America.

Paths toward a new world history in North America

Historians in North America—which for purposes of this chapter means the United States and Canada—did not invent global approaches to the past. In one form or another, global approaches have been features of historical writing since antiquity. The Greek historian Herodotus and the Chinese scholar Sima Qian wrote histories focusing principally on their own countries, but they located their own countries' experiences in a much larger geographical and cultural context. The Persian historians Ala'iddin Ata-Malik Juvaini and Rashid al-Din took the Mongol empires as their focus, but they recognized that a proper understanding of the Mongol empires required awareness of the hemispheric context in which the empires emerged, flourished and declined. Enlightenment historians took even more ambitious global approaches to the past: Göttingen historians Johann Christoph Gatterer and August Ludwig von Schlözer aimed to construct a professional *Universalgeschichte* that would illuminate the hidden connections between distant events. Global conflicts of the twentieth century prompted fresh rounds of global historical reflection, as H. G. Wells, Oswald Spengler, Arnold Toynbee and others looked into the past in search of keys to unlock understanding of the dynamics driving historical development. All these works were available to specialists in the North American academy, but in most cases, they appealed more to popular audiences than to professional historians. Indeed, since the mid-nineteenth century, professional historians in North America had taken the state, and particularly the nation-state, as their default unit of analysis. History, it seemed, was a property attaching to nation-states, not other social forms. How did it happen that some historians began to look beyond the nation-state and find larger and different units of historical analysis?

The world history project in North America arose from an effort to develop a new kind of world history that was quite different from the earlier versions associated with premodern historians, Enlightenment scholars and speculative visionaries like Spengler and Toynbee. This New World began to take shape after the Second World War. The epicenter of the movement in its early years was Chicago. William H. McNeill and Marshall G. S. Hodgson, both of the University of Chicago, and Leften S. Stavrianos of Northwestern University began to work independently to think about the global past from fresh perspectives. It was a missed opportunity that for personal, political, ideological and temperamental reasons, the three men did not collaborate, consult or even communicate much with one another. In his autobiography, McNeill recalls that he had a friendly relationship with Hodgson, but that the two men rarely spoke about historical matters—even though they occupied adjacent offices at the University of Chicago—and he refers to himself and Stavrianos as "rivals" who from the beginning of their acquaintance were "wary of one another." As a result, each man explored fresh perspectives individually, with no real opportunity to benefit from the insights, reactions and critiques that the others might have offered.[3]

Of the trio, McNeill seems to have been the first to begin thinking seriously about world history. As early as 1938, having just taken his baccalaureate degree from the University of Chicago, McNeill wrote a ninety-five-page paper (never published) entitled "Nemesis: A Study of the Rise and Fall of Civilizations." His interest deepened the following year when he happened upon the first three volumes, just published, of Arnold Toynbee's *Study of History*. He later became a friend and worked alongside Toynbee but eventually found himself disappointed in the man who had once piqued his imagination. During the late 1950s, by then a professor at the University of Chicago, McNeill worked on his magnum opus, *The Rise of the West: A History of the Human Community* (published 1963). More than any other single book, *The Rise of the West* influenced the early emergence of world history in North America. In an age of increasing specialization, McNeill explored the kinds of large-scale patterns of historical development that academic historians had largely abandoned in favor of highly precise and detailed studies. Yet he took an empirical approach and wrote in an idiom that historians recognized—unlike Spengler,

Toynbee and others who indulged speculative urges, allowing them to dictate their works. McNeill also presented an attractive and plausible thesis arguing that the main dynamic of world history was the transfer of knowledge, skills and technology from centers of high development to less-developed societies. Thus his work drew historians' attention to processes of cross-cultural engagements, which had been all but invisible in professional historical scholarship since the mid-nineteenth century. Even though McNeill had few graduate students at the University of Chicago, his influence radiated widely through *The Rise of the West* as well as later works reflecting his global vision of the past, including *Europe's Steppe Frontier* (1964), *Plagues and Peoples* (1976) and *The Pursuit of Power* (1982).[4]

While McNeill worked out his vision of world history, Hodgson developed his own sometimes quirky but nevertheless highly interesting and provocative views. An expert on Islam, Hodgson took a broad view of "Islamdom," the neologism he invented on the example of Christendom to refer to the Islamic world. His three-volume magnum opus, *The Venture of Islam*, located "Islamdom" in its hemispheric context, a framework that he took quite seriously. As early as 1941, he was writing papers and publishing articles arguing that a proper understanding of world history would entail investigation of interactions between societies on a hemispheric basis. As a devout Quaker and pacifist, Hodgson also brought a sharp moral sense to his work. He took it as his special mission to attack Eurocentric views that assumed industrial Europe as the standard of modernity. He even unleashed a withering attack against the Mercator projection of the world, which he savaged as a "Jim Crow projection," because of its exaggeration of Europe's size in relation to other world regions. Like McNeill, Hodgson had few students—partly because he died unexpectedly in 1968 at the age of forty-seven—but his ideas reverberated among scholars of the Islamic world as well as others who sought ways to think about large-scale historical processes. His contempt for Eurocentric views also resonated among younger historians who were increasingly taking critical approaches to inherited historiography and its assumptions about the superiority of European modernity.[5]

Stavrianos, a man of enormous passion and energy, concentrated his efforts on the reform of history education in both secondary schools and universities. After the Second World War, as the United States assumed ever more prominent roles in the larger world, Stavrianos came to believe that American students needed a new kind of global awareness. As early as 1952, he was working to launch a course in world history at Northwestern University. After the first Sputnik flight in 1957, he organized a World History Project to introduce global perspectives into high school curricula, later expanding the effort to higher education curricula as well. His efforts at curricular reform enjoyed modest success, but he laid a foundation for others to build upon in the form of numerous articles advocating global historical perspectives as well as his own textbooks and studies. He lambasted the so-called world history that failed to look beyond Western civilization, and he famously called for historians to adopt a global perspective on the past, to detach themselves from their own societies and traditions as if they were writing history from the moon: "What does this new perspective mean and what does it involve? It means the perspective of an observer perched on the moon rather than ensconced in London or

Paris or Washington." His college-level textbook—originally titled *A Global History of Man* (1962), abbreviated to *A Global History* in later editions—was among the earliest to take the world beyond Europe seriously. His Marxist accounts of the Third World (*Global Rift*) and long-term social and economic history (*Lifelines from Our Past*) also influenced younger scholars. Finally, by sheer force of his exuberant personality, he inspired like-minded historians to work on behalf of world history even though they faced obstacles.[6]

Chicago might have been the epicenter of the movement to develop new approaches to the global past, but it was not the only site of fresh thinking. In 1953, Philip D. Curtin began teaching his own brand of comparative world history at the University of Wisconsin, and in 1959 he collaborated with colleagues in the fields of southeast Asian, south Asian and Latin American history (John Smail, John F. Richards and John Leddy Phelan, respectively) in establishing a graduate-level Program in Comparative World History. Curtin and his colleagues did not favor the kind of synthetic world history that McNeill and Stavrianos produced. Rather, they encouraged a kind of global comparative history that analyzed several salient cases in different world regions in order to understand a general historical issue such as cross-cultural trade, European imperialism or plantation societies. Curtin began to publish his own comparative studies only in the 1980s, but he advocated his approach while supervising about a hundred graduate students at Wisconsin before departing for the Johns Hopkins University in 1975. Through the Program in Comparative World History, Curtin and his colleagues managed to imbue a deep sense of commitment to comparative analysis in many of their students. Indeed, Curtin's students make up a remarkable network of young historians who since the 1980s have constituted perhaps the core constituency of contemporary world historians in North America. Their numbers include Michael P. Adas, Ross E. Dunn, Richard M. Eaton, Myron Echenberg, Allen Howard, Craig A Lockard, Patrick Manning, Joseph C. Miller and Patricia Seed, among others from Wisconsin, as well as Lauren Benton and William K. Storey, from Johns Hopkins.[7]

Meanwhile, two additional scholars also made early contributions to the world history project: Alfred W. Crosby and Immanuel Wallerstein. Crosby broadened the thematic focus of world history by placing large-scale environmental developments on historians' agenda. Environmental history was just beginning to emerge as a distinct approach as the new world historians were developing fresh approaches to the global past. Since environmental processes often disregard national, geographical and cultural boundary lines, they became convenient focal points of analysis for world historians. In the hands of Crosby and others, environmental historical analysis was particularly helpful in explaining the process of European expansion after 1492. Wallerstein, a historical sociologist, devoted his early work to Africa, where he became well acquainted with the effects of European imperialism and exploitation. In seeking to apply his understanding of Africa to the larger world, he drew theoretical inspiration from Karl Marx, Fernand Braudel and the Latin American school of dependency economics. The result was world system analysis. Highly influential among historical sociologists, the world system approach experienced a cooler reception among professional historians, who found Wallerstein's construction excessively rigid and insufficiently attentive to the particularities of individual societies. Yet historians as well as sociologists appreciated Wallerstein's attention to the systemic linkages that helped to explain the patterns of global economic development.

What accounts for such a sudden, spontaneous, uncoordinated outpouring of scholarly effort seeking fresh perspectives on the global past? McNeill and Stavrianos spent their working lives in the United States, but they were both Canadian by birth, and I suspect that they were sensitive to assumptions of superiority among US historians who understood their own society as the heir of Europe and the highest expression of European modernity. Curtin and Wallerstein were both experts on Africa, and they certainly had no use for assumptions that European peoples had discovered a privileged path to modernity. Beyond that, all of the early world historians lived and worked at a moment when North America loomed large in world history. In his retrospective reflections on his magnum opus, McNeill readily conceded that

> *The Rise of the West* should be seen as an expression of the postwar imperial mood in the United States. Its scope and conception is a form of intellectual imperialism, for it takes on the world as a whole, and it tries to understand global history on the basis of cultural diffusion developed among American anthropologists in the 1930s.[8]

Indeed, world history emerged as a distinctive intellectual project in the context of a particular political economy. North Americans had economic and security interests in the larger world, and they possessed the resources to sponsor research and educational programs to develop and disseminate knowledge about that world. The postwar era was the age of flourishing area studies programs, when North American scholars ventured out into the world to familiarize themselves with the languages and cultural traditions of peoples in distant lands. It is hardly surprising that some historians working in this intellectual environment conceived a desire to construct a broader and more realistic understanding of the global past.

Thus as it took shape in the 1960s and early 1970s, the world history project in North America manifested several distinctive characteristics that combined to make up a new approach to the global past. The scholars who laid the foundations for the new world history worked to bring focus to large-scale historical processes and patterns that previous generations of professional historians had mostly ignored in favor of highly detailed empirical studies of local and national experiences. They recognized that since Leopold von Ranke, professional historians had taken the nation-state as the default category of their craft, and they consciously sought alternative frameworks of historical analysis and tested fresh ways of thinking about the dynamics of historical processes with large-scale effects. Their efforts entailed the recognition of geographical and cultural frameworks much larger than nation-states—civilizations, global economic systems, environmental zones and the like. The new world historians also took a rigorously empirical and largely materialist approach to the global past, rejecting the philosophical perspectives and speculative impulses that had characterized the works of Spengler, Toynbee and others. Recognizing that Eurocentric assumptions had contributed to a highly distorted understanding of the global past, these historians placed high value on comparative and cross-cultural analyses that took advantage of area studies scholarship and helped them develop alternatives to Eurocentric accounts. For the most part, the new world historians did not seek explicitly to advance any particular political or ideological agenda, but at the same time, and not coincidentally, they mostly held liberal and progressive political views. After all, they found serious problems with a tradition of historical scholarship that had served, among other things, to construct an image of Europe and Western civilization more generally as the standard of modernity while assuming that other lands and peoples were in one or more ways deficient with respect to Europe—an image that served to legitimize and justify conservative and imperialist policies.

Institutions: The World History Association, the *Journal of World History* and educational programs

Until the 1980s, the world history project was the work of individual scholars, some of whom knew one another and formed loose networks, but most of whom worked more or less independently. As individual scholars, the early world historians enjoyed the general respect of their colleagues for their basic research and publications, but the field of world history was invisible in the landscape of the history profession. There were numerous survey courses of world history at the levels of both secondary and higher education, although these courses varied wildly in approach: a few undertook a serious effort at global historical analysis, along the lines Stavrianos had promoted, but many were basically courses in Western civilization with perhaps a bit of attention to other parts of the world.

The world history project began to achieve institutional form in the 1980s. First came the WHA, which a group of young world historians founded in 1982. The WHA was the immediate outgrowth of a teaching conference sponsored by the American Historical Association (AHA) in cooperation with the United States Air Force Academy (USAFA) in Colorado Springs, Colorado. Opened in 1954 as the youngest of the US military academies, the USAFA recognized early on that it needed to educate cadets—many of whom would serve in distant lands—about the world beyond North America. In 1968, the USAFA established a survey course in modern world history, rather than Western civilization, as its required introductory course.[9] Firmly committed to this course, but without a large permanent faculty of professional historians, the USAFA called on the AHA for guidance. The result was the World History Teaching Conference (May 12–14, 1982), which was held on the campus of the USAFA.

The atmosphere of the 1982 conference was electric. Since they had publicly announced the conference only in April 1982, organizers anticipated no more than forty or fifty attendees. In fact, more than 180 historians made their way from New York, California, Hawai'i and elsewhere into the Rocky Mountains and converged on

Colorado Springs—at precisely the moment that a late spring blizzard also made its appearance—forcing the organizers to scramble to arrange lodging, transportation, food and logistics. World history was not yet a recognized field in the larger discipline of history, but there clearly was a deep reservoir of interest in the approach. The conference program featured major presentations by William H. McNeill, Ross E. Dunn, Kevin Reilly, Cyril E. Black and Craig A. Lockard, among others. Participants included many who later figured as prominent leaders of the WHA and the larger world history project. Although the announced focus of the conference was the teaching of world history, several participants—especially Lockard and myself—argued that in order to flourish, world history needed a research dimension that established comparative and cross-cultural analyses as appropriate approaches to understand the global past.[10]

The idea of founding a professional association of world historians had been an item of discussion at least since 1980. One effect of the 1982 conference at the USAFA was to bring a critical mass of energetic historians together, and one of the principal topics of conversation during the conference was the formation of a world history association. During the following months, a core group of individuals, including Reilly, Dunn, Lockard and others, worked out a plan for a group they proposed to call "World History Association." At the next annual conference of the AHA, they called a meeting of interested parties, and more than a hundred participants voted to found the WHA and elect Reilly president *pro tempore* until the organization could organize membership, draft a constitution and hold regular elections. As Reilly said in his public announcement of the events, "A World History Association was established December 28, 1982, at the AHA meeting in Washington, DC."[11] With support from Drexel University in Philadelphia, the WHA began to publish a biennial newsletter, the *World History Bulletin*, in the spring of 1983. The new organization also began to sponsor sessions on world history at the annual AHA conference, and a group of energetic members in the Rocky Mountain region teamed up with the USAFA to hold several additional teaching conferences in Colorado Springs. In 1992, the WHA organized the first of its own international conferences.

The purpose of the 1982 conference at the USAFA was to promote teaching in world history, and much of the early work of the WHA revolved around teaching issues. Yet from the beginning, the organization took research and publication as equally important dimensions of world history. To quote Article II of the WHA constitution: "The object of the association shall be the promotion of studies of world history through the encouragement of research, teaching, and publication."[12]

Toward that end, the WHA joined forces with a group of historians at the University of Hawai'i who proposed to found a new *JWH* that would reflect the interests of the new world history. From 1953 to 1972, UNESCO had published a highly interesting journal under the title *Cahiers d'histoire mondiale*, with the subtitles *Journal of World History* and *Cuadernos de historia mundial*. The UNESCO journal presented first-rate scholarship, much of which had broad appeal. Yet *Cahiers d'histoire mondiale* was a journal of world history primarily in the sense that it would publish articles dealing with historical events that occurred in any part of the world. Some of its essays addressed larger comparative or systematic issues, notably including two seminal contributions by Marshall G. S. Hodgson.[13] Yet for all their high quality and inherent interest, most of the articles in the UNESCO journal focused on individual lands, throwing light on the historical development of a single society, such as pharaonic Egypt, Renaissance Italy, colonial Mexico or modern Japan. In any case, the UNESCO journal was defunct.

By contrast, the new *JWH* would feature comparative, cross-cultural and global scholarship on large-scale historical processes such as mass migration, environmental change, biological exchanges, cross-cultural trade, technological diffusion, imperial expansion and the spread of religious and cultural traditions, all of which call for analytical frameworks larger than those conventionally adopted in historical scholarship. Published since 1990, the new *JWH* has indeed served as a forum for scholarship on these and other historical issues that require large-scale, transregional, continental, hemispheric, oceanic or literally global frames of reference. My analysis of the 195 articles that appeared in the first seventeen volumes of the *JWH* (1990–2006) argued that articles frequently explored issues over long periods of time, routinely crossed national, geographical and cultural boundary lines that historians and other scholars have conventionally observed, regularly took large regions as their geographical focus and often put historical experiences in conversation with conceptual, methodological and theoretical issues.[14] Thus alongside the WHA, the new *JWH* served the world history project in North America by making a forum available for new world historians to lay the foundations for fresh approaches to the global past. Since 2006, the *Journal of Global History*, which publishes articles much like those of the *JWH*, has also provided institutional support for the new world history. Although planned in Europe and published in England, North American scholars have figured prominently among the editors, contributors and reviewers of the *Journal of Global History*.

The organization of postgraduate programs in world history represented yet another form of institutional support for the world history project. The Program in Comparative World History at the University of Wisconsin largely disappeared after Philip D. Curtin departed in 1975, although Curtin continued to mentor PhD students on a less formal basis at the Johns Hopkins University. During the 1980s, however, as interest in the emerging field of world history surged—and as colleges and universities increasingly sought to hire faculty who could offer meaningful and thoughtful courses in world history—the demand for formal educational opportunities at postgraduate levels also rose dramatically. As early as 1983, Craig A. Lockard issued an impassioned plea for the development of postgraduate programs and research opportunities in world history.[15] Within two years, the Department of History at the University of Hawai'i had established a PhD field in world history.[16] Similar programs soon followed at Ohio State University, the University of Minnesota, Northeastern University, Rutgers University, University of California campuses at Santa Cruz and Irvine, Washington State University, University of Pittsburgh and others. These various programs undoubtedly have different emphases— the focus at Ohio State University is on world systems, for example, while the program at the University of Minnesota deals with the early-modern world—but all in various ways contribute to a larger effort to develop fresh visions of the global past.

Quite apart from postgraduate programs, the Advanced Placement (AP) course in world history also merits attention as a part of the institutional infrastructure supporting the world history project. "AP" is a trademark of the College Board, an independent, nonprofit corporation that administers the SAT and other standardized exams while also working in many ways to improve secondary school curricula in the interests of preparing students for higher education. AP courses are by definition college-level courses, but they are offered in secondary schools. Students who do well in the courses and post high scores on the ensuing exams receive recognition that they have succeeded in especially rigorous courses, and they sometimes receive higher education credit for their efforts.

The AP course in world history became available in the academic year 2001–02, and it quickly distinguished itself as a remarkable phenomenon on several counts. First, since the new world historians and members of the WHA had developed the curriculum of the course, AP world history reflects the new world history as it has emerged since the 1980s. This is significant, because the AP course is the single most influential course in world history in North American secondary education. As a high-profile course, AP world history tends to influence non-AP courses in world history, so that the perspectives of the new world history extend well beyond the AP program itself. Second, from its inception, AP world history was wildly popular. In 2002, its first year, it was the largest AP course ever launched, with 20,955 exams administered, and over its first decade it experienced explosive growth, with 188,417 students sitting for the tenth exam in 2011. This phenomenal growth of AP world history has attracted attention both for the course and for the new world history that is its foundation. Third, the AP course has created a powerful demand for increased attention to the new world history in the world of higher education. As the AP course grew, it became clear that most secondary school teachers lacked the educational preparation to offer sophisticated courses in the new world history. One reason for the growth of postgraduate programs in world history is precisely to make opportunities available for prospective teachers and in-service teachers to become better acquainted with the themes, theories, methods, concepts and scholarship of the new world history. Beyond postgraduate programs, the demand for education in the new world history has resulted in the organization of undergraduate curricula and literally thousands of institutes and workshops intended to familiarize secondary school teachers with the field. Thus a teaching program originally developed for secondary education has had considerable influence on the development of the new world history at the higher-education level.

Thus far I have mentioned efforts at establishing institutions that were stunningly successful. One notable effort was less successful, at least initially. This was the project to establish national standards for the teaching of world history in secondary schools, which, if it had realized its original plan, might have disseminated the perspectives of the new world history more broadly than the AP course. As things turned out, however, the effort to establish national standards for world history fell victim to the culture wars that raged in North America—particularly in the United States—during the 1990s.

In 1989, US president George H. W. Bush called the governors of the fifty states to a meeting at the University of Virginia to launch a movement to develop rigorous national educational standards in mathematics, natural sciences, English language, US history and world history. Over the following years, groups of scholars and educators worked diligently to hammer out standards and basic curricula for the chosen fields, striving to reflect both current scholarship and the practical possibilities of education at the secondary school level. Primary responsibility for the development of US and world history standards fell to the National Council for History in the Schools at the University of California, Los Angeles, led by Gary Nash, a distinguished historian of the United States. Nash himself led the effort to develop the US history standards, while Ross E. Dunn worked with a parallel team to develop standards for world history. With generous funding from the National Endowment for the Humanities—which Endowment Chairman [sic] Lynne V. Cheney (wife of future US vice president Richard B. Cheney) had personally approved and endorsed—the two groups duly produced a set of national standards and prepared to release them in 1994.[17]

On the eve of their publication, Chairman Cheney published an op-ed column in the *Wall Street Journal* denouncing the history standards that she herself had funded and previously lavished with high praise. The ensuing brouhaha revolved mostly around the standards for US history, which a motley clutch of critics, including radio personality Rush Limbaugh, found to be unpatriotic and insufficiently deferential to the notion that the United States was an exceptional nation that white men of European ancestry had fashioned into a guiding light for the rest of the world. The standards for world history attracted less attention, but they, too, came under attack as conservative critics construed them as attacks on Western civilization and found them insufficiently appreciative of conventional Western European and American exceptionalist ideologies.[18]

The movement to establish national standards in academic fields failed—largely because of resistance from the fifty states—but the controversy over national history standards was certainly not a bright moment for educators in the United States. But did the effort to establish rigorous standards for US and world history truly fail? As educators in individual states worked to develop their own state-level history standards, and as the designers of the AP course in world history developed that course, they all inevitably looked to the national standards prepared by the National Center for History in the Schools as the main published guide for their efforts. Many, though not all, recognized the thoughtfulness of the national standards and appreciated the fact that they reflected the best contemporary scholarship, and they drew considerable inspiration from the national standards for their own purposes. Thus in a peculiar way, the effort to develop national standards for world history ultimately had the effect of promoting the new world history and disseminating its ideas among educators, even if political ideologists and radio commentators railed against its principles.

Research and debates

With several very different forms of institutional support, the new world history emerged as a distinct and widely recognized field of professional historical scholarship. As far as research and publications go, the new world history has taken a largely materialist approach to the global past. A small but important cluster of studies has examined issues of cultural, religious and ideological exchanges in transregional and global contexts.[19] More commonly, however, research has focused on more down-to-earth topics that lend themselves (or at least seem to lend themselves) to fairly precise, highly empirical and often quantitative treatments—topics like cross-cultural trade, economic development, large-scale migration, imperialism, colonialism, epidemic disease, biological diffusion and environmental change.[20] Although it is only a few decades old, the new world history has dramatically influenced the work of professional historians in North America. Quite apart from establishing world history itself as a respectable approach to the past, it has stimulated research on transnational and borderlands issues, prompted efforts to devise alternatives to nation-centered and Eurocentric conceptions of the past and encouraged a reconsideration of national histories by locating them in global context.

Probably the most influential body of scholarship arising from the new world history thus far is that associated with the "California School." At the Third Pacific Centuries Conference held in 1998 at the University of the Pacific (Stockton, California), the historical sociologist Jack A. Goldstone bestowed this name on a group of historians who worked mostly in California and who engaged in the comparative study of Europe and China. Building on several generations' worth of area studies scholarship on Asian economic history, this group has emphasized the similarities in economic development between Europe and China up to about 1800. While no doubt reflecting the rise of China in the contemporary world, this view has also served the California School's larger agenda of developing fresh ways to think about the differential economic trajectories of the two lands after 1800—how to understand why Europe managed to industrialize while China did not. As of 1998, apart from Goldstone himself, the California School included Dennis O. Flynn, Andre Gunder Frank, Arturo Giráldez, James Z. Lee, Robert B. Marks, Kenneth Pomeranz, Richard von Glahn and R. Bin Wong, among others. Since that time, some representatives of the California School have left the Golden State, while other historians based elsewhere in North America (such as Prasannan Parthasarathi and Peter C. Perdue) or Europe (such as Patrick Karl O'Brien and Peer Vries) have engaged the issues and joined the debates first launched in California. Even if the geographical qualification has become less precise, the California School nevertheless has taken on big issues in such a way as to leave its mark not just on the new world history but on historical scholarship in general. As the economic historian Peter A. Coclanis recently noted, "this 'school' constitutes one of the most important, if not *the* most important intellectual complex to have emerged in historical circles over the past two decades."[21] A decade of critique has scored some points against some of the California School's views, and the debate seems to be shifting ground so as to recognize larger roles for science and the state than most of the Californians allowed. Nevertheless, most if not all knowledgeable observers would agree that the collective work of the California School has constructively changed the way scholars think about global economic history by taking Asian lands seriously and searching for alternatives to simplistic Eurocentric explanations for the rise of the West.[22]

The quest for alternatives to Eurocentric history was a prominent feature of the new world history from its earliest days. Hodgson and Stavrianos were especially vocal in their insistence that any world history worthy of the name must take seriously the world beyond Europe. McNeill rarely addressed the issue of Eurocentrism directly, but his historical praxis certainly represented a conscientious effort at global analysis.

In the early, heady days of the new world history, up through the 1980s, the scholars who made this field understood the problem of Eurocentrism somewhat simplistically. They were ready and eager to write the larger world into world history, and they were well aware that the practice of relying on European standards to evaluate the historical development of other societies was a recipe for distortion. Yet they did not seem unduly concerned about the possibility that professional historical scholarship in general relied on principles that imported Eurocentric elements into their work. There has been limited direct engagement of North America's world historians with either postmodern or postcolonial scholars—in spite of my own efforts on several occasions to instigate dialogue in the JWH. Dipesh Chakrabarty and others have argued that professional historical scholarship in all its forms, including world history, is so dependent upon analytical categories and research methods that were the characteristic products of European modernity that it inevitably, willy-nilly, represents a Eurocentric exercise of questionable reliability.[23] Some of the postcolonial critiques strike me as subtle and sophisticated as well as powerful, even if I cannot subscribe to all their details and implications. Speaking for myself only, not the larger community of world historians, I think postmodern and especially postcolonial critics have demonstrated that professional historical scholarship is more fraught with epistemological and conceptual problems than the early world historians realized—but the critics themselves have underestimated the possibility that by conscientious and reflexive practice, historians can produce good world history that, if not perfect, is meaningful and reliable.[24]

Notes

1. Jerry H. Bentley, "The Task of World History," in Jerry H. Bentley (ed.), *The Oxford Handbook of World History* (Oxford: Oxford University Press, 2011), 1–16.
2. Jerry H. Bentley, "Myths, Wagers, and Some Moral Implications of World History," *Journal of World History* 16 (2005), 51–82.
3. William H. McNeill, *The Pursuit of Truth: A Historian's Memoir* (Lexington, KY: University Press of Kentucky, 2005), 66–74, quoting from 67.
4. Apart from McNeill, *The Pursuit of Truth*, see also his account of his relationship with Toynbee in William H. McNeill, *Mythistory and Other Essays* (Chicago: University of Chicago Press, 1986), 174–98; and his retrospective essay, "*The Rise of the West* after Twenty-Five Years," *Journal of World History* 1 (1990), 1–21.
5. For a collection of Hodgson's writings on world history, see Marshall G. S. Hodgson, *Rethinking World History: Essays on Europe, Islam, and World History*, ed. by Edmund Burke, III (Cambridge: Cambridge University Press, 1993). The introduction and conclusion by Burke are valuable contributions in their own right.

6. For his famous view from the moon, see Leften S. Stavrianos, "A Global Perspective in the Organization of World History," in Shirley H. Engle (ed.), *New Perspectives in World History* (Washington, DC: National Council for the Social Studies, 1964), 616–20, quoting from p. 616. For a useful review of Stavrianos's work, see Gilbert Allardyce, "Toward World History: American Historians and the Coming of the World History Course," *Journal of World History* 1 (1990), 23–76, especially 40–62.

7. Curtin outlined his thoughts on graduate education in world history at least twice: Philip D. Curtin, "The Comparative World History Approach," *The History Teacher* 18 (1985), 520–27; and "Graduate Teaching in World History," *Journal of World History* 2 (1991), 81–89. See also the retrospective essay on Curtin and the Wisconsin program by Craig A. Lockard, "The Contributions of Philip Curtin and the 'Wisconsin School' to the Study and Promotion of Comparative World History," *Journal of Third World Studies* 11 (1994), 180–223.

8. McNeill, "*The Rise of the West* after Twenty-Five Years," 1–2.

9. On the USAFA course in world history and its role in the larger curriculum, see Captain Donald M. Bishop and Thomas F. McGann (eds.), *World History in Liberal Military Education* (Colorado Springs, CO: Department of History, United States Air Force Academy, 1979). Though rare in printed form, the volume is readily available on the Internet as ERIC Document ED 259960 (accessed November 28, 2017).

10. The official record of the conference is Major Joe C. Dixon and Captain Neil D. Martin, (eds.), *1982 World History Teaching Conference* (Colorado Springs, CO: Department of History, United States Air Force Academy, 1983). Though rare in printed form, the volume is readily available on the Internet as ERIC Document ED 259961 (accessed November 28, 2017). For reports and reminiscences of the conference, see Kevin Reilly, "Conference on the Teaching of World History," *AHA Perspectives* 20:9 (December 1982), 12–14; Kevin Reilly, "Further Recollections," *World History Bulletin* 24:1 (Spring 2008), 3–4.

11. Kevin Reilly, "World History Association Established," *AHA Perspectives* 21:4 (April 1983), 7. Early issues of the *World History Bulletin*, especially those dating from 1983 to 1985, include several reports that trace the development of the WHA. Archived issues of the *World History Bulletin* are accessible at the WHA website: http://www.thewha.org/world_history_bulletin.php (accessed July 8, 2017)

12. The text of the constitution is accessible at the WHA website: http://www.thewha.org/wha_constitution.php (accessed July 8, 2017).

13. Marshall G. S. Hodgson, "The Hemispheric Interregional Approach to World History," *Cahiers d'histoire mondiale* 1 (1954), 17–23; and "The Unity of Later Islamic History," *Cahiers d'histoire mondiale* 5 (1960), 879–914.

14. Jerry H. Bentley, *The Journal of World History*, in Patrick Manning (ed.), *Global Practice in World History: Advances Worldwide* (Princeton: Markus Wiener, 2008), 129–40.

15. Craig A. Lockard, "The Promotion of Graduate Study and Research in World History," *World History Bulletin* 2:2 (Fall/Winter 1984), 6–7.

16. Jerry H. Bentley, "A Graduate Education and Research in World History," *World History Bulletin* 5:2 (Spring/Summer 1988), 3–7.

17. National Center for History in the Schools, *National Standards for History* (Los Angeles: National Center for History in the Schools, 1994); and *National Standards for History*, rev. ed. (Los Angeles: National Center for History in the Schools, 1996).

18. For a thick description of the debates over national history standards, see Gary B. Nash, Charlotte Crabtree and Ross E. Dunn, *History on Trial: Culture Wars and the Teaching of the Past* (New York: Knopf, 1997).

19. For a discussion, see Jerry H. Bentley, *Cultural Exchanges in World History*, in Jerry H. Bentley (ed.), *The Oxford Handbook of World History* (Oxford: Oxford University Press, 2011), 343–60.
20. For a discussion of the empirical scholarship associated with the new world history, see Jerry H. Bentley, *Shapes of World History in Twentieth-Century Scholarship* (Washington, DC: American Historical Association, 1996); Jerry H. Bentley, "The New World History," in Lloyd Kramer and Sarah Maza (eds.), *A Companion to Western Historical Thought* (Oxford: Blackwell, 2002), 393–416.
21. Peter A. Coclanis, "Ten Years After: Reflections on Kenneth Pomeranz's *The Great Divergence*," *Historically Speaking* 12:4 (September 2011), 10–12, quoting from p. 11.
22. For critical but also appreciative and balanced assessments, see three detailed articles by Peer Vries, "Are Coal and Colonies Really Crucial? Kenneth Pomeranz and the Great Divergence," *Journal of World History* 12 (2001), 407–46; "The California School and Beyond: How to Study the Great Divergence?," *History Compass* 8:7 (July 2010), 730–51; "Challenges (Non-) Responses and Politics: A Review of Prasannan Parthasarathi, *Why Europe Grew Rich and Asia Did Not: Global Economic Divergence, 1600-1850*," *Journal of World History* 23 (2012), 639–64.
23. The most impressive of the postcolonial critiques is Dipesh Chakrabarty, *Provincializing Europe: Postcolonial Thought and Historical Difference* (Princeton: Princeton University Press, 2000). For other postcolonial critiques, see Ashis Nandy, "History's Forgotten Doubles," in Philip Pomper, Richard H. Elphick and Richard T. Vann (eds.), *World History: Ideologies, Structures, and Identities* (Malden, MA: Blackwell, 1998), 159–78; Vinay Lal, "Provincializing the West: World History from the Perspective of Indian History," in Benedikt Stuchtey and Eckhardt Fuchs (eds.), *Writing World History, 1800–2000* (Oxford: Oxford University Press, 2003), 271–89. For a very different critique of Eurocentric history based on Marxist rather than postcolonial principles, see two articles by Arif Dirlik: "History without a Center? Reflections on Eurocentrism," in Eckhardt Fuchs and Benedikt Stuchtey (eds.), *Across Cultural Borders: Historiography in Global Perspective* (Lanham, MD: Rowman & Littlefield, 2002), 247–84; and "Confounding Metaphors, Inventions of the World: What Is World History For?" in Benedikt Stuchtey and Eckhardt Fuchs (eds.), *Writing World History, 1800–2000* (Oxford: Oxford University Press, 2003), 91–133.
24. Apart from Bentley, "Myths, Wagers, and Some Moral Implications of World History," see also two contributions to the larger debate from beyond North-American horizons: Dominic Sachsenmaier, "World History as Ecumenical History?" *Journal of World History* 18 (2007), 465–89; and Heather Sutherland, "The Problematic Authority of (World) History," *Journal of World History* 18 (2007), 491–522.

PART II
CENTRAL THEMES IN GLOBAL HISTORY

CHAPTER 7
NEW PERSPECTIVES ON WORKERS AND THE HISTORY OF WORK: GLOBAL LABOR HISTORY
Andreas Eckert and Marcel van der Linden

Crisis! What crisis?

Very few terms summarize such manifold and fundamental issues as the word *work*. Our current understanding of the term is still very much determined by the conditions that industrial development and the labor movement imprinted on modern societies.[1] In the political discourse of most industrialized countries, work is regarded as one of the key issues, so much so that it is sometimes said that once the problem of work is solved, all other problems will be solved much more easily. For most people, work defines status: success and failure, both personally and professionally, are inextricably linked to the concept of work. The supposed unambiguity of the term, however, makes it easy to ignore the fact that *work* covers an enormous range of activities and concepts linked to very different experiences. Notwithstanding this fact, debates in industrialized countries are usually about one very limited concept of work, namely gainful employment, which is more or less clearly separated from the domestic sphere—no matter that this distinction no longer corresponds to most people's experiences.

Work has always been an important category in social theory, one discussed by thinkers such as John Locke, Karl Marx and Max Weber. In contemporary theories, however, work became almost irrelevant, replaced by, for instance, in Niklas Luhmann's scholarship, the category of communication.[2] Moreover, many critics have diagnosed "the end of the labor society."[3] However, the idea that work is over does not take into account that the traditional understanding of labor as wage work or gainful occupation no longer applies to the post–Cold War globalized world. It is becoming more and more evident that received understandings of labor closely associated with the powerful state under advanced capitalism have to be reconsidered. Partly as a result, labor history became a very diverse field, covering a wide array of themes and approaches. According to Jürgen Kocka, "it is not yet clear what the leading questions and viewpoints structuring the history of work as a general field of research might be."[4]

This uncertainty has been fueled by a widespread disillusionment about the possibilities of labor history. As Marcel van der Linden argues,

> many labour historians have viewed the state of their discipline as a protracted crisis. First, the emerging paradigms of women's and ethnic history showed that there had been giant blank spots on labour history's maps, and that filling in these

blanks would necessitate a complete rewriting of the old narratives. Second, the unilinear conception of class consciousness that had long been dominant came into question.[5]

Due to a growing uncertainty about its organizing categories, labor history began to lose its character as a discipline. The distinction between labor history and historiographical branches such as women's history, ethnic studies, anthropology or sociology began to dissolve. Conceptual difficulties and political disappointments further fueled the impression of a state of crisis.[6]

Adjacent disciplines proved to be of limited help. In anthropology, very few ethnographic studies focus on the subject of work. Nor are there many theoretical monographs and articles.[7] Social science research in labor focuses more or less exclusively on industrialized societies, usually concentrating on national labor markets and questions of current labor market policies, new employment risks and the relationship between labor market and welfare state.[8] In legal studies, the development of research on questions of labor is closely linked to the setup of labor relations in a nation-state (contract and status). In the context of globalization, this limited perspective becomes increasingly problematic; it becomes difficult, for instance, to do justice to "globalized labor relations" on the level of the European Union.[9]

More recently, labor history and the history of work as a field of research are thriving again. Global labor history has become one of the main approaches representing new directions in this field. This chapter attempts to provide an overview of this burgeoning historiographical branch. It has been divided into four sections. The section "The 'new' labor history of the 1960s and 1970s and its limitations" discusses the insights and (Eurocentric) limitations of the "new" labor history of the 1960s and 1970s represented, among others, by E. P. Thompson. "Toward a global labor history" charts the rise of global perspectives in labor historiography and its methodological implications. "Themes and approaches" presents some of the avenues and thematic issues in the writing of global history. "Conclusion: Complications" summarizes the potentials and pitfalls of this field.

The "new" labor history of the 1960s and 1970s and its limitations

In its first phase, starting in the 1870s and lasting well into the 1960s, labor history was predominantly institutional, focusing on the description of organizational developments, political debates, leaders and strikes. It was represented by Sidney and Beatrice Webb, the Wisconsin School of John Commons and others, but also by Marxists like Philip Foner. In the 1960s we saw the beginnings of the so-called new labor history, in which E. P. Thompson's *The Making of the English Working Class* was a crucial landmark. The new labor history Thompson represented attempted to *contextualize* workers' struggles. As Eric Hobsbawm put it, it accentuated "the working classes as such … [and] the economic and technical conditions that allowed labor movements to be effective, or which prevented them from being effective."[10] The differences between new labor history and its older counterparts are often exaggerated, but it cannot be denied that the new labor history of the 1970s and 1980s introduced a dramatic renewal of the discipline. Not just labor processes and everyday culture but also gender, ethnicity, race and age finally gained the attention they deserved, along with household structures, sexuality and informal politics. Although it was truly an intellectual revolution, the new approaches were also imprisoned in the old, limited perspective. This becomes visible when *The Making* is considered from a global point of view: Thompson reconstructs the English process of class formation (in the period 1792–1832) as a *self-contained process*. England is, according to his analysis, the logical unit of analysis—though external forces influenced it, they are specifically portrayed as *foreign* influences. Thus the French Revolution plays an important background role in Thompson's narrative, as an inspiration for working-class activities. But developments in neighboring countries always remain an externality. Added to this is the fact that Thompson pays no attention in *The Making* to imperial connections. Colonialism, with its increasingly significant influence on the lives of the lower classes in the nineteenth century, is simply disregarded.

Peter Linebaugh and Marcus Rediker have pointed out that the London Corresponding Society (LCS) (which plays such an important role in *The Making*) declared itself at its foundation in 1792 in favor of equality, whether "black or white, high or low, rich or poor." But in August the same year, the LCS declared this: "FELLOW CITIZENS, Of every rank and every situation in life, Rich, Poor, High or Low, we address you all as our Brethren." Here the phrase "black or white" has disappeared. Linebaugh and Rediker persuasively argue that this sudden change of phrase must be explained with reference to the revolt in Haiti that had recently begun: "Race had thus become a tricky and, for many, in England, a threatening subject, one that the leadership of the L.C.S. now preferred to avoid."[11] Such transatlantic linkages cannot be found in Thompson's writing. Thompson's insular approach is all the more surprising given that politically he was an internationalist, familiar from his childhood days with stories about British India, where his parents had lived.[12] Thus we can see that, despite its pathbreaking achievement, *The Making of the English Working Class* clearly had limitations.

Much of the new labor history was characterized by Eurocentrism and by what could be called methodological nationalism: the nation-state was more or less naturalized and considered as the basic analytical unit of historical research. Even in the fast-growing literature on international labor migration, the nation-state remained central, and migrants were perceived as people who either preserved the culture of their country of origin or assimilated into the culture of their new country. Eurocentrism took numerous forms: one was simple neglect or ignorance of developments outside (Western) Europe and the United States. The second form is prejudice: the authors do consider global connections, but nevertheless believe that Greater Europe (including North America and Australasia) shows the way. This Eurocentrism is especially evident among modernization theorists.[13]

On the other hand, in many non-European areas the interest in labor history is rapidly rising. This is especially the case in South Asia.[14] In Latin America, too, a real boom in labor studies has taken place in recent years.[15] In terms of the historiography on Africa, it would be an exaggeration to talk about a boom in labor history, yet, there is a steady flow of new studies, with many of the more influential ones analyzing wage labor as one of the most important factors influencing societal changes in sub-Saharan Africa.[16] At the same time, among historians of labor and work, there is a growing awareness of the necessity of transcending the limits of the nation-state, because borders are not very relevant to the object of study. Working-class formation and restructuring are not neatly contained within particular national borders; they are processes on which voluntary and forced immigration and emigration have a great deal of influence. Dramatic developments in one country may cause turbulence in other countries; strike waves often have a transnational character, with new forms of campaigning imitated elsewhere; national labor movements communicate with each other, learn from each other and create international organizations. [17]

From a global history perspective, it is important to note that while there is no doubt that Western ideas and practices profoundly shaped developments in the non-European world, there is evidence, too, that developments in Africa, Asia and Latin America exerted some influence in the West. The concept of entangled or shared histories is useful here.[18] This concept implies, on the one hand, the idea that the creation and development of the modern world can be conceptualized as a history in which different cultures and societies shared a number of central experiences and, through their interactions and interdependence, created the modern world. And on the other hand, this concept takes for granted that the growing circulation of goods, people and ideas produced not only common ground but also disassociations and differences, the search for particularities and the hypostatization of dichotomous structures. Moreover, the reference to interaction should not imply that inequality, power and violence are ignored. Relations between Europe and the non-European world were often hierarchical or even repressive. It is impossible to conceptualize European modernity and leave out colonialism and imperialism. Europe realized itself in the world by arguing and disputing with other societies beyond its own boundaries.[19] This consideration also applies to the issues of work and labor.

Toward a global labor history

After the Second World War, when labor history spread out over the world, it maintained a Eurocentric and methodologically nationalist approach. European and Western labor historians tended to universalize their views based on rather specific examples. They ignored, for instance, the work of Caribbean specialists who, following C.L.R. James and Eric Williams in the 1930s and 1940s, saw the relationship of plantation labor and global capitalism as central. Even the so-called peripheral historians who began working on labor in the 1960s focused—like their European counterparts—on mineworkers, dockers or plantation workers and neglected families and households and the work done there. They, too, mainly sought out strikes, trade unions and political parties. And most importantly, they used the development of the North Atlantic as a model that peripheral working classes did not yet match.[20] Gradually, attempts were made to develop a less Eurocentric approach. Path-breaking works include Walter Rodney's histories of the Upper Guinea Coast and of the Guyanese working people, Charles van Onselen's *Chibaro* on mine labor in Southern Rhodesia and the essays collected in Ranajit Das Gupta's *Labor and Working Class in Eastern India* on plantation workers, miners and textile workers in Assam, Bengal and elsewhere.[21] All these developments began to undermine Eurocentrism and methodological nationalism from different sides.

A first major influence was the rise of labor history in the periphery. The nation-state was increasingly historicized, and thereby relativized, and Eurocentrism increasingly came under fire. Although these two are two distinct tendencies, they run more or less parallel. Their appearance is linked to a series of changes, most importantly decolonization, as the new independent countries, especially in Africa and Asia, began to investigate their own social histories. In this way, labor history acquired not only an increasingly important peripheral component (the number of monads expanded), but it also quickly became clear that peripheral history could not be written without reference to the history of the metropole. In research about historical migration, historians realized that the perspective of nation-to-ethnic enclave misinterpreted the reality of migrant life, because migrants often live simultaneously in two worlds.[22]

The consequences of the contemporary wave of economic de-territorialization (globalization), including the dramatic casualization of labor, new forms of workers' protest, new labor movements and the growing consciousness of worldwide interdependence, also played an important role. These developments seemed to warrant a new type of historiography, one that transcends traditional labor history from North America and Europe by incorporating its findings in a new globally oriented approach. But what can be understood by the term *global labor history*? As far as *methodological status* is concerned, global labor history is more an area of concern than a theory to which everyone must adhere. As regards *themes*, global labor history focuses on the transnational and even transcontinental study of labor relations and workers' social movements in the broadest sense of the word. By transnational, we mean either the comparing of all historical processes, no matter how geographically small they may seem, to processes elsewhere in order to place them in a wider context, or the study of interactions between locations, or a combination of the two. The study of labor relations encompasses work that is free as well as unfree, paid and unpaid, and concerns not just the individual worker but also his or her family. The study of workers' social movements should cover both formal organizations and informal activities, and historians investigating labor relations and social movements need to pay as much attention to what we might call the other side—that is, employers and public authorities—as to workers themselves. Gender relations, of course, play an important role, within the family and in the work experiences of individual family members. Finally, as regards the *period* studied, the emphasis is on the study of labor relations and workers' social movements that have evolved along with the growth of the world market from the fifteenth century.

A global labor history faces numerous methodological problems. The core concepts of traditional labor history have primarily been based on experiences in the North Atlantic region and are thus in need of critical reconsideration. This applies to the concept of labor itself. In the most important Western languages (English, French, Spanish, Italian, etc.), a distinction is often made between "labor" and "work," in which "labor" refers to toil and effort (as in "woman's labor"), while "work" refers more to creative processes. This binary—to which, philosopher Hannah Arendt, for example, attached far-reaching analytical consequences—simply does not exist in many other languages, and sometimes there is even no single word for "labor" or "work," because these concepts do not consider the specific characteristics of separate labor processes.[23] We ought, therefore, to investigate carefully to what extent the concepts "labor" and "work" are transculturally usable, or, at the very least, we should define their content much more precisely than we are used to doing. Where does "labor" begin, and where does it end? How exactly do we draw the boundary between "labor" and "work," or is that boundary less obvious than is often assumed?[24]

And where are the boundaries between work and nonwork? The definitions of what constitutes work and what is excluded from it are of central importance for a global perspective on labor, as are practices and policies surrounding these definitions. Historical research has shown that the line of demarcation between work and crime, work and leisure, and paid and unpaid time has always been blurred. What is legitimate work and what is illegal has long been a matter of state policy. And not just when it comes to crime: as the history of unemployment shows, state law and other regulatory regimes have defined work in multiple ways and thus made it an object of regulation.[25] However, not all social regulations emanate from the state, and the interactions between state and nonstate modes of regulation very much need to be analyzed.

The concept of "working class" needs a critical reconsideration as well. It appears that this term was used in the nineteenth century to identify workers considered respectable and distinguish them from slaves and other unfree laborers, as well as from the self-employed or petty bourgeoisie, and the poor outcasts, or lumpen-proletariat. However, this interpretation does not seem appropriate to most parts of the world. While unfree labor may have been exceptional in the Global North in the last centuries, it has been the rule in large parts of Asia, Africa and Latin America. A new conceptualization of the working class, one that is less oriented to *excluding* than to *including* various dependent or marginalized groups of workers, is needed. Chattel slaves, indentured laborers and sharecroppers should be considered as segments of the working class as well. The implication is that the disciplinary boundaries of labor history will continue to become more fluid. The historiography of chattel slavery, until recently mostly ignored by labor historians, actually overlaps significantly with global labor history. Related research fields such as the history of indentured laborers and of the Indian coolies who were employed in Asia, Australia, Africa and the Caribbean are increasingly coming into the ambit of labor historiography. There is also the question of how the imagining of class shapes labor history—both for elites and for working people.

Recent global historical research, often building on area-based research, has shown numerous hybrid forms of work, for example, slaves who were ordered by their owners to leave the mansion or plantation and work for wages, but who still had to bring back part of their earnings.²⁶ Other combinations of slave and wage labor or serfdom and capitalism (such as in Russia *c.* 1900) would seem to relativize Karl Marx's and other classical writers' thesis of the outstanding importance of contractually free wage labor as a defining element of capitalism.²⁷ In the world of work relations and labor politics, the distinction between "free" and "unfree" labor has been crucial. "Free labor" has been a central element of a master narrative of Western societies being on a progressive path toward "freedom" and "emancipation." "Free labor" was contrasted to slave labor, forced labor or bondage. In societies where slavery was central—as in the Americas and Africa—the distinction between "free" and "unfree" became essential too, especially once slavery was formally ended. This distinction was also crucial to definitions and practices of unfree labor in Europe's colonies. For instance, indentured labor on the tea plantations in Assam (India) was not thinkable without the specific concept of English workers as "servants." Indentured laborers on plantations in Asia and the Caribbean were neither slaves nor proletarians—so what categories are appropriate to describe them?²⁸

The boundaries between wage labor and chattel slavery are not nearly as clear as they have seemed—in fact they are downright fuzzy. A more global view of labor invites us to use this fuzziness as a stimulus for rethinking the concept of the working class as such. Historians and sociologists now point out that the borderlines between free wage labor, self-employment and unfree labor are not clear. First, as mentioned, there are large gray areas where distinctions between free wage laborers and slaves, the self-employed and the lumpen-proletarians are not wholly clear. Second, almost all subaltern workers belong to households that combine several modes of labor. Third, individual subaltern workers can combine different modes of labor, both synchronically and diachronically. Finally, the distinctions between the different kinds of subaltern workers are not clear-cut.

The implications are far-reaching. We know there has always been a large class of people within capitalism whose labor power is commodified. Its members are enormously varied: they include chattel slaves, sharecroppers, small artisans and wage earners. To understand the historic dynamics of this multitude should be a central task for future global labor historians. In its long development, capitalism has utilized many kinds of work relationships, some mainly based on economic compulsion, others with a strong noneconomic component. Millions of slaves were brought by force from Africa to the Caribbean, Brazil and the southern states of the United States. Contract workers from India and China were shipped off to toil in South Africa, Malaysia or South America. The so-called free migrant workers left Europe for the New World, Australia or the colonies. And today slavery still exists, and sharecroppers continue to produce an important portion of the world's agricultural output. These and other work relationships are synchronous, even if there seems to be a long-term trend toward "free wage labor." Capitalists could and can choose whatever form of commodified labor they think best fits a given context: one variant seems most profitable today, another tomorrow. If this argument is correct, then it behooves us to conceptualize the wage earners as one (important) kind of commodified labor among others. Consequently, the so-called free labor cannot be seen as the only form of exploitation suitable for modern capitalism, but rather as one alternative among several.

Themes and approaches

The methodological and conceptual considerations presented above did shape in considerable ways efforts to "do" global labor history. This section presents some examples of themes and approaches that had been developed in order to cross boundaries and challenge the prevailing compartmentalization of the world. Slavery and the slave trade rank high among those research fields that already for a long time focus on entanglements between different world regions. In the long history of relations between Europe and Africa, labor always played a central role: by the early-modern period, slavery and the slave trade made links between Europe and the rest of the world in terms of work and labor apparent.[29] The creation of a world economy by European capitalists and the reordering of economic relations in virtually every part of the world created a huge need for labor that could only be satisfied by various forms of force and coercion.[30] The slave trade completely transformed labor regimes not only in most of the New World but also in Africa, where slaves became both a crucial commodity and also the main source of labor.[31] This raises the fundamental question of how colonialism has shaped labor history. Some authors, for instance, have called the Caribbean slave plantations "factories in the field" and argued that these industrial production methods and capitalist labor relations on these estates both anticipated and influenced production methods in industrialized Europe.[32] Certainly an important reference here is the slave plantation as a formative experience in developing large-scale, closely supervised enterprises. How did this experience shape the ideas, organization and practices of labor throughout the world?

In South Asian history, Ravi Ahuja has argued that the development of labor relations in India and Europe has been linked for at least two centuries.[33] This entanglement emerged against the backdrop of the colonial project, creating not only commonalties but also differences and new kinds of inequalities. In fact, the uneven development of capitalist labor markets not only preserved differences but deepened and recreated them again and again.

But what did these entanglements look like? South Asia was part of the social history of capitalism before it became part of the British Empire.[34] During the seventeenth and eighteenth centuries, the agrarian sector and some trades gradually commercialized, which meant that labor relations were at least partly based on contracts. Thus wage labor was on the scene before the establishment of colonial rule, and there was no need to import European terms to express the phenomenon of wage labor. In the Tamil language, a wage laborer was (and is) called a *Kuliyal* or *Kuli*. Indian workers were conscious of the difference between free and unfree labor: a *Kuli* was nobody's servant. However, the term had a negative connotation because it was linked to subordination and lower-caste background. During the nineteenth century, the British picked up the term (spelling it as "coolie") to denominate an unfree laborer, and from this colonial context, the term entered European languages as a term for the unlimited subordination of the labor force.[35]

Another form of entanglement that still has not been systematically explored is the way in which the practice of colonial labor regulations in the British Empire affected the situation in the metropole. The Master and Servant Acts, the cornerstone of English employment law for more than 400 years, gave largely unsupervised, inferior magistrates wide discretion over employment relations, including the power to whip, fine and imprison men, women and children for breach of private contracts with their employers. The English model was adopted, modified and reinvented in more than a thousand colonial statutes and ordinances regulating the recruitment, retention and discipline of workers in shops, mines and factories, on farms, in forests, on plantations and at sea.[36] The claim by some historians that the British colonies were used as laboratories of institutional reform still needs further evaluation. It is evident, however, that the globalization of English employment law did not lead to the leveling of difference; instead, the most repressive and anti-egalitarian legal practices were developed further and survived longer in the colonies. The system of indentured labor is a case in point: indenture (apprentice contract or contract of employment) refers to a specifically colonial legal form, one that was not restricted to South Asia. For the period of the contract (which the worker could not terminate), the plantation owner had nearly unlimited right of disposal of "his" workers. This practice was justified by the cynical argument that indenture was a school for Indian workers to teach them how to conclude and to keep to a contract.[37]

In the colonial world in general, Europeans saw work as helping to overcome the supposed backwardness of colonized people. Work promised to open access to civilization, but only slowly, since colonial ideology claimed that it would take a long time to instill a sufficient capitalist work ethic into Asians and, especially, Africans. The idea of the lazy native soon became a classic stereotype of colonial literature.[38] This was not just a racist view but also an indication that European rule in the colonies was far from omnipotent. The characterization of African workers, for example, as lazy suggests that in the end colonizers had to accept the limits of colonial power, that Africans were partially successful in struggles over work. Even in the harsh context of South African gold mining, Africans shaped the limits of their own exploitation, notably by pressuring for systems of day labor, by organizing workers' guilds in cities and by embracing various forms of labor tenancy on farms, all of which allowed them to control family labor and shape work rhythms to a significant extent.[39] On the other hand, colonizers consistently contrasted the way work was supposedly performed in Africa and other non-European regions with the allegedly high quality of "national types of work."[40]

Educating colonized peoples for work was a crucial element of colonial policies. Sebastian Conrad has argued that efforts to discipline the homeless in Germany in the late nineteenth and early twentieth centuries shaped the parallel project of "civilizing" Africans in the German colonies.[41] Moreover, he claims that the colonial mission had effects on debates and practices back in Germany. However, in the end there are few clues that show that there were indeed shared experiences, discourses and practices in East Africa and East Westphalia. To be sure, the parallel structure of educational projects in Germany and East Africa is striking. Yet it is far from clear whether discourses about and measures against the homeless in Germany had anything to do with colonial experiences and practices.

There are a number of further themes that can help explore global connections in the history of labor:

Labor processes in different locations can be linked via a global commodity chains analysis. Luis Valenzuela, for example, shows how from the 1830s through the 1860s a tight nexus existed between Chilean copper miners and British copper smelters in Swansea (South Wales):

> Large quantities of Chilean copper and regulus arrived in the Swansea docks to be smelted and refined in the South Wales furnaces. On the other hand, Welsh coal and firebricks as well as other British produce were shipped from South Wales to Chilean ports close to the mines to pay for that copper and, incidentally, stimulating mining and smelting production.[42]

Labor processes are themselves sometimes intrinsically international and can be explored as such. Transport workers such as seamen and longshoremen are liaisons between regions separated by long distances. Already in the sixteenth and seventeenth centuries, and perhaps even earlier, they made logistical connections between subaltern workers on different continents. Seamen "influenced both the form and the content of plebeian protest by their militant presence in seaport crowds" and "used their mobility … to create links with other working people."[43] Transport workers have figured prominently in the transcontinental dissemination of forms of collective action, as shown by the diffusion of the model of the Industrial Workers of the World (IWW) from the United States to places such as Chile, Australia, New Zealand and South Africa. Moreover, in 1911, the IWW was the first group to organize transcontinental collective action, conducting simultaneous strikes in Britain, the Netherlands, Belgium and on the East Coast of the United States.[44]

Migrants can bring their experiences to other workers in the country of settlement— as Indian workers did in the Caribbean and Southeast Asia, British workers did in Australia, Italian workers did in the Americas and Chinese workers did in the Asian diaspora. On the one hand, their presence in a new country may cause the segmentation of labor markets, and thus working classes divided by ethnicity. On the other hand, returning migrants may also import a repertoire of collective action from their respective temporary homes.[45]

Consumption by subaltern workers of products produced by subaltern workers elsewhere is another notable relationship that a global approach to labor history can illuminate. The increased use of sugar by workers in Europe in the eighteenth century, for example, influenced the activities of slaves in the sugar plantations of the New World. The inverse also seems to apply. For example, Sidney Mintz suggests that sugar made the diet of workers in England more varied and richer, therefore promoting the Industrial Revolution.[46]

Moreover, a global perspective brings transnational waves of collective action into view. To cite just one example: in addition to instigating the first Russian Revolution in 1905, the Japanese victory over Russia promoted nationalist and anticolonial forces throughout Asia and encouraged workers' collective action in many places. The second Russian

Revolution from March 1917 and the Bolshevik seizure of power inspired an explosive increase of workers' collective action on all continents. Similarly, the Hungarian uprising of 1956—influenced by the earlier unrest in Poznan—was a "powerful stimulus" for labor unrest in Shanghai the following year.[47]

Finally, at a somewhat different level, international organizations, especially the International Labour Organization (ILO), have recently been recognized as sites of globally entangled discourses about labor and work, with the ILO also providing an example of an institution that has propagated a broad range of international labor standards—albeit without being able to enforce their implementation.[48]

Conclusion: Complications

A global perspective on the history of work and labor does not mean simply expanding or complicating Western labor history, nor is it intended to direct the focus exclusively to the non-European world. Instead, such a perspective can provide tools to look at the ways the West and the rest have influenced one another.[49] One of the contributions of global labor history is its awareness that, first, free and unfree, paid and unpaid labor should be dealt with together, and, second, that there was no unilinear path from unfree to free labor. However, while it is easy to show how labor regimes and working practices in the Americas, Africa and Asia have been shaped by European influences, it is far more difficult to demonstrate how Europe has been influenced by its colonial experiences and practices.

Future research on global labor issues should be careful not "to subordinate the rich histories of labor, generated on multiple scales of social space, to the trajectory of globalization."[50] Frederick Cooper has warned us about the dangers of doing history backward and to limit ourselves to identifying only the flows and nodal points of globalization.[51] It is no accident that recent research has focused on seamen and other mobile sectors of the African and Asian labor force, which contributed to the emergence of global commodity and labor markets.[52] There is nothing wrong with this focus. However, we must not overlook other workers—nonplantation rural labor, for instance—as the globalization of labor meant not only unbounded mobility but spatial immobility as well, and we need to see the contradictions and unevenness of global incorporation processes.

Moreover, one of the virtues of labor history in recent decades has been its microhistorical focus on workers and work in relation to the range of social processes in a particular location—race, gender and ethnicity, for instance. Why does this matter? If we look beyond both locality and region toward wider spatial relationships, what do we learn besides the insight that we are confronted with fuzzy categories and fuzzy constellations? If we look at the African case, for instance, we can see that the history of labor there does not fit a linear model of proletarianization and the "making" of a working class. Power, whether on the shop floor or in mines and on plantations, is rooted in particular cultural structures—from the racially based system of colonial authority to Africans' efforts to use personal relations to shape work patterns to their own needs. Labor movements are more than automatic responses to becoming a proletarian as they are rooted in specific patterns of affiliation and strategies of mobilization and alliance-building. The challenge, then, "is to look at different modes of thinking, speaking and acting as a worker, patterns shaped not by statically conceived 'cultures,' but by history, by layers of experience and memory."[53] Labor historians of Africa, for instance, face the difficulty of focusing on the necessarily specific historical trajectories in certain localities in Africa and across specific patterns of regional migration, without losing sight of the wider context, in order to evaluate how much African labor has been shaped by its connections to the rest of the world and how much the world has been shaped by the labor of Africans. And what else can we call this kind of history, a history infused with both specificity and comparison, that sees shared entanglements as bi- or multidirectional rather than unidirectional, that does not impose a model from one period, nation or region onto another, but global?

Notes

1. This chapter is partly based on: Marcel van der Linden, "Labour History Beyond Borders," in Joan Allen et al. (eds.), *Histories of Labour. National and International Perspectives* (London: Merlin Press, 2010), 353–83; Andreas Eckert, "What Is Global Labour History Good For?," in Jürgen Kocka (ed.), *Work in a Modern Society. The German Historical Experience in Comparative Perspective* (Oxford: Berghahn, 2010), 169–81. For another essay mapping the field of global labor history, see Marcel van der Linden, "The Promise and Challenges of Global Labor History," *International Labor and Working-Class History* 82 (2012), 57–76. For a recent collection of important essays in the field of global labor history, see Andreas Eckert (ed.), *Global Histories of Work* (Berlin and Boston: De Gruyter, 2016).
2. See Reinhart Kößler and Hans Wienold, "Arbeit und Vergesellschaftung. Eine aktuelle Erinnerung an die klassische Gesellschaftstheorie," *Peripherie* 85/86 (2002), 162–83. Niklas Luhmann, *The Differentiation of Society* (New York: Columbia University Press, 1982).
3. This diagnosis, framed by, among others, Hannah Arendt, *The Human Condition* (Chicago: University of Chicago Press, 1958), became very popular during the 1980s. See also André Gorz, *Critique of Economic Reason* (London, 2011); Jürgen Habermas, "The New Obscurity," *Philosophy and Social Criticism* XI2 (1986), 1–18. For the German context, see for instance Ralf Dahrendorf, "Wenn der Arbeitsgesellschaft die Arbeit ausgeht," in Joachim Matthes (ed.), *Krise der Arbeitsgesellschaft? Verhandlungen des 21. Soziologentages in Bamberg 1982* (Frankfurt: Campus Verlag, 1983).
4. Jürgen Kocka, "Work as a Problem in European History," in idem. (ed.), *Work*, 1–15, here: 1. See also Kim Christian Priemel, "Heaps of Work. The Ways of Labour History," in H-Soz-Kult, January 23, 2014, http://www.hsozkult.de/literaturereview/id/forschungsberichte-1223 (accessed February 10, 2017).
5. Marcel van der Linden, *Transnational Labour History. Explorations* (Aldershot: Ashgate, 2003), 2.
6. Van der Linden, *Transnational Labour History*. According to William Sewell, Jr., this "crisis" is due to the fact that labor history is too embedded in the meta-narrative of proletarianization. The thesis of proletarianization brings together, as Sewell points out, a number of processes and, while acknowledging variation, treats the overall trend as

universal: cultivators and artisans are deprived of access to means of production, they move to cities or are forced into insecure wage labor jobs on farms, their skills are devalued and even tighter forms of managerial control are devised; meanwhile, workers acquire a sense of their collective identity as the sellers of labor power, and their tradition of artisanal autonomy and Republican assertiveness are rechanneled into class identity; they build organizations, go on strike and collectively challenge capital. According to Sewell, this proletarianization thesis pays "insufficient attention to the profoundly uneven and contradictory character of changes in productive relations, not to mention the role of discourse and politics in labor history." See William Sewell, Jr., "Toward a Post-Materialist Rhetoric for Labor History," in Lenard A. Berlanstein (ed.), *Rethinking Labor History: Essays in Discourse and Class Analysis* (Urbana: University of Illinois Press, 1993), 15–38 (quote: 18). On this also, see Frederick Cooper, *Decolonization and African Society. The Labor Question in French and British Africa* (Cambridge: Cambridge University Press, 1996), 12f. On the "crisis" of labor history, see also, among many others, Marcel van der Linden (ed.), *The End of Labour History?* (Cambridge, 1993); Thomas Welskopp, "Von der verhinderten Heldengeschichte des Proletariats zur vergleichenden Sozialgeschichte der Arbeit—Perspektiven der Arbeitergeschichtsschreibung in den 1990er Jahren," *1999. Zeitschrift für Sozialgeschichte des 19. und 20. Jahrhunderts* 8:3 (1994), 34–53; John Belchem, "Reconstructing Labor History," *Labor History Review* 62 (1997), 147–52.

7. Gerd Spittler is an exception. See his *Hirtenarbeit. Die Welt der Kamelhirten und Ziegenhirtinnen von Timia* (Cologne, Rüdiger Köppe Verlag, 1998), idem., *Anthropologie der Arbeit. Ein ethnographischer Vergleich* (Wiesbaden, 2016). With a focus on wage labor, see the review article by Sutti Ortiz, "Laboring in the Factories and in the Fields," *Annual Review of Anthropology* 31 (2002), 395–417.

8. See for instance Günther Schmid, *Wege in eine Vollbeschäftigung. Übergangsarbeitsmärkte und aktivierende Arbeitsmarktpolitik* (Frankfurt: Campus Verlag, 2002).

9. See Alain Supiot et al (eds.), *Beyond Employment. Report for the European Commission* (Oxford: Oxford University Press, 2001).

10. Eric J. Hobsbawm, *Labouring Men: Studies in the History of Labour* (London: Weidenfeld and Nicholson, 1964), 4.

11. Peter Linebaugh and Marcus Rediker, *The Many-Headed Hydra: The Hidden History of the Revolutionary Atlantic* (Boston: Beacon Press, 2000), 274.

12. Bryan D. Palmer, *E.P. Thompson: Objections and Oppositions* (London and New York: Verso, 1994), 11–51. See also E. P. Thompson, *Making History: Writings on History and Culture* (New York, 1994), 200–25; Tom Nairn, *The Break-Up of Britain: Crisis and Neo-Nationalism*, 2nd edition (London and New York, 1977), 303–04.

13. Leonard Binder, "The Natural History of Development Theory," *Comparative Studies in Society and History* 28:1 (1986), 3–33.

14. See the comprehensive overviews by Marcel van der Linden, "Die Geschichte der Arbeiterinnen und Arbeiter in der Globalisierung," *Sozial.Geschichte* 18:1 (2003), 10–40; idem., "Vorläufiges zur transkontinentalen Arbeitergeschichte," *Geschichte und Gesellschaft* 28:2 (2002), 291–304; idem., "Transnationale Arbeitergeschichte," in Gunilla Budde, Sebastian Conrad, and Oliver Janz (eds.), *Transnationale Geschichte. Themen, Tendenzen und Theorien* (Göttingen: Vandenhoeck & Ruprecht, 2006), 265–74; idem., *Workers of the World. Essays Towards a Global Labor History* (Leiden: Brill, 2008). Over the last fifteen years, many important monographs and collective volumes on South Asian labor history appeared, among them Samita Sen, *Women and Labor in Late Colonial India. The Bengal Jute Industry* (Cambridge: Cambridge University Press, 1999); Rajnarayan Chandavarkar, *The Origins of*

Industrial Capitalism in India: Business Strategies and the Working Classes in Bombay, 1900–1940 (Cambridge: Cambridge University Press, 1994); Chitra Joshi, *Lost Worlds of Labor. Culture and Community in North India* (Delhi: Permanent Black, 2002); more recently, Ravi Ahuja (ed.), *Working Lives and Working Militancy. The Politics of Labor in Colonial India* (New Delhi: Tulika, 2013); Rana Behal, *One Hundred Years of Servitude: Political Economy of Tea Plantations in Colonial* (New Delhi: Tulika, 2014); Nitin Varma, *Coolies of Capitalism: Assam Tea and the Making of Coolie Labour* (Berlin and Boston: De Gruyter: 2016); for an assessment of this historiography, see Ravi Ahuja, "Erkenntnisdruck und Denkbarrieren. Anmerkungen zur indischen Arbeiterhistoriographie," in Shalini Randeria, Martin Fuchs and Antje Linkenbach (eds.), *Konfigurationen der Moderne: Diskurse zu Indien* (Baden Baden: Nomos, 2004), 349–66; Rana Behal et al., "India," in Allen et al. (eds.), *Histories of Labor: National and International Perspectives* (London: merlin, 2010); Chitra Joshi, Histories of Indian Labor: Predicaments and Possibilities, *History Compass* 6:2 (2008), 439–54.

15. John D. French, "The Latin American Labor Studies Boom," *International Review of Social History* 45 (2000), 279–308; John Womack Jr., "Doing Labor History. Feeling, Work, Material Power," *Journal of the Historical Society* 5:3 (2005), 255–96; James P. Brennan, "Latin American Labor History," in José C. Moya (ed.), *The Oxford Handbook of Latin American History* (Oxford: Oxford University Press, 2011), 342–66. For a more skeptical view: Peter Winn, "Global Labor History. The Future of the Field?," *International Labor and Working-Class History* 82 (2012), 85–91. Especially Brazilian labor history currently belongs to the most vibrant areas within Latin American historiography. See Alexandre Fortes et al., *Cruzando Fronteiras. Novos olhares sobre a história do trabalho* (Sao Paulo: Editora Fundação Perseu Abramo, 2013).

16. See for instance Bill Freund, *The Making of Contemporary Africa. The Development of African Society since 1800* (London: Palgrave, 1998). For historiographical overviews, see Bill Freund, "Labor and Labor History in Africa. A Review of the Literature," *African Studies Review* 27 (1984), 1–58; idem., "Labour Studies and Labour History in South Africa: Perspectives from the Apartheid Era and After," *International Review of Social History* 58:3 (2013), 493–519; Andreas Eckert, "Geschichte der Arbeit und Arbeitergeschichte in Afrika," *Archiv für Sozialgeschichte* 39 (1999), 502–30; Frederick Cooper, "African Labor History," in Jan Lucassen (ed.), *Global Labor History. A State of the Art* (Berne: Peter Lang, 2006), 91–116. Among the numerous more recent monographs focusing on labor are Lisa A. Lindsay, *Working with Gender. Wage Labor and Social Change in Southwestern Nigeria* (Portsmouth, NH: Heinemann, 2003); Isaïe Dougnon, *Travail de Blanc, travail de Noir. La migration des paysans dogon vers l'Office du Niger et du Ghana (1910–1980)* (Paris and Amsterdam: Karthala, 2007); Babacar Fall, *Le travail au Sénégal au XXe siècle* (Paris: Karthala, 2011). A recent collective volume stresses the need for simultaneous consideration of local, national and transnational contexts in the field of African labor history. See Lynn Schler et al. (eds.), *Rethinking Labour in Africa, Past and Present* (London and New York: Routledge, 2011).

17. Van der Linden, *Transnational Labor History*, 3.

18. See Shalini Randeria, "Geteilte Geschichte und verwobene Moderne," in Jörn Rüsen (ed.), *Zukunftsentwürfe. Ideen für eine Kultur der Veränderung* (Frankfurt: Campus Verlag, 1999), 87–96.

19. Ann Laura Stoler and Frederick Cooper, "Between Metropole and Colony. Rethinking a Research Agenda," in Ann Laura Cooper and Frederick Stoler (eds.), *Tensions of Empire. Colonial Cultures in a Bourgeois World* (Berkeley: University of California Press, 1997), 1.

20. On the history written outside Europe as the historiography of the "(not) yet," and of "absences," see Dipesh Chakrabarty, "Postcoloniality and the Artifice of History: Who Speaks for 'Indian' Pasts?," *Representations* 37 (Winter 1992), 1–26. It is interesting to note that the Subaltern Studies project (in which Chakrabarty participated) could not escape this

problem. The announcement of the project was worded as follows: "The central problematic of the historiography of colonial India" is the "historical failure of the nation to come into its own, a failure due to the inadequacy of the bourgeoisie as well as of the working class to lead it to a decisive victory over colonialism and a bourgeois-democratic revolution of the classic nineteenth-century type." Ranajit Guha, "On Some Aspects of the Historiography of Colonial India," in Ranajit Guha and Gayatri Chakravorty Spivak (eds.), *Selected Subaltern Studies* (New York: Oxford University Press, 1988), 37–43 (here: 43). This "problematic," although couched in Comintern phraseology, is really a Western topos. Rajnarayan Chandavarkar, "'The Making of the Working Class': E. P. Thompson and Indian History," *History Workshop Journal* 43 (1997), 177–96 (here: 182).

21. Walter Rodney, *A History of the Upper Guinea Coast, 1545–1800* (Oxford: Clarendon Press, 1970); idem., *A History of the Guyanese Working People, 1881–1905* (Baltimore: Johns Hopkins University Press, 1981); Charles van Onselen, *Chibaro: African Mine Labor in Southern Rhodesia 1900–1933* (Johannesburg: Raven Press, 1976); Ranajit Das Gupta, *Labour and Working Class in Eastern India. Studies in Colonial History* (Calcutta: K.P. Bagchi and Company, 1994).

22. For important comprehensive contributions to the field of migration history, see Dirk Hoerder, *Cultures in Contact: World Migrations in the Second Millennium* (Durham, NC: Duke University Press, 2002); Jan Lucassen et al. (eds.), *Migration History in World History. Multidisciplinary Approaches* (Leiden: Brill, 2010); Patrick Manning, *Migration in World History* (New York: Routledge, 2013).

23. Hannah Arendt, *The Human Condition* (Chicago: Chicago University Press, 1958).

24. For a very broad and insightful discussion of the semantics of work, see Jörn Leonhard and Willibald Steinmetz (eds.), *Semantiken von Arbeit: Diachrone und vergleichende Perspektiven* (Cologne: Böhlau Verlag, 2016).

25. See the by-now classic study by Benedicte Zimmermann, *La constitution du chômage en Allemagne. Entre professions et territoires* (Paris: Editions de la Maison des Sciences de l'Homme, 2001).

26. João José Reis, "'The Revolution of the Ganhadores': Urban Labor, Ethnicity and the African Strike of 1857 in Bahia, Brazil," *Journal of Latin American Studies* 29 (1997), 355–93.

27. See Alessandro Stanziani, "The Legal Statute of Labour from the Seventeenth to the Nineteenth Century. Russia in a Comparative European Perspective," *International Review of Social History* 54 (2009), 359–389; idem., *Bondage. Labor and Rights in Eurasia from the Sixteenth to the Early Twentieth Century* (New York and Oxford: Berghahn, 2014).

28. Brazilian historians in particular have emphasized that during the nineteenth century there were no clear-cut divisions between slaves and "freed" workers with regard to the utilization of extra-economic coercion. At the same time, the concept of "freedom" was a very ambivalent but highly relevant ground-level social category. See for instance Sidney Chaloub, "The Precariousness of Freedom in a Slave Society (Brazil in the Nineteenth Century)," *International Review of Social History* 56 (2011), 405–39.

29. See David Eltis (ed.), *Coerced and Free Migrations. Global Perspectives* (Stanford: Stanford University Press, 2002).

30. See, among many others, Paul E. Lovejoy and Nicolas Rogers (eds.), *Unfree Labor in the Development of the Atlantic World* (London: Frank Cass, 1994).

31. Paul E. Lovejoy, *Transformations in Slavery. A History of Slavery in Africa*, 2nd edition (Cambridge: Cambridge University Press, 2000).

32. Sidney W. Mintz, *Sweetness and Power. The Place of Sugar in Modern History* (New York: Penguin, 1985); Albert Wirz, *Sklaverei und kapitalistisches Weltsystem* (Frankfurt: Suhrkamp Verlag, 1984).

33. Ravi Ahuja, "Geschichte der Arbeit jenseits des kulturalistischen Paradigmas. Vier Anregungen aus der Südasienforschung," *Geschichte und Zukunft der Arbeit*, 121–34; idem., "Die Lenksamkeit des 'Lascars.' Regulierungsszenarien eines transnationalen Arbeitsmarktes in der ersten Hälfte des zwanzigsten Jahrhunderts," *Geschichte und Gesellschaft* 31:3 (2005), 323–53.

34. See David Washbrook, "Progress and Problems. South Asian Economic and Social History, c. 1720–1860," *Modern Asian Studies* 22 (1988), 72; Ahuja, "Geschichte der Arbeit," 124. For a case study, see Ravi Ahuja, *Die Erzeugung kolonialer Staatlichkeit und das Problem der Arbeit. Eine Studie zur Sozialgeschichte der Stadt Madras und ihres Hinterlandes zwischen 1750 und 1800* (Stuttgart: Steiner Verlag, 1999); idem., "Labor Relations in an Early Colonial Context: Madras, 1750–1800," *Modern Asian Studies* 32:4 (2002), 793–826.

35. Ahuja, "Geschichte der Arbeit," 125.

36. Douglas Hay and Paul Cravan (eds.), *Masters, Servants, and Magistrates in Britain and the Empire, 1582–1955* (Chapel Hill and London: University of North Carolina Press, 2004).

37. See Ravi Ahuja, "Arbeit und Kolonialherrschaft im neuzeitlichen Südasien. Eine Einführung," in Dietmar Rothermund and Karin Preisendanz (eds.), *Südasien in der Neuzeit* (Vienna: Promedia Verlag, 2003), 200; Gupta, *Labor and Working Class in Eastern India. Studies in Colonial History*; Marina Carter, *Voices from Indenture. Experiences of Indian Migrants in the British Empire* (London and New York:: Leicester University Press, 1996).

38. Syed H. Alatas, *The Myth of the Lazy Native* (London: Frank Cass, 1977).

39. Frederick Cooper, "Africa in a Capitalist World," in Darlene Clark Hine and Jacqueline McLeod (eds.), *Crossing Boundaries. Comparative History of Black People in the Diaspora* (Bloomington: Indiana University Press, 1999), 399–418, especially 401.

40. Sebastian Conrad, "Circulation, 'National Work' and Identity Debates about the Mobility of Work in Germany and Japan, 1890–1914," in Wolf Lepenies (eds.), *Entangled Histories and Negotiated Universals. Centers and Peripheries in a Changing World* (Frankfurt: Campus Verlag, 2003), 260–80.

41. Sebastian Conrad, "Eingeborenenpolitik" in Kolonie und Metropole. "Erziehung zur Arbeit" in Ostafrika und Ostwestfalen, *Das Kaiserreich transnational. Deutschland in der Welt 1871–1914* (Göttingen: Vandenhoeck & Ruprecht, 2004), 107–28; idem., *Globalisation and the Nation in Imperial Germany* (Cambridge: Cambridge University Press, 2010), ch. 2.

42. Luis Valenzuela, "Copper: Chilean Miners—British Smelters in the Mid-Nineteenth Century," in Prodromos Panayiotopoulos and Gavin Capps (eds.), *World Development. An Introduction* (London and Sterling: Pluto Press, 2001), 173–80 (here: 177).

43. Marcus Rediker, *Between the Devil and the Deep Blue Sea: Merchant Seamen, Pirates, and the Anglo-American Maritime World, 1700–1750* (Cambridge: Cambridge University Press, 1987), 294; Linebaugh and Rediker, *The Many-Headed Hydra*.

44. On the IWW model, see Verity Burgman, *Revolutionary Industrial Unionism: The IWW in Australia* (Melbourne: Cambridge University Press, 1996); Erik Olssen, *The Red Feds: Revolutionary Industrial Unionism and the New Zealand Federation of Labor 1908–1914* (Oxford: Oxford University Press, 1988); John Philips, "The South African Wobblies: The Origin of Industrial Unions in South Africa," *Ufahamu* 8:3 (1978), 122–38; Lucien van der Walt, "'The Industrial Union Is the Embryo of the Socialist Commonwealth': The International Socialist League and Revolutionary Syndicalism in South Africa, 1915–1920," *Comparative Studies of South Asia, Africa and the Middle East* 19:1 (1999), 5–30. On the 1911 strike, see Marcel van der Linden, "Transport Workers' Strike, Worldwide 1911," in

Neil Schlager (ed.), *St. James Encyclopedia of Labor History Worldwide. Major Events in Labor History and Their Impact.* 2 vols. (Detroit: St. James Press/Gale Group/Thomson Learning, 2003), vol. II, 334–36.

45. See for example Sandew Hira, *Van Priary tot en met de Kom. De geschiedenis van het verzet in Suriname, 1630–1940* (Rotterdam: Futile, 1982); Chandra Jayawardena, "Culture and Ethnicity in Guyana and Fiji," *Man*, New Series, 15:3 (September 1980), 430–50; Prabhu Mohapatra, "The Hosay Massacre of 1884: Class and Community Among Indian Immigrant Laborers in Trinidad," in Arvind N. Das and Marcel van der Linden (eds.), *Work and Social Change in Asia: Essays in Honour of Jan Breman* (New Delhi: Manohar, 2003), 187–230; Seymour Martin Lipset, "Radicalism or Reformism: The Sources of Working Class Politics," *American Political Science Review* 77 (1983), 1–18; Donna Gabaccia, "The 'Yellow Peril' and the 'Chinese of Europe': Global Perspectives on Race and Labor, 1815–1930," in Jan Lucassen and Leo Lucassen (eds.), *Migration, Migration History, History* (Berne: Peter Lang, 1997), 177–96; Touraj Atabaki, "Disgruntled Guests: Iranian Subaltern on the Margins of the Tsarist Empire," *International Review of Social History* 48 (2003), 401–26.

46. Mintz, *Sweetness and Power*, 183.

47. Elizabeth Perry, "Shanghai's Strike Wave of 1957," *China Quarterly* 137 (March 1994), 1–27 (here: 11).

48. See Jasmien Van Daele et al. (eds.), *ILO Histories. Essays on the International Labour Organization and Its Impact on the World during the Twentieth Century* (Berne: Peter Lang, 2010); Sandrine Kott and Joelle Droux (eds.), *Globalizing Social Rights. The ILO and Beyond* (London: Palgrave Macmillan, 2012); Daniel R. Maul, *Human Rights, Development and Decolonisation: The International Labour Organization (ILO) 1940–1970* (London: Palgrave Macmillan, 2011).

49. Rana Behal et al. (eds.), *Rethinking Work. Global Historical and Sociological Perspectives* (New Delhi: Tulika, 2011); Sabyasachi Bhattacharya (ed.), *Towards a New History of Work* (New Delhi: Tulika, 2014).

50. Ravi Ahuja, "Scenarios of Labor Regulation and Transterritorial History. Some Preliminary Observations," Opening Lecture to the Conference *Rethinking Labor History from a Global Perspective* (Berlin, October 12, 2006).

51. Frederick Cooper, *Colonialism in Question. Theory, Knowledge, History* (Berkeley: University of California Press, 2005), ch. 4.

52. See for instance Golan Balanchandran, *Globalizing Labor? Indian Seafarers and World Shipping, c.1870–1945* (Delhi and Oxford: Foundation Books, 2012); Ravi Ahuja, "Mobility and Containment. The Voyages of South Indian Seamen, *c.* 1900–1960," in Rana Behal and Marcel van der Linden (eds.), *India's Labouring Poor: Historical Studies, c. 1600–c. 2000* (Delhi, 2007), 111–41; Leon Fink, *Sweatshops at Sea. Merchant's Seamen in the World's First Globalized Industry, from 1812 to the Present* (Chapel Hill: University of North Carolina Press, 2011); Diana Frost, *Work and Community among West African Migrant Workers Since the Nineteenth Century* (Liverpool: Liverpool University Press, 1999).

53. Cooper, "African Labor History," 116.

CHAPTER 8
SCALE, SCOPE AND SCHOLARSHIP: REGIONAL PRACTICES AND GLOBAL ECONOMIC HISTORIES
Kenneth Pomeranz

An emerging field: From national to global in economic history

Economic history, as an academic field, was for a long time mostly the history of national economies—just as history in general tended to be national history. To be sure, trade across borders was always a frequent object of study, especially since it was often the best-documented form of economic activity. But until very recently cross-border flows of money and goods were usually small relative to total economic activity, and the flow of people—that is, migration—was usually assigned to social historians. If anything, the increasing sophistication of national income accounting after the Second World War (stimulated by wartime planning and by the rise of computers), and the increasingly strong conviction that national economies constituted integrated units,[1] furthered this trend. Decolonization—which meant that combined statistics for metropoles and colonies no longer appeared—furthered that trend. Then came the rise of the new economic history in the 1960s, which made greater use of formal modeling to measure the significance of particular events, institutions, inventions and so on—modeling that required data that were, or seemed to be, available only for a relatively few, mostly North Atlantic, countries.[2]

For all these reasons, economic history that was global, or at least intercontinental, was rare. Equally rare was economic history written by people outside the North Atlantic that caught the attention of economic historians in the richer countries. Two important exceptions were Eric Williams (from Trinidad) and Walter Rodney (from British Guiana), who argued that European economic history could not be understood apart from its relations with Africa and Latin America; there were also Indian scholars who emphasized the importance to Britain of colonial extraction.[3] In the 1960s and 1970s, some scholars from the "global north" picked up this theme, with greater success in getting their colleagues' attention.[4] For the most part, though, these were colleagues in history rather than economics departments; consequently, they had relatively little impact on economic history as practiced in the Global North.[5] Work by Kawano Kenji, Iinuma Jiro and Tsunoyama Sakae, which emphasized the importance of supposed peripheries to the development of advanced economies, and insisted that it was essential to study global capitalism as a unified system, seems not to have been noticed by scholars outside Japan.[6]

But the picture was very different in the emerging field of world history. That field arose, of course, largely in history departments among scholars who were interested in tracing comparisons and/or connections across vast geographic spaces. Interestingly, economic trends (broadly understood to include phenomena such as migration) formed the backbone of many pioneering attempts to teach and write world history. That the nutritional value of a kilo of rice or the efficacy of a particular method of shaping iron did not vary across cultures in the same way as political, social and cultural values made thinking beyond borders easier in these realms; moreover, material exports and imports (and their possible influence) were much easier to follow than movements of ideas. In fact, it is quite common for both critics and supporters of global history to assert that thus far it has been *too* materialist.

As the field of world/global history grew in Western universities, the questions and debates it took as central reverberated, and in the context of contemporary globalization, they have provoked considerable discussion among economic historians not previously involved in the field. Over the decades beginning, probably, c. 1980, economic history became less important in both history and economics departments. Beginning in the 1960s, an increasing amount of economic history (though certainly not all) employed formal econometric models; when many history departments took the "linguistic/cultural turn" in the 1980s, people studying economics using quantitative approaches often found themselves on the intellectual margins of their discipline. Meanwhile, many economics departments became more theoretical and less empirical, so that economic historians often felt undervalued in those departments, as well; certainly it became increasingly difficult to reach large audiences in both disciplines simultaneously. In recent years, there have been signs that those trends are reversing,[7] and while the main reasons are quite likely external— for example, the global economic crisis—the new questions, approaches and data emerging from a specifically transnational economic history have probably played some role as well.

An impressionistic survey suggests that so far, the stimulus has been larger within history departments than economics departments. The rapid growth of world history curricula—especially, though certainly not exclusively, in North America—has all but guaranteed an audience for scholarship that holds out the promise of providing an organizing frame for such courses and/or a way to give historians of one region some entrée into others that they need to teach as part of these surveys. Economics courses, which are rarely conceived on time/place lines, have provided less of an incentive to pick up the literature described in this chapter. And since history as a discipline is more methodologically eclectic than economics, it has no doubt been more common for historians than economists to sample broadly from the many approaches surveyed here. But these are matters of degree, and insofar as scholars with very different methods respond to each other, even passive observers of their debates gain some exposure to unfamiliar approaches.

Thus far, the resulting conversations have mostly been among scholars based in the world's richer countries. However, the topics under discussion have become increasingly global, and the possibility that the economic experience of the West cannot be fully understood outside a larger framework has gained traction. This shift makes it easier for a wider range of people to play important roles; and that, one suspects, will lead to further shifts in content as well.

Three central issues and one recurring problem

Since much of economic history is, at least in principle, measurable, it is particularly prone to teleology—to seeking the roots of an inevitable present rather than exploring contingency and/or the quality of past experience. This may be even truer of global economic history, since it can be argued that its topic exists only in the modern and perhaps early-modern eras.[8] For any given date, the extent to which we should approach the global economy as a unit, rather than as an aggregate of parts, is controversial. I have, however, excluded from this survey work that goes the furthest in subordinating the whole to its parts: work that may well include multiple "cases" from around the world, but treats each case as a strictly national or regional story.[9]

Consequently, much of global economic history concerns three overlapping issues: integration/interdependence, hierarchy and measurement.[10] Integration here means not only the amount of goods, capital, workers, pollutants and so forth moving among regions but also the extent to which inter-regional dynamics determine local outcomes. Whether or not contemporary interdependence is unique in kind, it is surely unprecedented in extent. Today's world economy is also strikingly hierarchical. Though our measurements are uncertain, it is unlikely that the difference in per capita income between the richest and poorest large-scale societies 250 years ago exceeded 4:1; today it far exceeds 40:1. Inequalities in wealth are even larger. And because of increased integration, these differences create more consequential inequalities of *power* than those between, say, seventeenth-century London and Turfan. Integration and hierarchy are not the only stories worth telling in global economic history, but their prominence is easy to explain.

Measurement is clearly not entirely separable from integration and hierarchy: they are often what we want to measure. But it merits its own category since so much work aimed at measuring important features of global economic history does so without directly addressing integration and hierarchy. When Angus Maddison, for instance, made estimates of historical GDP, he provided considerable fodder for analyses of hierarchy, but he did not focus on interactions that make hierarchy more than just inequality or on the emergence of a global division of labor. The same generally applies for estimates of global population, deforestation, literacy levels and so on.

Collaborations

Today global economic history is a rapidly growing field; it would be impossible to discuss all its practitioners, or even come close. Fortunately for us—and for the field—much of the more notable work is at least loosely collaborative; we can therefore discuss several major groupings, each involving a number of scholars.

Global History, Globally

One can loosely distinguish between institutionalized research programs, usually supported by significant grants, and more informal groups, often catalyzed by a seminal publication. Recent examples of the former include the Global Price and Incomes History Group (headquartered at UC Davis, with collaborators in Europe and Japan); the Global Economic History Network and its successor projects (headquartered at LSE, with participants in Europe, the United States, Japan, China and India); various projects centered at the International Institute for Social History in Amsterdam; and the Eurasia Project (headquartered at Lund University, with participants in Europe, Japan, China and the United States). Examples of the latter include networks influenced by World Systems theory, by the Acemoglu et al. "reversal of fortunes" literature, and by the confluence of Japanese scholarship on the "East Asian path to modernity" and the so-called "California school." As even this superficial and incomplete list suggests, projects emanating from the "developed" countries predominate, despite widespread interest in "southern" perspectives on global economic history.

The very limited survey that follows begins with institutionally based groupings and moves to more informal ones. Within each category, I also move very roughly from older to newer groups, from data-gathering and measurement to explanatory models, and toward research agendas that are less heavily focused on dynamics originating in Western Europe. The chapter ends by arguing that we need relatively deep histories of multiple regions in order to construct a global economic history that avoids being overly teleological.

Institutional groupings

Unsurprisingly, institutionally based collaborations are often more devoted to collecting and standardizing data than to elaborating a particular explanatory framework. But they do have methodologies, and those methodologies are never completely neutral.

The OECD's projects—now continued by the Maddison Project, based at the University of Groningen[11]—mostly focus on estimating historical GDP for each part of the world, with little attempt to explain differences or interactions: the sum of these parts is called "the world economy," whether in 1000 CE or 2000 CE. These estimates require big assumptions: about whether purchasing power parity adjustments can yield truly comparable numbers across vastly different times and places,[12] about the best proxies to use for crucial missing data, and about how to estimate nonmonetized economic activity. These assumptions are sometimes contested, but when they are explicit, we can anticipate the resulting biases and use the data appropriately.[13] Besides Maddison's work, recent projects have included recalculating late-medieval/early-modern Dutch and English national income (suggesting that those two countries became relatively rich earlier than we thought), estimating gross regional product for the eighteenth-century Lower Yangzi (suggesting impressive prosperity) and comparing it with the Netherlands *c.* 1800/1820 (suggesting that it had fallen behind by that date).[14]

The IISH was opened in 1935, but until recently focused almost exclusively on Europe. Its recent global projects include one led by Jan and Leo Lucassen on histories of long-distance migration[15] and one coordinated by Marcel van der Linden that tracks the spread of wage labor (and other labor relations). Much of this work is being presented at the World Economic History Congress, another Dutch-based institution that has also worked hard in recent years to move beyond Europe.[16]

The Eurasia Project, a much more limited collaboration, brought together historians, demographers and economists from several (mostly European) countries to ask a tightly focused set of comparative questions. (It has not addressed transregional flows, however, and so would not fit some definitions of global history.) Moreover, the authors have mostly eschewed making claims about entire societies.[17] Instead they have looked at small communities that left records that allow scholars to ask a common set of relatively fine-grained, event-centered, questions about villages in, say, eighteenth-century Tuscany, Liaoning, Sendai, Flanders and so on. Topics have included how rural families fared after a household head died young; how much difference property-owning, household size and so on made; how upward mobility for one nuclear family affected their less immediate kin; and how bad harvests affected birth and death rates. The comparisons of, say, vulnerability to particular kinds of common shocks represent potential supplements or alternatives to per capita income as measures of popular material welfare in preindustrial societies (though the project has also looked at some conventional measures of living standards).

These comparisons are made in terms of externally imposed categories, rather than emic ones. Thus findings for "the bottom 20% by income" can be compared even if that group consists of small landholders in one place and proletarians in another; such results can generate important new questions for both economic and social history. But even if the cases come from many places, this approach is better for capturing local structures than for explaining the emergence of global dynamics, and though indices of, say, harvest vulnerability could in principle be as significant for global comparison as GDP per capita or real wages, they tend to rely on the availability of unusually detailed local data sets: examples include especially detailed and frequently updated population registers, which are necessary for tracking changes in infant and child mortality and connecting them to other short-run variables, such as grain price fluctuations. Consequently, it is not likely that these studies can be duplicated for most places in the world for any period before very recent times. This work thus contributes rather indirectly to any unified story of global economic history.

The Global Price and Income History Project employs more conventional measurements, but improves and extends them. In particular, it has been assembling wage and price data for early-modern cities around the world. (It has also compiled some material for the last 150 years, for places where this was not already done, and done preliminary work on the Roman Empire.[18]) In addition to the data itself, this work has so far produced three noteworthy, though, tentative conclusions.

First, English and Dutch real wages were already well above those elsewhere in Europe in the seventeenth century, though still below mid-fifteenth-century levels.[19] Second,

GPIH (Global Price and Income History Project) affiliates have made two important corrections to historical real wage indices for Europe compiled in the 1930s–1950s. For one thing, those older indices failed to deal adequately with housing rents, which were a (highly variable) expense for most people, but which provided income for others. Second, older indices ignored differences between the goods that poor and rich people bought. The main purchases of the poor (particularly grains) rose sharply in price during most of early-modern times, while the rich bought many items (e.g., exotic imports and the labor of servants) whose real prices fell.[20] Overall, then, early-modern Western Europe was wealthier but even more unequal than older data suggested, and comparisons of its popular living standards to those elsewhere might look much less favorable than those of average incomes that included all classes. Among other things, this distinction helps add precision to debates raised by the California school and others about the timing of European economic leadership. It also bears on arguments made by Giovanni Arrighi and others about the uniqueness or lack thereof of preindustrial European "capitalism"—defined by Arrighi (following Fernand Braudel) not in terms of either product or factor markets, but as a system in which power relations facilitate the accumulation and reinvestment of capital by privileged parties.

Third, the GPIH group's data—which is shaky, but better than before—suggest that real wages in early-modern England and Holland were also much higher than those in other Eurasian "cores": the urban wages they have compiled for Canton, Beijing, Delhi, Osaka, Istanbul and so on are generally close to those for some eighteenth- and nineteenth-century cities in poorer parts of Europe, such as Milan (which are also close to estimates for the first-century Roman wages[21]), and fall still further behind later.[22] A separate analysis of India and Britain reached similar conclusions.[23] The Indian comparisons have been challenged by Prasannan Parthasarathi and Sashi Sivaramakrishna, who see rough parity in earnings between South Indian and English workers c. 1780; they question the representativeness of the data, the categorization of skilled and unskilled workers and the treatment of noncash parts of Indian wages. To an outsider, there seem to be data problems on both sides, so that the quantitative issues remain inconclusive.[24] And as we shall see, wages are not always a reliable proxy for popular welfare.

One important contribution of this work is that it introduces an improved measurement: the "welfare ratio."[25] This begins by looking at Northern European laborer families' consumption in basic physical units (calories, grams of protein, BTUs of heat, liters of alcohol, etc.); day wages that would buy the cheapest goods meeting those standards in any given place represent a "welfare ratio" of 1.0. (This is not "subsistence": adults earning lower wages can drink less alcohol, have fewer children, work more days per year, etc.) This has many advantages over the measure of real wages based on unvarying market baskets that may be relevant to only one of the places being compared.

Still, any wage-based proxy for living standards is perilous. Beyond the problems already mentioned, wage labor has different positions in different societies. For instance, probably over half of all workers in eighteenth-century England and the Netherlands relied on wages, and most of those were unskilled; in the Yangzi Delta, the figure was probably under 20 percent. A rough estimate suggests that Delta tenants (the largest occupational group) earned 2.5 to 3.0 times as much as a laborer, and smallholders (also more numerous than proletarians) more still. Thus comparing unskilled wages compares something near the mid-point of the English or Dutch income distribution with a much lower point on the Yangzi Delta distribution, so that even the large real wages differences found by Allen et. al. do not necessarily indicate a significant difference in popular living standards.[26] In light of this and other problems, Kent Deng and Patrick O'Brien have recently argued that both wage and GDP data are too unreliable to be useful for assessing the onset of East/West economic divergence, and that data which reflect the basic nutritional status of poor people are probably safer to use.[27] But real wages can be used—though again, only cautiously—to estimate another important variable: labor productivity. Where labor markets function well, wages should roughly reflect comparative productivity—but only for similarly situated workers. For instance, weavers or farmers who were free and had secure access to loom or land would normally keep more of their output than either bound laborers or proletarians: thus comparable earnings might mask big productivity differences. Notably, those who argue for earnings parity between eighteenth-century South Indian and English laborers also argue that the former had a better bargaining position vis-à-vis their employers; this strengthens claims for comparable living standards, but may suggest lower labor productivity.[28] (This may also be true for some comparisons of eighteenth-century Chinese nonagricultural workers.[29]) Thus even sharply different wages may not indicate different living standards, while relatively equal earnings might conceal emerging productivity differences.

The last institutional network considered here is the Global Economic History Network (and its successors),[30] organized by Patrick O'Brien. It has focused on convening research conferences on a various global topics: the history of cotton textiles, regimes for creating and disseminating "useful knowledge," imperialism, state formation, factor markets and so on. Other activities have included faculty exchanges, postdoctoral fellowships, conferences and conference sessions held under other auspices and so on. While there has been some data collection and a number of publications,[31] the program's primary focus has been discussion among the participants themselves—chosen with an emphasis on diversity of topics, methodologies and opinions, rather than any shared outlook. Much of the group's output has therefore come in the form of work published by individuals but influenced by these interactions.

GEHN's publications have also tended to be more narrative than those of most groups discussed here. That tendency is reinforced by its focus on institutions, technology and "useful knowledge"—topics not very conducive to direct cliometric measurement. This agenda has led to discussions focused more on transregional comparisons than transregional connections; some of the resulting work has been explicitly global, but more has probably consisted of scholars placing whatever regional economies they work on in a global context. Consequently, the group has been particularly useful to people who come to global history from a time/place specialization; and since that is how historians generally work, GEHN's approach may be particularly conducive to exerting influence beyond *economic* history. However, this also means that it has had few consensus conclusions to offer.

Some problems of explanation

Global economic history, as we have seen, is particularly focused on cross-societal comparisons and interactions. It thus sometimes unsettles causal sequences inferred from the histories of single regions—when A was followed by B in one area but not in another—and opens up new questions about how inter-regional influences may have reinforced, undermined or otherwise altered more local dynamics. Meanwhile, any structural regularities we perceive behind long-distance influences or parallels must work through local institutions of some kind; consequently, dynamics on different scales cannot be completely isolated from each other for analysis. Identifying and evaluating explanations is thus particularly hard for global history—and it is hard enough for economic history on any scale. While data become more plentiful when we focus on the last two centuries, the changes to be explained become more rapid, and in some ways more elusive.

Before discussing groups defined by shared explanatory frameworks, it is worth noting some methodological problems in moving from measurement to explanation. The explanations for most economic growth during the last 200-plus years do not emerge directly from the canonical factors of production: land, labor and capital. Population growth clearly cannot explain rising *per capita* incomes; increases in labor time explain only a small fraction of modern growth. (Increased labor inputs—both through population growth and through the "industrious revolution"[32]—do explain a hefty share of *pre*modern growth, along with opening new land and some modest capital deepening.) Capital accumulation—as measured by increases in the market value of capital stock per person—explains only a quarter of post-1800 per capita growth in wealthy societies; increases in land under use explain very little. So unless market values grossly understate the contribution of these factors, most modern growth is left as an unexplained residual.

This residual is usually labeled "total factor productivity" or "efficiency," and attributed to "innovation," "improved institutions," "technology," "the quality of labor" and other factors that escape direct measurement. Education is one common proxy for many of these factors, but it explains a third or less of the residual.[33]

We must thus have recourse to less directly visible factors. Institutional influences—the impact of new laws, for instance—are hard to measure, but at least the institutions themselves can be seen, and narratives about their importance can be subjected to basic tests of plausibility. Do the changes occur when and where they should to explain the outcomes? Did contemporaries see them as important? Technological explanations can be interrogated the same way: What did a given machine or technique do? How big were the sectors that employed it? Did people perceive a bottleneck before these innovations came along, or did they say that these innovations had spillover effects? A complication is that new technologies may make some activity more rewarding (and thus prevalent), but may also free resources from activity X that get redeployed in a very different sector; this can play havoc with using regressions to link specific technological changes to overall output.[34] Cultural influences are even harder to capture.[35]

Meanwhile, a "productivity" residual that generally rises over time will appear correlated with many other series that do the same. For instance, the residual for American economic growth fit very nicely with time series data for "effective" energy use—until fairly recently, when computers and de-industrialization offer credible explanations for divergence.[36] This seems a plausible story, but the correlation itself tells us little: various other series (e.g., for water or newsprint) would show similar patterns. Moreover, all of these problems are greatly compounded when we look at less well-documented and/or less heavily monetized economies. Thus, although statistics are essential for global economic histories, they do not dispense with the need for other kinds of narrative, evidence and argument.

Group research programs based on intellectual affinities

Before discussing four particular groups, let me quickly acknowledge how much this leaves out. Many relevant groupings have not taken "the global economy" as their *explicit* focus, but have worked across national and regional lines on topics that are obviously relevant to global economic history. One such group studies commodities—coffee, cotton and cotton goods, silver, silk, grain, tobacco, contraband drugs and so on.[37] Another tracks merchant groups: Armenians, Fujianese, Parsis, Jews, Genoese and so forth.[38] A third examines techniques governing long-distance trade: methods of navigation, finance, contract enforcement, suppression of piracy, tariffs and so on. While the studies of commodity chains often have a good deal to say about hierarchy in the world economy, the other types of work more often address integration, explaining declines (or, less often, increases) in transaction costs that led to new patterns of interdependence. Due to space limitations, I have listed only a few of many possible examples here.

Another cluster of contributions has focused on modeling global economic integration. Here the work of Jeffrey Williamson and his collaborators has been particularly important, highlighting price convergence and/or correlations of price movements in different places. This has included work on migration and wage convergence[39] and on price correlations, both for single commodities and broad market baskets.[40]

This work has placed the onset of true globalization in the 1800s, with intercontinental (and especially transatlantic) price differences narrowing rapidly after three centuries of mostly directionless wandering.[41] It argues that trade expansion between 1492 and 1800 was largely driven by developments *within* the world's constituent societies (especially population growth), while expansion after 1800 was increasingly driven by market integration between trading economies. Only the latter qualifies as "globalization."

Thus defined, globalization is only part of "global economic history." It leaves out comparable phenomena that might have influenced equal numbers of people: Keller and Shiue, for instance, find more price integration in China *c.* 1780 than in continental Europe,[42] and China had considerably more people than the entire Atlantic world at that point. It also leaves out global currents with enormous effects that did not result in large-scale and repeated flows. The diffusion of American crops (corn, tobacco, potatoes, etc.), for instance, did not involve Ireland, Poland, Ghana or Yunnan importing them year after year; instead, they began to grow these plants themselves. The same would apply to many diffusions of machines, institutions and so on. Thus we have major economic transformations triggered by transcontinental contacts but falling outside "globalization." Effects mediated by politics would also be left out: for example, trade with tariffs that limited price integration, but that facilitated through those very tariffs the building of states that underwrote conditions for subsequent economic expansion. (Such effects are especially important in the "world systems" and "reversal of fortunes" literatures.) Some have argued that the inability to trace these effects makes the methods of Williamson et. al. the wrong tools for investigating the question, "When Did Globalization Begin?"[43] However, an approach that gives globalization a clear and testable meaning seems quite useful so long as we understand that such globalization does not exhaust the field of global-level economic history, even after 1800.[44]

O'Rourke and Williamson argue forcefully that the more or less continuous growth in what they call "global" trade (i.e., trade between Europe and non-Europe)[45] since 1500 masks two very different regimes of expansion. It is only under the second of these regimes, inaugurated after 1800 (or perhaps even 1840), that increases in trade volumes have been accompanied by striking declines in price and wage differences between sending and receiving ports. Some of this convergence reflects technological improvements in shipping and communications, but they estimate that institutional changes have been at least as important: tariff reductions, abolitions of monopolies, reductions in piracy and so on. The timing of price convergence tracks those changes more closely than it does purely technological ones. Moreover, Europe's external trade rose faster in the nineteenth century—the classic era of liberalization—than in the twentieth, even though income growth (which should increase trade) was much faster after 1900.[46] They also argue that globalization since 1800 has generally led to greater transnational equality in real wages—though they are very careful to note that this convergence has been driven overwhelmingly by migration (mostly to a few resource-rich countries[47]), not by other flows, and so can only be expected in times and places with relatively free migration.

O'Rourke and Williamson also find growing trade volumes under a first regime of global trade expansion, in place from roughly 1500 to 1800—but they see little price convergence in this period, due to trade restrictions and high protection costs.[48] Under those circumstances, they argue, increased volumes must have been driven by changes in either European demand or extra-European sources of supply. Skipping over possible changes in tastes, they argue that growing European demand must have resulted from rising income: specifically, the incomes of the rich, since most pre-1800 imports to Europe were luxuries. They then estimate income trends for the wealthy that correlate closely with imports.[49] But European developments cannot explain the periods in which volumes and/or prices of Asian and American imports diverged. O'Rourke and Williamson speculate that periods in which China, Japan and Korea retreated into "relative autarchy" may have been crucial, as they enabled Europeans to buy more of goods such as Southeast Asian pepper and spices without pushing up prices. This would, in turn, suggest that while the expansion of Europe's trade after 1800 was driven largely by increased global integration, its growth before 1800 was partly due to global *dis*integration.

This rough contrast between pre- and post-1800 worlds is intriguing, but should be viewed with caution. A massive contraction of Chinese trade seems unlikely, except in the mid-1600s; our data for the eighteenth century (and more tentatively, for most of the sixteenth) suggest the opposite.[50] The 1500–1800 era also seems marked by some overall trade liberalization, at least in South and Southeast Asia, and perhaps (despite some reversals) in China as well. Thus the discontinuity O'Rourke and Williamson suggest for Europe may have been absent in Asia.[51] Much of South Asia (and Java) may even have experienced a discontinuity opposite to Europe's *c.* 1800, with increasing British and Dutch territorial power creating more monopolistic trade regimes than had prevailed earlier, which would have had considerable costs to development[52].

More generally, assigning all true "globalization" to the nineteenth and twentieth centuries overlooks too many ways in which early-modern illiberalism laid foundations for later developments. Chartered monopolies certainly blocked some trade, but given very uncertain returns and high start-up costs for both long-distance trade and overseas settlement, it seems unlikely that these activities would have grown more rapidly without ways for investors to exclude rivals for an extended period of time, thus making them confident of future profits.[53] It is even harder to imagine how the Americas would have become positioned such that transatlantic trade could become a major driver of nineteenth-century integration without massive imports of unfree labor.[54] The de-emphasizing of technology by Williamson et. al. and their sharp separation of external and internal factors (made even sharper by focusing on noncompeting imports such as spices and pepper, rather than competing goods like cloth[55]) also suggest the need for other, complementary agendas. It is also important to remember that the "globalization" research agenda is very heavily focused on the integration side of our two-part agenda of explaining integration and hierarchy. Investigating the exercise of power, which is essential to distinguishing durable hierarchy from mere (and perhaps very temporary) inequality, takes us back more frequently to the early-modern period and the rise of Europe's overseas empires (along with Russian and Chinese expansion across the Eurasian landmass, giving them greater control of its trade routes). And there is no shortage of work suggesting that those relationships had effects that lasted into the post-1800 world, whether the specific colonial tie was severed soon thereafter (as in Latin America) or endured well into the twentieth century (as in India).[56]

By contrast, Wallersteinian World Systems theorists are more concerned with explaining hierarchy than integration. The basics of this view need not be reviewed here. It has stimulated an enormous amount of research in global economic history—including post-1990 attempts to apply the model to periods before 1500 and to places outside the sway of the Western "core," which Wallerstein himself excluded from his analysis. In the process, scholars have sought to clarify some key ideas, including the criteria that show that a "world system" exists.[57]

However, the original World Systems model seems at odds with much recent research. As more sources from within "peripheral" economies have been found, even the places that once seemed most completely dominated by the "core" (e.g., colonial Latin America and the Caribbean) have come to look much less dependent than World Systems theory suggests.[58] In addition, quantitative research has not shown that super profits gained in "peripheries" were crucial to European capital accumulation (though neither has it completely ruled out that possibility, much less claims that peripheries were essential for other reasons). [59] Third, various key terms seem to be vaguely or inconsistently defined. There has been particular debate about the concept of "semi-periphery," for instance, in part because, while Wallerstein has insisted that this represents a permanent condition, several countries originally relegated to that category (particularly on the edges of Europe and in East Asia) now have "core"-level incomes.[60]

The conceptualization of capitalism in much of World Systems research can also be problematic. Wallerstein made a point of utilizing Braudel's definition of "capitalism": a system (of whatever size) in which political power serves the project of ongoing accumulation of profit by investors of capital, generally through allowing the *circumvention* of truly competitive markets. This made it easier to think about how societies not based on wage labor could nonetheless be part of a "capitalist" system and become increasingly bound to cores without becoming like them. But it has sometimes invited a simplistic conflation of all profits based on exclusive rights—whether from patents based on years of research, armed trading monopolies or slave ownership—and encouraged invoking the supposed needs of an abstract capitalist system to explain too many disparate phenomena.[61] (The variety of routes to profit that World Systems theory considers to be consistent with capitalism should, on the contrary, make us very reluctant to assume that the system, as opposed to some specific actor, needs any particular mechanism to survive.)

As evidence of economic dynamism outside of Wallerstein's world system has mounted, World Systems scholars have responded in diverse ways. Some have latched on to this evidence to reinforce claims about the importance to Europe of appropriating contributions from elsewhere. (Sometimes, however, these contributions—from slave labor to the Muslim preservation and extension of Greek science to the potato to Third World resources—are so heterogeneous that the idea is not analytically useful.[62]) But only a minority have accepted the ideas that these "external" economies were already sufficiently dynamic that neither their evolution after "incorporation" nor that of the world economy should be explained solely in terms of European influence.

Giovanni Arrighi's *Adam Smith in Beijing* does take that idea seriously. It combines an essentially Wallersteinian account of Western economic development with arguments drawn from the "California school" (discussed below) and Kaoru Sugihara about a distinct East Asian growth path, and argues (again following Sugihara) that today's world economy is a fusion of the two.[63]

Daron Acemoglu and his associates agree that the impact of European colonialism on institutions elsewhere goes a long way toward explaining contemporary inequality, but similarities to World Systems theory stop there. For Acemoglu, economic performance is largely explained by a country's institutions, and those institutions stem from early colonial choices. Where population was very sparse—an indication, in this view, that indigenous institutions discouraged economic growth—Europeans founded settler colonies, and the settlers were usually able to secure a liberal property rights regime; this promoted growth, creating some of today's wealthiest societies. But where Europeans found dense populations—indicating, ironically, "better" indigenous institutions—exploiting this population through forced labor or tribute was more promising than displacing them. This entailed reinforcing coercive precolonial institutions (e.g., Incan labor tribute) and/or introducing others (e.g., chattel slavery). Saddled with such institutions, these colonies grew more slowly than settler colonies—and lagged even further after independence, since new rulers again took over exploitative systems rather than dismantling them, and their ill effects became ever more crippling as modern economies became more dependent on skilled workers.[64] Thus urbanization rates and population density *c.* 1800 (used, problematically, as proxies for output per capita at first contact[65]) are inversely correlated with per capita income today.[66]

The contrasts to World Systems theory here are far more significant than any superficial resemblances. In Wallerstein's view, an ever-evolving core acts *continually* on peripheries to reproduce institutions that keep peripheral resources and labor cheap and facilitate the export of profits. The "reversal of fortunes" argument instead posits a single critical intervention, which says nothing about any effects of subsequent global connections; the persistence of bad institutions is not fully explained, but seems to be internally driven.

The model is elegant, but has several problematic features. First, it narrows the impact of colonialism to one dichotomous variable—bestowing good or bad property rights—which ignores many other relevant policy areas. Second, it treats colonial preferences alone as decisive, even though most colonies had small bureaucracies and left much dispute settlement to "traditional" authorities wielding "traditional law." Third, sparse population sometimes led to *more* coercive institutions rather than to liberal policies: the extreme violence used to obtain miners, rubber collectors and so on in equatorial Africa is an obvious example. Precolonial population densities did influence European decisions about settlement, and the presence of white settlers did affect institutions, but the links are much less direct than Acemoglu et. al. suggest.

Indeed, several historians have argued that the distinction between "colonies of settlement" and "colonies of exploitation" is largely a retrospective creation, which would have made little sense to anybody, even as late as 1850. Others have emphasized that most places we now think of as "colonies of settlement," attracting mostly "free labor," began with largely unfree migrants who remained economically crucial well after free migrants began arriving in large numbers.[67] Neatly divided "property respecting" and "insecure property" systems probably *reflect* long-run development as much as they determined it. (The Sokoloff and Engerman version of the institutionalist argument, it should be noted, has feedback loops in it that mitigate this problem.) After all, colonization often involved violent dispossession of some people *in order* to confer property rights on others: not only homesteading settlers but collaborating local elites, such as in parts of India; creators of plantations using coerced labor; railway developers who received large grants of adjacent land; and so on. Where those who resisted the (re-)assignment of land, water, labor and other rights were crushingly defeated, what remained was the relatively secure property rights of the victors and their allies. Where that victory was incomplete—not just in places where colonizers settled for extractive strategies from the start but also in places where settler colonialism hit serious obstacles (e.g., Algeria or South Africa)—the original measures aimed at dispossessing the colonized often stayed in place alongside measures designed to protect a favored group.

An article by Ewout Frankema, moreover, follows Acemoglu in looking at correlations in large data sets rather than case studies, and finds no correlation one way or the other between white settlement and colonial extraction in the form of taxes, either in absolute terms or relative to incomes.[68] Rates of extraction were much more strongly shaped by other, mostly local, factors—access to ports (and thus export revenues), timing of colonization, metropolitan willingness to delegate administration to "natives" and so on. If the colonies of white settlement had a fiscal advantage, Frankema concludes, it lay not in their enjoying low taxes but in comparatively high rates of government spending on public goods.[69] This suggests more complicated connections between colonial institutions and development. Investments in public goods require *repeated* choices, and particular investments may be either good or bad choices; thus unlike the yes/no and relatively slow-changing decisions about, say, crown ownership of mineral rights, they do not suggest a story featuring one crucial "reversal of fortune."

The last research program I have room to address here is (like GEHN among the institutional groups) the one with which I have been most involved. Also like GEHN, it has tended toward "narrative" approaches, and toward transregional comparisons, retaining "regions" of various sizes and definitions alongside nations and global systems as units of analysis. It takes a particular interest in East Asia's role in global economic history—both for its own sake and as a foil that highlights neglected aspects of the more familiar Atlantic-centered stories. This regional basis is of course also limiting—raising questions about whether other regional histories might be used in similar ways.[70]

Since the 1980s, several Japanese scholars—Takeshi Hamashita, Heita Kawakatsu, Kaoru Sugihara and others—have traced the historic emergence of an East and Southeast Asian littoral region,[71] evolving (with interruptions) over many centuries, but especially between roughly 1400 and 1800. Intra-regional trade developed gradually, eventually outgrowing dependence on the scaffolding of China's state-centered "tribute system." Multilateral networks bypassing China also became stronger, though many of them used goods that could be sold there as "currency," with which to clear other balances and realize profit.[72]

Meanwhile, Japan undertook considerable import-substituting industrialization (in silk, porcelain, sugar refining, etc.) as the Tokugawa retreated from China's tribute system, created their own smaller system and modestly increased their trade with other parts of Asia.[73] By the 1800s, this had evolved into a Japanese ambition to replace China at the center of an East Asian regional system: an ambition that makes an intra-Asian frame much more important for Japanese development in the Meiji than most Western scholars have acknowledged. Many early Japanese textile mills, for instance, were financed by Chinese merchants based abroad and aimed at the Chinese market; the share of Asia in Japan's trade grew continually from 1890 (when that of the West briefly peaked) through the Second World War.[74]

This work reads like a prelude to economists' descriptions of the so-called flying geese pattern of postwar East Asian development, with Japan off-loading more labor-intensive industries to other East and Southeast Asian countries as it moved up the value-added ladder, and South Korea and Taiwan repeating this process decades later.[75] Research showing that Korea, Taiwan and Manchuria industrialized more rapidly under Japanese rule than most other colonies did—including more controversial claims that Japanese colonies were generally better off than colonies of other powers—provided a temporal link between the historical literature repositioning the rise of Japan and stories of more recent "economic miracles" elsewhere in Asia.[76]

More recently, this literature has also fused, to some extent, with a literature focused more on China, often labeled "the California school." These authors (Andre Gunder Frank, Jack Goldstone, James Lee, Li Bozhong, Kenneth Pomeranz, R. Bin Wong, Robert Marks and others) disagree on many points but have generally agreed on a rough comparability in economic performance between China and Europe—and between the Yangzi Delta, its most developed region, and Britain and Holland—until some time in the 1700s.[77] Notably, this chronology of divergence, which was once very much at odds with the estimates of scholars (mostly Europeanists) constructing historical GDP estimates, is no longer much of an outlier, though some gaps remain.[78] Some of these scholars have also argued that Western Europe's subsequent leadership owed much to its relations with areas outside Europe, which provided far greater relief from the ecological pressures created by early-modern growth than East Asian cores could gain from their peripheries.

It was nonetheless obvious that China's institutions worked very differently from those in Europe; some of my own recent work, for instance, has sought to sketch those institutions and argue that, despite multiple nineteenth- and twentieth-century upheavals, they remained relevant to the rapid growth of the late twentieth century.[79] Salient features this approach considers are a highly productive agriculture based on smallholders and relatively secure tenants and the subsequent low rates of proletarianization despite considerable commercialization; an unusually slow exit from the countryside during the first several decades of industrialization; and technological and organizational choices in both agriculture and industry that absorbed relatively large amounts of both skilled and unskilled labor and (until recently) relatively little capital, energy and natural resources. This partly reflects the fact that resource bonanzas accompanied industrialization in the West but not in East Asia, and—as Sugihara has noted—that Asians were largely excluded from the most resource-rich countries during the great global migrations of c. 1830–1930.

Many of these features also characterized Japanese development, though with very different underlying institutions.[80] Combining these China- and Japan-centered stories suggests an "East Asian path of development" that, given how many lives it has transformed, may be as historically significant as the North Atlantic story. Over time, the Eastern and Western paths have converged—especially since the post–Second World War order allowed Japan, Taiwan, Korea and later China equal access to global resources and markets—but that convergence has remained incomplete. Moreover, these scholars suggest, this convergence has been mutual, not just a result of East Asia "catching up." (One example is the drastic decline in Western energy intensities since the 1970s.) Sugihara has further argued that because the East Asian development path is more labor-absorbing and less resource-intensive, it represents a more sustainable model for future growth in general than the North Atlantic pattern.[81]

How much China's recent boom still fits this pattern is murky, however: development in its interior regions not only lags far behind the coastal provinces but is consistently more resource intensive.[82] The historical significance of the "East Asian path" does not, of course, require that this path turn out to be further extensible, but a sense of whether that path is likely to remain robust, peter out, converge unilaterally toward a Western one or remain one side of a mutual convergence will clearly influence how we understand its significance.

Many elements of this argument remain contested and continue to evolve in response to new evidence—generated by members of this group (notably James Lee and Li Bozhong) and by others responding to them (e.g., Debin Ma and Jan Luiten Van Zanden). For instance, as more research has suggested that Yangzi Delta living standards remained close to Western European ones much longer than real wages did,[83] explaining the causes and significance of China's low rate of proletarianization has become much more central to my work;[84] others are focusing more on related issues of urbanization and nonagricultural technological change.

Indeed, it seems increasingly clear that whatever the economically crucial differences between parts of "the West" and parts of "the Rest" may have been, they did not arise from a difference between advanced and backward countrysides. By the eighteenth century, the urbanization rates, capital intensity of urban production and productivity of urban workers in England and the Netherlands seem to have been exceptional.[85] For the still-rural majority, however, no such divergence is evident even in the early 1800s, and total factor productivity was still much higher in Yangzi Delta agriculture than anywhere in Europe.[86] "Agrarian fundamentalism"[87]—the once-common assumption that, as the basis of premodern societies, agriculture must be key to explaining why some places industrialized first—now seems discredited: high rates of agricultural labor productivity—not to mention total factor productivity—simply do not correlate with early industrialization.[88] But an emerging consensus on where not to look has not meant agreement on where or how we should look.

After arguing that Chinese and European institutions were probably comparably adaptive for a preindustrial world, Jean-Laurent Rosenthal and R. Bin Wong turn to considering how different political structures may have influenced manufacturing. They argue that the political disunity and frequent warfare of Europe (compared to China's *relative* unity and internal peace) encouraged placing fixed capital behind city walls; since urban labor generally cost more (largely due to food costs) and capital was cheaper there (because information was cheaper), urban locations encouraged more capital-intensive production techniques, which gradually raised industrial labor productivity.[89] Others have suggested guild structures, freedom from lordly power, relatively cheap energy and a distinctive European scientific tradition as alternate or complementary explanations.[90]

Regardless of how "California school" propositions fare in the light of future research, they address only one part of global economic history. However, they seem to have influenced work in various other areas. Some recent work on South Asia, for instance, has referenced this reframing of Europe/East Asia comparisons, even as it takes the "divergence debate" in other directions,[91] so has work on other regions and periods. This influence may be partly because the California school propositions avoid the sharp categorical distinctions central to some other approaches: in contrast to deducing a place's prospects based on its location in the core, semiperiphery or periphery, whether it was a settler colony, or whether it was "globalizing," this approach suggests multiple paths to modernity, based on several continuous rather than dichotomous variables, and makes global ties influential, but not decisive. Thus it also suggests various ways in which regional units of various kinds and sizes remain important to the story of global economic history.

Meanwhile, other kinds of histories are using transregional comparisons and connections to understand developments in Europe—thus looking afresh at the relationship between integration and hierarchy. In these stories, Europe remains central but is not the "unmoved mover" of economic modernity. I close, then, with two recent studies focused explicitly on Britain.

Robert Allen's *The British Industrial Revolution in Global Perspective* (2009) is, on one level, focused on a series of labor-saving, energy-using technical innovations. Most were invented in Britain and for decades thereafter mostly used there, but not, Allen insists, because nobody else could have adopted them. Rather, he says, "what made the Industrial Revolution British" was a unique combination of high wages and cheap energy. This made it uniquely worthwhile for Britons to develop and deploy labor-saving equipment, even when it used huge amounts of energy—early steam engines, for instance, converted less than 1 percent of heat energy used into motion. But as the market for these machines grew, it became profitable to make improvements, including ones that reduced the engine's energy needs. Eventually, these "micro-inventions" made the original "macro-invention" economical in places with relative prices that were very different from Britain's, spreading industrialization overseas.[92]

At first glance, there may seem to be little "global perspective" in this argument. Nor does it fit well with Parthasarathi's recent work on England and South Asia—which focuses on textiles and on British attempts to match Indian *quality*, rather than to cut production costs.[93] But Allen's focus on Britain's unusually low energy costs fits well with my own arguments about the steam engine,[94] and the focus on high nominal wages and technological choices fits well with Rosenthal and Wong's comparative argument, as well as Parthasarathi's earlier work.[95] And pursuing the origins of these high wages leads us beyond Britain itself.

Rejecting, as we have seen, "agrarian fundamentalism," Allen sees a boom in overseas trade pushing up British wages: workers were needed not only for the production of exported goods, but in a variety of trade-related service occupations (from dockworkers to sailors to insurance brokers). And Britain's naval victories and concomitant success in colonization were crucial in creating this dynamic. As Philip Hoffmann puts it, summarizing Allen, "When victories in warfare gave Britain the lion's share in [those] colonial goods and in intercontinental trade as a whole ... That was in large part what boosted British wages and created the incentive to mechanize."[96] He further suggests that Britain's victories may have shifted not just *where* early industrialization happened, but *that* it happened: given Britain's relatively small seventeenth- to eighteenth-century population, dominance in overseas trade raised its wages much more—creating much larger incentives to use fewer workers—than a similar boom could have done in more populous (and coal-poor) France.

Hoffmann, meanwhile, has argued convincingly elsewhere that well before Europeans had a clear lead in economic productivity, they had attained primacy in the production of cheap, reliable and sophisticated weapons.[97] That does not mean that Europe's growing military superiority directly raised the continent's wages; indeed, they did not rise much in most of Europe until mechanization was well underway (confirming the importance of micro-inventions that made machines useful in new places). Moreover, Hoffmann is at least as interested in technical spillovers from war-making as in direct returns to conquest. Nor is a claim that extra-continental trade raised wages the same as what Sugihara or I say about ecological relief. But an interesting link between these perspectives, at least for Britain, seems implicit in Kevin O'Rourke and Jeffrey Williamson's article "From Malthus to Ohlin."

In a Malthusian world, these authors argue, population growth should push wages down *relative to land rents*. (Wages could, of course, still rise absolutely if productivity improved enough.) In a modern economy, however, the wage-to-rent ratio can rise even while land is becoming scarcer relative to labor.

O'Rourke and Williamson then create a model based on Malthusian assumptions and use it to predict changes in the wage/rent ratio based on British population trends for 1500–1936. The model works almost perfectly up until about 1730. It works less well from 1730 to 1800, and much less well from 1800 to 1842: while population growth still depresses the wage/rent ratio, it does so less than the model predicts, and the fit deteriorates over time. The model fails completely after 1842, when the wage/rent ratio soared despite rapid population growth.

This much is unsurprising, though placing approximate dates on Britain's escape from quasi-Malthusian[98] dynamics is certainly useful. Next, however, O'Rourke and Williamson argue that two basic factors explain this turnaround: (1) unprecedented gains in labor productivity and (2) a much smaller increase in land prices than the population-based model would predict, because land-intensive imports increasingly competed with Britain's farms, pastures and forests. Running two sets of simulations—one in which labor productivity remained unchanged and one in which transatlantic trade (their proxy for all overseas trade) remained too small to influence British prices—Williamson and O'Rourke find that these two factors were about equally important. In other words, all of this century's famously productivity-enhancing changes put together—new technologies, organizational change, fossil fuels, better-educated and healthier workers and so on—were, according to these estimates, no more important in launching Britain's economic modernity than transatlantic trade alone. If Britain's enormous emigration and its trade with Asia, Africa and Australia were added to the model, extra-continental connections would loom even larger.

If land-intensive imports from beyond Europe were so important for changing wage/rent ratios after 1842, they were probably also central to the drift away from Malthusian dynamics in 1730–1842 (for which the data quality does not allow a similar simulation). After all, technological change was slower in that period and improvements in workers' health and education minimal; meanwhile agriculture and forestry had greater weight, both in productivity indexes and in consumers' market baskets, than they would later.

The real world is always messier than simulations, and this is only one study. Still, it does strongly suggest that overseas connections were central to launching and continuing Northwest Europe's "self-sustaining growth." And as I have suggested earlier, those connections are not as easily detached from either earlier colonization or continuing applications of coercion as some models would suggest.

Thus early-modern increases in both integration and hierarchy—albeit small compared to what followed after *c.* 1800—appear important to explaining how one part of the world became the center of a vastly more integrated and more unequal modern world economy. Our understanding of these processes remains quite limited, and we will need to explore them on multiple spatial scales. Interacting regional histories, rather than forces from a single source, made the world economy; at the same time, however, an emerging world economy was also remaking regions.

We thus find ourselves needing more regionally focused research, especially on parts of today's "Global South" as well as more research that takes as its object global structures and dynamics. And it is essential that global economic history maintains connections with the other kinds of global history that are now taking shape. Specialization is an inevitable part of the production of new knowledge, but since history emphasizes contextual understanding, "new knowledge" is of very limited significance without ongoing attempts at integration and synthesis. It is a good thing that a specifically global economic history is now more important to the general study of economic history. It is probably also a good thing that it is becoming somewhat less central than it once was to the field of global history, thanks to the increasing willingness of political, social, cultural and intellectual historians to attempt global narratives. But global economic history cannot afford to become fully absorbed into, or detached from, either of these fields, lest it lose the stimulus that it derives from the competing pressures exerted by diverse constituencies.

Notes

1. On national accounts, see for instance Yuval Yonay, *The Struggle over the Soul of Economics: Institutionalist and Neoclassical Economists in America between the Wars* (Princeton, NJ: Princeton University Press, 1998), 184–95. On the national economy as a unit, see Timothy Mitchell, "Economist and the Economy in the Twentieth Century," in George Steinmetz (ed.), *The Politics of Method in the Human Sciences* (Durham, NC: Duke University Press, 2005), 126–41 especially 132–38.
2. Since then, large amounts of quantitative data have been discovered and reconstructed for some other places, a trend which is likely to continue. But the gap remains large.

3. Eric Williams, *Capitalism and Slavery* (New York: Russell and Russell, 1944); Walter Rodney, *How Europe Underdeveloped Africa* (Washington, DC: Howard University Press, 1981); Romesh C. Dutt, *The Economic History of British India: A Record of Agriculture and Land Settlements, Trade and Manufacturing Industries, Finance and Administration from the Rise of British Power in 1757 to the Accession of Queen Victoria in 1837* (London: K. Paul, Trench, Trubner and Co., 1902); Romesh C. Dutt, *India in the Victorian Age: An Economic History of the People* (London: K. Paul, Trench, Trubner and Co., 1904).

4. E.g. Andre Gunder Frank, *Capitalism and Underdevelopment in Latin America: Historical Studies of Chile and Brazil* (New York: Monthly Review Press, 1967); Andre Gunder Frank, *World Accumulation, 1492–1789* (New York: Algora Publishing, 1978); Immanuel Wallerstein, *Capitalist Agriculture and the Origins of the European World Economy* (New York: Academic Press, 1974); Henrique Cardoso and Enzo Faletto, *Dependency and Development in Latin America* (Berkeley: University of California Press, 1979).

5. It should be noted that scholars in the North often granted or even emphasized the relevance of the Western past to the Global South's present, and took seriously noneconometric studies of that past: the journal *Economic Development and Cultural Change* is perhaps the most obvious among many examples. But fewer people accepted the relevance of the Global South's own past to modern economic issues, especially those in "advanced" countries.

6. Kawano Kenji and Iinuma Jirō, *Sekai shihonshugi no keisei* [*The Formation of World Capitalism*] (Tokyo: Iwanami Shoten, 1967); Kawano Kenji and Iinuma Jirō, *Sekai shihonshugi no rekishi kōzō* [*The Historical Structure of World Capitalism*] (Tokyo: Iwanami Shoten, 1970). Shigeru Akita argues elsewhere in this volume that this work anticipated some of the key ideas later made famous by Immanuel Wallerstein's World Systems theory.

7. Kenneth Lipartito, "Reassembling the Economic: New Departures in Historical Materialism," *American Historical Review* 121:1 (2016), 101–39; Jeremy Adelman and Jonathan Levy, "The Fall and Rise of Economic History," *Chronicle of Higher Education* (December 1, 2014), available at http://chronicle.com/article/The-FallRise-of-Economic/150247 (accessed November 28, 2017).

8. Some have argued for an earlier date: see, e.g., Janet Abu-Lughod. *Before European Hegemony: The World System, A. D. 1250–1350* (New York: Oxford University Press, 1989); Christopher Chase-Dunn and Thomas D. Hall, *Rise and Demise: Comparing World Systems* (Boulder: Westview, 1997); Andre Gunder Frank and Barry Gills, (eds.), *The World System: Five Hundred Years or Five Thousand?* (London: Routledge, 1993). But even if one accepts their arguments for Eurasia—as many do not—the Americas were clearly not part of the same global economy as Asia, Europe or Africa before 1500. These issues will be covered at greater length elsewhere in the chapter, particularly in the discussion of Jeffrey Williamson's work on globalization and on World Systems theory.

9. A well-known example here would be David Landes, *The Wealth and Poverty of Nations: Why Some Are So Rich and Some So Poor* (New York: W.W. Norton, 1998). It is also noteworthy that while Landes's views are shared by many—indeed, they represented something like the "common sense" of global economic history before the debates discussed here emerged—he was not part of a group of scholars working on global topics and united by either institutional ties or explicit and shared theory and/or methods.

10. I owe the "integration and hierarchy" formulation to Joseph Inikori, "Africa and the Globalization Process: Western Africa, 1450–1820," *Journal of Global History* 2:1 (2007), 63–86, here 64.

11. http://www.rug.nl/research/ggdc/ (accessed November 28, 2017).

12. For two critiques of the use of historical PPP, see Roberto Patricio Korzeniewicz and Timothy Patrick Moran. "Measuring World Income Inequalities," *The American Journal of*

Sociology 106:1 (2000), 209–14; M. Shahid Alam, "Global Disparities since 1800: Trends and Regional Patterns," *Journal of World-Systems Research* 12:1 (2006), 36–59. For an argument that PPP is unreliable even for comparing rich and poor economies today, see Sanjay Reddy and Thomas Pogge, "How Not to Count the Poor." Social Science Research Network (2005) working paper available at SSRN: http://ssrn.com/abstract=893159 (accessed November 28, 2017). For an application of this skepticism to a specific issue in global economic history, see Kent Deng and Patrick O'Brien, "Nutritional Standards of Living in England and the Yangzi Delta (Jiangnan) *c.* 1644–*c.* 1820: Clarifying Data for Reciprocal Comparisons," *Journal of World History* 26:2 (2015), 233–68. Deng and O'Brien argue that GDP numbers, whether PPP-adjusted or not, are not suitable for answering key questions about most early-modern economies. Morten Jerven criticizes GDP (and some other statistics) as measures of development in both historical and contemporary Africa; some of his (controversial) arguments are in principle equally applicable to various historical contexts, both in and beyond Africa, cf. Morten Jerven, *Poor Numbers: How We Are Misled by African Development Statistics and What to Do About It* (Ithaca, NY: Cornell University Press, 2013).

13. For instance, the idea that urbanization can be used as a proxy for agricultural productivity assumes that the urban population is a good rough measure of the number of nonfarmers that the society's agriculturalists fed in addition to feeding themselves (after adjusting for any significant food imports). This probably works reasonably well for societies like those of early-modern Britain and the Netherlands, with a more or less capitalist agriculture in which people not needed as agricultural laborers were free, had no land rights and had every reason to move to cities—though even in nineteenth-century Britain, urbanization was significantly slower than it "should have been," as Williamson pointed out years ago (Jeffrey Williamson, *Coping with City Growth during the British Industrial Revolution* (New York: Cambridge University Press, 1990), 193; Jeffrey Williamson, "Leaving the Farm to Go to the City: Did They Leave Fast Enough?" in John James and Mark Thomas (eds.), *Capitalism in Context: Essays in Honor of R.M. Hartwell* (Chicago: University of California Press, 1994), 159–82.) In societies where there were significant numbers of unfree people, or significant numbers of families with small plots sufficient to employ some but not all family labor, a very large rural industrial labor force could develop with relatively little urbanization: this was clearly the case, for instance, in parts of both Tokugawa Japan and Qing China. (For a very rough estimate of the share of rural industry in the work effort of the Yangzi Delta region, see Kenneth Pomeranz, "Beyond the East-West Binary: Resituating Development Paths in the Eighteenth Century World," *Journal of Asian Studies* 61:2 (2002), 539–90, here pp. 544–45.) The differences can be very significant: for instance, Van Zanden has shown that in 1750, when Maddison believes that European per capita income was already close to double China's, and England's 50 percent more than that, the China/Europe and England/Yangzi Delta differences both narrow to 10 percent simply by adjusting this one assumption to take account of the large number of nonfarmers in the Chinese countryside. (Jan Luiten van Zanden, *Estimating Early Modern Economic Growth*. Working paper. International Institute for Social History, Amsterdam, 2004. www.iisg.nl/research/jvz-estimating.pdf, pp. 21–22.) Given both the large degrees of uncertainty in all these numbers and the small size of such a difference in comparative perspective—it would make the Yangzi Delta closer to England in per capita income than any country in Europe except Luxembourg and Norway is to the United States—such a difference would be insignificant and require a very different narrative about the timing and nature of East-West economic divergence than we would need if we stick with Maddison's original numbers.

14. Jan Luiten Van Zanden, "The Dutch Economy in the Very Long Run," in Szirmai et al. (eds.), *Explaining Economic Growth* (Amsterdam: North Holland, 1993), 267–83; Stephen Broadberry et al., *English Economic Growth, 1270 –1700* (2011). Available at www2.lse

.ac.uk/economicHistory/pdf/Broadberry/Pre1700.pdf (accessed November 28, 2017); Debin Ma, "Modern Economic Growth in the Lower Yangzi in 1911–1937: A Quantitative, Historical, and Institutional Analysis." Discussion paper 2004-06-002, Foundation for Advanced Studies on International Development, Tokyo, 2004; Li Bozhong and Jan Luiten Van Zanden, "Before the Great Divergence? Comparing the Yangzi Delta and the Netherlands at the Beginning of the Nineteenth Century," *Journal of Economic History* 72:4 (2012), 956–89; Li Bozhong, *Zhongguo de zaoqi jindai jingji: 1820 niandai Huating—Louxian diqu GDP yanjiu* (The Economy of Early Modern China: Research on the regional GDP of Huating and Louxian in the 1820s) (Beijing: Zhonghua shuju, 2010).

15. Jan Lucassen and Leo Lucassen, "The Mobility Transition Revisited: What the Case of Europe Can Offer to Global History," *Journal of Global History* 4:3 (2009), 347–77; a set of responses to the project follow in 6:2 (2011). Most of the latter are focused on Europe, but for an exception, see Adam McKeown, "Different Transitions: Comparing China and Europe, 1600–1900," *Journal of Global History* 6:2 (2011), 309–19. For two other particularly relevant IISH contributions on global migration, see Ulbe Bosma, "Beyond the Atlantic: Connecting Migration and World History in the Age of Imperialism, 1840–1940," *International Review of Social History* 52:1 (2007), 116–23; Ulbe Bosma, "European colonial Soldiers in the Nineteenth Century: Their Role in White Global Migration and Patterns of Colonial Settlement," *Journal of Global History* 4:2 (2009), 317–36.

16. To cite just one example, the group had never met outside Europe until 2002, but has held two of its last four meetings in Argentina and South Africa, and will meet in Japan in 2015; its governing body has also added representatives from parts of the world not previously represented (e.g. China).

17. See for instance the papers published in Tommy Bengtsson, Cameron Campbell and James Lee, (eds.), *Life under Pressure: Mortality and Living Standards in Europe and Asia, 1700–1900* (Cambridge: MIT Press, 2004); Robert Allen, Tommy Bengtsson and Martin Dribe, (eds.), *Living Standards in the Past: New Perspectives on Well-Being in Europe and Asia* (Oxford: Oxford University Press, 2005); Renzo Derosas, Michel Oris and Osamu Saito, (eds.), *When Dad Dies* (Bern: Peter Lang, 2002); Noriko O. Tsuya, Feng Wang, George Alter and James Z. Lee, *Prudence and Pressure: Reproduction and Human Agency in Europe and Asia 1700–1900* (Cambridge: MIT Press, 2010).

18. Robert Allen, "How Prosperous Were the Romans? Evidence from Diocletian's Price Edict (301 AD)." GPIH working paper #7 (September 2007). Available at http://gpih.ucdavis.edu/papers.htm#7 (accessed November 28, 2017); Branko Milanovic, Peter H. Lindert and Jeffrey G. Williamson, "Measuring Ancient Inequality." GPIH Working Paper #8 (November 2007). Available at http://gpih.ucdavis.edu/papers.htm#8 (accessed November 28, 2017).

19. Robert Allen, "The Great Divergence in European Wages and Prices from the Middle Ages to the First World War," *Explorations in Economic History* 38:4 (2001), 411–47.

20. D. Philip Hoffmann, P. Levin Jacks and P. H Lindert, "Real Inequality in Western Europe Since 1500," *Journal of Economic History* 62:2 (2002), 322–55.

21. Allen, "How Prosperous Were the Romans?".

22. Robert Allen, Jean-Pascal Bassino, Debin Ma, Christine Moll-Murata and Jan Luiten Van Zanden, "Wages, Prices, and Living Standards in China: In Comparison with Europe, Japan, and India," *Economic History Review* 64: issue supplement s1 (2011), 8–38.

23. Stephen Broadberry and Bishnupriya Gupta, "The Early Modern Great Divergence: Wages, Prices, and Economic Development in Europe and Asia, 1500–1800," *Economic History Review* 59:1 (2006), 2–31.

24. In particular, his index consists largely of grain and cloth (see especially 709), which are two goods that were especially cheap in India as opposed to Britain; and though these goods did indeed make up a substantial portion of poor people's consumption basket, the assertion that these workers were fairly prosperous suggests they should have been consuming some other things as well.

25. R Allen, J Bassino, Ma, Moll-Murata and Luiten Van Zanden, "Wages, Prices, and Living Standards in China: 8–38.

26. See the discussion of these points in Kenneth Pomeranz, "Standards of Living in Rural and Urban China: Preliminary Estimates for the Mid 18th and Early 20th Centuries." Paper for Panel 77 of International Economic History Association Conference, Helsinki, 2006; Kenneth Pomeranz, "Chinese Development in Long-Run Perspective," *Proceedings of the American Philosophical Society* 152:1 (2008), 83–100; Kenneth Pomeranz, "Ten Years After: Responses and Reconsiderations," *Historically Speaking* 12:4 (2011), 20–25.

27. Deng and O'Brien, "Nutritional Standards of Living in England and the Yangzi Delta (Jiangnan) *c.* 1644–*c.* 1820."

28. Prasannan Parthasarathi, "Rethinking Wages and Competitiveness in the Eighteenth Century: Britain and South India," *Past and Present* 158 (1998), 79–109. Prasannan Parthasarathi, *Why Europe Grew Rich and Asia Did Not: Global Economic Divergence, 1600–1850* (Cambridge: Cambridge University Press, 2011); Sashi Sivaramkrishna, "Ascertaining Living Standards in Erstwhile Mysore, Southern India, from Francis Buchanan's Journey of 1800-1801: An Empirical Contribution to the Great Divergence Debate," *Journal of the Economic and Social History of the Orient* 52:4 (2009), 695–733.

29. See the brief argument for earnings parity in Kenneth Pomeranz, "Beyond the East-West Binary: Resituating Development Paths in the Eighteenth Century World," *Journal of Asian Studies* 61:2 (2002), 549–51; but note that it compares independent producers with English textile workers who often had considerably less independence from merchants or who had become employees of manufacturers. And as we have seen, wage comparisons seem to favor England. Agricultural labor productivity, however, remained very close even *c.* 1820: Robert Allen, "Agricultural Productivity and Rural Incomes in England and the Yangtze Delta, *c.* 1620–1820," *Economic History Review* 62:3 (2009), 525–50.

30. The most notable of these successor groups has been the network for the study of Useful and Reliable Knowledge, East and West (URKEW). However, because this group has been largely focused on the history of ideas and technologies, rather than on economic history per se, I have excluded it here.

31. The first cluster of publications to emerge from a GEHN conference (other than GEHN's own working papers) was a set of comparative papers on land markets in *Continuity and Change* 23:1 (2008).

32. For varying uses of this term, see Hayami Akira, "Kinsei Nihon no keizai hatten to Industrious Revolution" (Modern Japanese Economic Development and the Industrious Revolution), in Hayami Akira, Saito Osamu and Sugiyama Chuya (eds.), *Tokugawa shakai kara no tenbo: hatten, kozo, kokusai kankei* (*A View from Tokugawa Society: Development, Structure, and International Relations*) (Tokyo: Dobunkan, 1989), 19–32; Jan de Vries, "The Industrious Revolution and the Industrial Revolution," *Journal of Economic History* 54:2 (1994), 249–70; Jan deVries, *The Industrious Revolution: Consumer Behavior and the Household Economy 1650 to the Present* (Cambridge: Cambridge University Press, 2008). Kenneth Pomeranz, *The Great Divergence: China, Europe, and the Making of the Modern World Economy* (Princeton: Princeton University Press, 2000).

33. For a quick estimate, see Gregory Clark, *A Farewell to Alms: A Brief Economic History of the World* (Princeton: Princeton University Press, 2007), 201–2.

34. To cite just one well-known example, statistics fail to show either significant short-term gains in the efficiency of American industry or sudden surges in investment with the coming of electrification, which common sense suggests should have had an important impact. As it turns out, however, looking at engineering magazines reveals gains that kicked in more slowly and were more subtle. The electric motors that firms could use if they were connected to an electric utility were cheaper than steam engines; they were also smaller, less bulky and less dangerous, allowing firms to deploy lots of machinery without needing heavily reinforced floors and letting them set up the shop floor with fewer impediments to movement. Thus much of the impact of electrification came by making certain older kinds of investment unnecessary, which in purely quantitative measurements canceled out the visible effects of the investment they stimulated; they also often reduced labor costs by allowing workers of all sorts to move more freely around the shop floor rather than increasing the efficiency of those who worked on electrical machinery in particular. Moreover, all of these changes appeared gradually, as new plants were built that took advantage of the possibilities of electricity. (For instance, people might build a new factory, when the time came, without reinforced floors; they didn't stop using existing factories with reinforced floors that had already been paid for.) See Gavin Wright and Paul David, "General Purpose Technologies and Surges in Productivity: Historical Reflections on the Future of the ICT Industry," *Oxford University Discussion Papers in Economic and Social History* #31 (1999), http://www.nuff .ox.ac.uk/economics/history/papers1/a4.pdf (accessed November 28, 2017). Needless to say, these kinds of problems are multiplied many times over when we deal with broad-ranging technological changes for which the timing of invention and dissemination is already very hard to track: the rise of double-cropped rice, the use of clover in crop rotations, improved knowledge of oceanic wind patterns and so on.

35. A recent attempt that has gotten considerable attention is Clark, *A Farewell to Alms*. For reviews, see Samuel Bowles, "Genetically Capitalist?" A Review of Gregory Clark, A Farewell to Alms. *Science* 318 (2007), 394–95 and Kenneth Pomeranz, "Review of Gregory Clark, "A Farewell to Alms: A Brief Economic History of the World," *American Historical Review* 113:3 (2008), 775–79.

36. Energy consumption multiplied by an index of the average energy efficiency of all machines in use. The paper is Robert Ayres and Benjamin Warr, "Accounting for Growth: The Role of Physical Work," homepage of the International Energy Agency (Fontainebleau, France: Center for the Management of Environmental Resources; http://www.iea.org/dbtw-wpd /Textbase/work/2004/eewp/Ayres-paper1.pdf, accessed August 2, 2005).

37. Beckert Sven, *Empire of Cotton: A Global History* (New York: Alfred A. Knopf, 2014); Dennis Flynn, "Arbitrage, China, and World Trade in the Early Modern Period," *Journal of the Economic and Social History of the Orient* 38:4 (1995), 429–48. Dennis Flynn and Arturo Giraldez, "Born with a Silver Spoon: The Origin of World Trade in 1571," *Journal of World History* 6:2 (1995), 201–21; Steven Topik, Carlos Marichal and Zephyr Frank, (eds.), *From Silver to Cocaine: Latin American Commodity Chains and the Building of the World Economy, 1500–2000* (Durham: Duke University Press, 2006); Mark Kurlansky, *Salt: A World History* (New York: Penguin, 2003); Barbara Freese, *Coal: A Human History* (Cambridge, MA: Perseus, 2003).

38. Shelomo Dov Goitein, *A Mediterranean Society: The Jewish Communities of the Arab World as Portrayed in the Documents of the Cairo Geniza* (Berkeley: University of California Press, 1967–1993); Sebouh Aslanian, *From the Indian Ocean to the Mediterranean: The Global Trade Networks of Armenian Merchants from New Julfa* (Berkeley: University of California

Press, 2011); Claude Markovits, *The Global World of Indian Merchants, 1759-1947: Traders of Sind from Bukhara to Panama* (Cambridge: Cambridge University Press, 2000); Ng Chin-keong, *Trade and Society: The Amoy Network on the China Coast*, 1683-1735 (Singapore: Singapore University Press, 1979); Wang Gungwu, "Merchants without Empire: The Hokkien Sojourning Communities," in James Tracy (ed.), *The Rise of Merchant Empires: Long-Distance Trade in the Early Modern World, 1350-1750* (Cambridge: Cambridge University Press, 1990), 400-21.

39. Timothy J. Hatton and Jeffrey Williamson, *The Age of Mass Migration: Causes and Economic Impact* (New York: Oxford University Press, 1998).

40. E.g. A.J.H. Latham and Larry Neal, "The International Market in Rice and Wheat, 1868-1914," *Economic History Review* 36:2 (1983), 260-80 on the making of a global grain market.

41. E.g. Kevin O'Rourke and Jeffrey Williamson, *Globalization and History: The Evolution of a Nineteenth Century Atlantic Economy* (Cambridge: MIT Press, 1999); Kevin O'Rourke and Jeffrey Williamson, "When Did Globalization Begin?" NBER Working Paper 77632 (April 2000). Available at http://www.nber.org/papers/w7632 (accessed November 29, 2017); Kevin O'Rourke and Jeffrey Williamson, "After Columbus: Explaining Europe's Overseas Trade Boom, 1500-1800." *Journal of Economic History* 62:2 (2002), 417-56; Kevin O'Rourke and Jeffrey Williamson, "Once More: When Did Globalization Begin?" *European Review of Economic History* 8:1 (2004), 109-17.

42. Wolfgang Keller and Carol Shiue, "Markets in China and Europe on the Eve of the Industrial Revolution," *American Economic Review* 97:4 (2007), 1189-216.

43. See Dennis Flynn and Arturo Giraldez, "Path Dependence, Time Lags, and the Birth of Globalization: A Critique of O'Rourke and Williamson," *European Review of Economic History* 8:1 (2004), 81-108. See also the reply by Kevin O'Rourke and Jeffrey Williamson, "Once More: When Did Globalization Begin?," *European Review of Economic History* 8:1 (2004), 109-17.

44. For cogent objections to many uses of "globalization," see Frederick Cooper, "Globalization" in Frederick Cooper, *Colonialism in Question: Theory, Knowledge, History* (Berkeley: University of California Press, 2005), 91-112.

45. In most of their work, O'Rourke and Williamson equate "global" trade with intercontinental trade—above all, flows of goods from the Americas and Asia to Europe and of labor from Europe to the Americas. This simplification has its uses, but it rules out any likelihood that they would notice long-distance integration that did not involve Europe, such as the growing trade between China and/or India and Southeast Asia. This is important for any arguments that Europe was not the sole motor of early-modern commercialization, growth and increasing global contacts. It is also of some theoretical interest, since looking at intra-Asian trade would give us a chance to compare spheres in which government-licensed monopolies and war on the high seas—which Williamson and others plausibly argue kept Europe's trade with the rest of the world c. 1500-1800 from growing even faster—were much less widespread, with those in which they clearly were central. It also omits early-modern flows that did not go through Europe even if Europeans played important roles in them: above all the slave trade from Africa to the Americas, but also the flow of silver from the Americas to East Asia.

46. Kevin O'Rourke and Jeffrey Williamson, *Globalization and History: The Evolution of a Nineteenth Century Atlantic Economy* (Cambridge: MIT Press, 1999).

47. Marvin McInnis, "Review of O'Rourke and Williamson, Globalization and History." Published by EH.NET (2000). Available at http://www.h-net.msu.edu/reviews/showrev.cgi?path=2441965413322 (accessed November 28, 2017).

48. The argument summarized from here on comes from Kevin O'Rourke and Jeffrey Williamson, "After Columbus: Explaining Europe's Overseas Trade Boom, 1500–1800," *Journal of Economic History* 62:2 (2002), 417–56.

49. Williamson and O'Rourke use land rents as a proxy for the incomes of the rich in Europe, justified by an argument (see 442–43) that dovetails nicely both with the work of Hoffmann et al. cited above and with one of their later articles, discussed near the end of this chapter, which seeks to explain England's transition to economic modernity largely through effects of long-distance trade.

50. Li Tana, "Rice from Saigon: The Singapore Chinese and the Saigon Rice Trade of the Nineteenth Century," in Qang Gungwu and Ng Chin-keong (eds.), *Maritime China in Transition 1750–1850* (Wiesbaden: Harrassowitz Verlag, 2004), 261–69; Anthony Reid, "A New Phase of Commercial Expansion in Southeast Asia, 1760–1850," in Anthony Reid (ed.), *The Last Stand of Asian Autonomies* (London: MacMillan, 1997), 57–82; Paul Van Dyke, *The Canton Trade: Life and Enterprise on the China Coast, 1700–1845* (Hong Kong: Hong Kong UP, 2005); Victor Lieberman, *Strange Parallels: Southeast Asia in Global Context c. 800–1830* (2 vols.) (Cambridge: Cambridge University Press, 2003, 2009); Sarasin Viraphol, *Tribute and Profit: Sino-Siamese Trade 1652–1853* (Cambridge: Harvard Council on East Asian Studies, 1977); Robert Marks, *Tigers, Rice, Silk, and Silt: Environment and Economy in Late Imperial South China* (New York: Cambridge University Press, 1998); Flynn and Giraldez, "Born with a Silver Spoon"; Leonard Blussé, *Strange Company: Chinese Settlers, Mestizo Women, and the Dutch in VOC Batavia*, 1619–1740 (Dordrecht, Netherlands: Foris Publications, 1986); Leonard Blussé, *Visible Cities: Canton, Nagasaki, Batavia, and the Coming of the Americans* (Cambridge, MA: Harvard University Press, 2008); Takeshi Hamashita, "The Tribute Trade System and Modern Asia," *Memoirs of the Research Department of the Toyo Bunko* 46 (1988), 7–25; Takeshi Hamashita, "Kindai Dō Ajia kokusai taikei" (The International System of Modern East Asia) in Takeshi Hamashita et al. (eds.), *Chi-iki Shisutemo to kokusai kanken* (Regional Systems and International Relations), volume 4 of *Kōzai gendai Ajia* ([Writings from the] Chair for Modern Asia) (Tokyo:Tōdai shuppankai, 1994), 285–325; Ng Chin-keong. *Trade and Society: The Amoy Network on the China Coast, 1683–1735* (Singapore: Singapore University Press, 1983).

51. Kaoru Sugihara, "Introduction," in Kaoru Sugihara (ed.), *Japan, China, and the Growth of the Asian International Economy, 1850–1949* (Oxford: Oxford University Press, 2005). Pages six and seven show that the 1914–39 reversal of integration in the Atlantic world also is absent in intra-Asian trade.

52. For arguments along these lines, see Debendra Biyoy Mitra, *The Cotton Weavers of Bengal, 1757–1833* (Calcutta: Firma KLM Private Limited, 1978); Parthasarathi, *Why Europe Grew Rich and Asia Did Not*. For Java, see Jan Luiten Van Zanden. "Colonial State Formation and Patterns of Economic Development in Java, 1800–1913" (2008), http://www2.warwick.ac.uk/fac/soc/economics/news_events/conferences/econchange/programme/luiten_-_venice.pdf (accessed November 28, 2017). Note that Van Zanden integrates the most monopolistic period of Dutch rule into a long-run story of progress by arguing that though the Dutch extracted very high rents in the mid-nineteenth century, they also built institutions that helped make a more liberal regime possible later on—an argument that requires the kinds of connections across periods and between foreign and domestic changes that, as I argue below, need more emphasis for the Atlantic world as well.

53. For one version of this argument, see Pomeranz, *The Great Divergence*.

54. For one of many versions of this argument—one that is particularly relevant here since it accepts a post-1800 beginning for true "globalization," and for reasons similar to those of Williamson, see Inikori, "Africa and the Globalization Process."

55. In fairness, goods that Europe simply could not produce at home (e.g. pepper) do seem to have formed the bulk of exotic imports in the sixteenth and seventeenth centuries, though how much this appearance would change if we had figures on smuggled goods remains unclear. (For obvious reasons, it was imports which did compete with domestic products which were most often heavily taxed or otherwise restricted, and thus were most likely to be smuggled.) By the eighteenth century, however, cloth was becoming a very important item in long-distance trade profiles for Europe. Moreover, even some goods that could not be produced at home competed with goods that did (sugar with honey, for instance, and tea and coffee with other beverages). The share of goods that were also produced at home seems to have been much larger in early-modern long-distance trade within Asia—another way in which the nineteenth-century divide may have been less marked there.

56. For Latin American examples, see Daron Acemoglu, Simon Johnson and James A. Robinson, "Reversal of Fortune: Geography and Institutions in the Making of the Modern World Income Distribution," *Quarterly Journal of Economics* 117:4 (2002), 1231–94; Kenneth Sokoloff and Stanley Engerman, "Factor Endowments, Inequality, and Paths of Development among New World Economies," *Economia* 3 (2002), 41–102. For India, see for instance Dutt, *The Economic History of British India*; A. K. Bagchi, *Perilous Passages: Mankind and the Global Ascendancy of Capitalism* (Lanham, MD: Rowman & Littlefield, 2005); Parthasarathi, *Why Europe Grew Rich and Asia Did Not*.

57. Frank and Gills, *The World System*; Immanuel Wallerstein, "Hold the Tiller Firm: On Method and the Unit of Analysis," in Stephen Sanderson (ed.), *Civilizations and World Systems* (Walnut Creek, CA: Alta Mira Press, 1995), 239–47; Abu-Lughod. *Before European Hegemony*; Chase-Dunn and Hall, *Rise and Demise*; Andre Gunder Frank, *ReOrient: The Silver Age in Asia and the World Economy* (Berkeley: University of California Press, 1998). To some extent, these controversies have stemmed from the fact that World Systems theory has been so much more concerned with explaining hierarchy than with tracking integration. Wallerstein has claimed that there is a clear criterion distinguishing places that are "peripheries" in a world system to those that are "external areas" to it—which in turn tells us whether there is a world system covering a given area at all. Essentially, Wallerstein's criteria come down to whether the goods exchanged between a given area and the more developed "core" it interacts with are "mere "preciosities" or are "essential staples." But these are much more subjective standards than those proposed by people like Williamson—essential to whom, and for what? Christopher Chase-Dunn has tried to add greater rigor to these discussions by mapping different kinds of systems that overlap in space and for which different standards of importance apply: for example: distinguishing a "prestige goods network," in which the goods exchanged may be a tiny percentage of GDP and irrelevant to most people, but are important for confirming elite status and patronage networks that structure a region's politics, from a "political-military network" in which all the polities are potential allies or enemies of each other, from a "staple goods network" within which people depend on others for economically necessary goods like food and fuel, cf. Thomas D. Chase-Dunn and Andrew K. Jorgenson, "Regions and Interaction Networks: An Institutional Materialist Perspective," *International Journal of Comparative Sociology* 44:1 (2003), 433–50. However, these modifications have not yet become a generally accepted part of World Systems theory.

58. On colonial Latin America in particular, see the debate between Wallerstein and Steve Stern in the *American Historical Review*, beginning with: Steve J. Stern, "Feudalism, Capitalism and the World System in the Perspective of Latin America and the Caribbean," *American Historical Review* 93:4 (1988), 829–72. Response by Wallerstein, Comments on Stern's Critical Tests 873–85; rejoinder to Wallerstein's response by Stern, Reply: Ever More Solitary 886–97.

59. See e.g. Patrick O'Brien, "European Economic Development: The Contribution of the Periphery," *Economic History Review*, 2nd series 35:1 (1982), 1–18; Patrick O'Brien, "The Foundations of European Industrialization: From the Perspective of the World," in José Casas Pardo (ed.), *Economic Effects of European Expansion, 1492–1824* (Stuttgart: F. Steiner, 1992), 463–502; Pomeranz, *The Great Divergence*; Joseph Inikori, *Africans and the Industrial Revolution in England* (Cambridge: Cambridge University Press, 2002).

60. Japan, Taiwan, South Korea, Iceland and Finland now have about the same per capita GDP as Germany, France, Belgium and the UK; Norway is significantly higher, and Spain (despite its current depression) not far below. 2012 IMF data at http://en.wikipedia.org/wiki/List_of_countries_by_GDP_(PPP)_per_capita (accessed February 1, 2014).

61. Several examples of this tendency are evident in Bagchi, *Perilous Passages*. I discuss the problem at greater length in my review of that book Kenneth Pomeranz, "Review of Amiya Kumar Bagchi, Perilous Passage: Mankind and the Global Ascendancy of Capitalism," *Economic and Political Weekly* 42:9 (2007), 752–54.

62. Bagchi, *Perilous Passages*; John Hobson, *The Eastern Origins of Western Civilization* (Cambridge: Cambridge University Press, 2004).

63. Giovanni Arrighi, *Adam Smith in Beijing: Lineages of the 21st Century* (London: Verso, 2007). Interestingly, a number of other people strongly influenced by World Systems theory who have moved in this direction are people trained as East Asianists, such as Bruce Cumings and Mark Selden. I have not made a systematic survey, but my sense is that people working with a World Systems research agenda and focused on Latin America, Africa and perhaps South Asia have been more inclined to stay within the classical version of that agenda. But there are important exceptions there, too: most obviously Andre Gunder Frank (originally a Latin Americanist), but also, for instance, the Africanist Joseph Inikori.

64. Acemoglu et al., "Reversal of Fortune." A more popular version of essentially the same argument, published after most of this chapter was written, is Daron Acemoglu and James Robinson, *Why Nations Fail: The Origins of Power, Prosperity, and Poverty* (New York: Crown Books, 2012).

65. As a result, St. Domingue and Jamaica—which had high per capita incomes *c.* 1790, but are poor today—contribute to the inverse correlation that this work relies on. Note, however, that the oppressed labor force of these colonies was not generally descended from an already-dense and exploited population living in these places at first contact: they were imported after initial colonization devastated the native population, and the forms of oppression used upon them were new as well. Thus, had the populations and urbanization rates of these places *c.* 1500 or 1600 been available—instead of being replaced by proxy data from 1800—they would have weakened the observed correlation between "good institutions" (as indicated by dense population) and subsequent economic misery, rather than reinforcing it.

66. Sokoloff and Engerman (2002) (and other versions) make a related but distinct argument (limited to the Americas) in which the bad institutions of colonial economies heavily based on labor-intensive resource extraction became self-perpetuating. Such societies, they argue, tended to generate a small elite that benefited from primary product exports, and a large, mostly unskilled, frequently unfree, population that did the work for very little compensation. In such a situation, elites had little interest in democratization, and thus tended to support authoritarian politics (with predictable ill effects on transparency, the reliability of courts, etc.). These elites and regimes, in turn, were disinclined to make large public investments in nurturing human capital (e.g. through high-quality universal public education). This fostered a situation in which the only comparative advantage of these states was in resource extraction and products produced using cheap unskilled labor. Note that while this argument does posit a mechanism that keeps growth-suppressing institutions in

place, that mechanism requires no further action by "advanced" countries once the original system takes shape.

67. Thomas Holt, *The Politics of Freedom: Race, Labor and Politics in Jamaica and Britain, 1832–1938* (Baltimore: Johns Hopkins University Press, 1992); Gunther Peck, *Reinventing Free Labor: Padrones and Immigrant Workers in the North American West, 1880–1930* (New York and Cambridge: Cambridge University Press, 2000); Bosma, "Beyond the Atlantic."

68. Ewout Frankema, "Raising Revenue in the British Empire 1870–1940: How 'Extractive' Were Colonial Taxes?" *Journal of Global History* 5:3 (2010): 447–77, here 458. Van Waijenberg suggests that adding the value of forced labor would raise the tax rates of most colonies significantly, but the increment decreases over time, and there is no reason to think that it would upset Frankema's conclusion, cf. Marlous van Waijenberg, "Financing the African Colonial State: The Revenue Imperative and Forced labor," *African Economic History Network, working paper*, #20 (2015), https://www.aehnetwork.org/wp-content /uploads/2016/01/AEHN-WP-20.pdf (accessed November 28, 2017). Indeed, the more white settlers a colony had, the more likely that some forced labor was diverted from public to private projects, making it still less likely that a "better" property rights regime demanded by white settlers led to residents of the colony in general getting a better ratio of government services received to extraction suffered.

69. Frankema, "Raising Revenue in the British Empire 1870–1940," here 469.

70. Gareth Austin suggests ways of doing just this from the perspective of sub-Saharan Africa (see Gareth Austin, "Reciprocal Comparison and African History: Tackling Conceptual Eurocentrism in the Study of Africa's Economic Past," *African Studies Review* 50:3 (2007), 1–28), but this is not yet very far advanced as a collective research agenda.

71. In some formulations, this maritime zone extends past Singapore to coastal India; in others it does not.

72. Hamashita, "The Tribute Trade System and Modern Asia"; Takeshi Hamashita, "Kindai Dō Ajia kokusai taikei" (The International System of Modern East Asia) in Takeshi Hamashita et al. (eds.), Chi-iki Shisutemo to kokusai kanken (Regional Systems and International Relations), volume 4 of Kōzai gendai Ajia ([Writings from the] Chair for Modern Asia) (Tokyo: Tōdai shuppankai, 1994), 285–325; Reid, "A New Phase of Commerical Expansion in Southeast Asia, 1760–1850."

73. Kawakatsu Heita, *Nihon Bunmei to Kindai Seiyō: "Sakoku" Saikō* (Japanese Civilization and the Modern West: "The Closed Door Policy" Reconsidered") (Tokyo: Nippon Hōsō, 1991); Kawakatsu Heita, "Nihon no kōgyōka o meguru gaiatsu to Ajia kan kyōsō" (Outside Pressures Surrounding Japanese Industrialization and Intra-Asian Competition) in Hamashita Takeshi and Kawakatsu Heita (eds.), *Ajia kōekiken to Nihon kōgyōka 1500–1900* [*The Asian Trading Sphere and Japanese Industrialization*] (Tokyo: Riburopōto, 1991); Kawakatsu Heita, "Datsu-A katei to shite no Nichi, Ō no kinsei" (The Japanese and the European Early Modern Periods as Processes of "Escape from Asia"), *Rekishi hyōron* 515 (1993), 43–58; Christian Daniels, "Jushichi, hachi seiki Higashi, Tōnan Ajia ikinai boeki to seisan gijutsu iten: seitō gijutsu o rei to shite" (The Intra-Regional Trade in Seventeenth and Eighteenth Century East and Southeast Asia and the Transfer of Productive Technologies: The Case of Sugar Refining) in Hamashita Takeshi and Kawakatsu Heita (eds.), *Ajia kōekiken to Nihon kōgyōka 1500–1900* [*The Asian Trading Sphere and Japanese Industrialization*] (Tokyo: Riburopōto, 1991), 69–102. Some Japanese trade with Southeast Asia was really an indirect trade with China that replaced the old tributary framework. This was true, for instance, of some of the trade along the Vietnamese coast.

74. Andō Yoshio, (ed.), *Kindai Nihon Keizai Shi Yōran* (*Overview of Modern Japanese Economic History*) (Tokyo: Tokyo Daigaku Shuppankai, 1979), 23.

75. E.g. K. Akamatsu, "A Historical Pattern of Economic Growth in Developing Countries," *Developing Economies* 1 (1962), 3–25; Kaoru Sugihara, "The East Asian Path of Economic Development: A Long-term Perspective," in Giovanni Arrighi, Takeshi Hamashita and Mark Selden (eds.), *The Resurgence of East Asia: 500, 150 and 50 Year Perspectives* (London: Routledge, 2003), 78–123.

76. E.g. Samuel P. S. Ho. "Colonialism and Development: Korea, Taiwan, and Kwantung," in Ramon Myers and Mark Peattie (eds.), *The Japanese Colonial Empire*, 1895-1945 (Princeton: Princeton University Press, 1984), 347–98 on industry; Lewis Gann, "Western and Japanese Colonialism: Some Preliminary Comparisons," in Ramon Myers and Mark Peattie (eds.), *The Japanese Colonial Empire, 1895–1945* (Princeton: Princeton University Press, 1984), 497–525, here: 522–24 for a positive overall assessment of economic impact; Mark Peattie, "Introduction" in Ramon Myers and Mark Peattie (eds.), *The Japanese Colonial Empire, 1895–1945* (Princeton: Princeton University Press), 3–52 for a relatively positive view generally, see Kawakatsu. For a sharply dissenting view, rejecting the idea that Japanese colonialism had more positive economic implications than others in Southeast Asia, see Anne Booth, *Colonial Legacies: Economic and Social Development in East and Southeast Asia* (Honolulu: University of Hawaii Press, 2007). Beyond these economic debates, of course, lie very sensitive arguments about the history of Japanese aggression in Asia more generally, arguments that touch on questions of atrocities, war guilt, reparations, nationalism and memory and so on.

77. In work left unfinished when he died, Frank argued that this parity actually extended well into the nineteenth century.

78. See for instance Stephen Broadberry, Hanhui Guan and David Daokui Li, "China, Europe, and the Great Divergence: A Study in Historical National Accounting, 980–1850" (2014). Available at http://eh.net/eha/wp-content/uploads/2014/05/Broadberry.pdf (accessed November 28, 2017), suggesting that the Yangzi Delta had fallen behind the richest parts of Europe by about 1700: a big difference from earlier claims by two of these authors that such a divergence was clear by 1400 (Guan Hanhui and Li Daokui, "Mingdai GDP ji jiegou shitan" (An Exploration of Ming Dynasty GDP and Its Structure), *Jingji jikan* (*China Economic Quarterly*) 9:3 (April 2010), 787–828 and by many others that the decisive divergence had happened by 1500, 1000 or, in some cases by even earlier dates.

79. E.g. Kenneth Pomeranz, "Is There an East Asian Development Path? Long-Term Comparisons, Constraints, and Continuities," *Journal of the Economic and Social History of the Orient* 44:3 (2001), 3–41; Pomeranz, "Chinese Development in Long-Run Perspective"; Pomeranz, "Ten Years After: Responses and Reconsiderations"; Kenneth Pomeranz, "Labor Intensive Industry in the Rural Yangzi Delta: Late Imperial Patterns and Their Modern Fates," in Gareth Austin and Kaoru Sugihara (eds.), *Labor-Intensive Industrialization in Global History* (London: Routledge, 2011), 122–43. See also Sugihara, "The East Asian Path of Economic Development"; Kaoru Sugihara, "Introduction," in Kaoru Sugihara (ed.), *Japan, China, and the Growth of the Asian International Economy, 1850–1949* (Oxford: Oxford University Press, 2005). For a series of East-West institutional comparisons, see Jean-Laurent Rosenthal and R. Bin Wong, *Before and Beyond Divergence: The Politics of Economic Change in China and Europe* (Cambridge: Harvard University Press, 2011).

80. It should be noted, however, that Kawakatsu rejects the idea that Japan and China (or even Japan and parts of China, as far as I can tell) had comparable dynamics. See especially Kawakatsu Heita, "Datsu-A katei to shite no Nichi, Ō no kinsei" (The Japanese and the European Early Modern Periods as Processes of "Escape from Asia") *Rekishi hyōron* 515 (1993), 43–58. Hamashita, Suighara and Saito, on the other hand, seem to endorse the general idea of different institutions producing similar kinds and degrees of early-modern dynamism in different parts of East Asia.

81. Kaoru Sugihara, "The European Miracle and the East Asian Miracle: Towards a New Global Economic History," *Sangyō to Keizai* 11:2 (1996), 27–48; Kaoru Sugihara, "The East Asian Path of Economic Development: A Long-Term Perspective," in Giovanni Arrighi, Takeshi Hamashita and Mark Selden (eds.), *The Resurgence of East Asia: 500, 150 and 50 Year Perspectives* (London: Routledge, 2003), 78–123. This issue is revisited, with varying conclusions, by several of the essays in Gareth Austin, (ed.), *Economic Development and Environmental History in the Anthropocene* (London: Bloomsbury Academic, forthcoming).

82. For some general comments, see, e.g., Pomeranz, "Is There an East Asian Development Path?" and my essay in Gareth Austin, (ed.), *Economic Development and Environmental History in the Anthropocene* (London: Bloomsbury Academic, forthcoming). See Peter Sheehan and Fiona Sun, "Energy Use in China: Interpreting Changing Trends and Future Directions," *Centre for Strategic Economic Studies, University of Victoria, Working Paper # 13* (2007). Available at http://www.cfses.com/documents/climate/13_Sheehan_&_Sun_Energy_Use_China.pdf (accessed November 28, 2017). They are arguing for a reversal of improvements in energy intensity; others see only a slowdown in efficiency gains. Ma and Oxley (2012: 65–68) show much lower (and still declining) energy intensities for some rich areas than for the country as a whole. On data problems clouding all of these arguments, see Wang Yanjia and William Chandler, "Understanding Energy Intensity Data in China," Carnegie Endowment for International *Peace Policy* Outlook March 24, 2011, available at http://www.carnegieendowment.org/files/chinese_energy_intensity.pdf (accessed November 28, 2017).

83. Robert Allen, "Mr Lockyer Meets the Index Number Problem: The Standard of Living in Canton and London in 1704" (2004). Available at http://www.economics.ox.ac.uk/Members/robert.allen/default.htm (accessed November 28, 2017); Robert Allen, "Agricultural Productivity and Rural Incomes in England and the Yangzi Delta, c. 1620–1820" (2005). Available at http://www.economics.ox.ac.uk/Members/robert.allen/default.htm; Robert Allen, Tommy Bengsston and Martin Dribe, (eds.), *Standards of Living and Mortality in Pre-Industrial Times* (Oxford: Oxford University Press, 2005); Ma Debin, "Modern Economic Growth in the Lower Yangzi in 1911–1937: A Quantitative, Historical, and Institutional Analysis" (2004). *Discussion paper 2004-06-002*, Foundation for Advanced Studies on International Development, Tokyo. See also Stephen Morgan, "Economic Growth and the Biological Standard of Living in China 1880–1930," *Economic and Human Biology* 2:2 (2004); Joerg Baten, Debin Ma, Stephen Morgan and Qing Wang, "Evolution of Living Standards and Human Capital in China in the 18th–20th Centuries: Evidences from Real Wages, Age-Heaping, and Anthropometrics," *Explorations in Economic History* 47 (2010), 347–59.

84. Parts of the explanation are sketched in Pomeranz, "Standards of Living in Rural and Urban China"; Kenneth Pomeranz, "Land Markets in Late Imperial and Republican China," *Continuity and Change* 22:3 (2008), 1–50, forthcoming; Pomeranz, "Chinese Development in Long-Run Perspective" and Pomeranz, "Ten Years After: Responses and Reconsiderations."

85. Rosenthal and Wong, *Before and Beyond Divergence*; Bozhong and Van Zanden, "Before the Great Divergence?"; Philip Hoffman, "Why Was It that Europeans Conquered the World?" (2010) http://www.econ.barnard.columbia.edu/~econhist/papers/Hoffman_01Apr2010.pdf (accessed November 28, 2017).

86. Robert Allen, "Agricultural Productivity and Rural Incomes in England and the Yangtze Delta, c. 1620–1820," *Economic History Review* 62:3 (August 2009), 525–50; Bozhong and Van Zanden, "Before the Great Divergence?".

87. Robert Allen, *Enclosure and the Yeoman: The Agricultural Development of the South Midlands 1450–1850* (Oxford: Clarendon Press, 1992), 2–3.

88. The data in Robert Allen, "Agricultural Productivity and Rural Incomes in England and the Yangzi Delta, c. 1620–1820." (2005) Available at http://www.economics.ox.ac.uk/Members

/robert.allen/default.htm (accessed November 28, 2017) and Robert Allen, *The British Industrial Revolution in Global Perspective* (Cambridge: Cambridge University Press, 2009) are instructive here.

89. Rosenthal and Wong, *Before and Beyond Divergence*.
90. Joel Mokyr, *The Gifts of Athena: Historical Origins of the Knowledge Economy* (Princeton: Princeton University Press, 2002); Joel Mokyr, *The Enlightened Economy* (New Haven: Yale University Press, 2009). Patrick O'Brien. "The Needham Question Updated: A Historiographical Survey and Elaboration," *History of Technology* 29 (2009), 7–28; Jan Luiten Van Zanden, *The Long Road to the Industrial Revolution: The European Economy in a Global Perspective, 1000–1800* (Leiden: Brill, 2009); Jan Luiten Van Zanden, "The Skill Premium and the 'Great Divergence,'" *European Review of Economic History* 13:1 (2009), 121–53. Nor have older arguments based on property rights disappeared, as we have seen. See also C. Douglass North, John Wallis and Barry Weingast, *Violence and Social Orders: A Conceptual Framework for Interpreting Recorded Human History* (Cambridge: Cambridge University Press, 2009); Tuan-Hwee Sng, "Size and Dynastic Decline: The Principal-Agent Problem in Late Imperial China, 1700–1850" (2010). http://www.econ.upf.edu/docs/seminars/sng.pdf (accessed November 28, 2017).
91. E.g. Parthasarathi, *Why Europe Grew Rich and Asia Did Not*.
92. Robert Allen, *The British Industrial Revolution in Global Perspective* (Cambridge: Cambridge University Press, 2009), 135–81.
93. Parthasarathi, *Why Europe Grew Rich and Asia Did Not*.
94. Pomeranz, *The Great Divergence*, 59–628; Kenneth Pomeranz, "Le machinisme induit-il une discontinuité historique? Industrialisation, modernité précoce et formes du changement économique dans l'histoire globale," in P. Beaujard, L. Berger and P. Norel (eds.), *Histoire globale, mondialisations, capitalisme* (Paris: La découverte, 2009), 335–73. I did not say much about wages in that context, in part because early steam engines, being largely deployed at coal mines to pump water, replaced horses more than they did men. I discuss this in greater detail in Kenneth Pomeranz, "Le machinisme induit-il une discontinuité historique? Industrialisation, modernité précoce et formes du changement économique dans l'histoire globale" in P. Beaujard, L. Berger and P. Norel (eds.), *Histoire globale, mondialisations, capitalisme* (Paris: La découverte, 2009), 335–73 and Pomeranz, "Ten Years After: Responses and Reconsiderations."
95. Parthasarathi, "Rethinking Wages and Competitiveness in the Eighteenth Century."
96. Philip Hoffmann, "Comment on Ken Pomeranz's The Great Divergence," *Historically Speaking* 12:4 (2011), 16–17.
97. Hoffman, "Why Was It that Europeans Conquered the World?" Some have questioned this, at least for weapons used on land, and with respect to India: Parthasarathi, *Why Europe Grew Rich and Asia Did Not*. But at least for naval weaponry, it seems indisputable; and one way or the other, Europeans clearly gain the upper hand militarily, even on the Indian sub continent, by the late eighteenth century.
98. I add the qualifier "quasi" here to indicate that neither the authors nor I are suggesting that all the grim logic of Malthusianism applied to eighteenth-century Britain; wages did not inevitably return to biological "subsistence" levels, and living standards could rise over time. But the term "Malthusian" captures Malthus's broader insight that in a world in which almost all necessities came from the land, land supply was a constraint on growth, and land/labor ratios did have a profound economic impact.

CHAPTER 9
GLOBAL HISTORIES OF MIGRATION(S)
Amit Kumar Mishra

[T]he world we live in is one in which human motion is more often definitive of social life than it is exceptional.

—Arjun Appadurai[1]

In recent years, owing primarily to the forces of globalization that have led to tremendously increased interaction and integration among disparate regions, historians have attempted to move away from the territorial restrictions of their understanding of the past and toward an analysis of networks and connections that transcends the territorial boundaries of nation-states. This global turn aims to investigate the historical roots of global conditions and connections. It does so without being overly generalizing or ignoring the regional specificities or disparities. Moreover, the global turn wants to contribute to a better understanding of complexities and limitations of prevailing narratives of history. One such limitation is the implication of territorial political boundaries as epistemological boundaries known as centrism—for example, Eurocentrism. Global history attempts to tackle this inadequacy by embracing a "spatial turn"—a conceptual departure from essentialized Eurocentrism, a recognition of the historical significance of non-Western regions and people in the making of the modern world and a repudiation of the methodological hegemony of any "centrism."[2] Transregional flows, exchanges and transitions cannot be explicated through a singular, fixed spatial framework that fails to capture the dialectics of transborder networks and flows. No mono-spatial approach can be posited as the determinant discourse for the historical processes and progression of the entire world.[3]

Global history is neither an attempt to write a meta-narrative of everything and every part of the globe nor, as Marcel van Linden suggests in the context of global labor history, a bid to provide an alternative to earlier explanatory models such as the world system.[4] The essential point of departure is the attempt to overcome narrow national/regional readings of historical events and processes by shifting the analytic focus to historical processes of global integration, inclusion and connectedness through networked flows of capital, commodities and ideas. Adding to the comparative framework of historical analysis, global history makes an attempt to look at connections across space.

The global historical turn means that human mobility has been recognized as a "significant force in historical change"[5] and a historical constant that has shaped the contours and character of political, economic and social-cultural formations across space and time, meshing and moving spatial references and boundaries. Unlike other historical subjects and processes that do not necessarily involve and invoke connections and crossings, migration is a unique phenomenon in which movements, crossings and therefore connections[6] and comparisons are at the very core of this process. Migration history pertains directly to connections and crossings and can be used as a measure of global integration, making it a core theme in global history. Global migration history is a crucial subset of writing global history because "the story of human coexistence is always also the story of migrations."[7] Patrick Manning makes a similar assertion about human migration being "so fundamental an element of our history that it needs to be considered in the study of every aspect of our experience."[8] This increased recognition of the historical significance of human mobility brings migration history, which for a long time has been relegated to the footnotes of the economic and social histories of nation-states, into the center of study, a place it so richly deserves.[9]

Studying migration from the perspective of global history has gained enormous currency in the contemporary world because the movement of people across borders challenges regimes of territorialization and spatialization, challenges fundamental to the very process of globalization. This means we must recognize that "migration trends and patterns contribute to the definition of global history."[10] Yet despite this recognition, most historical studies of migration are segmented by region, time period and social situation.

This chapter posits that migration has been influenced by global factors and therefore must be studied and evaluated within the historical contexts and conceptual framework of global history. I do not aspire to build a grand narrative and a single overarching theory for global migration history; I have drawn on diverse literatures to extract ideas, terms, approaches and concepts that resonate with different migration flows and processes and allow me to extrapolate certain universals without undermining specificities. I also attempt to consider fundamentals like the role of empire in determining the flows, directions and attributes of migration—in the context of the Global South in general and the Indian context in particular.

Before proceeding, I want to offer several caveats that will help delineate the scope and purpose of this chapter. Mobility has always been manifested in temporal and spatial contexts, thus the first caveat is about temporal scope. Although migration has been a constant in human history, the nineteenth century and early decades of the twentieth century witnessed an unprecedented movement of people across regions, nations, oceans and continents, ensuing its recognition as the century of "men moving."[11] *International Migration and the Global Economic Order*, a World Bank report, estimates that around 10 percent of the world's population moved from their homelands to another country between 1850 and 1914, whereas today, in the age of globalization, migration is barely around 3 percent.[12] It is not just the quantity but qualitative features such as the role of empire and the specifics of capitalist economic development that make this period distinct. Nineteenth- and early-twentieth-century migrations occurred at a juncture of history when the world economy, territorial borders and political entities, under the aegis of imperial expansion and capitalist development, were undergoing a tremendous reordering. It is thus imperative to study this distinctive period separately. This chapter suggests that this period of distinctive migration patterns ended only in the 1950s: after that decade, the process of decolonization, unequal integration of erstwhile colonial economies and the creation of postcolonial nation-states in former colonies introduced particulars of citizenship and identity to regulate transnational movements which fundamentally altered the very essentials of migration process.

The second caveat is about the spatial scale of migration—many parts of the world experienced movements of people within their territorial boundaries, but this chapter will explore only transborder migrations. Internal migrations and transborder migrations operate within distinct paradigms. Because of the dissimilar influence of determinants like state intervention, social-cultural contexts, possibility of return, and so on, on both migration flows, any attempt to incorporate both streams into a single chapter may lead to inconsistent interpretations and problematic inferences. Therefore I have tried to map the contours and trajectories of transborder migration only. Embracing such a perspective is not intended to dismiss the fact that most of the transborder migrations are facilitated by and connected with local and regional mobility.

Writing migration history: The global turn

The dominant mode of writing about the history of human mobility has been case studies intended to demonstrate what is unique about specific flows of people.[13] This historiographical trend perceived and explained human migration in terms of statist regimentation and the territorialization of mobility. The methodological and conceptual rationale behind this approach was the assumption that transborder migrant flows are products of specific, social, economic and political histories, and therefore a single analytical frame cannot successfully discuss migration at a global scale. This territorial approach has provided multiple viewpoints for migration history based on divergent regional perspectives and priorities and local conditions; in the process, however, it has created a series of migration narratives that do not always fit with one another.

Another approach of migration history, espoused mostly in the 1980s and 1990s, looked at broader trends and included more than one region, but was essentially centered in the West—Europe or North America—and, following the core-periphery model, explained developments in other parts of the world solely as consequences of events in the West. The general trend in these studies was to turn toward characteristic studies of Western patterns and processes or to study migration in other parts of the world as an outcome of European expansion into those regions. An archetypical work might be *European Expansion and Migration: Essays on the Intercontinental Migration from Africa, Asia and Europe* (1992), edited by P. C. Emmer and M. Morner, which perceives and propounds the causative connections between European expansion and international migration.[14] The Atlantic-centric approach, which omits the Asian migrations as "short" and "ephemeral," is based on an imagery of permanence—those who go to America never want to return. However, this has been effectively challenged by scholars such as Walter Nugent, who have shown that "returning home after a season, a year or a few years"[15] was quite common among European migrant groups arriving in the Americas, including the United States.[16]

Euro- or Atlantic-centric perspectives on migration are based on an essential differentiation between European/North American migrations and waves of migration in other parts of the world. These differentiations use the history of mobility, factors for migration and the nature of migration as the most significant markers. The Eurocentric approach represents Asian regions as stagnant and without significant trends in human mobility and explains the nineteenth-century surge in Asian migrations as a consequence of European economic-political intervention. Within the binary of push and pull, European and North American migrations have been conceived as an outcome of pull factors that represent the informed economic choices of the migrants, while Asian migrations have been seen as determined by push factors that present migration as the only choice for survival. In terms of the nature of migrant flows, European and North American migrations were all too often depicted as freely undertaken, while Asian migrations are imagined to have occurred largely under contract and other forms of servitude.[17] At the core of these disparities is the migrants' agency—the standard narrative works on a racial taxonomy that gave European/North American migrants agency while assuming that Asian migrants were subject to larger political-economic structural compulsions. More broadly, African migrants were to be enslaved, Asian to be indentured and atop the pyramid were white free migrants.[18] These attitudes determined the differentiation and subsequent segmentation of nineteenth-century migrations and seriously diminished the possibility of comparative analysis and thus the creation of a coherent historical narrative of global migrations.

However, the omnipresent global turn in academia over last two decades has now reached migration history, with more and more scholars working to situate migration within that context. From a global history perspective, they postulate a basic premise of universality among various migration flows, despite their enormous exceptionalities and distinctive local characteristics. The global turn is primarily an attempt to initiate a dialogue between migration historians to develop a better understanding of the differences and commonalities of various migrations and then to put forth a comprehensive global perspective. This is a difficult ontological task for a historian—to find a coherent synthesis of dissimilar points and counterpoints while simultaneously remaining receptive to the exclusive, existential and implicit physiognomies of territorially and temporally different migrations. In order to map the trajectories of this global turn, to trace the theoretical and methodological innovations and to identity the critical issues in global migration history, I will evaluate some of the symptomatic and determinative writings and institutional efforts.

Earlier writings on the transregional expanse of migration, like David Northrup's *Indentured Labor in the Age of Imperialism* (1995), focus on regimes and regulations rather than processes and people.[19] The genesis of the process of making a comprehensive study of global migrations can be traced within the gigantic volumes presenting different flows of migrations over very long periods. One noteworthy attempt to present a collective narrative of various migration flows was the *Cambridge Survey of World Migration*

(1995), edited by Robin Cohen. Although this and similar volumes do not offer much of a comparative approach, they provide the background and awareness required to draw parallels and trace the points of commonality and divergence of migrations in many regions of the world.[20]

For historians interested in addressing the problems of territorial specificity, one methodological possibility is to shift the analytic focus from region-specific to issue- and theme-specific analysis of migration. David Eltis edited work titled *Coerced and Free Migration: Global Perspectives* (2002) offers a comparative analysis of global migration that uses freedom and coercion as its conceptual lens. This work also effectively shows the ways in which global networks and connections are maintained through migration and brings in divergent experiences of migrants within a singular framework of analysis.[21] However, the binary of coerced versus free migrations has reductionist implications, and, unfortunately has been used by territory-centric scholars to segment migrations and divide them from one another.

Global perspectives on migration history, in contrast, are based on the longue-durée approach, and among the first significant works of this kind was Dirk Hoerder's magnum opus *Cultures in Contact: World Migrations in the Second Millennium* (2002). Hoerder argues for a move from national/spatial limitations to a global view of migration because territorial boundaries fail to capture how transnational networks and economies function in an increasingly integrated world, particularly from the nineteenth century onward.

Migration flows are often seen as conditioned by larger political-economic contexts and constraints, but this approach often diminishes or even dismisses the role of migrants themselves and human agency in general in the process. By bringing in the cultural context and the negotiations of migrants themselves, which does the crucial work of humanizing them, Hoerder makes human agency a critical determinant in global migrations. And in underlining the significance of human agency, he argues that migration processes are induced, structured and shaped by individuals trying to determine their destinies. Rather than being meek subjects in larger schemes of human relocation strategies, migrants have minds of their own and plans for their future, and they evaluate losses and opportunities according to their own terms of reference.

A transborder, transcultural comparative approach suggests fundamental similarities between migration processes in different cultures and regions. However, as Hoerder demonstrates, "within this global framework, migrations were unique to each society, depending on economic practices, social structures, and power relationships, as well as on the right to relocate, gender hierarchies, and children's positions," which makes global migration history more difficult to study than "bowls of spaghetti or grains in sacks of rice."[22] Hoerder advocates an integrated chronological, topical and spatial perspective that addresses some of these challenges through connections of economic regions, social-cultural linkages and polities. To address these concerns and challenges in writing global migration history, Hoerder proposes a "human-centered" systems approach that introduces new paradigms and concepts for the theoretical-methodological discourse of global migration history.[23] He defines a migration system as "a cluster of moves between a region of origin and a receiving region that continues over a period of time and is distinct from non-clustered multidirectional migrations" and that joins "two distinct societies," each characterized by degrees of differences in industrialization, political structures, demographic factors and distance of movement.[24] The systems approach combines an analysis of the position of the society of origin in the global order, as well as its cultural practices, and rituals, among other such factors, with an examination of the receiving society's structure, its formation of ethnic enclaves, networks and its interaction with new social values and norms.[25]

Hoerder's use of a wide framework and the longue-durée perspective of human mobility enables him to trace the crucial links between migrations and economic-social developments and political transitions and shows that migration was an integral part of Africa, China and India before European intervention. This model, however, is too focused on only three actors and is trapped in the typical Euro- and Atlantic-centric differentiation between European and Asian migrations; Asian migrations are analyzed as having been influenced by the push factors (desperate situations and difficulties at home), while European migrations are depicted as "free" economic choices.

Following the logic of longue-durée approach, Patrick Manning, one of the leading advocates for global history, has presented the history of human migration across possibly the longest temporal span in *Migrations in World History* (2005). In order to establish the scale of human migrations in world history, Manning describes two waves of migration in the nineteenth and earlier twentieth centuries—first, the migration of about fifty million Europeans across Europe and then to North and South America and beyond, and second, the movement of about eighty million migrants across East and South Asia. Manning argues for exploring connections between global-level changes and micro levels of migration flows in order to evaluate the effects of migration over the course of history and to delve into continuity and change in the migration flows over time.

Each migratory movement has its unique conditions and produces its own experiences. The foremost methodological challenge for writing migration history from a global perspective is to reconcile the dialectic between generalization and intrinsic distinctiveness. Manning introduces a model that makes "it possible to generalize about migrations at the same time as emphasizing their distinctiveness."[26] This model focuses on the interaction of five elements—the boundaries of human communities, major categories of migration, migratory movement, the short-term social development brought about by migration and the long-term influences of migration—to consider the underlying logic and recurring choices of migrations.[27] Other valuable additions made by Manning to the rubric of global migration history are linked to the role of networks (discussed below) and the consequences of migration in terms of hopes, costs and risks. Manning's global overview of migrations was complemented by the methodological formulation for writing global migration history that he introduced in his collaboration with Netherlands-based scholars Jan and Leo Lucassen. In *Migration History: Multidisciplinary Approaches* (2010), which Manning coedited with Jan and Leo Lucassen, the authors argue for a universalizing long-term approach, in order to include the full range of the human migration experience.[28] Looking at the existing disciplinary approaches and their inability to address the problematic of global migration history, particularly the historical approach that segments migration history, these scholars propose a more general framework that entails a long time period, a wide geographical range and an interdisciplinary approach.[29] Although this "long term" can be problematic for its oversimplification, this idea was nonetheless a major step in developing a framework for global migration history by offering a way to move beyond conformist disciplinary precincts.

Migration has been recognized as a crucial component of writing global history, and there has been tremendous advancement in methodology and conceptual frameworks for writing global migration history.[30] Still, most of these works considered global issues through the lens of European or Atlantic migrations and did not attempt to go beyond the historical experiences of Euro- and Atlantic-centric migrations. The initial exclusion of Asia from larger migration narratives was based on perceptions of the scale and spread of migration and the theory of divergence—Asian migrations were seen as numerically trivial in comparison to European or Atlantic migrations.[31] Disdain for Asian migration can be seen in these works, as when, for example, Emmer suggests that it is not worth even discussing whether Asian migration was beneficial for migrants or not "given the relatively small volume of both internal and external migration." Emmer points to an explosion in European migration and estimates that "between 1800 and 1960 at least 61 million Europeans participated in intercontinental migration." In comparison, the share of non-European migrants was smaller, both in absolute and relative terms, and in the same period, the total number of Asian and African migrants was only about five to six million.[32] The other rationale given for excluding "third world" migrations has been the highly segmented nature of migration flows from these regions.[33]

This scale-based rationale for exclusion was not tenable for long. An early attempt to situate Asian migrations within global history, indeed, can be found in *Global History and Migrations*,[34] edited by Wang Gungwu (1997), along with a pessimistic note on what contributors to the volume saw as historians' failure to engage with the global panorama of migration. This work uses the universality thesis to elaborate and explain the global history of migration by tracing common points of analysis such as the role of political-economic conditions and migrants' perceptions and ambitions within various migration streams across the world. However, when Gungwu dates Chinese migration as starting post the Opium War period (1860s), he essentially still subscribes to the Eurocentric view that Asian societies were immobile before European intervention.

The truly momentous shift from Euro- and Atlantic-centric perspectives came with the publication of Adam McKeown's provocative article "Global Migration, 1846-1940" (2004). This article is seminal for many reasons, most importantly McKeown's take on the sources of segmentation and his looking beyond both the Europe-centered normative migration model and that of global history. McKeown highlights the involvement of non-Europeans, particularly Asians, in the expansion and integration of the world.[35] His agenda is to get Asian movements, particularly Chinese migrations, included in the global wave of migrations, arguing that they were part of the same processes of global integration that shaped migrations across the world, and thus cannot be contained solely within categories of indenture, sojourning or response to famine and overpopulation.[36] McKeown's framework for global migration history is based on the assumption of broad similarities between various migrations in the world; it has two essential vectors—commonality and comparability between migrations. McKeown's argument for including Asian migrations within the global migration framework comes from his rejection of the conventional differentiation between European/Atlantic migration and Asian migration. Using data from China, India, Siberia, Southeast Asia, Central Asia and Japan, McKeown argues that Asian migration from the mid-nineteenth to the mid-twentieth century was comparable in scale to transoceanic migrations from Europe.[37]

McKeown's work also disproves another previously asserted difference between European-Atlantic and Asian migration—the binary of free and unfree. He recognizes the role of coercion and violence in mid-nineteenth-century Asian migrations, but argues that the bulk of these migrations was channeled through independent networks of friends, families and villagers and that less than 10 percent of Asian migrants were indentured.[38] In his consideration of Asian migrants under indenture (and other contract labor migrations), he does not find them qualitatively different from European migrants to the Americas. Europeans, after all, were also signing employment contracts both before and after departure, as well as obtaining employment through more informal ties or debt and personal obligations in places where contract migration was outlawed.[39] The *a priori* distinction of European migrations as free and non-European as unfree is based, McKeown shows, on a racialized discourse of segmentation and on drawing boundaries rather than doing real history. As McKeown's work shows, freedom of migration flows is an untenable marker to differentiate between European and non-European migrations because *all* migrations have been shaped by a variety of regulatory and coercive factors.

McKeown's study of the regimes of regulation and restrictions imposed upon migrants from Asian regions into Europe and the Americas is also crucial. He considers this not as a characteristic reluctance to migrate, as the Western models would argue, but as a product of the authority of imperial powers. According to his estimates, about 2.5 million migrants from South and East Asia had migrated to the Americas by the 1880s when anti-Asian immigration regulation began to take effect. He argues that the number of Asian immigrants would have been far greater absent those restrictions.[40]

Nineteenth-century migrations were embedded in global political-economic conditions and conditioned by the global economy and internal changes. There was a symbiotic relationship between economic progression and the expansion in migration flows. The rise of the global economy that centered on Europe and North America caused economic transformations across the world that disrupted previous migration patterns and created the conditions, contexts and inducement for long-distance migrations. This rise in migration then furthered economic growth and consolidation. Therefore global migration history needs to engage with the contexts and transitions of the global economy. McKeown argues that the plantations, mines and agricultural regions in the Global South were as much part of the expanding global economy as Western European and North American factories and fields and therefore migrations to those destinations should also be included in the global narrative of migrations along with the European and Atlantic migrations.[41] However, in order to establish Asian migrations as free migrations that can be equated with European migrations, McKeown downplays the discourse of racialization into the framework of global migration history in the nineteenth century.

One critical issue relating to writing global migration history is periodization. Migration has been a constant in human history, but deciding how much of it should be analyzed is a trying task for reasons of both achievability and conceptual/methodological coherence. Periodization in global migration history is a tricky affair—too short a period can result in a very selective and constrained narrative. Additionally, features such as economic considerations and racial, geopolitical predispositions transcend the closures of period, though their contexts, forms, intensities or even taxonomic orders may change over time. One needs a long-term perspective to understand the historical complexities, but the temporal span cannot be left open-ended: Patrick Manning has embraced a span of 5,000 years,[42] while Dirk Hoerder uses a millennium. We need to trace quantitative and qualitative specificities in every historical context; only then can they be compared and appraised across various historical contexts over a longer time period.

As mentioned, the nineteenth century marked a particular historical juncture, and thus serves as a good unit of analysis, as the expansion of European imperial authority was concomitant with the abolition of slavery. To meet the ever-increasing demands to support their territorial-economic growth, Europeans created new labor regimes based largely on the migration of Asian (Chinese and Indian) laborers. These labor regimes reflected racial hierarchies and the segmentation of migrant labor, and they mobilized migrant laborers—in a very structured institutional manner—to be moved to Burma, Ceylon and Malaya within the Asian region as well as to South American and African territories. This was reversed from the 1940s onward with decolonization and the moves of newly independent former colonies to regulate immigration flows within their territories. These large-scale shifts changed the nature, dynamics and destinations of global migration.

Focusing on the nineteenth century as a period for studying migrations across the world brings the discourse of racialization into the framework of global migration history. Patterns of global migration in the nineteenth century were determined by racial prejudices, hierarchies, discrimination and exclusion that created a taxonomic order of global migration in which migrants from non-European origins were placed either on the margins or on the lowest rung, or both. In many places, Asian migrants were introduced into the debris of recently ended slavery, and they faced punitive actions and demoralizing subjugation.

One alternative to Eurocentric schema that see European colonial intervention and strategies of mobilization as the factors responsible for Asian mobility in the nineteenth century is the view that, just as in European migration, network-induced mobilizations were the key factor for Asian migration. In a social network perspective, networks are described as the vital sinews that provide channels for migration and "migration itself can be conceptualized as a process of network building, which depends on and in turn reinforces social relationships across space."[43] In a suggestive essay on the "interpersonal trust network within migration streams," Tilly argues that "trust networks play central parts in the organization, maintenance, and transformation of long-distance migration streams across much of the world."[44] For Tilly, it is actually the networks that migrate.[45] Social networks are crucial in finding jobs and accommodation and circulating goods and services, along with ongoing social and economic information and moral support.

This network model describes the migration process as a self-sustaining order that does not necessarily require stimuli like state intervention to keep going. As Monica Boyd suggests, "networks connect migrants across time and space. Once begun, migration flows often become self-sustaining, reflecting the establishment of networks of information, assistance and obligations which develop between migrants in the host society and friends and relatives in the sending area. These networks … ensure that movements are not necessarily limited in time, unidirectional or permanent."[46] McKeown argues that in the context of Asian migrations, attention to these networks as a fundamental organizing rubric is key to understanding broad global patterns of migration,[47] as these networks facilitate migrations across regions.[48] My own work and that of other historians show that the family-, kinship- and locality-based networks facilitated the migration of Indians and Chinese during colonial times.[49] Specific configurations of network ties, including organizational, composite and interpersonal ties, result in different migration flows and occupational outcomes.[50] The dynamic effects of migrant networks make the world different from the familiar mosaic of geographically discrete territories. They create complex and overlapping migrant flows and nodes, none of which can be captured in entirety within a single national or regional migration history.[51]

Methodological approaches and theories based on social networks have considerable analytic power and provide valuable insights about the complexities of global migration. However, they do not offer much analysis of the discourse of political-economic authority, hierarchies of social order within migrants in terms of origin and destinations, roles of actors and agencies employed by the employers such as recruiting agents and, above all, the involvement of regimes in creating and exploiting these networks to mold migration flows to their preferences and requirements.

On this theme as well, McKeown's work marks a major departure from the prevailing Eurocentric perspectives because of the way he traces the similarities between European and non-European migrations and highlights the significance of non-European patterns of migration in shaping the contours of global economic formations in the nineteenth and twentieth centuries. However, his proposal that free migration is a distinctive feature and normative model for global migration is problematic. Many Asian migrants, particularly from India, were subjected to racial slurs, discrimination and exclusion inside and outside Asia. Highly punitive labor legislations like the antivagrancy laws in British plantation colonies were only one way their freedom was effectively curtailed, and one way these labor regimes were very nearly slavery. Migrants' freedom was also restrained by the legally enforced conditions of indenture or debt advances (as in the Kangani- and Maistry-facilitated migration from India[52] that was part of the intra-

Asian migrations).⁵³ Millions of Europeans left via state support to Latin America, Cuba and Australia in the nineteenth century and worked under binding conditions very similar to indentured migrants. This fact, of course, challenges the explicit Eurocentric assumption that European migrations were free migrations in which migrants made rational independent choices to migrate for better prospects.

McKeown's other contribution to the universalization of global migrations is reading Asian migrations as an outcome of networks rather than of European colonial intervention, but this can be contested as well because most of the intra-Asian migrations took place either in regions that were under direct European colonial rule or where European colonial presence was dominant. McKeown proposes moving beyond a Eurocentric approach, but his analysis and arguments slip into a universalization of European model when he argues that free movement is the norm for global migration history. McKeown brings perspectives from non-European migrations, but his arguments are based largely on the historical experiences of Chinese migration and do not address Indian experiences, making his case more China-centric than truly global.

A significant recent effort to bring Asian perspectives into the framework of global migration history is Sunil Amrith's *Migration and Diaspora in Modern Asia* (2010). This work argues for revision of the Eurocentric mobility transition perspective that portrays Asian people as static and immobile prior to colonialism.⁵⁴ At the same time, however, it attributes most of the drivers for the Asian mobility revolution in the mid-nineteenth century to colonial intervention, therefore essentially falling back into the conventional Eurocentric approach.⁵⁵

Amrith also highlights a serious constraint for comprehensive analyses of Asian migrations: the scarcity and objectivity of data. Unlike European migrations for which ships' logs and passenger registers are available, detailed information on arrivals and departures is not easily available for Asian migrations, particularly for intra-Asian movement.⁵⁶ This means that the analysis depends heavily on census figures, which is problematic, not only because such figures carry the perceptions and prejudices of the state but also because they do not count circular migrations, a significant part of intra-Asian migrations.⁵⁷

In addition to individual scholars, the agenda of global migration history has also been endorsed and strengthened by institutional programs. One such institutional effort to "fully understand the causes and effects of migration and settlement processes in the current globalizing world" is the Global Migration History Program, initiated in 2005 and based at the International Institute of Social History in Amsterdam (the Netherlands).⁵⁸ This institutional initiative includes the elaboration of explanatory frameworks through thematic workshops, publication series and creation of a digital repository of meta-sources on migrations across the world.⁵⁹ In terms of conceptual understanding, this program reinforces two major propositions of global migration history—first, the importance of global perspectives in fully understanding the causes and effects of migration in a globalizing world and, second, the necessity of including the migration experiences of the non-Western world along with the long-focused-on experiences of the European and Atlantic regions.

Role of empire and Indian exceptionalism

The Eurocentric description of nineteenth-century Asian migrations as solely an outcome of imperial economic-political interventions has been refuted by scholars like McKeown in order to trace similarities between European and Asian migrations. The Eurocentric emphasis on European intervention has also been faulted for espousing historical determinism and negating the agency of Asian migrants. However, a detailed survey of intensities of European expansion and intervention in Asian regions and the quantum increase in migrations within and from Asia reveal that the history of nineteenth-century migrations cannot be separated from histories of imperial expansion and capitalism, even though this makes it more difficult to decenter Europe, as imperialism and capitalism are both rooted in Europe. Scholars like Jan Breman have revealed how colonial states and European capitalists used all the means of coercion and control at their disposal to uproot people and communities from the impoverished Asian countryside so they could work on plantations and in other sectors important to expanding the empire. Asian labor in the colonial era was mobile but unfree. Given this oppressive intervention, it has been argued that the violence of European empires must remain a crucial part of the narratives of global migrations.[60]

I would like to exemplify this conceptual dilemma through an examination of the exceptionalism of Indian migrations in the nineteenth century. Most attempts to study migration from India through the theoretical models of Atlantic- or European- or China-centric models have led to less clarity, not more. While there has been a long history of Indians migrating—slaves, traders, laborers and so on—to different parts of the world, nineteenth-century migration from India consisted primarily of laborers who were strategically mobilized to migrate and did so under punitive contractual obligations. Historical evidence from nonindentured migration from India to Southeast Asia and Ceylon (Kangani to Malaya, Maistry to Burma, and Tundu in Ceylon, about 90 percent of total migration) show that mobilization of migrants worked via systems of debt and advances that tied laborers to particular employers through the mediations of labor contractors. Even though, unlike indentured migration, these systems were not structured and regulated at the recruitment level, there were elaborate regulatory mechanisms in place for legal and extralegal coercion of migrants at their destinations. This was significantly different from China, the other Asian region with a significant outmigration, where indentured labor constituted a very small segment of migration flows, making clear that analytic categories like capitalism and empire have to be included into the framework of global migration history because of their overarching impact on migrations in certain parts of the world like Asia, and particularly India, in the nineteenth and early twentieth centuries.[61]

Limitations of the state of the art in global migration history

As the preceding discussion illustrates, it is very challenging to develop critical paradigms and concepts applicable to different migration regimes and different eras without privileging one particular region or time. There has been an agreement among scholars of migration history about the "demographic, socioeconomic, and cultural differences that existed and still exist between different waves of international migration."[62] This conundrum in historiographies of migration—showing sensitivity to the regional specificities which may eventually lead to the old territorial paradigm—may be attributable to a relative dearth of writings on migration from the perspectives of global history. On a rather pessimistic note, Hatton and Williamson conclude that the stark inequalities, coupled with the segmentation of different migration flows and regimes, make it impossible to find a unifying paradigm to develop a global migration history.[63]

This chapter does not agree with the conclusion of Hatton and Williamson, and suggests instead how the conceptual framework can evolve toward a more comprehensive, inclusive analysis. Migration history needs to consider the consequences of migration-caused intensification that results in a rapid formation of migrant communities within host communities, thus creating new "ethnoscapes" or landscapes of people. Most historical writing on migration has not moved beyond the causes and processes, and many historians refer to migrants as statistical abstractions, paying little attention to migrants' process of settlement and accommodation and the ways they negotiate through the distinct social-cultural norms and political-economic contexts of their destinations. There have been works on these done by scholars of diasporas and of cultural studies, but then there are apprehensions of theoretical abstraction and oversight of historical insights.

In the context of the contemporary transnational global world order, peoples' places and redistribution arrangements are often determined by their ethnic and territorial/national markers. In many instances, migrants are constantly reminded, even, as in the case of descendants of Indian immigrants in Malaysia or Fiji, after several generations, about their distant origins in another location. This approach is both official and unofficial, infecting popular perceptions and becoming a determinant for exclusion and discrimination. Examples include the Bhumiputera policy in Malaysia, and, in the most extreme cases, expulsion of Indian immigrants as has happened in East Africa. Little analysis is offered by those writing in the tradition of diaspora studies—engaging large sociological binaries—of the effects of the movement of people transcending regional, national and continental boundaries on the lives of immigrants, particularly extra-economic corollaries like exclusion from the social, cultural and political realms.

This lacuna, even given the efforts to expand the conceptual boundaries and methodological frameworks of migration history, seriously limits the scope of global migration history, because these movements of people create communities across nations, continents and oceans with a wide range of fortunes and futures. Another understudied issue is the consequences of immigration on the native population—how the influx of people has affected their lives—have they been marginalized, displaced or brutalized by the migrants, or have they been able to retain their position?

Migrations from India and China and Africa have often been explained in terms of the desperate conditions in those locations that act as push factors. They are extolled as beneficial to the migrants in terms of survival, income generation and subsequent generational transformations. This in turn portrays them as the beneficiaries of the empire, and current trends in global migration history do little to consider the benefits of these migrations to the receiving countries (like sugar production for the empire or building necessary infrastructure like roads, railroads, ports to fortify the imperial enterprise) and the empire as a whole.[64] This is particularly significant because these contributions were made by migrants at considerable sacrifice of their personal freedom, family and social life and even their lives.

Conclusion

Like global history, which attempts to narrate the complicated and entangled stories of world history, global migration history is confronted with the challenge of disentangling conceptual and methodological complexities, rethinking established analytical categories and the problem of retaining the hegemonic dominance of one "centrism" while arguing against another. Fashioning appropriate language, analytical concepts and methodological approaches that can capture and square the dialectics of divergent perspectives is the foremost challenge for global migration history. Looking at transoceanic migrations as the normative model, as most of the works so far seem to do, helps address one dimension of global processes. Better knowledge of the densities and destinations of overland and domestic migrations in diverse areas like Asia is necessary to better understand the causes of migration and comprehend the varieties of integration and differentiation. An enhanced engagement with regional differences will lead to a better understanding of global migration history, and thus to more grounded narratives. A better sense of how some differences disappeared over time while others became more pronounced will provide insights into how the world was divided into West and East, rich and poor, developed and developing.

This chapter also attempts to suggest that a possible way forward is to move beyond the predefined teleological frameworks often used in national histories, to read and write global migration history as open-ended narratives with opportunities for inclusion and amendment, and to include concepts introduced by the rubrics of transnationalism and diaspora. Practitioners of global migration history should adopt a polymorphic approach that allows them to see beyond binaries and consider contradictions as inherent characteristics of migration flows and processes.

This chapter underlines a need to historicize the agency, motives and negotiations of migrants by situating migration flows within the larger historical context and moving from just measuring mobility to considering a discourse analysis of causes and consequences of this mobility. A heuristic approach in writing global migration history would gloss over the differences between specific migratory movements to articulate a "grand narrative of global migration." Instead, historians should understand distinct processes within similar conceptual and analytic frameworks in order to touch upon essential questions, concerns and debates around migration and to explicate the differential impact of migration on different parts of the world. Global migration has acquired a new theoretical and historical significance in the contemporary world order as borders and boundaries are being transcended, blurred, eradicated, remade and renegotiated through migration. This chapter has made an attempt to make the necessary spatial turn toward the Global South and to argue for writing the global migration history as multivocal dialogic stories that appreciate and underscore migrants' agency by recognizing the fact that human mobility, operating within a complex set of events and contexts, has shaped the world we inhabit. As Frantz Fannon has argued, "I am asking to be considered. I am not merely here-and-now, sealed into thingness. I am for somewhere else and for something else. I demand that notice be taken of my negating activity insofar as I pursue something other than life; insofar as I do battle for the creation of a human world—that is a world of reciprocal recognitions."[65]

Notes

1. Arjun Appadurai, "Sovereignty Without Territoriality: Notes for a Postnational Geography," in Patricia Yeager (ed.), *Geographies of Identity* (Ann Arbor, MI: Michigan University Press, 1996), 40–58, especially 43.
2. Barney Warf and Santa Arias (eds.), *The Spatial Turn: Interdisciplinary Perspectives* (London: Routledge, 2008).
3. Arjun Appadurai, "Sovereignty"; Saskia Sassen, "Spatialities and Temporalities of the Global: Elements for a Theorisation," *Public Culture* 12:1 (2000) 215–32.
4. Marcel van der Linden, "The Promise and Challenges of Global Labour History," *International Labour and Working-Class History* 82 (Fall 2012), 57–76, especially 60.
5. Judith M. Brown and Rosemary Foot (eds.), *Migration: The Asian Experience* (London: Palgrave MacMillan, 1994), 1.
6. Patrick Manning, *Migration in World History* (New York: Routledge, 2012) (second edition), 2.
7. Ludger Pries, "New Migration in Transnational Space," in Ludger Pries (ed.), *Migration and Transnational Social Spaces* (Aldershot: Ashgate, 1999), 1.
8. Manning, *Migration in World History*, 2.
9. Leo Lucassen, Jan Lucassen and Patrick Manning (eds.), *Migration History in World History* (Leidedn: Brill, 2010), 6.
10. Wang Gungwu, "Migration and Its Enemies," in Bruce Mazlish and Ralph Buultjens (eds.), *Conceptualising Global History* (Boulder, CO: Westview Press, 1993), 131–51, especially 132.
11. Eric Hobsbawm, *The Age of Capital: 1848–1875* (New York, NY: Vintage, 1996).
12. http://www.globalization101.org/uploads/File/Migration/migration.pdf (accessed on March 10, 2014).
13. Madhavi Kale, *Fragments of Empire: Capital, Slavery and Indian Indentured Labor in the British Caribbean* (Philadelphia, PA: University of Pennsylvania Press, 1999); Leslie Page Moch, *Moving Europeans: Migration in Western Europe Since 1650* (Bloomington, IN: Indiana University Press, 1992); James H. Jackson, *Migration and Urbanization in the Ruhr Valley, 1821–1914* (Boston, MA: Humanities Press, 1997); Steven Hochstadt, *Mobility and Modernity: Migration in Germany, 1820–1989* (Ann Arbor, MI: University of Michigan

Press, 1999) and Colin Pooley and Jean Turnbull, *Migration and Mobility in Britain Since the Eighteenth Century* (London: UCL Press, 1998); Kernial Singh Sandhu, *Indians in Malaya: Some Aspects of Their Immigration and Settlement, 1786-1957* (Cambridge: Cambridge University Press, 1969); G. William Skinner, *Chinese Society in Thailand: An Analytical History* (Ithaca, NY: Cornell University Press, 1957); Akram Fouad Khater, *Inventing Home: Emigration, Gender, and the Middle Class in Lebanon, 1870-1920* (Berkeley, CA: University of California Press, 2001); J. C. Moya, *Cousins and Strangers: Spanish Immigrants in Buenos Aires, 1850-1930* (Berkeley, CA: University of California Press, 1998).

14. Pieter C. Emmer, "European Expansion and Migration: The European Colonial Past and Intercontinental Migration; An Overview," in Pieter C. Emmer and Magnus Morner (eds.), *European Expansion and Migration: Essays on the Intercontinental Migration from Africa, Asia and Europe* (New York, NY: Berg, 1992), 1-12, especially 2.

15. Walter Nugent, *Crossings: The Great Transatlantic Migrations* (Bloomington, IN: Indiana University Press, 1995), 35.

16. Walter Nugent shows that the return rate for European migrants was about 25 percent between 1846 and 1924 in the Americas overall; from Argentina between 1857 and 1914, the return rate was 43.3 percent; and from Mexico for 1899-1912, it was 66 percent. The return rate was an extremely high 52.5 percent for the period 1908-1914—effectively showing why it does not make sense to attribute permanency to one set of migrations over another. Nugent, *Crossings*, 35-36. Period is not important; important is the trend of return: what I am trying to underline is that there was more that 50 percent return in American migration as well (which was argued to be permanent in nature) similar to Asian migrations (considered to be seasonal or temporary).

17. David Eltis, "Introduction: Migration and Agency in Global History," in David Eltis (ed.), *Coerced and Free Migration: Global Perspectives* (Stanford, CA: Stanford University Press, 2002), 1-32.

18. Ulbe Bosma, "Beyond the Atlantic: Connecting Migration and World History in the Age of Imperialism, 1840-1940," *International Review of Social History* 52 (2007), 116-23, especially 117.

However, this essentialized racial segmentation of migration flows has been effectively challenged by a large number of scholars who have questioned the assertion for free migration being a "white prerogative." Bosma, "Beyond the Atlantic," 116-23; Thomas C. Holt, *The Problem of Freedom: Race, Labor and Politics in Jamaica and Britain, 1832-1938* (Baltimore, MD: Johns Hopkins University Press, 1992); Adam McKeown, "Global Migration: 1846-1940," *Journal of World History* 15 (2004), 155-90.

19. David Northrup, *Indentured Labor in the Age of Imperialism, 1834-1922* (Cambridge: Cambridge University Press, 1995), published under the series Studies in Comparative World History from CUP.

20. Robin Cohen, *The Cambridge Survey of World Migration* (Cambridge: Cambridge University Press, 1995).

21. David Eltis, *Coerced and Free Migration: Global Perspectives* (Stanford, CA: Stanford University Press, 2002).

22. Dirk Hoerder, *Cultures in Contact: World Migrations in the Second Millennium* (Durham and London: Duke University Press, 2002), 4.

23. Ibid., 15.

24. Ibid., 16.

25. Earlier works on migration system as an analytic concept to understand global interactions include Mary M. Karitz, Lin Leam Lim and Hania Zlotnik (eds.), *International Migration*

Systems: A Global Approach (Oxford: Clarendon, 1992) and Douglas S. Massey et al. (eds.), *Worlds in Motion: Understanding International Migration at the End of the Millennium* (Oxford: Clarendon, 1998). However, these works use "systems" within a more statist paradigm and policy perspective primarily to explore causes and impacts of the international migration.

26. Manning, *Migration in World History*, 2.
27. Ibid.
28. Jan Lucassen, Leo Lucassen and Patrick Manning (eds.), *Migration History in World History: Multidisciplinary Approaches* (Leiden and Boston: Brill, 2011), 17.
29. Ibid., 18.
30. Dona Gabaccia (ed.), *Gender and Migration Revisited* (Staten Island, NY: Center for Migration Studies of New York, 2006); J. Lucassen and Leo Lucassen, "The Mobility Transition Revisited, 1500–1900: What the Case of Europe Can Offer to Global History," *The Journal of Global History* 4:4 (2009), 347–77; Adam McKeown, *Melancholy Order: Asian Migration and the Globalization of Borders* (New York, NY: Columbia University Press, 2008); L. P. Moch, "Connecting Migration and World History: Demographic Patterns, Family Systems and Gender," *International Review of Social History* 52:1 (2007), 97–104; R. S. Parreñas, *Servants of Globalization. Women, Migration and Domestic Work* (Stanford, CA: Stanford University Press, 2001); P. Sharpe (ed.), *Women, Gender and Labour Migration. Historical and Global Perspectives* (London and New York: Routledge, 2001); Ian Goldin, Geoffrey Cameron and Meera Balarajan, *Exceptional People: How Migration Shaped Our World and Define Our Future* (Princeton, NJ: Princeton University Press, 2011) and most Jan Lucassen and Leo Lucassen (eds.), *Globalising Migration History: The Eurasian Experience, 16th–21st Centuries* (Leiden: Brill, 2014).
31. Pieter C. Emmer, "Was Migration Beneficial?" in Jan Lucassen and Leo Lucassen (eds.), *Migration, Migration History, History* (Peter Lang), 111–30, especially 113.
32. Emmer, "European Expansion and Migration," 3.
33. Timothy Hatton and Jeffrey Williamson, *The Age of Mass Migration: Causes and Economic Impact* (New York: Oxford University Press, 1998), 249.
34. Only introduction by Wang Gungwu and a few essays dealing with Asian migration particularly China.
35. McKeown, "Global Migration, 1846–1940," 156.
36. Adam McKeown, "Chinese Migration in Global Context, 1850–1940," *Journal of Global History* 5:1 (2010), 95–124, especially 119.
37. About 29 million Indians and over 19 million Chinese migrated to Southeast Asia and the lands around the Indian ocean and the South Pacific. McKeown, "Global Migration, 1846–1940," 156–57.
38. Ibid., 167, 157. For Chinese migrants only, it was less than 4 percent (McKeown, "Chinese Migration in Global Context, 1850–940," 102).
39. McKeown, "Chinese Migration in Global Context, 1850–1940," 103.
40. McKeown, "Global Migration, 1846–1940," 157, 174–75.
41. Ibid., 166.
42. However, in the revised edition of *Migration in World History* (2013), Manning expands his coverage to the entire history of humankind because "migration is one of those human

patterns that can be seen from the start of human experience to the present." Preface to the second edition.

43. A. Portes and R. Bach, *Latin Journey: Cuban and Mexican Immigrants in the United States* (Berkeley, CA: University of California Press, 1985), 10.

44. Charles Tilly, "Trust Networks in Transnational Migration," *Sociological Forum* 22:1 (2007), 3–25, especially 5.

45. Charles Tilly, "Transplanted Networks" in V. Yans-MacLoughlin (ed.), *Immigration Reconsidered: History, Sociology and Politics* (New York, NY: Oxford University Press, 1990), 79–95.

46. Monica Boyd, "Family and Personal Networks in International Migration: Recent Developments and New Agendas," *International Migration Review* 23:3 (1989), 638–70, especially 641.

47. McKeown, "Global Migration, 1846–1940," 178.

48. Manning, *Migration in World History*, 8–9.

49. Amit Kumar Mishra, "Sardars, Kanganies and Maistries: Intermediaries in the Indian Labour Diaspora during the Colonial Period," in Sigrid Wadauer, Thomas Buchner and Alexander Mejstrik (eds.), *The History of Labour Intermediation: Institutions and Finding Employment in the Nineteenth and Early Twentieth Centuries* (New York, Oxford: Berghahn Books, 2014) 368–87; Marina Carter, *Servants, Sirdars and Settlers: Indians in Mauritius, 1834–1874* (Delhi: Oxford University Press, 1995); Gary Hamilton and Tony Waters, "Ethnicity and Capitalist Development: The Changing Role of the Chinese in Thailand," in Daniel Chirot and Anthony Reid (eds.), *Essential Outsiders: Chinese and Jews in the Modern Transformation of Southeast Asia and Central Europe* (Seattle, WA: University of Washington Press, 1997), 254–84.

50. Maritsa V Poros, "The Role of Migrant Networks in Linking Local Labour Markets: The Case of Asian Indian Migration to New York and London," *Global Networks* 1:3 (2001), 243–59, especially 243.

51. McKeown, *Global Migration*, 180.

52. Kangani and Maistry were sort of intermediaries who facilitated and financed the mobilization of labor in southern parts of India for emigration to Southeast Asia. For a more detailed discussion, see Mishra, "Sardars, Kanganies and Maistries:.

53. There is large volume of writings discussing the nature of these labor migrations, particularly the Indian indentured emigration, starting from the seminal writing of Hugh Tinker titled "A New System of Slavery." Some critical issues of this debate are summarized in Amit Kumar Mishra, "Indian Indentured Labourers in Mauritius: Reassessing the New System of Slavery vs Free Labour Debate," *Studies in History* 25:2 (2009), 229–51.

54. Sunil Amrith, *Migration and Diaspora in Modern Asia* (Cambridge: Cambridge University Press, 2011), 5.

55. Amrith lists four factors as drivers of Asia's mobility revolution in the nineteenth century: first, colonial invasion and regional conflicts; second, uneven economic development in Asia; third, expansion of colonial state and displacement of people in the process; fourth, environmental insecurity. Sunil, *Migration and Diaspora in Modern Asia*, 6.

56. For emigration of Indians across the oceans to countries like Mauritius and Fiji, ship lists and other detailed documents about the lives of migrants are available, but there is severe scarcity of similar data for intra-Asian flows.

57. Sunil, *Migration and Diaspora in Modern Asia*, 13.
58. http://socialhistory.org/en/projects/global-migration-history-programme (accessed November 29, 2017)
59. GMHP has published some very valuable books for furthering the agenda and understanding of global migration history. They are as follows: Jan Lucassen, Leo Lucassen and Patrick Manning (eds.), *Migration History. Multidisciplinary Approaches, Studies in Global Social History* (Leiden and Boston: Brill Publishers, 2010), 3; Ulbe Bosma, Gijs Kessler and Leo Lucassen (eds.), *Migration and Membership Regimes in Global and Historical Perspective* (Leiden and Boston: Brill Publishers, 2011); Jan Lucassen and Leo Lucassen (eds.), *Globalising Migration History. The Eurasian Experience (16th–21st Centuries)* (Leiden and Boston: Brill Publishers, 2012).
60. Jan Breman, *Labour Migration and Rural Transformation in Colonial Asia* (Amsterdam: Free University Press, 1990).
61. Amit Kumar Mishra, *Survivors of Servitude: Indian Labour Diaspora in Mauritius* (Delhi and Thousand Oaks: Sage, forthcoming).
62. Emmer, "European Expansion and Migration, 2.
63. Timothy J. Hatton and Jeffrey G. Williamson, *Global Migration and World Economy: Two Centuries of Policy and Performance* (Cambridge, MA: MIT Press, 2005).
64. However, the pathbreaking recent work of Sven Beckert tries to correct some of these inaccuracies of historical analysis of global capitalism under the aegis of empire. Sven Beckert, *The Empire of Cotton: A Global History* (New York: Alfred A. Knopf, 2014).
65. Frantz Fanon, *Black Skin, White Masks* (translated by Charles Lam Markmann) (London: Pluto Press, 1986), 218.

CHAPTER 10
THE CHALLENGE OF THE GLOBAL IN INTELLECTUAL HISTORY
Dominic Sachsenmaier and Andrew Sartori

Trajectories of Global Intellectual History

Intellectual historians make no exception to the global landscapes of historiography: they have long been transnationally connected through movements of people and ideas. It is hence hardly surprising that many changes to the field can be observed across a variety of countries. For instance, in different parts of the world, an older history of ideas has now given way to forms of intellectual history that have been influenced by social and cultural historical perspectives. As a research area, today's intellectual history no longer primarily focuses on great minds and famed works. Much rather, the field has come to pay more attention to more general intellectual environs, ranging from facets of public opinion to conceptual transformations. As part of that process, the body of primary source materials explored by intellectual historians has grown significantly wider. It now includes not only the writings of lesser known thinkers but also documents like newspapers, pamphlets or private letters.[1]

Yet while such transformations can be observed in many academic systems, intellectual history has certainly not grown into a globally standardized field. To put it in a different way, despite all global entanglements, the contours of intellectual history continue to be shaped by local factors. This is already evidenced by the varied standing of the field within and across various historiographical landscapes. For example, while intellectual history has until recently carried little weight in India, it has been quite prominent in France and Japan. And whereas in several European countries, especially after the end of the Second World War intellectual historians tended to focus chiefly on academic pursuits, parts of this field could be decidedly politicized—and publicly visible—in some Latin American societies.[2]

During the past ten or twenty years, there has been another trend in the field of intellectual history—a trend that can be observed in quite dissimilar academic settings: the growing presence of global and transregional perspectives. This development was facilitated by a complex pattern of interactions between scholars based in different countries. Rather than trying to sketch the complex global patterns of the field, this article will particularly focus on relevant academic developments in the United States and China.

We do not suggest that it is possible to juxtapose both sites of global intellectual history in a reductionist manner. Contrasting single facets of global intellectual history would not get us very far, for two main reasons. Firstly, in both China and the United States the field is extremely diversified, and many scholars are engaged in transnational collaborative projects. It would thus simply not be possible to clearly demarcate the contours of US-American or Chinese approaches to global intellectual history in either of these two academic systems. Secondly, the wider academic contexts of global intellectual history in the United States and China are far from similar to each other; this means they cannot be ignored. For example, while since the Second World War many US universities have come to figure as hubs of global intellectual exchange, Chinese peer institutions have only recently mounted more sustained efforts to become internationally influential. Similarly, the English language has continued to play an internationally dominant role during the past few decades whereas Chinese has not even regained its status as a lingua franca in East Asia.

Developments in the United States

In the United States, intellectual history, as it has been practiced by people who identify as intellectual historians, has long overwhelmingly treated literate intellectual life in non-Western world regions as largely irrelevant to its endeavors. True, if one were to define the core agenda of intellectual history as the interpretation of ideas and meanings in context, one could readily consider much of the scholarship commonly identified as postcolonialist as intersecting the field's major concerns. Yet for the most part neither self-identified intellectual historians nor the producers of postcolonial scholarship have tended to view this literature as "intellectual history." Similarly, much scholarship on non-Western literate civilizations, as in the fields of area or religious studies, for example, could easily be considered intellectual history. Yet it seems to have rarely been considered relevant to the major trajectories of inquiry in the field—even when it was highly elaborated, as in the case of twentieth-century Japanese scholarship. This has been so despite the fact that there were no obvious theoretical or methodological gaps between intellectual historians on the one hand and their colleagues studying non-Western parts of the world on the other hand.

While intellectual history was relatively open disciplinarily, it had implicit geographical connotations and remained centered on Europe and North America.[3] As a field, it was commonly oriented around the history of "Western thought" from Athens and Jerusalem to the present (institutionalized in the form of the "Western civilization" survey that rose to prominence after the Second World War), and the history of modern political and social thought. Whether in the case of Max Weber's notions of Confucianism or in the approaches of the most prominent modernization theorists half a century later, the history of Western thought was often identified with the unfolding of universally valid precepts. This implied that other world regions often featured only as a recipient of ideas whose inception and elaboration had already been accomplished elsewhere. [4]

Since then, intellectual history has been slower than many other subfields of history to embrace a less parochial vision of its subject matter. Still, it would be grossly inadequate to suggest that the entire field of intellectual history in the United States and many other Western countries represented merely crude forms of Euro-centrism or that its research parameters have remained frozen in time. For one thing, intellectual history has been significantly affected by some transformations in the humanities. The rise of first social and later cultural history at least notionally paved the way for a rapprochement between scholarship on Western history and area studies. Yet although intellectual history was most certainly impacted by the innovations of cultural history, the field participated at best minimally in any such rapprochement. Instead the larger conceptions of space framing the field stood firm, even as methodological assumptions and other conventional boundaries crumbled. During the 1960s and 1970s, pressure grew on those forms of intellectual history that marginalized the larger historical contexts within which ideas and concepts were being articulated. At the same time, intellectual history was subject to the broad criticism that it featured an elite-centered perspective and an essentialist conception of nations, cultures and civilizations. In this context, many currents of intellectual history emerged that sought to decenter these visions and become more attentive to hitherto marginalized voices and texts. Abandoning their faith in the possibility of depicting entire societies in a unified manner, many researchers turned their attention to individual biographies or localized groups. At the same time, many became more interested in the non-elite voice, even in the inarticulate—not least as a means to render more clearly the historically situated intentions and meanings of better known texts from the canon.[5]

Much of the energy in intellectual history has turned on debates over the proper way to mediate between conceptions of ideas as free-floating, textually immanent or radically contextually contingent. It became increasingly difficult for historians to depict societies essentialistically, as organized around key determinative ideas or values, or to rely confidently on organizing dichotomies like elite/popular and rational/religious. Along the way, the authority of some of the implicit or even explicit formulations of West/non-West differences were opened up to questioning, while the appropriate parameters within which even canonical texts might be studied began to blur and shift.

For example, starting in the 1970s in the United States, some scholars argued that mainstream academic historiography was not doing justice to the diversity of the country and that existing histories represented the privileged perspective of elites more than the wider and more varied experience of society.[6] As identity claims assumed greater significance on university campuses and in political arguments, some history departments became the sites of significant contestation over the very possibility of historical objectivity and the givenness of conceptions of nation and culture.[7] And as the basic coordinates of historical research were fracturing, conventional spatial parameters of investigation (nation, culture, civilization) came to be questioned. So even before global history emerged in its currently vigorous form, historians of gender, race and religion, for example, were criticizing the adequacy of unitary and linear "national" histories as well as civilizational categories like "Europe" and "the West;" these historians fragmented those wholes and traced trajectories and connections that confounded their boundaries. If the history of, say, race spilled over the borders of the United States, then how could a contextualized history of corresponding ideas respect those boundaries? At the same time, many scholars working on regions outside the West rejected the spatial constraints within which their areas of research had been constituted—a rejection that resonated with the efforts of non-American scholars such as Anouar Abdel-Malek and Abdallah Laroui, who were inspired by visions of postcolonial emancipation.[8] Border-crossing as such was hardly new in intellectual history: after all, though largely enclosed within the West, intellectual historians were long accustomed to following conversations and networks that had never much respected political or geographical frontiers. But what has become possible, and is finally (albeit belatedly) coming to be realized on a broad scale, is the study of intellectual interactions across the Western/non-Western divide.

For example, when the journal *Modern Intellectual History* was founded in 2004, it declared itself "a focal point for scholarship on intellectual and cultural history from the mid-seventeenth century to the present, with primary attention to Europe and the Americas and to transnational developments that encompass the non-West."[9] While initially focused on uniting the fields of European and American intellectual history within a single publishing forum, the journal's subsequent history shows that the field of intellectual history is becoming more open to scholarship on other regions and to the study of transregional entanglements and engagements. In 2006, the journal's third year, it began publishing a series of articles on unambiguously non-Western topics; in 2007, it published a special issue entitled "An Intellectual History for India" (edited by Shruti Kapila); and in 2010, it published a series of essays on "The Bhagavad Gita and Modern Thought" (edited by Shruti Kapila and Faisal Devji). Of course, given the distribution of expertise and the relative recentness of the emergence of self-identified intellectual historians engaging with non-Western locations, most intellectual history, including in the pages of *Modern Intellectual History* (let alone the older and more conservative *Journal of the History of Ideas*), remains focused on Western cases. Yet a loosening of the geographical parameters of the field is unmistakable. The effort to decenter understandings of global intellectual entanglements was also strong outside the United States; its strength in US academic circles may relate to domestic developments including the ethnic pluralization of faculty and student bodies at American research universities and the ensuing "history wars," that is, the debates on patterns of inclusion and exclusion in national and world historical narratives. In this context, widespread criticisms emerged in the 1970s of the "Western civilization" paradigm, as well as of the related assumption that core ethical values, philosophical insights and scientific knowledge had emerged definitively in the West and then undergone a complicated and incomplete process of diffusion to the Rest.[10]

Not all intellectual histories of circulation and exchange necessarily take the critical history of the West as their object. Much of the writing of the "spatial turn," for example, has sought to rethink the formation of non-Western regions—"India" and "China," for example—as the spatial parameters organizing historical research.[11] In Anglo-American scholarship, there have been calls to consider the relationship between West and non-West beyond the colonizer/colonized framework—focusing, for example, on the relationship between Indian intellectuals and Central European, Italian or Soviet intellectuals.[12] There has also been a striking impulse to think about processes of circulation and exchange that bypass Western centrality entirely. In 1997, for instance, Sanjay Subrahmanyam's widely read "Connected Histories" announced a new agenda for intellectual historians: first an emphasis on lateral relationships among different locations, with the West just one among several, and second, the correlative claim that "thinking globally" emerged across Afro-Eurasia in the sixteenth and seventeenth centuries. Subsequent work has elaborated on these ideas, in work that, for example, traces the connections between South and Central Asia in the early-modern period or between South and East Asia in the era of Pan-Asianism.[13]

Indeed, in the hands of Subrahmanyam and many of his collaborators around the world, the concept of early modernity has emerged in South Asian studies—as well as in the fields of Chinese, Persian and Ottoman history—as a powerful analytic frame that seeks to locate the emergence of the "modernity" that has been so closely identified with "the West" in a "global and conjunctural" moment defined by "diverse phenomena" that might include "the Mongol dream of world conquest, European voyages of exploration, activities of Indian textile traders in the diaspora, the 'globalization of microbes.'" From such a perspective, "modernity" is a phenomenon generated on an Afro-Eurasian scale, no matter how it may have been subsequently hijacked by European imperial powers. Correlatively, the intellectual histories of, say, diverse imaginings of the "global" across early-modern Afro-Eurasian space not only open up to multilateral explorations of their intellectual interconnectedness, but also take as their proper explanatory context the network of social, cultural, religious, economic and political connections that constituted early modernity as a transregional spatial formation. Where the invocation of "early modernity" has primarily served to prolong the force of the mediaeval within European historiography, in historiographies focusing on other parts of the world it has served a contrary function of providing at least some privileged non-Western locations with their own "ambiguous 'early modernity.'" Such a modernity has its own distinctive vectors that may conflict with, qualify, confound or resonate with the subsequent, more parochial conceptions of "Western" modernity established in the wake of colonialism and imperialism.[14] The compensatory appeal of this paradigm in the context of postcolonial anxieties about derivativeness is hard to miss, but its productivity in opening new vistas for intellectual historical inquiry that traverse and confound the emphasis on the axis of colonial domination and developmentalism is equally clear.

The "early modernity" paradigm has not only been used to relocate Afro-Eurasian histories within wider networks of connectedness that may or may not include European nodes, it has also been taken up as a means to mediate between two different dimensions of historicization—on the one hand, the depth of any particular tradition's intellectual history, and on the other, the breadth of that tradition's embeddedness within transregional processes. If a self-conscious intellectual tradition developed in China, India or Europe over the course of many centuries, one would be hard-pressed to explain every phase of that (retrospectively constituted and imagined) tradition with equal recourse to transregional processes. Presumably at some moments these regions were more deeply and powerfully embedded within transregional processes than at others, and over several centuries such embeddedness might have been more or less powerfully felt by intellectuals across those several different locations. In the face of this unevenness, intellectual historians—especially intellectual historians focusing on world regions where the disjuncture between tradition and modern knowledge appears especially sharp—have used the category of early modernity as an intermediary space that provides the basis for thinking about how the experience of "modern history" (mainly taken to mean the rise of the West) was shaped by the hermeneutic horizons of tradition.

The journey from a preoccupation with "early modernity" to a conception of "alternative modernities" is a relatively short and intuitive one: if European modernity is just one hypertrophic and overbearing impulse that emerged out of a larger Afro-Eurasian complex, then it becomes immediately more plausible to imagine that there might be ways to inhabit the modern world without necessarily standing either in supplicated subordination to processes of convergent modernization or in incommensurable disjuncture from any such global process. Dilip Parameshwar Gaonkar thus invokes a "narrow but critical band of variations consisting of site-specific 'creative adaptations' on the axis of convergence (or societal modernization)."[15] Sudipta Kaviraj, an early advocate of taking the intellectual history of modern South Asia seriously despite contrasting views of many progressivists, has argued that, while "political modernity" in India has turned as elsewhere on the importance of "the modern state, nationalism, and democracy," nonetheless insofar as the new practices with which these ideas were associated were "not written on a clean slate," insofar as political modernity was itself composed of heterogeneous elements. As the problems to which political thinkers addressed themselves necessarily varied across space and time, the articulation of political modernity in India was unsurprisingly something more than a mere repetition of a Western original. As a result, "these institutions or movements have evolved in ways that are different from recognized Western equivalents."[16] And indeed, in the absence of some such claims about specificity, whether pitched at the level of local histories or otherwise, it can be difficult to see why we should contemplate the intellectual history of the modern non-West at all.

As Sheldon Pollock loves to remind us, we cannot grasp the specificity of whatever it is we might like to call modernity without some determinate sense of what preceded it in different world regions.[17] In this context, we are—among other directions research has taken—also beginning to see intellectual histories built around the problematic of comparison. Pollock's own work is crucial here: he is perhaps the first to undertake a major synthetic study of Sanskrit cosmopolitan literary culture and the emergence of vernacular languages in the subcontinent, structured around a systematic comparison with Latinitas, the Imperium Romanum, and the emergence of European vernaculars. Siep Stuurman advocates the notion of meta-analytic categories of comparison that can be used to compare across traditions while laying the groundwork for a cosmopolitan conception of intellectual interaction in which multiple traditions converge around particular themes of global relevance—"humanity" and "equality," for example.[18] Harry Harootunian has also embraced the centrality of comparison to an intellectual history whose horizons extend beyond the West, but he sees the task as more difficult. Instead of positing meta-analytic categories that are then validated by comparative empirical work,

Harootunian takes the work of comparison itself as a historical problem, focusing on the ways in which comparison emerged as an inescapable condition of modern political and social thought. Japanese intellectuals, for instance, generated claims about alternative modernities in the context of the Second World War, and Harootunian looks at these claims to understand the historical conditions under which the comparative urge is felt as imperative.[19] This is a theme that has been developed with great sophistication by Manu Goswami in his work on nationalist political economy in India and by Rebecca Karl, on nationalist anti-imperialism in China.[20]

In addition, one of the preeminent tasks of intellectual historians will thus no doubt be to undertake a detailed and careful *Begriffsgeschichte*, or conceptual history, or conceptual history to chart the terrain of various intellectual traditions, not only to better understand the traditions themselves, but also to be able to specify the nature of changes that have occurred in the wake of modern transformations, whether understood in terms of European colonialism or capitalism or whatever else. For example, while the changing semantics of political, economic and other forms of life during the nineteenth and twentieth centuries have been studied for single languages, research is only beginning on the history of single terms, concepts and expressions such as "progress," "world order," "nation," "society," or "culture" from a perspective that is both global and locally sensitive.[21] In some cases, transnational research networks—rather than individually scholars—have started investigating the history single concepts in terms of both, their transformations within single languages and their global entanglements.[22]

Andrew Sartori has argued that certain concepts have assumed something like a "global" significance over the course of the last two centuries and has suggested that intellectual history should address itself to systematically examining the processes that made this possible. He points out that the global availability of such key concepts represents not only the adaptation of European concepts across diverse world regions, but also the de-Europeanization of such concepts due to their insertion into social contexts in which their provenance ceases to matter. In that sense, the global history of such concepts implies a serious rethinking of European intellectual history itself rather than an extension or add-on to an already constituted field.[23]

More developed than global conceptual history is scholarship on globally circulating translations but here, too, many detailed studies and modes of contextualization are needed.[24] Still, as a general trend most of the emergent work on intellectual histories outside of the West remains organized around area specializations, even if comparative work has begun to put these literatures into conversation. Where those boundaries have been breached, it is most often at contiguous spaces such as the North-West India/Central Asia/Persia nexus, or the maritime rims of the Indian or Atlantic Oceans.[25] The problem of comparison brings us, however, to a major issue that most intellectual historians have thus far carefully evaded: namely, the question of whether a "global" intellectual history is primarily the multiple histories of the many world regions, histories that traverse the conventional boundaries around which most research has been organized, or whether it is histories of concepts or ideas that can themselves be thought of as "global."[26]

Nonetheless, what is clear is that historians need to clarify the differences between the various possible conceptions of the task of a "global" intellectual history and elaborate positions on their feasibility, desirability, and mutual relatedness as explicitly and rigorously as possible. However belatedly, the "global turn" has arrived in intellectual history as it is being practiced and debated in the Anglo-American World—and it is now time to think as clearly as possible about what that should mean for the field.

Part of the task of opening intellectual history further to the horizon of the global will require a process of historical introspection within the historiography of the West, as a way of giving us a historical perspective on the process by which the parochial inwardness of Western intellectual history was institutionally and intellectually established. Such a history would have to extend beyond the limits of historiography itself to investigate the ways in which hierarchies of knowledge were produced in the contexts of imperial expansion, migration, economic developments, social transformations and/or disciplinary formations. Such inquiries might potentially lead us far from the more familiar trajectories of postcolonial theory with its sometimes rather monolithic conceptions of Europe and the West.

Debates in China

In the first decades of the twentieth century, large parts of the history of ideas (*sixiangshi*) were based on the assumption that a new historiography needed to contribute to China's nation-building process, and that it had to be inspired by the pathways of more "advanced" societies in the West and Japan. While numerous historians advocated more cautious approaches, strong currents in the history of ideas were based on the notion that China's scholarly, philosophical and epistemological heritage needed to be reevaluated through historical inquiry.[27] Chinese intellectual traditions were now being analyzed with categories and methods inspired by modern Western historiography. At the same time, a growing number of historians studied the history of philosophy, science and political thought in societies including the United States, Germany, Great Britain and Japan.

After the Communist Revolution in 1949, a rather quickly emerging hegemony of Stalinist and Maoist historiography marginalized the history of ideas.[28] What remained of the field grew into a forum to attack Confucianism as well as other, allegedly feudal, traditions in China. Sometimes other "traditional" teachings could be studied in this context. For instance, in their attacks on Confucianism some scholars drew on the ancient school of legalism (*fajia*), even though at that time the latter was also subject to criticism. After Mao's death and particularly under Deng Xiaoping's reforms during the 1980s, the academic climate in China changed profoundly. A loosening political control over the academic sector and increasing emphasis on market-driven models of economic growth coincided with renewed international academic exchange and increased availability of translations of foreign, mainly Western, academic publications. As a result, a growing number of scholars openly went against the rigid theoretical frameworks, analytic categories and modes of periodization that had characterized much of Chinese historiography in earlier decades.[29]

Within this context, "intellectual history" also experienced a growing importance. There were tendencies to conflate critiques of Maoism and critical assessments of much older Chinese intellectual and political traditions. Within this mindset, quite a few scholars regarded the Mao era as a continuation of earlier forms of Chinese anti-individualism. In many circles, newly acclaimed commitment to scientism went hand in hand with an interest in the Enlightenment and Western humanism.[30] A number of influential historians of ideas now operated on the assumption that Chinese intellectual history needed to help the country reenter the world and transform Chinese culture accordingly.[31] For instance, some scholars portrayed the intellectual and philosophical cultures of China as rather inward-looking and hostile to both change and domestic and international openness.[32] Here a vaguely defined "West" often figured as a reference when seeking to overcome allegedly stagnant and repressive domestic traditions.

At the same time, there was a renewed interest in Chinese tradition, which in a very complex manner was entangled with the interest in themes such as the Enlightenment. While there was a wide variety of opinions, most intellectual historians were cautious not to endorse a wholesale Westernization in their own work. This was certainly supported by the strong critiques of Eurocentrism in much of the historical literature (a large proportion of which originated in the United States) that found its way into China starting from the 1980s.[33] The idea that intellectual history could not and ought not be based on paradigms of Westernization gained further currency from the mid-1990s onward. Around that time, many intellectuals started emphasizing a history of incremental changes over one of sudden ruptures through wholesale cultural import.[34] From this background, the historiography of ideas took a new interest in prominent late-nineteenth- and early-twentieth-century advocates of a Chinese modernity such as Liang Qichao, Wang Guowei or Hu Shi who in various regards remained doubtful about the prospects of dramatic, revolutionary change.

Since the early 2000s, intellectual history as a loosely defined research field has become even more diversified, particularly due to the impact of cultural-historical, social-historical and other approaches. These developments have certainly been entangled with similar transformations in the field elsewhere, particularly at US universities which remained very influential in the Chinese academic landscapes. For instance, during the last one or two decades, a growing number of intellectual historians working on modern China began focusing on the history of newspapers, academic journals, women's magazines and other media. In a related movement, interest in the history of artistic milieus, academic societies, universities and publishing houses also surged.

As a general trend, much of the new intellectual history in China still faces significant challenges to open up new analytic spaces. For instance, despite efforts to the contrary, many scholarly publications in intellectual history and surrounding fields still tend to fall into the divide between "Chinese history" and "world history."[35] In Chinese historiography, the latter field focuses chiefly on Western Europe, North America and Japan. Inside and outside of the field of world history, there are extremely few scholars who can qualify as experts in South Asian, Middle Eastern or Latin American history. For the study of global intellectual history in China this usually means that there is hardly sufficient manpower to study topics such as the flow of ideas within parts of the Global South.

However, there have now been significant efforts to overcome such institutional divides in intellectual history and adjacent fields. This is particularly the case with studies transgressing the gaps between world historical and China-related research. For example, the historiography of concepts has become more and more influential, and as a field it increasingly seeks to relate the history of semantic changes in China to the study of global conceptual transformations. There has been increased research activity in the late-nineteenth- and early-twentieth-century linguistic exchanges that greatly transformed the Chinese, Japanese and other languages.[36] Other scholars, have, for instance, investigated the history of early-twentieth-century Chinese neologisms, using the lens of a transnationally oriented cultural history of politics.[37]

There have also been other attempts at exploring intellectual history within hitherto understudied spatial formations. For instance, a small research community is now investigating East Asia as a historical region. While many publications in this field focused on the study of social and economic networks, intellectual historical perspectives have not been altogether irrelevant. During the early 2000s, one could observe a small but growing research interest in themes like the history of forms of regional consciousness in premodern East Asia as well as in later forms of East Asian, Pan-Asian or related identities.[38]

As a general trend with great implications for the study of global intellectual history in China, debates on the position of "West" as the prime reference model have received new stimulus and taken new directions. An example is a movement often called the "national studies fever" (*guoxue re*), which has antecedents in the early twentieth century, got rekindled in the 1980s and grown more influential during the 2000s.[39] The national studies fever has been characterized by a growing interest in Chinese intellectual traditions. Many protagonists of this movement see the idea of Chinese nationhood not primarily as the outcome of Western influence or the impact of nationalism as a global ideology.

While they do not deny the role of Western influences, numerous scholars emphasize much older historical trajectories in China's nation formation; in other words, they try to put this historical process onto deeper historical ground. Intellectual historians play an important role in this area of research. An important example is the renowned Fudan scholar Ge Zhaoguang who sometimes resorts to historical comparisons between Europe and China. Among other points he argues that unlike in European history, East Asia had not witnessed the emergence of a transregional Republic of Letters and that flows of ideas in the Far East only occurred between much more loosely knit networks among thinkers in Japan, Korea and China. Moreover, a universal faith with a supranational organization did not exist in East Asia. In that sense national history is foundational to the East Asian experience, Ge argues, while at the same time he distances himself from narrow nationalist interpretations of history.[40] By contrast, other scholars in authoritative positions define the mission of global history, including global intellectual history, as more closely related to themes of national interest.[41]

As this example suggests, many academic debates in the field of intellectual history in general and global intellectual history in particular are entangled with public debates on issues of wider political and societal concern. This is for instance the case with the core problem of how to evaluate China's cultural heritage as well as the multifarious questions emanating from it. Since the 1980s, particularly during more recent decades, there has been a renewed interest in the relevance of Confucian and other Chinese traditions for twentieth-century Chinese intellectual history.[42] A controversial issue is, for instance, how values such as liberalism, individualism, civic consciousness or legalism are related to the China of the past and of the present. Whereas some scholars see them chiefly as Western ideologies or even as Western power instruments, others regard them as universal ideas and values. Additional groups stress the compatibility of certain forms of modern political culture with key elements of Confucian philosophy. Concepts ranging from Confucian democracy to Confucian socialism have all found their proponents, while a strong group of scholars—both in the Marxist and liberal camps—still disputes the suggestion that Confucianism carries any major relevance for China's future sociopolitical order.[43] Others in turn seek to develop visions for a new global relevance of Confucianism, for instance, as an ethicopolitical tradition that can help find new ways of conceptualizing the relationship between nature and humankind, or as a teaching from which supposedly more peaceful forms of international order can be derived.[44]

Needless to say, these debates on themes related to global intellectual history are formed by a myriad of individual positions, many of which would deserve more thorough discussion. Among the most influential—and internationally visible—figures in this field is Wang Hui, who authored a widely acclaimed history of modern Chinese thought.[45] This multivolume work places intellectual history at the very center of a call for the renewal of sociopolitical debates in contemporary China. More importantly, it seeks to stimulate a partial reversal of some key facets of this debate.

Wang's history of modern Chinese thought starts with historical reflections which partly speak to concepts such as "early modernity" or "indigenous modernity." Wang Hui in no way suggests that as a proto-modernity, if in fact it was one, this period could be said to teleologically anticipate a later European modernity, except through retrospective reconstruction. In one of his subsequent steps, Wang looks at the responses of Chinese scholars of the late 1800s and early 1900s to the twin problematics of national political forms and capitalist development. Wang maintains that key scholars of this epoch did not merely seek to balance indigenous traditions with accommodation to Western economic and political forces. Rather they simultaneously embraced the need to modernize and envisaged that process of modernization as imperfect and incomplete. According to Wang, central currents in modern Chinese political and social thoughts subsequently went into dissonant or even violent directions. This process, symbolized strikingly by Maoism, was the result of an intellectual project developed within the transregional conjuncture of modern imperialism and capitalism, and yet it was rooted deeply in the traditions of Chinese neo-Confucianism. At the same time, he argues that many central tenets of neo-Confucianism were lost during the ruptures of the nineteenth and twentieth centuries.

Global History, Globally

Decidedly opposed to programs advocating a blunt "return of tradition," Wang nevertheless argues that Chinese intellectual history should seek to excavate concepts and tropes from an earlier Chinese proto-modernity. He hopes that such an epistemological step will enable Chinese thinkers to assess and critique derivatives of current Chinese and global modernization discourses such as progressivism, socialism, capitalism or developmentalism from an outside perspective. It can be expected that parts of this debating field will figure as important arenas for future Chinese studies in global and local intellectual history.

Concluding remarks

This brief, largely comparative look at Chinese and Anglo-American scholarship shows that on both sides of the Pacific, intellectual history has witnessed efforts to strengthen the presence of global and transnational perspectives. In both cases, this trend has been accompanied by field-specific debates which, however, were entangled with wider social and political contestations. For example, in both research communities prominent protagonists of intellectual history have problematized the lasting impact of Eurocentric traditions on the field. Moreover, in both China and the United States there have been discussion on how to strike a balance between global and local perspectives or between universalizing assumptions and claims to particularism.

However, despite such similarities—and in fact direct connections—between relevant Chinese and Anglo-American research communities, the landscapes of global intellectual history in both academic systems continue to differ. One can easily see this with the debates on universalism and Eurocentrism. For instance, in China the notion of universal political values (particularly such of Western origin) is often used to counter claims to cultural nationalism that are voiced by quite some influential circles of scholars. By contrast, for a variety of reasons in the United States, it is usually the same group of scholars that critiques nationalism and universalism; in other words, there is a dominant tendency to see both universalizing master narratives and methodological nationalism as part of the same problem. This outlook is only shared by a minority camp of Chinese intellectual historians.

Some differences are related to global hierarchies of academic languages and the concomitant divergent positionalities of scholarly communities operating in them. For example, in Chinese academic circles the critique of Eurocentric perspectives is often closely connected with the search for making Chinese scholarship more globally influential—an intellectual vision which in quite a few prominent cases has been tied to the articulation of rather nationalist agendas when ruminating on the future trajectories of intellectual history in China.

In addition, the highly dissimilar distribution of regional expertise in China and the United States may account for parts of these disparities. Whereas at US research universities, departments belonging to the humanities usually employ a substantial body of regional experts working on regions ranging from South Asia to Latin America, the equivalent is not the case in China. Actually there is hardly any historian—let alone an intellectual historian—who works on world regions outside of the West, China and East Asia. This is so despite the fact that quite a few non-Western world regions, including India, have played a significant role in Chinese history. Given this institutional dominance of Chinese and "First World" studies at Chinese universities, it is small wonder that "the West" figures as a central reference space in much of the Chinese scholarship in the field of global intellectual history. This is even the case with most currents that are decidedly critical of the scale of Western academic influence. In the global historical landscapes of the United States, however, no central outside reference space is discernible. Needless to say, such differences in the role, standing and distribution of regional expertise are related to much wider factors and forces, including global hierarchies of academic influence.

Such wider academic configurations also contribute to differences in the relationship between critiques of Eurocentrism on the one hand and national conceptions of history on the other hand. In the United States, already several decades ago scholars with expertise in world regions like South Asia or Latin America were among the key agents in the mounting critiques of Eurocentrism in the humanities. In this context one may think of such important groups as the Subaltern Studies movement. These groups, however, stood professionally very far apart from the study of US history, and also in terms of their own worldviews their main protagonists stood far apart from any US-centered claim to methodological nationalism. A combination between critiques of Eurocentric narratives and a search for ways of looking at global history through decidedly national lenses was thus very unlikely to develop in the US setting. In China there is thus far no solid regional studies base from which conceptual or epistemological critiques are being articulated. Much rather, the critiques of Eurocentrism often come from the side of scholars who are mainly working on Chinese and/or Western intellectual history. From this array emerge quite influential attempts to overcome Western epistemological influence while at the same time retaining the main frameworks of Chinese national historiography.

Institutional patterns, academic geopolitics and many other factors matter when we compare the trajectories of global intellectual history in China and the United States. As this brief assessment of the situation in China and the United States confirms, differences in the field of global intellectual history cannot be deduced to artificial notions of pristine intellectual traditions. The diversity between research communities in today's rather closely connected academic world is related to a far more complex arrangement of factors. All this makes global intellectual history a fascinating field, with much potential for further research and debates.

Notes

1. On this transformation see for example Anthony Grafton, "The History of Ideas: Precepts and Practice, 1950–2000 and Beyond," *Journal of the History of Ideas* 67:1 (2006), 1–32. See also Samuel Moyn and Andrew Sartori (eds.), *Global Intellectual History* (New York: Columbia University Press, 2013).

2. On Latin America see for example Walter D. Mignolo, *Global Histories/Local Designs: Coloniality, Subaltern Knowledges, and Border Thinking* (Princeton, NJ: Princeton University Press, 2000).

3. A statistical account of the disciplinary background of the members of the editorial board of the *Journal of the History of Ideas* in 2004 revealed that almost half came from a rather wide array of disciplinary backgrounds outside history. See Alan Megill, "Intellectual History and History," *Rethinking History* 8:4 (2004), 549–57.

4. For example, Joseph R. Levenson, *Confucian China and Its Modern Fate: A Trilogy* (Berkeley, CA: University of California Press, 1968).

5. For the history of intellectual history and the history of ideas, see for example Donald R. Kelley, *The Descent of Ideas. The History of Intellectual History* (Burlington, VT: Ashgate, 2002); Anthony Grafton, "The History of Ideas: Precepts and Practice, 1950–2000 and Beyond," *Journal of the History of Ideas* 67:1 (2006), 1–32.

6. A very influential work was Howard Zinn, *A People's History of the United States* (New York: HarperCollins, 1980).

7. Michael N. Bastedo, "Curriculum in Higher Education: The Historical Roots of Contemporary Issues," in Philip G. Altbach, Robert Berdahl and Patricia Gumport (eds.), *American Higher Education in the Twenty-First Century: Social, Political, and Economic Challenges* (Baltimore, MD: Johns Hopkins University Press, 2005), 462–85.

8. Dominic Sachsenmaier, *Global Perspectives on Global History: Theories and Approaches in a Connected World* (Cambridge: Cambridge University Press, 2011); Anouar Abdel-Malek, "L'orientalisme en crise," *Diogène* 44, 4e trimestre, 109–42 (1963); Abdallah Laroui, *La crise des intellectuels arabes* (Paris: Maspero, 1974).

9. Taken from the journal's online description: http://journals.cambridge.org/action/newsTop?jid=MIH (accessed November 29, 2017).

10. See Gilbert Allardyce, "The Rise and Fall of the Western Civilization Course," *American Historical Review* 87 (1982), 695–725; and Katja Naumann, "Von 'Western Civilization' zu 'World History'—Europa und die Welt in der historischen Lehre in den USA," in Matthias Middell (ed.), *Dimensionen der Kultur- und Gesellschaftsgeschichte* (Leipzig: Leipziger Universitätsverlag, 2007), 102–21.

11. See for example Manu Goswami, *Producing India: From Colonial Economy to National Space* (Chicago: University of Chicago Press, 2004).

12. Bayly and Biagini, *Giuseppe Mazzini and the Globalization of Democratic Nationalism, 1830–1920* (Oxford: Oxford University Press, 2008); Sugata Bose and Kris Manjapra (eds.), *Cosmopolitan Thought Zones: South Asia and the Global Circulation of Ideas* (New York: Palgrave, 2010).

13. Sanjay Subrahmanyam, "Connecteld Histories: Notes Towards a Reconfiguration of Early Modern Eurasia," *Modern Asian Studies* 31:3 3 (1997), 735–62; "Historicizing the Global, or Labouring for Invention?" *History Workshop Journal*, 64 (Autumn 2007), 329–34.

14. Sanjay Subrahmanyam, "Hearing Voices: Vignettes of Early Modernity in South Asia, 1400-1750," in S. N. Eisenstadt and W. Schluchter (eds.), *Early Modernities*, a special issue of *Daedalus* 127:3 (Cambridge MA: American Academy of Arts and Sciences, 1998), 75–104. See for the further elaboration of these initial calls his two volumes of *Explorations in Connected Histories* (Delhi: Oxford University Press, 2004), and, co-authored with Muzaffar Alam, *Indo-Persian Travels in the Age of Discoveries, 1400–1800* (Cambridge: Cambridge University Press, 2007).

15. Dilip Parameshwar Gaonkar, "On Alternative Modernities," *Public Culture* 11:1 (1999), 1–18, particularly p. 16.
16. Sudipta Kaviraj, "Modernity and Politics in India," *Daedelus* 129:1 (2000), 137–62.
17. Sheldon Pollock, *Language of the Gods in the World of Men: Sanskrit, Culture and Power in Premodern India* (Berkeley, CA: University of California Press, 2006).
18. Siep Stuurman, *De uitvinding van de mensheid. Korte wereldgeschiedenis van het denken over gelijkheid en cultuurverschil* (Amsterdam: Prometheus, 2010).
19. Harry D. Harootunian, *Overcome by Modernity: History, Culture and Community in Interwar Japan* (Princeton, NJ: Princeton University Press, 2001).
20. Goswami, *Producing India*; Rebecca Karl, *Staging the World: Chinese Nationalism at the Turn of the Twentieth Century* (Durham, NC: Duke University Press, 2002).
21. An example for the study of nineteenth and twentieth century influences on the Chinese languages and their underlying webs of exchanges is Lydia H. Liu, *Translingual Practice: Literature, National Culture, and Translated Modernity—China, 1900–1937* (Stanford, CA: Stanford University Press, 1995). See Dominic Sachsenmaier and Margrit Pernau (eds.), *Global History and Conceptual History—A Reader* (London: Bloomsbury, 2016).
22. A team project exploring the concepts of "society" and "the economic" from global historical perspectives with case studies on European and Asian languages has resulted in the following publication: Hagen Schulz-Forberg (ed.), *A Global Conceptual History of Asia, 1869–1940* (London: Pickering & Chatto, 2014). In addition, the *Thesaurus Linguae Sericae*, an international collaborative project led by Christoph Harbsmeier of the University of Oslo and involving scholars from China, Europe and the United States, is a major exemplar. See http://tls.uni-hd.de (accessed November 29, 2017).
23. Andrew Sartori, *Bengal in Global Concept History: Culturalism in the Age of Capital* (Chicago, IL: University of Chicago Press, 2008).
24. For example Lydia H. Liu, *Tokens of Exchange: The Problem of Translation in Global Circulations* (Durham, NC: Duke University Press, 1999).
25. For example, the Centre for Indian Studies in Africa at the University of Witwatersrand in South Africa; the SSRC's new Inter-Asian Contexts and Connections post-doctoral fellowships; and the National University of Singapore's Asia Research Institute Metacluster on Asian Connections.
26. This is the central question posed in Samuel Moyn and Andrew Sartori (eds.), *Global Intellectual History* (New York: Columbia University Press, 2013).
27. See for example Prasenjit Duara, *Rescuing History from the Nation: Questioning Narratives of Modern China* (Chicago, IL: University of Chicago Press, 1995), and Tang Xiaobing, *Global Space and the Nationalist Discourse of Modernity: The Historical Thinking of Liang Qichao* (Stanford, CA: Stanford University Press, 1996).
28. A general account of world history during that time period is offered by Q. Edward Wang, "Encountering the World: China and Its Other(s) in Historical Narratives, 1949–89," *Journal of World History* 14:3 (2003), 327–58.
29. See Susanne Weigelin-Schwiedrzik, "History and Truth in Marxist Historiography," in Helwig Schmidt-Glintzer, Achim Mittag and Jörn Rüsen (eds.), *Historical Truth, Historical Criticism, and Ideology. Chinese Historiography and Historical Culture from a New Comparative Perspective* (Leiden: Brill, 2005), 421–64.
30. See for example Li Zehou, *Zhongguo xiandai sixiangshi lun* (History of Contemporary Chinese Thought) (Beijing: Dongfang chubanshe, 1987).

31. For more details, see Wang Jing, *High Culture Fever: Politics, Aesthetics, and Ideology in Deng's China* (Berkeley, CA: University of California Press, 1996). See also Edward X. Gu, "Cultural Intellectuals and the Politics of Cultural Public Space in Communist China, 1979–1989," *Journal of Asian Studies* 58:2 (1999), 389–431. See also Chen Xiaomei, *Occidentalism. A Theory of Counter-Discourse in Post-Mao China* (Oxford: Oxford University Press, 1995); Zhang Xudong, *Chinese Modernism in the Era or Reforms: Cultural Fever, Avant-Garde Fiction, and the New Chinese Cinema* (Durham, NC: Duke University Press, 1996).

32. This was, for example, the case with Jin Guantao who served as an adviser for the prominent television series "River Elegy" (Heshang). See for example Wang Jing, *High Culture Fever*.

33. See Q. Edward Wang, "Western Historiography in the People's Republic of China" (1949 to the Present), *Storia della Storiografia* 19 (1991), 23–46.

34. Zhang Ming and Li Shitao (eds.), *Zhishifenzi lichang* (The Standpoint of Intellectuals), (Changchun: shidai wenyi chubanshe, 1999).

35. See Dominic Sachsenmaier, *Global Perspectives on Global History. Theories and Approaches in a Connected World* (Cambridge: Cambridge University Press, 2011), ch. 4. About the divide between world history and Chinese history in general see Xu Luo, "Reconstructing World History in the People's Republic of China Since the 1980s," *Journal of World History* 18:3 (2007), 235–50.

36. For example, Jin Guantao and Liu Qingfeng, *Guannianshi yanjiu: zhongguo xiandai zhongyao zhengzhi shuyu de xingcheng* [*The Historiography of Ideas: The Formation of Important Chinese Modern Political Terms*] (Beijing: Falü chubanshe, 2009). In the United States, this research field has been prominently advanced by Lydia Liu who is also affiliated with Tsinghua University. See idem., *Translingual Practice. Literature, Culture, and Translated Modernity: China, 1900–1937* (Palo Alto, CA: Stanford University Press, 1995).

37. Huang Xingtao, "Xin mingci de zhengzhi wenhua shi—Kang Youwei yu riben xin mingci guanxi zhi yanjiu" (Cultural Policital History of New Terms—Research on the Relationship between Kang Youwei and Japanese New Terms) in idem. (ed.), *Xin shixue* (vol. 3)—*Wenhuashi yanjiu de zai chufa* [*New Historiography, vol. 3, A New Perspective of Culture History Studies*] (Beijing: Zhonghua shuju, 2009).

38. For example, Li Wen, *Dongya hezuo de wenhua chengyin* (*Cultural Roots for East Asian Cooperation*) (Beijing: Shijie zhishi chubanshe, 2005); and Chen Fenglin, "Dongya quyu yishi de yuanliu fazhan jiqi xiandai yiyi, (The Origin and Development of East Asian Consciousness and Its Modern Significance)" *Shijie lishi* (World History) 3 (2007), 66–75.

39. For the historical roots of this movement, see for example Shang Xiaoming, "A New Trend in the 'National Studies Fever' of the Post-May Fourth Era. The Establishment of National Studies Departments in Universities and Its Outcomes," *Chinese Studies in History* 43:4 (2010), 6–19.

40. Ge Zhaoguang, "Zai quanqiushi chaoliu zhong guobie shi you yiyi ma?" (Is There a Meaning of National History in the Trends of Global History?"), *Zhongguo wenhua* 2 (2012), 26–30.

41. For instance Qian Chengdan, "Shijieshi yanjiu de ruogan wenti" (Several Questions of World Historical Research), *Lishi jiaoxue* 20 (2012), 3–9; and Pei Yu, "Global History and National Historical Memory," *Chinese Studies in History* 42:3 (2009), 25–44. On this topic, dealing with the situation in the 1990s, see for example Xu Ben, "From Modernity to 'Chineseness': The Rise of Nativist Cultural Theory in Post-1989 China," *Positions* 6:1 (1998), 203–37.

42. For the 1990s, see for example See Tang Yijie, "Some Reflections on New Confucianism in Mainland Chinese Culture of the 1990s," in Gloria Davies (ed.), *Voicing Concerns: Contemporary Chinese Critical Inquiry* (Lanham, MD: Rowman & Littlefield, 2001), 123–34.

For the early 2000s, see Daniel Bell, *China's New Confucianism: Politics and Everyday Life in a Changing Society* (Princeton, NJ: Princeton University Press, 2008).

43. A critical overview of relevant debates is provided by Chen Jiaming, "The National Studies Craze. The Phenomena, the Controversies, and Some Reflections," *China Perspectives* 1 (2011), 22–30.
44. See for example Zhao Tingyang, "The Ontology of Coexistence: From Cogito to Facio," *Diogenes* 57:4 (2012), 27–36.
45. Wang Hui, *Xiandai Zhongguo sixiang de xingqi* (*The Rise of Modern Chinese Thought*), 4 vols. (Beijing: Sanlian shudian, 2004–2008). See Viren Murthy's review essay, "Modernity Against Modernity: Wang Hui's Critical History of Chinese Thought," *Modern Intellectual History* 3:1 (2006), 137–65.

PART III
PROBLEMS IN THE PRACTICE OF GLOBAL HISTORY

CHAPTER 11
WRITING WORLD HISTORY IN AFRICA: OPPORTUNITIES, CONSTRAINTS AND CHALLENGES
David Simo

During the last few years in Africa, there has been an increasing call for the humanities, especially history, to focus more thoroughly on the writing of global history or universal history and to redefine the place of Africa in the past and thus to consider its future in the world.[1] It may seem natural for research to want to fill existing gaps, but the awareness of a gap only leads to action if there is a felt need to compensate. There are other gaps in other areas that do not appear to arouse the same concern or desire for remedy. The awareness of the gap in existing research can generally be traced to the appearance of a new research topic. And a new research topic only takes on scope and clarity when there is a change in the paradigm of categories that shape the perception and identification of topics. Hence the need for a global or universal history is felt only when it becomes visible or is deemed necessary or inevitable. We must ask ourselves, what makes a topic visible and what makes it indispensable as a research topic? This question is especially important to our understanding of the research goals, the potential methods and the underlying issues. I can identify three sets of reasons or, better, three drives that together compel participation in the writing of global history in Africa. The first drive is the staggering increase in the writing of global history around the world during the last twenty years. The second is the intensive debate over African historiography during the last few years. The third is the experience of globalization.

The development of global history throughout the world and the pressure to write universal history in Africa

Analysts have noted a considerable upsurge in interest in global history writing. German historian Matthias Middell has observed that world history has taken on a prominent place within historiography over the last decades.[2] The writing of global history has not emerged as a new phenomenon; it is reemerging, having undergone a notable transformation. What sort of transformation has occurred and to what extent can we speak of a reconstitution? Middell speaks of transformations in research, publishing and teaching method; the major transformations are in the nature of scientific practice, which is increasingly transnational. While in the past, the writing of universal history tended to be part of national traditions, currently writing is done at the international level. Middell talks about "multilevel organizational patterns, namely the simultaneity of national audiences, local traditions of history writing, and continental as well as worldwide networks of scholars."[3] Here he is referring to a trend that can best be observed in North America and Europe. Although other parts of the world are following suit, they are impelled by a movement that started in the United States, where the need to write world history gained ground because of the growing awareness of America's central position in today's unipolar world, the sense of responsibility deriving from it and the possibility to think of it as a global field of action. Although the backdrop for global history writing has changed, fundamentally, its traditional motivations and vital character have not, that is, the awareness of the globality of the world—an awareness whose scope is directly proportional to the global role and position of the historian's collective research environment and perspective.

The more a country is affected by globalization, the more its people are aware of the trend's reality, inevitability and permanency, and the more they take steps to design and develop adaptive forms of organization. The dialectic of compartmentalization and decompartmentalization inherent in the new trend in world history writing thus reflects the real functioning of the world and reproduces a global dialectic. Whether they want to or not, the peripheral regions must adhere to a trend initiated elsewhere. The transnationalization of sites producing historical knowledge about the world has not eliminated the asymmetrical character of global networks, especially in the field of science. This asymmetry can be observed in the definitions of programs and goals, as well as in research methods and categories. In this vein, what seems to have changed is nationals from peripheral regions coming to study in universities located at the center of knowledge production, particularly North American universities and, to a lesser extent, European universities. Their physical presence and their access to the major channels of production and dissemination have given rise to a set of voices that, unlike in earlier times, cannot be easily ignored. These so-called postcolonial voices started to strongly question certain dominant paradigms and challenging certain categories.

As for writing global history, postcolonial and postmodern critique has led to a demand for multiple approaches and greater acceptance of perspectival variety as a condition for the reconstruction of a decentralized writing of history. The writing of global history is increasingly offering a platform for expressing a variety of different experiences and subjectivities for which earlier modes of historical narrative left no room. Its writing, then, appears as a stage for a complex dialectic approach, a place for a cross-evaluation of approaches hitherto inscribed in national or even nationalistic, regional, continental or cultural traditions, approaches that aspire to shed themselves off the ethnocentric prisms of the past and strive for the deconstruction of the major instances of appeal—nations, Europe, the West and so on—that form the basis of most of the master narratives that have spawned the ideas about geography and topology of the world. It is also the place where hitherto inaudible or excluded perspectives can reveal other modes of perception, other experiences and other regimes of truth.

The debate on universal history writing involves two epistemological models that cannot be easily reconciled: the representational empirical model and the representational relativistic model. The first model recognizes that our idea of the world corresponds to a representation, in other words, that it reveals our individual construction. It is still realistic, however, since it is based on the postulate that some representations reflect reality more closely than others and that the truth of representations can be verified through empirical research. Absolute historical truth might exist, and it is incumbent on the professional researcher, the historian, to get as close as possible to this truth through an approach that distinguishes fact from myth and reality from phantasm.

The second model, which I call a representational relativistic model, is based on the postulate that absolute, objective truth about reality cannot be attained. It supports the idea that knowledge is no more than a construction that forms part of a regime of truth structured by more or less voluntary paradigms, desires and interests. In this perspective, there is no hierarchy based on truth, but rather a balance of power between representations.

What does it mean when debates on global history writing seem to allow for both models? There are two conceivable stances. The first is a radical and substantial challenge to the hierarchy that exists between universal narratives in different parts of the world; this challenge is presented by the emergence of diversity in the writing of global history, with each version individually reporting, with no universal pretensions, from a culturally and historically identifiable perspective. The second would involve the reintroduction of a hierarchy between writing sanctioned by science, that is, writing based on rationality that could be considered universally valid, and voices sunk in subjectivity, myth and other simplistic prisms. This latter type of voice might be deemed fascinatingly authentic and utterly charming; it would be legitimate as far as it went, but from the point of view of science and truth, its status would be questionable. This would lead to the repetition of a well-known situation with knowledge and scientific reason on one side, and, on the other, the informer who provides material that science can use to produce knowledge about his ethos and about humankind in general. This voice would offer little more than the vague trace of a reality that would still need to be reconstructed by those who have the means to do so.

Indian historian Gopalan Balachandran gives this word of warning:

> But new is not the same as distinct. Hence it is also necessary to be alert to whether, in encountering global history/ies, we are hearing distinct new voices narrating their own stories as they experienced them. Or are we in the presence of a master ventriloquist re-telling a master narrative in several seemingly different voices.[4]

Writing global history from the periphery is therefore inscribed in the first epistemological model, which aims at disrupting a hierarchy of narratives. The focus on writing history in Africa, on formulating Africa's own writing of global history, is undoubtedly part of a will to deconstruct certain traditions, certain dominant narratives. This deconstruction should interest Africa for several reasons, but it represents an ambiguous expectation with traps that must be avoided. It can support a finicky, simplistic nativism and contribute to efforts to build up oneself to look like the "Other" of the West, an undertaking that Valentin Mundimbé has shown to play a role in the reproduction of the colonial library.[5] It can also offer an opportunity for a seemingly egalitarian dialogue, but great care must be taken to avoid sliding into a tailored role, reproducing language, script and time-tested frameworks that cause a person to produce only what is desired and expected by others. The difficulty and quasi-impossibility of speaking up in the postcolonial period comes from a permanent challenge that Stuart Hall described in his report on the situation in the Caribbean, but which applies equally to Africa:

> The dialogue of power and resistance, of refusal and recognition with and against "Présence Européenne" is … complex. How can we stage this dialogue so that, finally, we can place it, without terror or violence, rather than being forever placed by it? Can we ever recognize its irreversible influence, whilst resisting its imperializing eye? The enigma is impossible, so far, to resolve. It requires the most complex of cultural strategies.[6]

What are the stakes involved in writing global history if not the positioning of oneself and of others in a specific geography of the world and in the future of the world? If the African perspective is to be part of this reconstruction, how can it participate without contributing to a revision of the master Western narratives, narratives that previously and still today assign a marginal place to Africa, if they do not exclude it completely? Writing world history in Africa is necessary key to deconstructing the Hegelian teleological constructs that simply exclude Africa from universal history and all history. How can the global history of Africa be written without reacting to the colonial library, whose maps create a hierarchy of places, cultures and states and legitimate the power play that cost Africa so dearly? Global history writing in Africa, and probably everywhere else in the world, must be the product of dialogue and critical analyses of representations, past and present, which must not be seen as part of an individualized imaginary but as part of a historically, geographically and culturally identifiable collective discourse. We will present an outline of a plan for such writing, as it seems to be taking shape, but we need to stress from the outset that the true voice coming from Africa must be seen as part of a shared dialogue.

The internal debate on African historiography and its impact on the understanding of universal history writing

In 1996, Senegalese historian Mamadou Diouf (now working in the United States but then teaching at Cheikh Anta Diop University in Dakar) participated in a panel discussion organized at Jawaharlal Nehru University in New Delhi on "Alternative Histories: Current Debates in Asia, Africa, Central and South America." In 1999, his article in the

African Sociological Review and the *Canadian Journal of African Studies*[7] referred back to the panel and expanded upon issues related to history writing in Africa. Since that time, the debate has moved forward, especially thanks to the book by Jacques Delpechin (Dar-es-Salaam, 2005) entitled *Silences in African History: Between the Syndromes of Discovery and Abolition*,[8] to which Paul Tiyambe Zeleza responded in a programmatic article entitled "Banishing the Silences: Towards the Globalization of African History."[9] Then there was the Third Congress of the Association of African Historians held in Mali in September 2001 and the Ninth General Assembly of CODESRIA held in Maputo, Mozambique, in December 2005, both devoted to African historiography. The article by Mamadou Diouf is significant because, in many ways, his assessment of the intra-African debate takes other debates into account, especially the ones in India focusing on Subaltern Studies, as well as debate in Europe and the United States. He anticipated the positions that the African Historians' Congress in Bamako and then Paul Zeleza would adopt as alternatives to the impasse observed in African historiography, that is, whether or not the writing of African history should be included in a global history.

Mamadou Diouf's discussion of the complex, contradictory trajectory of African historiography highlights the 1950s, the 1960s and then the period starting in the 1980s. In the first period, tension arises between the Pan-Africanist understanding of African space and the nationalist reading. The former allows the history of the continent's integration to be written from a long-term perspective, with the colonial period appearing as a mere interlude that cannot have a lasting effect on the history of Africa; the latter imposes spatial configurations stemming from colonialism as the major shapers of historical research. Despite heated debate over geography, so essential to African history, African historiography in this period shared the same epistemological bases. Writes Diouf:

[African history writing] was interested in a line of history that needed to first depict a past that is worthy of the present, with the main elements being freedom from the colonial yoke and its related ethnological knowledge, the unearthing of a memory that flows into commemorative expression, sites of memory, a hymn, indigenous appellations, victories and defeats.[10]

The writing of history sought to confirm the existence of an African civilization which legitimated the present and staked out the future, or else confirmed the historical reality of the nascent nation-states, a reality that contributed to their legitimation.

In the 1980s, the credibility of nationalism was called into question following the many crises that shook the nation-states, at a time when local ethnic and ethnicist identities were being asserted. This challenge was accompanied and supported by in-depth epistemological debate on the writing of history and by critical questioning of historiography by both writers and anthropologists. The epistemological debate challenged the Enlightenment idea that sees history as a great narrative structured by two postulates: continuity, homogeneity and coherence, on the one hand, and the idea of unilinear progress and teleology, on the other. The critique of these postulates made it necessary to read historical writings as a narrative. Their constructions were shaped so they would fit into regimes of truth. Furthermore, Mamadou Diouf points to the critique of writers such as Sembene Ousmane,[11] the famous Senegalese novelist, or Archibald Mafeje, the South African anthropologist, arguing that African historiography silences some—notable local—actors and historical forces whose sole source of revival comes from other types of writing.

> The historian and the politician who trekked together and looked in the same direction, even though their relations were turbulent and sometimes violent, are no longer the sole masters of their historical narrative. Their claim to be able to propose master fiction has been called into question. Other historical narratives and other actors are now vying with them for fragmented public space. They are calling for plurality in the spheres of historicity and for the African historical conscience.[12]

According to Diouf, although the historian saw historical understanding shift toward extreme communitarization and a severely splintered, polymorphous geography, he found it difficult to accept. Historians agreed with the critique of nationalist historical writing, whose main aim is to authenticate the state and postcolonial powers, but they recognized the justification for criticizing the linear, structuralist and teleological writing of history and defended the preeminence of rigorous, professional, academic writing. Diouf also discreetly and carefully pointed out that alongside these criticized historiographical traditions, there is at least one tradition of which he himself is part. Concerning this tradition, he writes as follows:

> Alongside these spatial constructions, there are approaches like Samir Amin's history of economics, with the formation of centers and peripheries during the rising phase of capitalist accumulation and the construction of the world economy, as well as the innovative perspective of Abdoulay Ly, the first Senegalese academic historian whose research was part of a geography centered on the Atlantic region. His work in the field of geography focused on the Atlantic and the capitalist connection between continents and against the cultural nationalism of Cheikh Anta Diop and the *ethnologism* of Léopold Sédar Senghor.[13]

Mamadou Diouf does not dwell at any length on this alternative, which he feels has been marginalized—or even omitted—from dominant African historiography. He therefore does not connect it explicitly to the debate on the writing of global history. But the American historian Frederick Cooper, who refers to Diouf in a long article that he introduces as a sequel to Diouf's, is very explicit:

> There is a lot at stake in studying history in Africa: histories offer not only one particularity to be set against other particularities, but the possibility of examining interconnections and the changing meanings of the "universal."[14]

As an alternative to a historiography that vacillates between complete focus on the notion of a nation-state, and a communitarization that uses it increasingly to make ethnic identity claims, Mamadou Diouf recommends that world history be written in Africa.

While Diouf is worried about the communitarization of historical circles that increasingly marginalize the professional historian and academic history writing, Jacques Depelchin sees this evolution as the ultimate solution to the epistemological impasse of African historiography. His approach to African historiography is part of a fundamental preoccupation with the particularization, peripheralization and pathologization of Africa in the world, relating both to the production of knowledge and the institutional practices of capitalism. With this focus, his critique joins those of several generations of African intellectuals.

Paul Zeleza took up and reformulated some of these issues, changing their direction. Like Mamadou Diouf, Zeleza does not seem to believe in the need to overhaul the practices and paradigms of historical knowledge production through democratization and decentering that would render them less isolated and introduce them into a critical, creative and friendly community conversation. He is mainly concerned with extracting the writing of African history from the clutches of Western epistemology. In his words: "Is autonomy of African history possible, can this history be written without European referents? Is it possible to liberate African history from the epistemological traps of Eurocentricism?"[15]

This concern is not new to the debate on African historiography. It was already fundamental to the nationalist writing of history, but Zeleza made it topical again by including new ideas. The need for updating came from the observation that various attempts to transcend Eurocentricism did not provide release from European epistemology—that, in fact, veritably new African knowledge had not emerged. For Zeleza (2005), nationalist writing of history, as well as *dependentist* and Marxist, postmodernist and postcolonial, feminist and environmentalist writings, continue to give Europe immanent teleology. Attempts to reconstitute otherness are bogged down in the logic of negative difference, while attempts to show that modernity has not been confined to Europe and to confirm the existence of asynchronous modernities, are nothing more than corrected writings of history that fail to challenge European epistemic hegemony. The categories and concepts still come from European historiography. Zeleza thus doubts that the ties to ethnocentrism can be broken by reappropriating self-criticism based on the Western tradition. Zeleza, in other words, criticizes the solutions being proposed by both nationalist historiography and postcolonial theorists such as Dipesh Chakrabarty (2000) or even Achille Mbembe (2002). For Zeleza, the alternative is

> producing new and alternative histories based on a fundamental reconstitution of world history, or what I would call human history, and the reconstitution of provincial histories of the world's major regions including Africa and Europe in that history. The process of reclaiming and rewriting African history needs to proceed not only through critiques of prevailing silences in western Africanist historiographies, but also vigorous reconstructions of African histories that have temporal depth and spatial breadth.[16]

Like Mamadou Diouf, Zeleza recommends the writing of world history as a solution to the problems he sees in African historiography, even if he does not emphasize the same issues. Both historians are convinced that a global perspective is likely to reshape African history and that a new approach to African history is likely to totally transform the writing of world history, notably through the reconstitution of a past that is outside of European time and thus set free from Europe's usurpation of universal history. This can be achieved mainly through a long-term (*longue durée*) approach to African history, which would allow the colonial period to be seen only as a passing event; some nationalist historians have already adopted this perspective. In shifting our gaze away from the excessive focus placed on the European intrusion and its consequences, a long-term approach would also allow for the discovery of collections other than the colonial library, for example, the Arab archive.

African historiography takes two positions regarding the importance of the colonial period. Nationalist historiography—which accepts the colonial past and focuses its research on states that were, for the most part, products of colonialism—tried to construct a precolonial past or reconstruct a culture independent from colonialism. It sought either deep history, which found its roots in a distant past, or continuity beyond the colonial intervention. And yet it also based national legitimacy on acts of resistance against the colonial invader. Even though colonialism was a painful interlude that had to be overcome, for many it remained a founding moment that provided the national conscience with examples of bravery and heroism, as well as faith in the lasting grandeur of the nation and the desire for freedom and willingness to make the sacrifices required to obtain it.

In contrast, world systems theory and dependency theory, like postcolonial theory, offered a paradigm that saw colonialism as a crucial turning point in African history, one that created new types of relationships and a new framework for economic, social, political and cultural interactions. In this paradigm, Africa's place in the world and all aspects of its reality came from this deep, enduring, perhaps even definitive, transformation. The fundamental question for African academics is thus how to think about Africa within its new framework. How can it integrate into and act in a globalized world? There are two types of response to this question.

First, the structuralist or systemic response posits that in the new world system created by colonialism and capitalist imperialism, Africa can only occupy a marginal space. Africa has lost its historical initiative and is nothing but a powerless victim of forces that benefit from the asymmetrical balance thus created and that seek by all means possible to ensure that the continent remains dependent. From this perspective, Africa's only chance resides in a transformation of the world system and the creation of a new economic and political world order.

The second response, which I would describe as constructivist, relational or interactionist, seeks to move away from the approach that places self-realization only in an indefinite future in which the balance of power will be transformed, finally providing Africa with the opportunity to once again become a full-fledged subject of history. It obviously interprets colonialism as a time of great transformation, but one in which Africans never totally lost initiative or their subject positions. The way the world works is thus not seen as the sole result of the colonizer or of imperialist will, but rather as the result of interactions between the dominant subject and the dominated subject, who, despite the asymmetrical relationship, was never passive. Both the overall system and everyday economic, social, political and cultural life are considered to be proof of a hybridity that combines the pressure of structural forces with the imagination and representations of the marginalized. And the marginalized can dream of another world without having to wait for future liberation to contribute—via a variety of cultural, economic and social strategies—to its coproduction. The fact that decolonization in some ways altered international relations and restored some—albeit relative—autonomy to Africans is seen as further proof that Africans help shape the world and impose their own modernity.

Although these responses form multiple bases for historical research and provide a theory of Africa's relationship with the world, Zeleza (2005) is critical of both since he feels they contribute to enrolling Africa into European time and endorsing Europe's centrality in the world. For him, giving depth to African history and enrolling it in a new geography are effective means for enacting Chakrabarty's program of provincializing Europe, that is of making it merely one region of the world rather than its center. In doing so, he takes up the thesis of the episodic nature of colonialism in the history of Africa. We can of course counter that Zeleza's whole argument is also based on a corrective approach and as such is a reaction to a postcolonial situation. In this respect, it arguably remains dependent on the intellectual reality created by colonialism. We can reconstruct a history in which colonialism is not the central focus; in doing so, we can also develop an intellectual strategy to address the challenges that arise from a world that is the product of colonialism. Why should we refuse to think about this period as essential in the process of defining our condition in the world?

Africa and human history beyond European time

After debates inaugurated in the late 1990s, notably by Mamadou Diouf, the third congress of the Association of African Historians held in Bamako, Mali in September 2001 deemed it necessary to consider how historians can help us understand globalization. The following is part of the conference summary:

> In a world, more and more united by trade, but also marked by the apparent paradox of increased marginalization and exclusion of many groups, historians felt the need to contribute to the understanding of the process of globalization. The concept itself is quite recent and covers realities resulting from a long historical process. The papers presented in Bamako cover several areas of main concerns.
>
> First they attempt a critical assessment of recent African historiography, thus leading to a debate on the historical profession and its relevance. What kind of History? For what audience? For what purpose? The relevance of our understanding of globalization partly depends on answers to those questions.[17]

When our preoccupations change, so does the way we look at the past. Research into an autonomous and self-sufficient past in which Africa is seen to exist for itself, by itself and of itself interests historians. Given the lively debate over globalization, historians are increasingly interested in spatial connections. The crisis of the nation-state encouraged the concentration of historical research on subnational topics and focused attention on what Mamadou Diouf calls "autochthonous narratives"[18] that "made nationalist and pan-African narratives inaudible."[19] Debate over globalization has caused the construction of new spaces that go beyond the continent's geographical boundaries, thus connecting it with other places. The Pan-African preoccupation with historical movements within Africa that shaped its unity and homogeneity has given way to a perspective that was already tacitly part of the Afro-centrist approach taken by Cheik Anta Diop. This approach does not only postulate the unity of Africa but also postulates its anteriority, which means the idea that human civilization started in Africa and was then exported to other areas. Mamadou Diouf criticizes two aspects of Cheik Anta Diop's approach that, he says, should be avoided when writing a new history of Africa's connections with other areas. First, giving human universalism an origin and precise trajectory, which, Diouf says, leads Diop to take up the European narrative and simply substitute Africa for Europe as the origin and end of the world. In this way, Diop has not freed himself from the grip of linear history and the master narrative of progress. The second criticism concerns a lack of methodological and conceptual precision.

The desire to examine large-scale connections was prominent at the Bamako congress. The congress was organized around five topic areas:

1. Africa in the world in the precolonial period: globalization *avant la lettre*
2. From the first explorers to the colonial conquest: the passage of Africans from the status of actors to that of subjects in international relations
3. Myths and realities of African integration from the colonial period to the early years of independence
4. Present experiences and perspectives of African unity from the Organization of African Unity to the African Union
5. Africa in the "big game" of current international relations, or globalization as seen by historians[20]

Although the program did include discussions on interconnections before colonialism, the colonial and postcolonial periods were at the center of attention.[21] It is in reaction to this trend that Zeleza (2005) has suggested writing African history with enough breadth and depth to ensure that the colonial period is just a parenthesis.

As mentioned, Zeleza is not only interested in filling in the blanks of Africa's written history. His project is part of an ambitious attempt at epistemological emancipation from Europe and part of a radical desire to rehabilitate Africa. In this respect, he is part of the great challenge that Stuart Hall talks about and of which nationalist and Pan-African writings were important components that now need to be dialectically surpassed, not by changing the goals but by addressing the weaknesses, impasses and contradictions of this prior work.

Zeleza thus engages in two preliminary intellectual moves that help him overcome certain impasses in European and American Africanist historiography as well as in African historiography. The first operation involves challenging the racial definition of Africa as a black continent that *de facto* excludes from African history anything not initiated by black people. He also challenges the racialization of Islam and its presentation as a strictly Arab religion, as it allows any movement or event fueled by Islam to be excluded from African history, even when it was initiated on the African continent.

The second move involves rehabilitating all collections upon which African history may be written and challenging the tendency to favor the colonial library. Zeleza reminds us of the existence of the "ancient library" as well as of the "Islamic library," thus agreeing with Mamadou Diouf and other historians. Such libraries would allow a new African historiography to emerge that would not limit the research on African history to sources in colonial languages produced by intellectuals whose writing is either the product of colonialism or a reaction to it. Zeleza goes even further in demanding that authors of African origin usually classified as part of European or American historiography be included in African historiography. This is to challenge the European narratives that so willingly appropriate and use them in narcissistic and linear constructions. That is why he insists on the contribution of St. Augustine, a theologian of African origin, being at the foundation of Christianity, as well as on the contributions of an intellectual of African origin such as W.E.B. Dubois in the discursive construction of American modernity.

These different operations allow for the forging of a new academic and historiographical tradition, one that can harbor contemporary African intellectual research that no longer needs to be aligned with European traditions and paradigms. These works further allow research perspectives to be defined that, by giving depth and spatial fullness to African history, can forge another world or human history. This construction is much more a projection of what is possible than a description of what already exists; it is thus a program whose feasibility we can question.

A few examples, however, can offer a glimpse at the likely results of a wide-scale application of this program.

The findings of a research project based on the famous Timbuktu manuscripts provide access to a whole facet of African intellectual history hitherto unknown and force us to reexamine the path of African historiography as it is generally accepted.[22] Similarly, an article published by Adil H. Mouhammed in the *International Journal of Business Research*[23] reveals how taking new sources into account allows the history of some theories and categories to be reshaped, freeing them from the confines of Eurocentric discourse and providing historical depth to African intellectual thought. In "Early African Contributions to Economic Development, the Business Cycle, and Globalization," Mouhammed shows how Ibn Khaldun, born on May 27, 1332, in Tunis, thought about economic issues in 1380 that would not be addressed and theorized until the eighteenth and nineteenth centuries in Europe. This article demonstrates that Ibn

Khaldun used history as a veritable science, using a demanding methodology before the discipline even existed in Europe. Calls for a new scientific tradition free from the prism of the colonial library are thus not at all illusory.

The shift from the notion of world history to human history proposed by Zeleza is extremely significant. It involves an important change in what is understood as the driving force and measure of history and, as such, orchestrates a change in what is to be studied by history as a scientific discipline. Indeed, according to Zeleza, historical science has focused most of its attentions on power. Some topics have merited attention only because they embody power, and some transformations seem to have become meaningful only when they were the result of a powerful entity's actions.

> But power cannot be the measure of history in all its complexities and ramifications; to equate history to power is to write impoverished histories of victors of war and genocide, colonialism and imperialism, of those whose glories have exacted heavy ethical costs for the value of human life and high entropic costs for the visibility of the planet itself.[24]

Refocusing the writing of history on the human species clearly allows us to move beyond the 5,000 years on which historians generally tend to focus and more away from a history that overvalues the history of empires and their conflict, supremacy and decline. A broader understanding of human history would allow African historians to put Africa at the center of this history: Africa is the cradle of humanity, the place where humans have lived the longest and accomplished most of their conquests, against both nature and humankind. Zeleza thus seems to be calling on historians to look at a discipline such as biohistory. Despite his distrust in introducing biology into the humanities—a reticence born from Social-Darwinist abuse—he appreciates the role that biohistory can play in understanding the future of humanity. Similarly, he draws on other sciences such as archaeology (unfortunately rarely practiced by Africans in Africa), as well as paleontology, evolutionary biology, epidemiology, ecology, anthropology and historical linguistics. All of these disciplines are likely to help provide African history with a depth that would place it at the center of human history.

And how might we achieve a spatial fullness in African history that would help Africa to return to its rightful place? Zeleza suggests focusing on the progressive dispersal of Africans into other regions of the world via migration and conquests. This would involve examining both voluntary migration, which led to the foundation of kingdoms outside of Africa, such as the empire of the Moors in Andalusia, and forced migration, such as slavery.

Zeleza's (2005) writings are above all programmatic. They point out the silences and impasses of an Africanist historiography of Africa, but they also identify research by non-African academics that should serve as an example. He refers to the research of Christophe Ehret and more particularly to his *The Civilization of Africa: A History to 1800*, as well as to that of Patrick Manning. The African perspective in the writing of world history thus needs to be understood in two ways. The first is connected to the historian's origins or place of residence, since the goal is to renew world history through the infusion of an academic or intellectual tradition in Africa or to redefine it based on new questions and new challenges confronting Africa. The second is connected to the research area itself—Africa, which, once remapped spatially and historically, provides subject matter that allows us not only to redefine the universal but also to develop a perspective from which the future of the world and humanity can take on a new shape and trajectory. Regardless of their origins, African historians as well as historians of Africa coming from elsewhere are confronted with subject matter and knowledge that enable them to have entirely different visions of the world.

At the same time, history writing is too important to be left only by historians. The desire to give the writing of global history an academic and scientific basis in order to include global history in an international scientific tradition should not lead us to lose sight of questions raised by writer Sembene Ousmane and anthropologist Archibald Mafeje about the form that history texts should take (see Diouf 1999). As Mamadou Diouf has said, there is no need to partition the different types of history writing or to create an unfounded hierarchy between these different forms. Whether oral or written, different scientific and artistic genres and different types of narrative should nourish and mutually enrich one another. Professional historians are not the only people producing historical knowledge from which it is possible to acquire a perception and representation of the world. That is why the reconstitution of a tradition or library for writing world history should not favor certain types of writing at the expense of others.

Conclusion

As we have seen, debate in Africa over the writing of world history is the product of several types of intentionality: first, a desire to be present in the international debate and in an academic tradition which, although based on a plurality of voices, tends to marginalize Africa and reproduce common asymmetrical patterns in the production of knowledge, particularly of historical knowledge. It is the product also of a desire to move beyond certain trends in African historiography that confine the writing of African history to communitarian and nationalist narratives, narratives which are increasingly developing outside of formal academic spheres. And it is the product of a desire to free the African production of historical knowledge from the blinders and shortsightedness of Eurocentrism, which, with regard to the writing of global history in particular, tends to favor an understanding of interactions built on an examination of long-distance trade, mass migration and empire building.

Even if this programmatic perspective of writing world history from Africa is part of a desire to provincialize all regions of the world, including Africa (i.e., to deconstruct all claims that one region has a central position in human history), it has no choice but to first dialectically take on a corrective role that challenges dominant discourses and emphasizes the role played by hitherto marginalized regions, notably including Africa, in the shaping of humanity. While looking ahead, the debate over African world history writing is also an attempt to recreate and find a place in a long historiographical tradition that allows Africans to think outside the European tradition.

Notes

1. I will refer only to a few books that I feel are especially relevant: Valentin Y. Mudimbe, *The Idea of Africa* (Bloomington, Indiana University Press, 1994); Mamadou Diouf, "Des historiens et des histoires, pour quoi faire, L'historiographie africaine entre l'État et les communautés," *Revue africaine de sociologie* 3:2 (1999), 99–128; Fatou Sow (eds.), *Engendering African Social Sciences* (Dakar: CODESRIA, 1997); Paul Tiyambe Zeleza, *A Modern Economic History of Africa*, vol 1; *The Nineteenth Century* (Dakar: CODESRIA, 1993); *Manufacturing African Studies and Crises* (Dakar: CODESRIA, 1997); "Banishing the Silences: Towards the Globalization of African History," paper presented at the Eleventh General Assembly of the Council for the Development of Social Science Research in Africa (CODESRIA), Maputo Mozambique, December 6–10, 2005; Achille Mbembé, "African Modes of Self-Writing," *Public Culture* 14:1 (Winter 2002), 239–73; Abolade Adeniji, "Universal History and the Challenge of Globalization to African Historiography," *Radical History Review* 91 (Winter 2005), Duke University Press, 98–103.
2. Matthias Middell, "Die Verwandlung der Weltgeschichtsschreibung. Eine Geschichte vom Beginn des 21. Jahrhunderts," *Comparativ, Zeitschrift für Globalgeschichte und vergleichende Gesellschaftsforschung*, 6/10 (2010), 7–19, especially 7.
3. Ibid.
4. Gopalan Balachandran, "Writing Global History: Claiming Histories beyond Nations," Working Paper in *International History and Politics*. Editor: Jaci Eisenberg. Department of International and Development Studies, 7 (2011), 7.
5. Cf. Mudimbe, The Idea of Africa note 1.
6. Stuart Hall, "Cultural Identity and Diaspora," in Bill Ashcroft, Gareth Griffith and Helen Tiffin (eds.), *The Post-Colonial Studies Reader*, 2nd edition (New York: Routledge, 2006), 435–42, 437.
7. Diouf, Des historiens et des histoires, note 1.
8. Ibid.
9. Ibid.
10. Ibid., 99.
11. Sembene Ousmane was a prolific Senegalese novelist and filmmaker whose writings and cinematographic productions carry a strong political and social commitment.
12. Ibid., 118.
13. Ibid., 99–100.
14. Frederick Cooper, "Africa's Pasts and African's Historians," *Canadian Journal of African Studies* 34:2 (2000), 298–336, especially 303–04.
15. Paul Tiyambe Zeleza *Banishing the Silences: Towards the Globalization of African History*, https://www.codesria.org/IMG/pdf/zeleza (accessed November 29, 2017) note 1.
16. Ibid.

17. Issiaka Mandé and Blandine Stefanson, eds., *African Historians and Globalization.*, *Actes du 3ème Congrès international des historiens africains* (Paris: AHA/ASHIMA & Éditions KARTHALA, 2001).
18. Diouf, Des historiens et des histoires p. 100.
19. Ibid. (translated here).
20. 3rd Congress of the Association of African Historians, Mali, 09/01, University of Pennsylvania—African Studies Center in URL: http://www.africa.upenn.edu/Current _Events/malihist0901.html (accessed March 15, 2013).
21. The published proceedings show that no participant actually addressed a subject related to the first topic.
22. Shamil Jeppie and Souleymane Bachir Diagne (eds.), *The Meanings of Timbuktu*, CODESRIA/HSRC (Dakar, 2008).
23. Adil. H. Mouhammed: Early African contributions to economic development, the business cycle, and globalization: in the International Journal of Business Research May, 2009. Source Volume: 9, Source Issue: 3 http://www.freepatentsonline.com/article/International-Journal-Business-Research/208535101.html.
24. Ibid., p. 4.

form
CHAPTER 12
WORLD HISTORY, NATIONALLY: HOW HAS THE NATIONAL APPROPRIATED THE TRANSNATIONAL IN EAST ASIAN HISTORIOGRAPHY?
Jie-Hyun Lim

The configuration of the national and the global

As a modern academic discipline, national history has been a product of worldwide cultural interactions and transnational discourses. A history of cultural encounters between "East" and "West" reveals the ways that non-Europeans have been obliged to respond to the conceptual categories brought into play by "Western" modernity. Confronting challenges of European modernity, East Asian historians have tried to prove their civilizational potential by finding European elements such as rationalism, science, freedom, equality and industrialism in their own national histories. Any national history lacking "Western" modernity would risk being branded as the history of "history-less people." Modern historiography in Japan and Korea was partly a struggle for recognition of the national *raison d'être* by proving their national potential for modernist development to skeptical Westerners. This struggle for recognition was more successful when it was written to be intelligible and appealing to Western readers.[1]

In order to satisfy their expectations, East and West, Orient and Occident had to be configured and structured in a grammar familiar to European history. Thus it is more appropriate to stress the configuration of national *and* world history rather than the bifurcation of an either/or rivalry. This configuration helps to position national histories sequentially in a linear trajectory of world history. In this historicist *schema*, Western countries occupy the higher positions that are to be followed as models by backward Easterners. Thus, making national histories in East Asia was not conceivable without referring to a world history based on the dichotomy of "normative-universal-developed-modern" Western history and its "deviated-particular-underdeveloped-premodern" Eastern variation.[2] The configuration of norm and deviation, of East and West and of the national and the global is crucial to understanding the historicist complicity of national history and world history.

However, the accommodation of national history or even promotion of nationalist agendas through world history is hardly unique to East Asia. The thesis of German *Sonderweg* debates originated in the same schematic configuration: the English history of a universal-normal-democratic path is posited as a yardstick against which to measure the German history of a particular-abnormal-fascist path.³ "Western civilization," designed as a part of the core curriculum of many American universities, is another good example. The "Western civilization" course was created during the First World War to encourage the national integration of massive numbers of immigrants of diverse nationalities. The history of "Western civilization" presented the United States as the culmination of a civilized "Western" tradition and imprinted the American national identity with a more "Western" than European identity.⁴ This "patriotic world history" highlights and celebrates American political and ideological values, and its parochial understanding of humankind's history has a century-long tradition.⁵

Similar to Eurocentric world history, Asia-centric world history played a role in consolidating a nationalist rationale in East Asia. Discourses of "Pan-Asianism" and a "Greater East Asia Co-Prosperity Sphere" before the Second World War, and the postwar discourses of an "Asiatic value-system," "East Asian Community," "East Asia as a Project" and "East Asia as a Methodology" can be listed in the catalogue of Asiatic regionalism. From the beginning, the discourses of regionalist Asia have been loaded with nationalist repugnance, impulses and aspirations. What is most revealing in the trajectory of regional histories is the discursive complicity between the Eurocentric Orientalism of "Western civilization" and the anti-Western Occidentalism of "Asian civilization" in the promotion of the idea of civilization as a self-regulating entity. This realization reveals the urgent task of problematizing the complicity of national, regional (Oriental) and world (Western) history in abusing history for a nationalist rationale.⁶ This chapter will explore the world history debates in conjunction with the national and regional history in East Asia where world history functioned as a nationalist rationale.⁷

World history as a nationalist rationale: From Enlightenment to Marxism

World history came to Japan in the 1870s with the *Meiji Ishin* (Meiji Regeneration). The Japanese government took the initiative of introducing world history in the name of *Bankokushi*, meaning "the history of all countries of the world." The project stressed information about current world affairs rather than the study of the histories of others. Its aim was to introduce Western things to Japan in order to speed the Japanese nation's adaptation to the new conditions and its entry into civilization. Among the various "world history" and "universal history" books, the most popular one initially was *Bankokushi* (1876), a Japanese translation of Samuel G. Goodrich's *Universal History on the Basis of Geography* (1870). This book was a simple compilation of many histories, covering every region on earth like a travel guidebook. Some of the other *Bankokushi* books carried more explicitly Eurocentric messages than Goodrich's book. For example, William Swinton's *Outlines of World History* viewed world history as the histories of the European people (Aryan races), who led the progress of civilization. The Swinton line of *Bankokushi* was called "Civilization History," and its Eurocentric interpretation of world history became dominant in Japan during the 1880s.⁸

It is intriguing to see that national history textbooks were preceded by world history textbooks. It was at the request of the Paris international exposition bureau that the first national history of Japan, *A Brief History of Japan* (日本史略), appeared in 1878. The final version of the text, *View of National History* (國史眼), was adopted as the official history textbook in 1888 by the newly created history department of Tokyo Imperial University. Thus the first official Japanese national history textbook had Western readers as its primary target. The first book on the history of Japanese art, *Histoire de l'art du Japon*, was also published originally in French upon the request of the Paris international exposition bureau in 1900.[9] The motivation to write this book was to glorify the Japanese state by highlighting its national heritage and encouraging "our own artistic spirit" to stay abreast with the European standard. The cognitive sequence from the world to the nation was approved also by Fukuzawa Yukichi, who, in championing modernity in Meiji Japan, famously said that "the knowledge of oneself develops in direct proportion to the knowledge of others: the more we know about them (the West), the more we care about our own destiny."[10]

In other words, writing national history was nothing but an "attempt to posit the identity of one's own ethnicity or nationality in terms of the gap between it and the putative West, that is, to create the history of one's own nation through the dynamics of attraction to and repulsion from the West."[11] Japanese Enlightenment intellectuals were stuck in a dilemma: the more they learned about European history, the wider the gap grew between Japan and Europe. The more they tried to find a symmetrical equivalent to the history of the West, the more they suffer from a sense of inferiority. When historicism adapted vertical evolutionary time for the horizontal space of an "imaginative geography," Japan discovered that it lagged behind the unilinear development scheme of world history. In order to escape this dilemma, Japanese modern historiography developed its own Orientalist strategy to highlight Japanese difference from the rest of Asia. Inventing the Orient of their Asian neighbors let the Japanese compensate for anything they feared they lacked. By inventing Japan's own Orient, Japanese historians forced China and *Chosŏn* to take the place of Japan while Japan joined the West in the imaginative geography of the period.

Thus *toyoshi* (history of the Orient) was established as a Japanese version of Orientalism in a broad scheme of world history. *Toyoshi* aimed at inventing its own Orient of China and *Chosŏn*, while Japanese national history (*kokushi*) tried to capture European historical elements in Japan's past. By wielding discourses of *toyoshi* and *kokushi* simultaneously, Japanese historians tried to escape from the image of Oriental Japan invented by European Orientalists. Perhaps it is not a coincidence that the establishment of *toyoshi* had the Sino-Japanese War (1894–95) and Russo-Japanese War (1904–05) as its historical background; the two victories over Great World Powers enhanced Japanese national pride. As a result, the historical research and pedagogy was divided into three departments: national, Oriental and Occidental.[12] This tripartite structure helped to elevate the strategic placement of Japan in world history into the "West" by differentiating Japanese history (*kokushi*) from the *toyoshi* (Oriental History) of China and Korea. That noble dream of de-Asianizing and Europeanizing Japan could best be realized through the trilateral discursive complicity of national (Japanese), regional (Asian) and world (Western) history. This tripartite structure of national history, regional/Oriental history and world/Occidental history still dominates historical research and education in contemporary Japan and Korea.

World history also throve in late nineteenth-century Korea, but here it was based on national crisis. The first world history textbook was *The Short History of the World*, published in 1896. In tandem with this, many other works of Western history were published in translation, including *The Outline of English History* (1896), *A Short History of Russia* (1898), *History of American Independence* (1899), *History of the Fall of Poland* (1899), *A History of Modern Egypt* (1905), *History of the Independence of Italy* (1907), *World Colonial History* (1908) and biographies of Napoleon, Otto von Bismarck and Peter the Great. World history was promoted as a means of inspiring patriotism and justifying "civilization and enlightenment" (*munmyŏng kaehwa*). In this regard, Korea can be seen as a predecessor to many other countries in creating a "patriotic world history." The dual historical tasks of modernization and independence urged Korean intellectuals to study world history in the belief that globalism and nationalism would be the path toward "civilization."

The newly acquired knowledge of world history provoked comparisons between Korea and the Great Powers, between East and West. World history, with its Western accent, signaled the deconstruction of the traditional Sino-centric world order and the repositioning of East Asia in the new international order. Korean Enlightenment intellectuals adopted Japanese Orientalist thinking in order to decenter and provincialize China. For Korean nationalists, appropriating the Western concept of civilization was in the interest of national sovereignty, as it helped them remake China as an Asian province. The repositioning went so far as claims by Korean journalists that even Denmark would soon shame China. Public history was much more active in decentering China than official history.[13] However, at the same time, world history reinforced a Eurocentric definition of a historically inferior East by replacing the traditional Sino-centrism with Eurocentrism. The configuration of Korea and the West underscored Korea's potential for following and catching up to the West, but at the cost of presenting Korea as lacking or backward.

The newly emerging Korean historiography compared Korea to Western countries through a temporalization of space in a homogenous and unified time of "history." The periodization was also based on European historiography and its division of time into the following epochs: ancient → medieval → modern → contemporary. Topics like liberalism, democracy, the bourgeois revolution, the industrial revolution and nationalism were the most popular problematics in world history textbooks, which in turn reinforced the Eurocentric understanding of world history. The sequence of "first world history, then national history" seems to reflect the "first in Europe, then elsewhere" structure of global historicist time that accommodated the Eurocentric diffusionism from Europe to the "Rest."[14] This explains why Korean national history based on the configuration of East and West gave rise to a consequential Eurocentrism.

The Eurocentric nexus of national and world history has been reinforced in post-1945 historiography in East Asia.

As a result, research subjects focused heavily on the transition from feudalism to capitalism in Western history. The rise of capitalism, the Renaissance and Reformation, the German Peasant's War, the English Revolution and the gentry debates, the American Revolution and slavery, Enlightenment and the French Revolution, agrarian reforms in Prussia and the Industrial Revolution were among the most popular topics for Western history-oriented world historians. Eurocentric world history was promoted to accelerate the historical process of industrialization, political democracy and modern nation-building. Japanese historians relatively free from Cold War imposition could expand their research frontiers to Eastern Europe, Latin America, the Middle East and Africa in 1970s, and leftist critical historiography has been relatively strong in Japan. But it is undeniable that an amalgam of Marxism and modernization theory, represented by Ōtsuka Hisao's economic history scheme, has been a main framework to explain the Japanese transition from the feudal to the modern on a world history scale.

Although Marxist historiography has been regarded as a potential alternative world history for its criticism of capitalist modernity, it was hardly free from Eurocentrism. A history of the complex cultural transfers and interactions of Marxist ideas, however, clearly shows that a broad range of movements and ideologies were invoked in the name of Marx. When Marx's *Das Kapital* was translated into Russian, for example, the Russian bourgeoisie was second to none in welcoming it, because they saw in it an argument for the historical necessity of capitalist development in Russia.[15] Indeed, Marxist historiography has never been free from the practice of configuring East and West hierarchically in historical thinking and writing. The Marxist dictum in *Das Kapital* that a "country that is more developed industrially only shows, to the less developed, the image of its own future"[16] proclaimed the manifesto of Marxist historicism. If one views Marx as a theorist of modernity, one may easily argue that "Marx's account of modernisation was inextricably a description of Westernisation, and therefore that his view of global history was a general history of the West."[17] Although Marxist historians were searching for an alternative modernity, Marxist historiography in twentieth-century East Asia was still the offspring of the Eurocentric world history.

What distinguished Marxist historiography was its comparative history of capitalist development on a global scale. The famous Marxist controversy over the *Meiji Ishin* of 1868 and subsequent capitalist development between the *Kōza-ha* (lecture's faction) and the *Rono-ha* (labor-peasant faction) is a good indication of this. While the *Kōza-ha* saw the "Meiji Restoration" as the transition to an absolutist state, the *Rono-ha* interpreted it as a bourgeois revolution. Thus *Rono-ha* Marxists insisted that the socialist revolution in Japan was imminent, given the universal crisis of world capitalism in the interwar period. In opposition to the *Rono-ha* group, the *Kōza-ha* Marxists emphasized Japanese backwardness and the peculiarities of military and semifeudal capitalism in Japan as indications that Japanese Marxists should complete the bourgeois democratic revolution as Russian Marxists in the revolution of 1905 had thought. Caught in the Marxist unilinear scheme of the development of socioeconomic formations, both factions presumed that every country must experience a bourgeois revolution prior to the institution of the worker state. The *Kōza-ha*'s definition of Japanese capitalism closely resembled Lenin's description of the "Prussian path" of capitalist development. But the *Kōza-ha*'s insistence on the contrast between Japan's distorted and crooked capitalist development and English autogenous capitalism, as well as between the Prussian path and American path, was also imprinted by historicist Eurocentrism.[18]

Marxist historiography in post-1945 Japan was not that far from the *Kōza-ha* tradition. The dominant discourse in the historical evaluation of Japanese modernity was that Japanese militarism and colonial expansion could be attributed to the pathological factors of an immature civil society, its semifeudal backwardness and authoritarian political culture, both of which are inherent in its "premodern residues." Postwar Japan should be reformed to eliminate premodern irrationality and complete democratic revolution. This diagnosis can be seen as the partial convergence of the SCAP's official view of the "Pacific War" and the *Kōza-ha* Marxist faction's interpretation of Japanese modernity.[19] Democratic liberals participated in this interpretation mainly through the work of Ōtsuka Hisao, who bridged the gap between *Kōza-ha* Marxists and modernization theory. Contrary to ideas of sharp ideological antagonism, Rostow's theory of the stages of historical growth was similar to the Marxian concept of the unilinear history. Developmental historicism explains why world history books in Japan, especially in the 1950s and 1960s, were full of tropes about the necessity of a "follow and catch up" strategy of countries in the periphery.[20]

Despite its attempts to combine a nationalist agenda with a Marxist understanding of world capitalism, Marxist historiography in colonial Korea was also marked by the Eurocentric vision of world capitalist development in a unilinear scheme. Among the various Marxist arguments, Paik Namwoon represented the most common interpretation. His periodization of Korean history corresponded exactly with the Marxist model of developmental stages: primitive commune → slave economy → Asiatic feudalism → capitalism. In his book, the most influential Marxist history in colonial Korea, Paik vehemently opposed any particularistic interpretation of Korean history and tried to locate Korean history within the universal history of Marxism.[21] By relying on the unilinear scheme of world capitalist development, Paik invoked a consequential Eurocentrism. But the Eurocentrism inherent in his universalist conception of history was a "weapon of criticism" to defend the theory of endogenous development of capitalism against the idea of the stagnancy of the Asiatic mode of production in Korea. It is intriguing to witness how the Eurocentric unilinear development model ended up defending the autogenous capitalist development of the colonized-Korea against the colonizer-Japan's stagnancy theory. Confronting red Orientalism arguing for the Asiatic mode of production and stagnancy in precolonial Korea, Marxist universal history, and its consequential Eurocentrism, was able to accommodate the nationalist rationale with its stress on the autogenous development of capitalism.

The peculiar amalgam of Marxist historicism and the Rostovian takeoff model of economic growth was influential in postwar Korean historiography, too. It is not surprising that the dominant Marxist historical narrative in Korea is the "sprouts of capitalism" and "endogenous development of capitalism" thesis.[22] Nationalist-Marxist historiography in postcolonial Korea tried very hard to locate the polarization of the rural population and the emergence of "enlarged scale farming"—a historical process that they argued produced an agrarian bourgeoisie and proletariat in the premodern *Chosŏn* period. They then sought a blueprint for utopia in historical phenomena such as the development of commercial production of specialized crops, wholesale commerce, handcraft industries that relied on merchant capital in the putting-out system, mercantilism and modernist thought. Along with looking at emerging capitalist relations of production, this line of historical inquiry goes back to ancient and medieval history to find an enslaved and feudal society. The main currents in Marxist historiography preferred the Marxian universalist scheme to the Asiatic mode of production in order to avoid justifying Japanese colonialism. Whether Marxist or not, the desire for modernity has been a locomotive that has driven the study of—and education in—world/Western history.

In less developed countries, socialism under the slogan of "the creative application of Marxism-Leninism" became a development strategy of rapid industrialization intended to catch up and overtake advanced capitalism at the cost of the working masses. To many East Asian intellectuals suffering from the schizophrenia between Westernization and national identity, socialism came as a two-bird-with-one-stone solution. Socialism was expected to solve the historical dilemma of anti-Western modernization because of its vision of anti-imperialist national liberation and rapid industrialization from above.[23] The popularity of the dependency theory among Korean left historians and social scientists in the late 1970s can be understood in the same vein. It stressed the one-way transfer of capital from the colony to the metropolis and the additional transfer of surplus to the metropolis through the process of unequal exchange between the center and periphery. Dependency theorists based colonial history on the basic premise that at the heart of colonialism lay surplus appropriation from the colony to the metropolis. The hated Japanese colonial rule was seen as the prime cause of contemporary Korean economic backwardness, military dictatorship, an immature civil society, the division into two Koreas and all sorts of premodern residues.

Dependency theory and its aftermath in historical research did not shatter the dichotomy of the normative West and the deviated East, nor of model modernization and deviated modernization. With its sharp criticism of the unequal exchange and unilateral surplus transfer between center and periphery, dependency theory and its historical arguments were more often than not based on an oversimplified opposition between East and West as well as essentialized regional differences represented by the concept of the "Third World." Thus, it fails to notice historical tensions inherent in any specific unit of either peripheries or centers. It tends to essentialize the homogeneity and heterogeneity of both nation-states and the region. In the final instance, dependency theory and its worldview came to serve world history as a nationalist rationale by justifying the accumulation of capital by the nation-state for rapid industrialization. Once again both modernist and Marxist world history in postwar East Asia were overcome by Western history.

Making Pan-Asian history: Between de-territorialization and re-territorialization

Along with the Japanese Orientalist discourse of *toyoshi* or history of the Orient discussed above, "East Asian" intellectuals intermittently heralded visions of a peaceful, united and racially defined Asia. Inspired by Social Darwinism, Pan-Asianism originated in Japan and quickly spread to China and Korea; it was not reluctant to connect the political ideas of Asian unity with the racial physiology of "yellow peoples." Ideologically, the category of "yellow race" included all Asian peoples, but practically it was equated with a narrowly conceived East Asia comprising only Korea, China and Japan, which all shared the Confucian culture. Leading Chinese intellectuals such as Liang Qichao and Sun Yatsen promoted peace and unity in a racially defined East in their speeches. Pan-Asianism translated the struggle for national survival into a racial struggle between "white people" and "yellow people." The ideal of Pan-Asianism as an antithesis to the European imperialist racism was shared by Japanese, Chinese and Korean intellectuals. They supported Pan-Asianism to assure their own national independence and regional security against Western imperialism.

The Pan-Asianist ideal attracted many a Korean intellectuals. Alongside *Ilchinhoe*, who were in collaboration with Japanese colonialism because of the unity of the yellow race, Korean Enlightened intellectuals advocated a unity of Asian people on different grounds. Enlightened Reformists assumed Pan-Asianism as an ideological weapon to guarantee national independence and regional security and peace. To the Korean Enlightenment activists, Pan-Asianism meant an alliance of three individually sovereign nations. The 1905 treaty establishing a Japanese protectorate over Korea was thus read as a betrayal of Pan-Asianism.[24] Upon the colonial conquest of Taiwan and annexation of Korea, Pan-Asianism revealed its hidden agenda of Japanese regional hegemony as it was meant to integrate the multinational colonial subjects into the Japanese empire. Later, it proved to be a stepping-stone toward the transnational ideal of the "Greater East Asian Co-Prosperity Sphere," helping to persuade colonial subjects more effectively into a total war system based on "voluntary mobilization."

Pan-Asianism posed a serious dilemma to Japanese imperial nationalists too. Applied to history, linguistics and anthropology, Pan-Asianism became *Ilseontongjoron* (日鮮同祖論), contending that Koreans and Japanese shared a bloodline. This bloodline discourse served to justify the Japanese integration of the Korean nation into its growing empire. *Ilseontongjoron* argued for ethnic/racial homogeneity between colonizers and colonized, a stark contrast with the racist discourse of European colonialism. The Japanese-Korean same bloodline thesis was asserted as a sort of official historiography by professors such as Kume Kunitake in the national history department at Tokyo Imperial University.[25] It is an irony that *Ilseontongjoron* as the first version of transnational history in East Asia was formulated by pioneer historians of the national history of Japan. Transnational history served Japanese nationalism recurrently and in a variety of contexts.

But *Ilseontongjoron* met furious opposition from the combative nationalist wing of Japan which believed in the cultural uniqueness of Japanese *Kokutai* (國體)—a complex of imperial family and nationality. They thought the family tree of the Japanese emperor should not be traced back to ancient *Chosŏn*. When professor Kume was sacked by Tokyo Imperial University in 1892, the Japanese minister of education explicitly criticized the thesis that Japanese and Koreans shared an ancestry.[26] At the turn of the twentieth century, pioneer historians of *toyoshi* such as Kuroita Katsumi and Shiratori Kurakichi began to distance themselves from *Ilseontongjoron*, too. They admitted the affinity of Japanese and Korean languages and ethnicity, but argued that the nationality difference was much greater than any cultural or ethnic affinity. Perhaps the originism immanent in the national history paradigm did not allow these *toyoshi* historians to accept the theory of a common origin of the Japanese and Koreans. It was unthinkable for Japanese Orientalists to equate Japanese with Koreans—in fact, *Ilseontongjoron* undermined the very basis of Japanese Orientalism.

What divided Japanese scholars on *Ilseontongjoron* was the internal tension of the Japanese nationalism between the multiethnic nationalism of imperial integration and the ethnic nationalism of bio-cultural authenticity, which foreshadowed the strain between transnational and national historiographic variants. Yet a common thread binding these two divergent currents is found in the historical discourse about the Japanese commandery, called *Imna*, supposedly established in *Kaya* (on the southern shore of the Korean peninsula) around the fourth century CE. The Japanese interpretation of the inscription on a monument of *Koguryŏ* King Kwanggaet'o led them to conclude that the *Yamato* royal court had led its army across the sea to *Chosŏn* and established a military base on the southern coast of the Korean peninsula.[27] This Japanese enclave in ancient Korea provided historical justification not only for *Ilseontongjoron*, but also for Japanese claims to Korean territory and for its Orientalization of Korea.

The Japanese annexation of the Korean peninsula in 1910 revived the theory of a common origin for Japanese and Koreans. Thanks to the contributions of physical anthropologists, *Ilseontongjoron* could now take the form of scientific (or pseudo-scientific) discourse. Across more than 400 articles, Japanese physical anthropologists surveyed the physical characteristics of ancient and contemporary Koreans, collaborating with archaeologists to study the remains of ancient Koreans and with physiologists to study contemporary Korean physiognomy. The theory of common origins of Japanese and Koreans backed up by physical anthropology was easily connected with the ethnological thesis of ancient migration between the Korean peninsula and the Japanese archipelago. The most salient point of this thesis is that authentic Japanese were composed mainly of immigrants from the Korean peninsula.[28]

The scientific discourse of *Ilseontongjoron* became more influential immediately after the March First Movement for Korean independence in 1919. The thesis of common origins of Japanese and Koreans was used to assert that Korean national self-determination and independence was wrong and that unification of peoples of common origins, a euphemistic expression for justifying Japanese colonial rule, was right. At the same time, there was strong opposition to *Ilseontongjoron* by anthropologists—eugenics-oriented scholars opposed to the assimilation policy and what they saw as miscegenation between inferior Koreans and superior Japanese, and emphasized the linear development of the Japanese nation from the Stone Age.[29] These scholars failed to dominate historical discourse, however, because the Japanese empire had to deploy the *Kokuminka* (nationalization of colonial subjects) policy in order to mobilize colonial subjects to sustain the "total war" system. The *Kokuminka* movement was an extreme form of assimilation designed to transform colonial subjects into "true Japanese," not only in action, but also in spirit.[30] Needless to say, *Ilseontongjoron* provided the ideological backbone of the *Kokuminka* movement.

The historical discourse of the common origins of Koreans and Japanese experienced a nationalist turn in postliberation Korean historiography. Korean nationalist historians rejected the Japanese *Imna* commandery, a historiographical by-product of *Ilseontongjoron*, as an invention of Japanese colonialism. But at the same time they highlighted the entangled history of ancient Korea and Japan in their stress on a unidirectional cultural transfer from ancient Korea to Japan. They argued that the Korean writing system of *idu* and *hyangch'al* influenced Japanese *Man'yō-gana* as a system of transcribing Chinese characters. They also alleged that the highly developed fine arts in ancient Korea contributed to Japanese art, which was proved by the superiority of Korean immigrant-made works such as the murals at the Hōryūji temple and the portrait of Shōtoku Taishi.[31] The thesis of the high culture transfer from Korea to Japan in ancient history fitted nicely with their nationalist argument.

It was Kim Sŏk-hyung, a famous North Korean Marxist historian, who published the most extreme account of this one-way cultural highway from Korea to Japan, arguing that emigrants from the three Korean kingdoms (Koguryo, Baekche Silla) had settled in Western Japan and were cultural pioneers who contributed to the progress of Japanese history.[32] What one finds in his writings is not Marxism but "national communism."[33] Kim's argument upset a group of Japanese historians and provoked angry counterarguments. Inoue Mitsusada described in highly emotive terms of "attack" and "defense" a quasi-physical battle between himself and Kim. Indeed, Inoue attributed the heart attack he suffered to the tension caused by this controversy.[34] The controversy took material form in arguments about how to interpret the inscription on the monument of King Kwanggaet'o. Paradoxically, although the two sides differed sharply in their reading of the texts, they stood on the same platform of *Ilseontongjoron*. For both, the cultural and anthropological homogeneity of Koreans and Japanese was a given; the only issue was which ethnicity was dominant.

Ironically, the transnational history of Korea and Japan, initiated by the Japanese colonial discourse of the common origins of Japanese and Koreans, became a battleground on which two opponents competed for hegemony over a shared heritage. Indeed, world history tended to be supplanted by Pan-Asianist regional history in colonial Korea and to a lesser extent in imperial Japan, but the grand narrative of Pan-Asianist regional history was oversimplified and one directional. Petty actors, everyday practices, minor events and historical ambiguities all escaped from this grand narrative. The reciprocal relations between colonizers and colonized and between the colonies and the Japanese metropole were simply disregarded in place of an abstract Pan-Asianism. Pan-Asianist regional history could not articulate that the empire (Japan) was made by its imperial projects.

The structure of the history department at Keizo (Seoul) Imperial University, the only university in colonial Korea (opened on May 1, 1926), is a good indication of this problem. In his speech inaugurating the university, Hattori Unokichi, the university's president, emphasized the academy's duty to serve the state. Paralleling the policy of the imperial university, he announced a blueprint for making the Keizo Imperial University a center for Oriental studies. Due to this Orient-centered research strategy, the history department offered only three history majors: national (Japanese) history, *Chosŏn* (Korean) history and Oriental history. Kaneko Kosuke had taught Western history at the university since 1928, but there was no official Western history major in the department. What distinguished Keizo Imperial University from other imperial universities in the Japanese archipelago was that Western history was replaced by Korean history. Of the eighty graduates from the history department between 1929 and 1941, eighteen students majored in Japanese history, thirty-four in Oriental history and twenty-eight in Korean history.[35] In fact, Seoul National University (the postliberation successor to Keizo Imperial University) had no professor lecturing on Western history until 1962, long after liberation.

The outbreak of the Second World War in the pacific hastened the decline of world history in East Asia. As the war against the West broke out, the Japanese national "modernists against modernity" stopped looking to "Western civilization" as a model for Japan's future. Under the strident slogan of "overcoming modernity," the West became an object to be vanquished by Japanese national culture.[36] "Asian civilization," as represented by Japan, was thought to deserve much more serious investigation than Western history. World history was diagnosed as having been infected by the Western disease, and Japanese intellectuals who supported "overcoming modernity" lamented the way that Western modernity had distorted the Japanese spirit. The Kyoto school tried to postulate an alternative world history based on a new "Asian" world order through which European dominance of world history could be overcome. This alternative world history would be one that emanated from the Japanese empire. The intellectual project of "overcoming modernity" was seen as the theoretical lever that would lift Asia into the context of world history and make an alternative world history of "overcoming Western history." This Asia-centric new world history was much discussed, but never articulated, structured or written.

De-territorialization or re-territorialization? The joint history textbook and history committee

In the midst of the tumultuous historical debates provoked by the publication of the revisionist Japanese "New History Textbook" (*Atarashii rekishi kyōkasho*) in 2001, *Sankei Shinbun*, a conservative Japanese newspaper that fully supported the textbook, published a peculiar series of articles analyzing South Korean history textbooks. While clearly their stance on Japan's colonization of the Korean peninsula differed markedly from the neo-nationalist Japanese account, the tone of the articles was not negative at all; indeed, the

Korean textbooks were praised by *Sankei Shinbun*'s Seoul correspondent for their firm basis in ethnocentric national history. In dozens of articles dedicated to the analysis of these textbooks, the *Sankei* correspondent justified the "New History Textbook" by referring repeatedly to ethnocentric Korean history textbooks. In comparing Korean and Japanese history textbooks, he located a shared master narrative, one in which "our nation" is the subject of history. Korean history textbooks thus confirmed the paper's conviction that history textbooks should teach children, regardless of nationality, "national pride" and "love for our own history" (*Sankei Shinbun*, 25/06 and 26/06/2001).

This explains how national histories in East Asia, and perhaps in many other regions, have formed a relationship of what we may term "antagonistic complicity" that operates behind the scenes of open conflict.[37] The parallel lines of nation-centered histories have no meeting point at which a reconciliation of historical interpretations can occur, and this prevents the opposing parties from moving "beyond national history" toward a reconceptualization of their shared pasts as entangled history, transnational history, border history, overlapping history and so forth. Instead, nation-centered histories force the general public to choose between "our own national history" and "*their* own national history." Any serious academic attempt to go "beyond national history" can be and has been denounced as "antipatriotic" or treason. Korean and Japanese national histories have thus been trapped in a mutual siege. What the recent history of "history wars" in East Asia shows is that this antagonistic complicity strengthens the discursive hegemony of national history and enriches the parties who perpetuate the "mutual siege." This is particularly unfortunate, as a close look at the century-long history of competing national histories in this region reveals numerous instances of cultural transfers between ostensible rivals as well as examples of "antagonistic acculturation" in which, for example, the hegemonic discourses of the colonizers have been appropriated by the colonized as the basis for anticolonial resistance and their own nationalist projects.[38]

Despite all of this, an East Asian history textbook, *History that Opens the Future* (HOF), was jointly produced and published simultaneously in Korea, Japan and China in 2005.[39] It was a watershed in textbook cooperation, designed to counteract the war over history in East Asia. In the midst of the turbulent historical controversy ignited by the Japanese *New History Textbook*, HOF achieved a remarkable marketing success. In 2005 alone, roughly 120,000 copies of the Chinese version were sold, along with about 70,000 Japanese copies and nearly 30,000 copies of the Korean version. More than fifty historians, history teachers and citizens of three countries participated in this project, and thirteen related conferences have been held consecutively in China, Japan and Korea since 2002.[40] The HOF encouraged hopeful thoughts about the future topography of East Asian historiography, and it has been credited with leading historical discourse in East Asia toward regional peace and historical reconciliation. The vast press coverage of that book, in Korea at least, disseminated this optimistic vision, and indeed HOF may deserve credit as the first transnational history book in postwar East Asia. Given the current East Asian "history war," this book is indeed an impressive achievement.

Yet a scrupulous reading of HOF raises questions about its transnational character. In short, it is a transnational history based on the national history paradigm. First of all, many nationalist historians from the three countries took part in the project. On the Korean committee, nationalist (left) historians constituted the majority. The Japanese committee was composed mainly of the so-called postwar historiography historians who express remorse for Japan's wartime past. In China, the main contributor was the Institute of Modern History of Chinese Academy of Social Sciences (CASS). Regardless of whether they are nationalists, left-leaning democrats or Marxists, a common positivist thread connects the contributors' different political approaches. They all claim to have sought "historical truth and lessons" through the textbook project, a position of which constructivists would be justifiably very skeptical. Perhaps the positivist stance helped to narrow down the scope of the book because trilateral agreement on the facts was a prerequisite, which explains why the book is rather simplistically focused on Japan's war of aggression and invasion.

Second, as Narita Ryūichi has rightly pointed out, the book never questions the idea that the nation-state is the collective subject. The editorial committee's proud declaration that HOF stands on the viewpoints of women, minorities and the oppressed is partly true. The goal of the HOF to be "free from narrow-minded chauvinism" seems partially accomplished. But one should pay attention to the intentional usage of "chauvinism" instead of "nationalism": the target of HOF was not "nationalism" per se, but perceived "bad nationalism"—that is, narrow-minded chauvinism. The problem the (Korean) editorial committee did not recognize is that even "good nationalism" betrays the principle of standing for minorities. Insofar as the nation-state continues to occupy the subject position of history, a transnational East Asia has no place for national minorities who lack their own nation-states. It should be noted, too, that HOF represents East Asia exclusively as the three countries of South Korea, Japan and China. Taiwan, Vietnam, Mongolia and even North Korea are completely excluded from the HOF project.[41]

Third, HOF sacrificed issues of transnationality and translocality for its own national history paradigm. The global context of modernity is missing in the first chapter on the "opening of ports and modernization." HOF arranges China, Japan and Korea's separate responses to the challenge of the Western "Great Powers" along parallel lines. It presupposes each nation-state, then not yet fully formed, as separate agents reacting against the Western impact. There is no description of how the geo-cultural East Asia came into being in the dialectical interplay between East Asia and the transatlantic Great Powers. Without Europe, Asia is not imaginable and vice versa. But the historical positivism immanent to the HOF tends to regard "East Asia" as a positivist rather than as a constructed reality. This means that the HOF has essentially bundled together the histories of three nation-states rather than achieving its stated goal of creating a transnational East Asian history.

Despite all these defects, however, HOF is a significant step in making a new regional history of East Asia. Compared to the final reports of the Chinese-Japanese and the Japanese-Korean Joint History Research Committee released respectively in January and March of 2010, the HOF has many merits. Covering the bilateral relations of China and Japan from ancient to contemporary history in 549 pages, the Chinese-Japanese Joint Committee final report contains a series of essays on the same subjects written separately by both Japanese and Chinese scholars. The *Asahi Shinbun* described this Sino-Japanese joint history effort as "an unprecedented undertaking," but despite this reserved optimism, the *Asahi* newspaper could not hide its disappointment with the wide gaps between Chinese and Japanese historians. What is worse than these gaps and disagreements is the committee's decision to block public access to the part of the report on the history of the postwar era. Allegedly the Chinese side justified the decision on the grounds that the report could hurt the feelings of ordinary Chinese people who suffered under Japan's aggression during the Second World War. But no one can doubt that it was in fact Chinese concerns about political turbulence, including the Tiananmen massacre, that was behind the decision not to make the report open to public.

In principle, differences in interpreting histories among East Asian historians are not necessarily a problem in itself. Without mentioning constructivism, dissenting voices and different opinions are inherent to historical research, and thus differences are inevitable to some extent. The question is not whether any kind of difference exists, but why historical interpretations diverge in parallel with national borders. Despite its recurrent stress on "objective understanding," "facing history squarely," "fact-based research" and its general positivistic stance, the report could not but be politicized by projecting the present nation-state into the past. Despite the Chinese *People's Daily* using positive metaphors such as "thaw," "the latest sign of warming ties between Beijing and Tokyo," "a milestone for the authoritative version of history acceptable to both nations,"[42] words cannot erase doubts about the nature of the historiographical conflicts. As long as national history is used as a lever to gear up national conflicts and as long as a national lens dominates the perception of the past, no political blueprint comprising East Asia is possible. This in part explains why this joint history research project was initiated not by scholars but by politicians.

The Chinese-Japanese report was followed by the more than 3,000-page report produced by the Japanese-Korean Joint History Research Committee and opened to the public on March 23, 2010.[43] While the Chinese-Japanese report is composed of two parts, "ancient" (ancient-medieval-early modern in Japanese terms) and modern/contemporary history, the Japanese-Korean report consists of four parts—ancient, medieval, modern/contemporary and textbooks. The compartmentalization of the report reflects the organizing principle of the Joint Committee, which divides participants into subcommittees based on historical periodization. Each subcommittee under the umbrella of the Japanese-Korean Joint History Research Committee has been relatively autonomous and has kept its own running principles and research agendas. The whole report including the roundtable discussion is open to the public via the Internet, and anyone can download its PDF files in both Korean and Japanese versions.

Greater public access does not necessarily mean the Japanese-Korean Joint History Research Committee's report is free from tensions. A cursory look at the report reveals the paradigm of national history and its ensuing problems. The joint preface under the names of the chairpersons of the Korean and Japanese delegations expresses their belief that the committee's effort will be "a stepping stone to make a scholars' community for common prosperity in the future with mutual trust." But each chairperson's individual preface, which immediately follows the joint preface, contains nuanced complaints about their counterpart, which suggests the difficulty of historical dialogue. Despite the desire to improve the ties between Japan and South Korea, according to the *Asahi*, this joint history project "spiraled into disagreement, criticism and heated exchanges mainly over Japan's colonial rule of the Korean peninsula." Bitter disagreements can be found in many places, especially in the minutes of the modern/contemporary history and history textbooks subcommittees. The polemical comments and countercomments in these two panels often led to radical doubts about the project itself, with members in both countries saying bluntly that they found little reason to continue the project. A Japanese participant on the textbook panel said that "this Korean presentation proves the Japanese-Korean joint-history research was to no avail."

Perhaps the *Asahi Shinbun*'s description that the committee turned into something of a "proxy war" may sound too gloomy and pessimistic. The situation is much less heated, for instance, in the ancient and medieval history subcommittees. Of course, disagreements, discrepancy, discord and even quarrels are found there, but they are still scholarly debates because they remain nonantagonistic. Given the circumstances of ancient history—especially the alleged Japanese *Imna* commandery in the southern part of the Korean peninsula, which has been the site of a century-long nationalist contestation between Korea and Japan—the fact that the disagreements remained nonantagonistic can be considered a breakthrough. This tells us once again that what is in question is not a choice between agreement and disagreement. Total agreement is neither possible nor desirable. The upshot is if the differences and disputes in interpreting the common past are symbiotic or exclusive. Symbiotic dissenting voices give a productive tension to historical research and make historical dialogues dialectical. Exclusive differences in historical interpretation give rise to destructive antagonisms. The prospect of bilateral or multilateral historical dialogues depends on whether disagreements remain antagonistic or are symbiotic contradictions. Antagonistic conflicts about historical interpretations make dialogue at best a political compromise rather than a true discussion of history.

Unfortunately, these two bilateral historical dialogues in East Asia are dotted with arguments that are more antagonistic than symbiotic. The ways that China, Japan and Korea distinguish true and false in historical epistemology reflect their different ways of governing themselves and others. In this game of true and false, the problem of truth represents political problems that culminate in national history. As long as the national history paradigm is allowed to render a verdict on historical truth, no stress on "objective understanding," "facing history squarely," "fact-based research" and a positivistic general stance can resolve the antagonistic contradiction. What is required as "a stepping stone to make a scholars' community for common prosperity in the future with mutual trust" is a change of episteme in historical thinking and reasoning. The goodwill to improve ties through historical reconciliation won't be realized unless historical disputes, historiographical disagreements and different opinions can be symbiotic and free from egocentric national history paradigms. Historical dialogues in East Asia, represented by two joint national history research committees, should shift from international to transnational dialogues, beyond national history.

Notes

1. See Jie-Hyun Lim, "The Configuration of Orient and Occident in the Global Chain of National Histories: Writing National Histories in Northeast Asia," in Stefan Berger, Linas Eriksonas and Andrew Mycock (eds.), *Narrating the Nation: Representations in History, Media and the Arts* (New York: Berghan Books, 2008) 290–308.
2. It is noteworthy that *The Rise of Great Powers* (*Daguo jueqi*), a popular Chinese history documentary on CCTV intended to justify the contemporary modernization project, deals with nine foreign countries in sequence: Portugal, Spain, the Netherlands, Great Britain, France, Germany, Japan, Russia and United States. See Q. Edward Wang, "'Rise of Great Powers' = Rise of China?" *Journal of Contemporary China* 19 (March 2010), 273–89.
3. See Jie-Hyun Lim, "A Postcolonial Reading of *Sonderweg*: Marxist Historicism Revisited," *Journal of Modern European History* 12:2 (2014), 280–94.
4. Ross E. Dunn, "Rethinking Civilizations and History in the New Age of Globalization," in *Proceedings of the 34th International Symposium at the National Academy of Sciences*, Korea, October 12, 2007.
5. Jerry Bentley, "Myths, Wagers, and Some Moral Implications of World History," *Journal of World History* 16:1 (2005), 51–82.
6. In this context "world history" has been more than often identified with "Western history" as a hegemonic discourse in East Asia.
7. In this chapter, I will use the terms "global history," "world history" and "transnational history" alternately from context to context. Arguments for "global history" as an alternative term for "world history" are convincing in that "world history" has been (mis-)used as an alibi for national history in East Asian modern historiography. Indeed, naming is important, but a new term does not necessarily guarantee a new perspective. What one witnesses in the history of East Asian historiography is that "world history," "global history," and "transnational history" have frequently been subjected to nationalist appropriation. Although conscious of subtle differences among these terms, I will not insist on their categorical differences in investigating the issue of nationalist appropriation.
8. Shingo Minamizuka, "How to Overcome Euro-Centrism in the Western History in Japan—Some Lessons from '*Bankokushi*' in the Meiji Era," *Proceedings of the Conference of Commemorating the Fiftieth Anniversary of the Korean Society for Western History* (unpubl., Seoul National University, July 5–6, 2007), 190–91.
9. Hiroshi Takagi, "Nihon bijutsushi no seiritsu/Shiron" (History of the Establishment of Japanese Art History), *Nihonshi Kenkyu* 320 (1989), 74.
10. Kazuhiko Kondo, "The Studies of Western History in Japan and the Understanding of Modernity," *Proceedings of the Conference of Commemorating the Fiftieth Anniversary of the Korean Society for Western History* (unpubl., Seoul National University, July 5–6, 2007), 117.
11. Naoki Sakai, *Translation and Subjectivity: On "Japan" and Cultural Nationalism* (Minneapolis: University of Minnesota Press, 1997), 50.
12. Stefan Tanaka, *Japan's Orient: Rendering Past into History* (Berkeley: University of California Press, 1993).
13. Andre Schmid, *Korea Between Empires, 1895–1919* (New York: Columbia University Press, 2002), 32–36, 56–59, 80.
14. Dipesh Chakrabarty, *Provincializing Europe: Postcolonial Thought and Historical Difference* (Princeton: Princeton University Press, 2000), 7.

15. Albert Resis, "Das Kapital Comes to Russia," *Slavic Review* 29 (June 1970), 219–37.
16. Karl Marx, "Preface to the German Edition," in idem (ed.), *Das Kapital. A Critique of Political Economy* 1:3. (1906).
17. Bryan S. Turner, *Orientalism, Postmodernism and Globalism* (London: Routledge, 1994), 140.
18. See Sebastian Conrad, *The Quest for the Lost Nation*, English trans. by Alan Nothnagle (Berkeley: University of California Press, 2010).
19. J. Victor Koschmann, "Introduction to the English edition," in Y. Yamanouchi, J. V. Koschmann and R. Narita (eds.), *Total War and Modernization* (Ithaca: Cornell University Press, 1998), xi–xii.
20. Yuji Geto, "Ilbonui segyesa gyogwasŏ" (Japanese World History Textbook) in Nakamura Satoru (ed.), *Dongasia yŏksa gyogwasŏnun ŏttŏge suyeoittulka? (How Have East Asian History Texts Been Written?)* (Seoul: Editor, 2006), 166.
21. Kijung Bang, *Hankook gunhyundai sasangsa* yŏngu (Seoul: Yŏksabipyungsa, 1992).
22. See Carter J. Eckert, *Offspring of Empire: The Koch'Ang Kims and the Colonial Origins of Korean Capitalism, 1876–1945* (Seattle: University of Washington Press, 1996).
23. Jie-Hyun Lim, "Befreiung oder Modernisierung? Sozialismus als ein Weg der antiwestlichen Modernisierung in unterentwickelten Ländern," *Beiträge zur Geschichte der Arbeiterbewegung* 43:2 (2001), 5–23.
24. Schmid, Korea Between Empires 86–100.
25. Mitsui Takashi, "Ilseontongjoron ŭi hakmuhjŏk kibane kwanhan siron" (A Study on the Origins and Development of Ilseontongjoron in Modern Japanese Academism before and after Japanese Annexation of Korea), *Hankukmunhwa* 33 (2004), 249–52.
26. Ibid., 253–54.
27. Lee Sung-si, *Mandlojin godai* (The Ancient Invented), Korean trans. by K. H. Park (Seoul: Samin, 2001), 41–45.
28. Pak Sunyoung, "Ilche sikminjuŭiwa Chosŏnŭi mome daihan inryuhakjŏk sisŏn" (The Anthropological Gaze at the Korean Bodies Under Japanese Colonialism)," *Bikyomunhwa yŏngu* 12:2 (2006), 57–92.
29. Ibid., 65, 72, 73 and *passim*.
30. Wan-yao Chou, "The Kōminka Movement in Taiwan and Korea: Comparisons and Interpretations," in Peter Duus et al. (eds.), *The Japanese Wartime Empire 1931–1945* (Princeton: Princeton University Press, 1996), 41–68.
31. Ki-baik Lee, *A New History of Korea* (Cambridge, MA: Harvard University Press, 1988), 57, 64.
32. Lee *Mandlojin godai*, 47.
33. For the nationalist historiography of the Marxist party in North Korea, see Jie-Hyun Lim, "The Nationalist Message in Socialist Code: On Court Historiography in People's Poland and North Korea," in Sølvi Sogner (ed.), *Making Sense of Global History* (Oslo: Universitetsforlaget, 2001), 373–88.
34. Lee *Mandlojin godai*, 51.
35. Gwanghyun Park, "Sikminji Chosŏnesŏ dongyangsahakun ŏttŏke hyungsongdoiŏttna?" (How Was East Asian History Formulated in Colonial Chosŏn)," in Do Myunhoi and Yoon Haedong (eds.), *Yŏksahakui Segi* (Seoul: Humanist, 2009), 217–34.

36. Harry Hartoonian, *Overcome by Modernity: History, Culture, and Community in Interwar Japan* (Princeton: Princeton University Press, 2000).
37. Jie-Hyun Lim, "Chōsen hantō no minzokushugi to kenryoku no gensetsu [Nationalism on the Korean peninsula and the power discourse]," Japanese trans. by Itagaki, Ryuta, *Gendai shisō*, 28 (June, 2000), 126–44; *Chŏkdaejŏk kongbŏmjadŭl* [*Antagonistic Accomplices*] (Seoul: Sonamu, 2005).
38. Ashis Nandy, *The Intimate Enemy: Loss and Recovery of Self Under Colonialism* (Oxford: Oxford University Press, 1989).
39. *Miraerŭl yŏnŭn Yŏksa (History Open to Future)* (Seoul: Hangyŏrechulpan, 2005).
40. https://www2.gwu.edu/~memory/issues/textbooks/jointeastasia.html (accessed November 29, 2017).
41. Narita Ryūichi, "Dongasiasaŭi Ganŭngsŏng (possibility of East Asian history)," *Changjakgwa Bipyŏng* 131 (Spring, 2006), 406.
42. http://english.peopledaily.com.cn/90001/90776/90883/6850633.html (accessed July 8, 2017).
43. One can find both Korean and Japanese versions of full report here: http://www.historyfoundation.or.kr/?sidx=119&stype=1 (accessed November 29, 2017).

CHAPTER 13
WRITING THE GLOBE FROM THE EDGES: APPROACHES TO THE MAKING OF GLOBAL HISTORY IN AUSTRALIA
Marnie Hughes-Warrington

Global history research has burgeoned in the last decade, as seen in the emergence of journals (i.e., *Comparativ*, 1990– and *Journal of Global History*, 2006–), publications lists, professional organizations, electronic discussion forums and historiographical collections such as Hopkin's *Global History* and Grantner's *Globalgeschichte und Globalisierung*. There has also been a dramatic shift toward the provision of postgraduate global history programs in schools and universities across the United States, Australia and parts of Europe.[1] At the same time, however, it is a reasonably common assumption that Australian historians have done little to shape the historiography of global history or to develop a distinctive approach to the analysis of world events. This assumption appears well founded, for an Internet or database search for publications on global history by Australian academics delivers few returns. But rather than simply concluding that Australians have little to offer to a global conversation on global history, it will be argued that a wider historiographical terminology and view is needed to see past, contemporary and potential Australian contributions to the field.

Global history in Australia: The view from which window?

In 1968, the Australian anthropologist Bill Stanner gave a series of radio lectures entitled *The Great Australian Silence*. Arguing that Australians wrote a past that they wished to see, a past that excluded Aboriginal peoples, he drew upon the imagery of a window. Inattention to Aboriginal history and issues, he wrote,

> Cannot be explained by absent-mindedness. It is a structural matter, a view from a window which has been carefully placed to exclude a whole quadrant of the landscape. What may well have begun as a simple forgetting of other possible views turned under habit and over time into something like a cult of forgetfulness practised on a national scale ... the Great Australian silence reigns; the story of the things we were unconsciously resolved not to discuss.[2]

Stanner's words spearheaded activism that led to the recognition of indigenous land rights ("native title" claims) in judgments such as *Mabo v. Queensland* (1992) and the impact of separating Aboriginal peoples from their lands, ways of life and families. His imagery of an historical window serving silence has been cited repeatedly in scholarship on Aboriginal-settler relations. But his imagery might be given wider application, one that takes in Aboriginal historiography, but that also offers an account of the Australian silence about global history.

> Australia is assumed not to have much to offer to the historiography of global history for at least three reasons.

Education, not research

First, global history is more often than not grouped with world history, and both are categorized as teaching fields rather than research and teaching fields. Just over half of Australian universities now offer a world or global history course to first-year students.[3] Not all university educators, though, see this as a positive phenomenon. In their view, the rise of world or global history courses does not mark the emergence of new fields, but rather confirms the decline of student exposure to the study of history in secondary school, increased provision for generalist, nonmajor students and the relentless downsizing of history departments. This view is apparent in the 2004 curriculum report published by the Australian Historical Association:

> If many students have been exposed to little, if any, history before attending university, the response of history programs is to attempt to provide that introduction, and a sampling of the rich possibilities of history, in the first year and to a range of students, a good number of whom will not pursue history much further. For those who do, the common expectation is of a corresponding shift in the curriculum: from accounts of the sweep of national or global change to more specialised thematic subjects.[4]

Underpinning this view is the idea of world and global history as undifferentiated and as a thoroughfare—one that compensates for educational poverty and that prepares students for more specialized studies—or as a one-stop destination for students with majors other than history. The same report confirms the growth of upper-level undergraduate programs in world and global history, usually organized on thematic lines (e.g., studies of childhood, gender, religion or warfare in world or global history). There is a perception, though, of these being overshaded by the ever-present first-year survey that surveys change on a large scale in a way that cannot satisfy upper-level students.

As currently conceived, the world or global history survey addresses those with a limited historical knowledge in a fashion that is itself historiographically limited. In the breadth of the survey, details are omitted, events are telescoped and the uncertainties or perhapses that historians use when evidence is lacking, inconclusive or contradictory are pushed aside in the rush to master the textbook. The past becomes a warehouse that is plundered for test questions, and history making is collapsed into the activity of getting through the content. This stereotype of the world or global history survey as content mastery is problematic for at least two reasons. First, it rests on the untested assumption that world history is outside of the optimal spatial and temporal scales for studying and making history. Second, it is mistaken to assume that the large spatial and/or temporal scales implied in world or global history surveys come at the expense of historiographical form. Compare texts or curricula, and it will be evident that even "sweeps" have different narrative forms. As I have argued elsewhere, writing world history involves multiple decisions.[5] The past is not packaged for interpretation and telling—there is no necessary or absolute beginning, end or size to any event nor any one necessary or absolute way of analyzing or presenting it.

Globalization as the Global North

Second, an Australian approach to global history is thought to be absent because global history is perceived to be the product of globalization as metropolitan North modernization. Some accounts of globalization, like that of Zygmunt Bauman, describe the growth of social diversity, the growing challenge of forming social norms, the difficulty of rational planning, the dominance of consumption over production and the transformation of politics into media spectacle.[6] Similarly, as Mike Featherstone puts it,

> [t]he process of globalization, then, does not seem to be producing cultural uniformity; rather it makes us aware of new levels of diversity. If there is a global culture it would be better to conceive of it not as a common culture, but as a field in which differences, power struggles and cultural prestige contests are played out.[7]

Other theories, though, equate globalization with the unification of the world into a single modern mode of production and the integration of different countries into a single global economy.[8] Antony Gidden's *Runaway World*, for instance, sees in globalization the spread of the liberal market, democracy and civil society.[9] This is the view of globalization that has shaped comments on the field of global history. Patrick Manning, for instance, has spoken of world and global history as fields dominated by European and American perspectives, and therefore of internationalization of methods as a key priority. This view is even clearer in Daniel Headrick's question about whether the global history movement is "unwittingly, part of the same Anglo-American conspiracy to 'globalise' the planet that has given us Coca-Cola, rock-and-roll, and the internet."[10]

Domination by the "metropolitan North" is also assumed by the Australian social theorist Raewyn Connell. Writings on globalization, she argues,

> share an intellectual strategy. They leap straight to the level of the global, where they reify perceived trends as the nature of global society. The trends thus reified are based on concepts that have previously been worked out, not for speaking

about colonies, empires or world affairs, but for speaking about *metropolitan societies*—that is, the cluster or modern, industrial, postmodern or postcolonial countries that have been the focus of theoretical debates ... for decades.[11]

Against the global "North," which she claims seeks " to close down, rather than open up, the self-knowledge of society," Connell calls for "southern theory," an approach to writing the global that foregrounds periphery-center relations, authority, exclusion, hegemony, sponsorship and appropriation. Together with Ann Curthoys, Marilyn Lake and John Maynard, for instance, she expresses concern that writing beyond the national may lead to a disconnection with politics, and that that connection is particularly important for indigenous communities.[12] Further, she establishes the credentials of Southern theory as southern, or at least as Australian, through the endorsement of analysis built upon the appreciation of local places.[13]

To "see" the Southern, Connell enjoins us to look beyond the academy to find a new intellectual foundation in Aboriginal narratives. Synchrony is a key characteristic of many Aboriginal narratives; they narrate an "everywhen," to use Stanner's phrase.[14] This is not a random combination of phenomena from different times, but rather, as Jeremy Beckett notes, an "attempt to negotiate the contradiction that colonization sets up between otherness and incorporation," a dialogue of similarity and difference.[15] The sequences of Aboriginal narratives are the sequences of space and moral judgment, and "before and after" sequences are contingent upon the spatial locus of the speaker and the moral point to be made.[16] In his "history of the world, or Australia," for instance, Walter Newton draws together biblical and local "dreaming elements" to narrate tales of geography as judgment, as with the creation of Ganduwandi:

> God picked out a number to go on in the world again. He stood them apart, and he punished the people all round him. There were convulsions, the ground blew up. They were standing up and he said, "You can stay as you are." He threw dust over them and they're now formed into rocks. That's Ganduwandi. They rose up a thousand feet high. He made a flat top. Just a little bit—300 yards away from his temple at Noontherungie—that's the Holy Jerusalem of Australia. At one end it's rough and cliffs. That's where the people were saved. They had to live there.[17]

As this excerpt suggests, events and persons who are temporally distant may be connected in Aboriginal narratives if they share the same moral content.[18] Further, the narrated events "take place": the teller's primary objective is to establish the names of local places and establish a connection with the landscape.

Connell seeks a future for the global in politically aware, place-based studies and in anthropology rather than history. While this is an option, it is not the only one for scholars of the global. If Connell had adopted a view of globalization more akin to those of Featherstone and Bauman—and expected divergence and contestation as well as unification and hegemony—she might have been more alert to local practices in historiography that set Australian scholars in conversation with, or even against, other practices in global history. Few Australian scholars write under the rubrics of "world" or "global" history; an increasing number, however, have declared an affiliation with "transnational" history. Transnational history, as Curthoys and Lake define it, clearly has affinities and overlaps with global and world history:

> It is the study of the ways in which past lives and events have been shaped by processes and relationships that have transcended the borders of nation-states. Transnational history seeks to understand ideas, things, people, and practices which have crossed national boundaries. It is generally in a complex relation with national history; it may seek to interrogate, situate, supercede, displace, or avoid it altogether. In their reaction against what they see as rigid and confining national histories, many of those enthusiastic about transnational history reach for metaphors of fluidity, as in talk of circulation and flows (of peoples, discourses, and commodities), alongside metaphors of connection and relationship.[19]

Their edited volume, *Connected Worlds*, includes studies of the circulation of cosmopolitan subjectivities between Australia and Hollywood, Australian missionary women in India, the migration of "ten pound Poms"—British people who came to Australia after the Second World War—and the role that Marcus Garvey's views played in stimulating Aboriginal activism in the 1920s.[20] It is typical of Australian work in that it reflects the varied forms of study collected under "transnational" label.

Transnational history in Australia is commensurate in the minds of scholars with new British imperial history and "settler society" history.[21] Elizabeth Elbourne and Alan Lester have shown how British imperial policy on the treatment of Aborigines, for example, bound the settler societies of Australia, Canada, New Zealand and South Africa together.[22] Their work joins that of Patricia Grimshaw, David Phillips, Julia Evans and Shirley Swain in providing a comparison of the rights and statuses of indigenous peoples across the British Empire.[23] This complements the work of Dirk Moses, who has written on the emergence of the "genocidal moment" in settler societies.[24] Further, there is a strong transnational element in studies of Aboriginal history such as Ann Curthoy's study of the American and Australian, African American and Aboriginal "freedom rides" of the 1960s.[25] Transnational histories written in Australia also favor the study of international organizations such as the United Nations, the movement of individuals or subcultural groups across national boundaries,[26] feminist and race relations,[27] crime and punishment,[28] resources development[29] and cross-national thinking about environment and environmental problems.[30]

Practiced this way, transnational history in Australia is cultural history across national boundaries, history written on a local-enough level to escape the generalizations thought to be associated with world history, and a relatively recent historiographical phenomenon. Curthoys and Lake see transnational history as having come to the fore in the 1990s,[31] although they offer a longer past in connection with feminist historiography.

As Lake has argued, history emerged as a "handmaiden" to the Australian state, with advancing masculine ideals, ambitions and interests. Women wrote history, but more often than not on the edges of the state or on other levels of community.[32] The lack of space for women in the state, Jill Roe has claimed, led them to engage with and write about other communities, and in the case of Australia, that community was the international one.[33] That Australian interest in transnational history—which is predominately cultural in nature—can be explained in part as a feminist response to marginalization by the state is a fascinating historiographical story, one that perhaps marks out Australia as distinct. Feminist historiography, however, was part of a wider internationalism, one that also has strong roots in the New Idealist philosophical movement in Britain in the late nineteenth and early twentieth centuries.

New Idealist philosophy, also called British Idealist philosophy, is probably best known through the writings of Thomas Hill Green. Green, however, was part of a much-larger intellectual community that included Edward Caird, F. H. Bradley, Henry Jones, Bernard Bosanquet, John Henry Muirhead and David George Ritchie and that connected Oxford, Cambridge and the Universities of Glasgow, Edinburgh and Aberystwyth, Wales. Jeannie Morefield has written of a "spiderweb" of linkages that connects New Idealists to one another, their universities, voluntary and political organizations and government initiatives.[34] These links stretch across the globe, taking in individuals, schools, universities, voluntary and political organizations and governments in Australia, Canada, South Africa, India and the United States.

The writings of Australian New Idealists, like those of their British counterparts, covered a wide range of topics, including education, federation, citizenship, war, peace settlements, the League of Nations, the United Nations, social services, industrial arbitration and health care. But there were a number of closely related themes throughout these writings, themes that can be described as global in outlook and aspirational in tone. The New Idealists showed a clear preference for demonstrating how social and political phenomena were part of larger "wholes" of "empire," "civilization," "humanity" and the "international order," rather than of the "state." For them, the state was best understood as one human community on a spectrum extending from family to humanity. They also placed war in the context of the story of human progress: despite being the result of injustice, poverty or greed, its ability to break up closed societies and force greater levels of cooperation gave it a central role in shaping civilization.

The first professor of philosophy at the University of Sydney—Francis Anderson—for instance, believed that war was instrumental in shaping civilization because it prompted people to adopt an international consciousness and support global institutions like the League of Nations. War for Anderson was, as Hegel put it, "the rational becoming real." He conveyed this view explicitly in his 1911 undergraduate course in ethics, in which he characterized war as an evil stemming from moral imperfection, but said that to condemn it would be "to condemn the whole history of the past." It is "only one of a number of evils each of which reacts on and strengthens the others. We cannot expect to abolish one unless we attack the other at the same time." Moreover, he stressed that peace requires more than treaties and reparations: it necessitates a reorientation in society—and in us—toward justice.[35]

Anderson developed his vision of civilization most fully in his 1922 essay "Liberty, Equality, and Fraternity," which is something of an encomium to the universalizing spirit of Latin-Franco civilization.[36] He claims here that "[t]he progress of civilisation is not a uniform and orderly advance, like that of an army with banners. The rhythm of human history is broken and fragmentary. The drama of human history is not the development of a single idea, moving onwards to the inevitable finale." Nevertheless, the central principle of civilization can be found in the idea of personality, and its development can be traced through three great revolutions: Buddhism, Christianity and the French Revolution. The idea of human personality connects the individual to society and to humanity itself:

> Without society there are no persons. ... Without persons, there is no society, no rights, and no duties, for all rights and all duties have their source and centre in the human person as a moral and spiritual being. Even the rights of nations are a deduction from the rights of man. What is Humanity, if it is not the human person, transfigured and symbolically conceived?

"Personality" is the "saving principle" of Christianity, as well as the preeminent civilizing principle: "the only principle which gives any moral right to revolution, which supplies a goal to global progress and unites justice and mercy."[37]

The South Australian historian G. V. Portus also had much to say on the development of civilization in world history, expanding on the arguments of his teacher, Anderson. In 1915, Portus preached a sermon entitled *The Cult of Kultur*, in which he argued for the recognition of two distinct forms of imperialism. The first, a "German sort," is characterized by the belief that nationalities other than that of a dominant people must be stamped out. The second, apparently typified by the British Empire and, to a lesser extent, the United States, is a "world commonwealth" in which separate nationalities are neither favored nor crushed but recognized as sovereign contributors to a global community.[38] Delivered after heavy Australian casualties at Gallipoli, Portus's words may at first sight be read as the isolation and rebuttal of a specific German or even Prussian "cult" of nationalism. On further consideration, however, it is clear that his comments on Germany can also be read as instantiations of his wider belief that the formation of communities beyond the state is the key to civilization.

We do not have to look far to see Portus's wider views at work. In *The Cult of Kultur*, German nationalism is not singular, but cast as a repeat of an "ancient Jewish imperialism," in which "The nation, tutored by its priests and rulers, was firmly convinced that the Jewish people were God's elect, and were destined to extend God's kingdom over all the earth."[39] This nationalism, we are also told, runs contrary against human evolution toward the formation of

> associations and political partnerships which are no longer nation states, but ... rather commonwealths of nations, inside which room may be found for the particular contribution which each nation has to bring to the commonwealth ideal.[40]

Finally he concludes that Australians, not just the Germans, are held in the grip of a selfishness that is expressed in nationalism and its inevitable product: war. He again puts German aggression into a wider backdrop of a sick civilization in work written during the Second World War. In *The Price of Peace* (1944), for example, Portus makes it clear that while the Germans and Japanese are currently enemies, the time is approaching in which hate must give way to cooperation for the greater good of humanity. If we are to have an abiding peace, difficult economic and political actions have to be taken. Barriers to international trade such as tariffs must be removed, all peoples must be guaranteed equal access to the world's resources and stable currency relations must be established. Economic changes of this sort will be "steps into the larger world of interdependence, and, I believe, steps forward to higher standards of living all around."[41] And peace demands giving up the traditional emotional and irrational desire for national sovereignty, which is "the gravest menace that exists to the establishment of justice in international relations."[42]

Portus reiterates his call for a wider historical and cultural view in *They Wanted to Rule the World* (1944), his historical study of dictators. While not denying that the actions of Alexander of Macedon, Julius Caesar, Charlemagne, Genghis Khan, Charles V and Napoleon Bonaparte were nothing "to boast about" morally, they often paved the way for unforeseen, beneficial social and political outcomes. Alexander's military conquests, for instance, encouraged Greeks to think of themselves as a part of a wider, human community. More importantly, by weaving in comments on Adolf Hitler and Mussolini, and representing them literally as small postscripts in his world history, Portus again sets German and Axis actions in context. This leads him to a provocative conclusion, framed in the form of two questions:

> How far has the turmoil of the years from 1934 to 1944 cleared the way to a Europe through which new ideas of social organization may run more easily than before? Is this the long run effect of dictators to promote such clearances by which new ideas, quite other than their own, may come to fruition?[43]

Anderson also presented war as pushing along the evolution of humanity, but he never offered as explicit—and for the time period, surely radical—an assessment of Nazi programs.

The process of civilization is difficult and slow, and Portus was never convinced that many will "reach beyond that area of community which is embraced within the frontiers of their own nation."[44] This would certainly have been his verdict about Walter Murdoch's world history *The Struggle for Freedom* (1912), which culminated with Australian Federation.[45] The process of civilization begins with the family and the long helplessness of infants who require parental care.[46] Since the sixteenth century, however, it has been joined by the state. The family is not superseded by the state, but complementary to it: larger communities emerge from and improve on the principles of civil association inherent in smaller communities. One such community is the British Empire, which in Portus's view is something like a family. He explains thus:

In some families the children are sternly governed by their parents who say proudly: "Our word is law." In other families the children have grown up and have begun to earn their own living, and have been given latch-keys. They are really independent. Yet they continue to pay respect and even obedience to their parents, not because the parents are able to enforce it, but because both parents and children wish to keep the family together and preserve the idea of family life. The British Empire is somewhat like a family of this kind. ... The word "empire" is not a very good name for a partnership like this. So it has begun to be called, not "the British Empire," but the "British Commonwealth of Nations."[47]

The British Empire contributes to the process of civilization through its fostering of international relations predicated on the recognition of diverse qualities, rational discourse and mutual respect. This distinguishes it from more uncivilized empires, or states, or families that are governed autocratically. It is not, however, the end point of civilization. "Perhaps the most important thing about the British Commonwealth of Nations," he writes, "is that it points the way to a still larger world partnership."[48] Although the attempt at global partnership in the League of Nations had failed because of petty national jealousies, Portus thought the United Nations offered a second chance. And even if that were to fail for the same reasons, "we shall be driven by the awful destructiveness of modern warfare to set up once gain some similar international body." International partnership is inevitable, and it will eventually lead to freedom, including freedom from war. Thus he concludes: "We hear a great deal about the blessings of freedom, but only when world unity is won can we begin to be free men and women in a free world."[49]

Nation and globe

The British Idealists in Australia were optimistic about the possibility of transcending—without leaving behind—local, particular allegiances and developing a humanity community built upon freedom and mutual respect. They allowed for the growth of this world consciousness and community to be providential. But they were also unlike other idealists—particularly the British—in the form and content of some of their arguments, most notable in their interest in developing and sustaining communities larger than the state and their persistent embrace of the concept of culture. This interest clearly does not arise—as with the case of feminist historiographies—from marginalization by the state. We recall above that feminist writers saw the women's global movement in Australia arising from their exclusion from state politics.

An interesting assumption that underpins their thinking—and indeed much of historiography—is that the national community precedes the global community. Put simply, national history is developed and written ahead of global history. This notion of expanding historiographical frames does not imply that national approaches to history making are incompatible with those on a global level, but it might serve to underpin what

Derrida would refer to as a "logocentric" view of history.[50] Under that view, histories focused on the national level are assumed to be a better-foundational instantiation of historical research. Successful global history making by historians is assumed to be predicated on successful history making at the national level. This metaphysical stance can be translated down to the individual level, as seen in the instruction that history PhD candidates need to master approaches to national history before they write world history. Global history is thus cast as a late career, reflective move.

If this idea is applied at the national level, it might be assumed that a state needs to be well developed before it evidences the foundations needed to make valid and meaningful global histories. If you assume that Australia is a young nation, then it should come as no surprise that it does not have a strong tradition of global history making. This might be advanced as a third reason why Australian approaches to global history have not taken the world by storm in a sustained and systematic fashion.

Embracing global history making ahead of the maturation of national history making might herald the conflict of the two approaches or the undermining of the strengths of both. It is unclear which, because these statements about positioning are metaphysical assumptions. One of the key insights of the early-twentieth-century British Idealists in Australia was that state maturation is not necessary for successful engagement in global affairs. Although they did not realize it at the time, this claim provides a thought-provoking challenge to wider statements about the relative positioning of national and global history. Global history is not after national history; national history is not a precedent for a wider frame of view. So too globalization does not imply a northern takeover, and global history is not an education movement. From the shores of a relatively young nation, then, it is possible to see global history as something of value in and of itself.

Notes

1. Antony G. Hopkins (ed.), *Global History: Interactions between the Universal and the Local* (Basingstoke: Palgrave, 2006); Margarete Grantner, Dietmar Rothermund and Wolfgang Schwentker (eds.), *Globalisierung und Globalgeschichte* (Vienna: Mandelbaum Verlag, 2005).
2. William Edward Hanley Stanner, *The Great Australian Silence* (St Leonards: ABC books, 1969).
3. Carly Millar and Mark Peel, "Canons Old and New?: The Undergraduate History Curriculum in 2004," *History Australia* 2:1 (2004), 1–13.
4. Ibid.
5. M. Hughes-Warrington, "Shapes," in M. Hughes-Warrington (ed.), *Palgrave Advances in World Histories* (Basingstoke: Palgrave Macmillan, 2005).
6. Zygmunt Bauman, *Globalization: The Human Consequences* (Cambridge: Polity, 1998).
7. Mike Featherstone, *Undoing Culture: Globalization, Postmodernism and Identity* (London: Sage, 1995), 13–14.
8. See for example William Robinson, "Social Theory and Globalization: The Rise of a Transnational State," *Theory and Society* 30:2 (2001), 157–200, especially 159.

9. Anthony Giddens, *Runaway World: How Globalization Is Reshaping Our Lives*, 2nd edition (London: Profile, 2002).
10. Patrick Manning, Navigating World History: Historians Create a Global Past (New York: Palgrave Macmillan, 2003); Daniel Headrick, "Review of *The New World History Reader*," *The Journal of World History* 13:1 (2002), 183–86.
11. Raewyn Connell, *Southern Theory: The Global Dynamics of Knowledge in Social Science* (Crows Nest: Allen and Unwin, 2007), 55.
12. See Ann Curthoys and Marilyn Lake (eds.), *Connected Worlds: History in Transnational Perspective* (Canberra: ANU E Press, 2006), 15. See also Ann Curthoys, "We've Just Started Making National Histories, and You Want Us to Stop Already?," in Antoinette Burton (ed.), *After the Imperial Turn: Thinking with and Through the Nation* (Durham, NC: Duke University Press, 2003), 70–89.
13. Connell, *Southern Theory*, 206.
14. William Edward Hanley Stanner, *White Man Got No Dreaming: Essays 1938–1973* (Canberra: Australian National University Press, 1979), 24.
15. Jeremy Beckett, "Walter Newton's History of the World—or Australia," *American Ethnologist* 20:4 (1993), 675–95, especially 685.
16. See for example Deborah B. Rose, "The Saga of Captain Cook: Remembrance and Morality," in Bain Attwood and Fiona Magowan (eds.), *Telling Stories: Indigenous History and Memory in Australia and New Zealand* (Sydney: Allen and Uniwin, 2001), 61–79; Stephen Muecke, Alan Rumsey and Banjo Wirrunmurra, "Pigeon the Outlaw: History as Texts," *Aboriginal History* 9 (1985), 81–100.
17. Beckett, "Walter Newton's History of the World—or Australia," 682.
18. See also Tony Swain, "The Ghost of Space: Reflections on Walpiri Christian Iconography and Ritual," in Tony Swain and Deborah B. Rose (eds.), *Aboriginal Australians and Christian Missions* (Canberra: Australian Association for the Study of Religion, 1988), 452–69.
19. Curthoys and Lake, *Connected Worlds*, 5–6.
20. See Margaret Allen, "'Innocents Abroad' and 'Prohibited Immigrants': Australians in India and Indians in Australia 1890–1910," 111–24 A. James Hammerton, "Postwar British Immigrants and the 'Transnational Moment': Exemplars of a 'Mobility of Modernity?'" 125–37; Desley Deacon, "'Films as Foreign Offices': Transnationalism at Paramount in the Twenties and Early Thirties" 139–56; John Maynard, "Transnational/Transcultural Interaction and Influences on Aboriginal Australia," 195–208, all in Ann Curthoys and Marilyn Lake, *Connected Worlds*.
21. On settler societies, see Daiva Stasiulis and Nira Yuval-Davis (eds.), *Unsettling Settler Societies: Articulations of Gender, Race, Ethnicity and Class* (London: Sage, 1995).
22. Alan Lester, "British Settler Discourse and the Circuits of Empire," *History Workshop Journal* 54 (2002), 24–44, 26; Alan Lester "Colonial Settlers and the Metropole: Racial Discourse in the Early Nineteenth Century Cape Colony, Australia and New Zealand," *Landscape Research* 27:1 (2002), 39–49; Elizabeth Elbourne, "The Sin of the Settler: The 1835-6 Select Committee on Aborigines and Debates over Virtue and Conquest in the Early Nineteenth Century British White Settler Society," *Journal of Colonialism and Colonial History* 4:3 (2003), online at: http://muse.jhu.edu/journals/journal_of_colonialism_and_colonial_history/v004/4.3elbourne.html (accessed November 29, 2017).
23. Julie Evans, Patricia Grimshaw, David Phillips and Shurlee Swain (eds.), *Equal Subjects Unequal Rights: Indigenous People in British Settler Colonies, 1830–1910* (Manchester: Manchester University Press, 2003).

24. Dirk Moses (ed.), *Empire, Colony, Genocide: Conquest, Occupation and Subaltern Resistance in World History* (New York: Berghahn Books, 2008); Dirk Moses and Dan Stone (eds.), *Colonialism and Genocide* (London: Routledge, 2007); Dirk Moses (ed.), *Genocide and Settler Society: Frontier Violence and Stolen Aboriginal Children in Australian History* (New York: Berghahn, 2004).

25. Ann Curthoys, *Freedom Ride* (Crows Nest: Allen and Unwin, 2002). See also Sean Scalmer, "Translating Contention: Culture, History, and the Circulation of Collective Action," *Alternatives* 25 (2000), 491–514.

26. See David Lambert and Alan Lester (eds.), *Colonial Lives across the British Empire: Imperial Careering in the Long Nineteenth Century* (Cambridge: Cambridge University Press, 2006).

27. See for example Marilyn Lake, "The White Man Under Siege: New Histories of Race in the Nineteenth Century," *History Workshop Journal* 58:1 (2004), 41–62; Patricia Grimshaw, "Settler Anxieties, Indigenous Peoples, and Women's Suffrage in the Colonies of Australia, New Zealand and Hawaii, 1888 to 1902," *Pacific Historical Review* 69:4 (2000), 553–72; Fiona Paisley, "Citizens of the World: Australian Feminism and Indigenous Rights in International Context, 1920s and 1930s," *Feminist Review* 58:1 (1998), 66–89.

28. David Goodman, *Gold-Seeking: Victoria and California in the 1850s* (Crows Nest: Allen and Unwin, 1994).

29. Hamish Maxwell-Stewart and Cassandra Pybus, *American Citizens, British Slaves* (Melbourne: Melbourne University Press, 2002); Cassandra Pybus, Marcus Rediker and Emma Christopher (eds.), *Many Middle Passages Forced Migration and the Making of the Modern World* (Berkeley: University of California Press, 2007); Cassandra Pybus, *Black Founders: The Unknown Story of Australia's First Black Settlers* (Sydney: University of New South Wales Press, 2006).

30. See for example Tom Griffiths and Libby Robin (eds.), *Ecology and Empire: Environmental History of Settler Societies* (Keele: University of Keele Press, 1997).

31. Curthoys and Lake (eds.), *Connected Worlds*, 7.

32. Marilyn Lake, "Nationalist Historiography, Feminist Scholarship, and the Promise and Problems of New Transnational Histories: The Australian Case," *Journal of Women's History* 19:1 (2007), 180–86.

33. Jill Roe, "What Has Nationalism Offered Australian Women?," in Norma Grieve and Alisa Burns (eds.), *Australian Women: Contemporary Feminist Thought* (Melbourne: Oxford University Press, 1994), 29–39.

34. Jeannie Morefield, "Hegelian Organicism, British New Liberalism and the Return of the Family State," *History of Political Thought* 23:1 (2002), 141–70, especially 142.

35. E. H. Burgmann, "Philosophy 2 (1911): Ethics [notes from Francis Anderson's Lectures]," Nat. Lib. Australia, Burgmann Papers, Box 32, Lecture 20.

36. Francis Anderson, *Liberty, Equality and Fraternity* (Sydney: O'Loughlin Bros, 1922).

37. Francis Anderson, *Liberty, Equality and Fraternity*, 9.

38. Garnet Vere Portus, *The Cult of Kultur: A Comparison of Ancient Jewish and Modern German Imperialisms* (West Maitland: Thomas Dimmock, 1915), p. 6.

39. Portus, *The Cult of Kultur*, 3.

40. Portus, *The Cult of Kultur*, 7.

41. Garnet Vere Portus, *The Price of Peace* (Adelaide: South Australian League of Nations Union, 1944), 6–7, see also idem, *Report on the Drafting Committee's Report on the Project for a Scientific and Cultural History of Mankind* [1952], Portus papers, State Library of South Australia PRG204, series 25.

42. Portus, *The Price of Peace*, 9
43. Garnet Vere Portus, *They Wanted to Rule the World: Studies of Six Dictators and Other Essays* (Sydney: Angus and Robertson, 1944), 18.
44. Portus, *The Price of Peace*, 13.
45. Walter Murdoch, *The Struggle for Freedom* (Melbourne: Whitcombe and Tombs, 1911).
46. Garnet Vere Portus, *The Family and the Community* (Adelaide: WEA Press, 1947).
47. Garnet Vere Portus, *Australia since 1606* (Melbourne: Oxford University Press, 1957 edn [1932]), 218. See also 217.
48. Garnet Vere Portus, *Australia since 1606*.
49. Garnet Vere Portus, *Australia since* 1606, 232. On the growth of the Australian state and its need for international association, see Garnet Vere Portus, *Britain and Australia* (London: Longmans, Green and Co., 1946), 41 and 55.
50. Jacques Derrida, *Limited Inc.*, (ed.) by Gerald Graff, trans. by Samuel Weber (Evanston: Northwestern University Press, 1998), 236.

CHAPTER 14
JAPANESE EFFORTS TO OVERCOME EUROCENTRIC PARADIGMS IN THE STUDY OF GLOBAL HISTORY
Shigeru Akita

World history in postwar Japan

In Japan, the study of "world history" developed in parallel with the creation of a new "world history" curriculum at the senior-high-school level in 1949 and with the great demand from schoolteachers as well as general readers for world history writings. According to the Digital Library (book reviews) of the Research Institute for World History in Tokyo,[1] Japanese scholars have published more than twenty book series on world history: one in the 1950s, seven in the 1960s, four in the 1970s, four in the 1980s, nine in the 1990s and two in the 2000s.[2] Most of the contents were merely an assemblage of national histories in chronological order, from ancient to contemporary times. However, a few series were part of strong academic initiatives by world historians in intimate collaboration with prominent academic publishers like Iwanami-shoten.[3]

This chapter aims to explore new approaches to the creation of global history in Japan. It introduces attempts by Japanese scholars to create "world/global history"[4] studies from Asian perspectives. World history studies in Japan started in the late 1940s with comparative histories of economic development and modernization, framed in Eurocentric paradigms. However, through a unique joint research effort in the Kansai area (Kyoto/Osaka), world/global history studies in Japan shifted from comparative history to "relational history." There have been significant Japanese efforts to overcome Eurocentric perspectives since the mid-1980s.

The Tokyo and the Kansai School

After the Second World War, Japanese scholars started to write "world history." It became a new subject at the senior-high-school level in April 1949 (and was made compulsory in the 1980s) at the behest of the Ministry of Education and the American SCAP. The original aim was very vague: schools were to teach the history of foreign countries rather than continuing the exaggeratedly nationalist Japanese approach used before and during the Second World War. The ministry did not set up any clear standard for contents, however, which inevitably led to a domination of the histories of Europe and China.

Since then, the Japanese academic world has had two major schools of world history writings and research: (a) Tokyo: Marxist historians centered on the Rekishigaku-Kenkyukai (the Historical Science Society of Japan: HSS)[5] and (b) the Kansai region (Kyoto and Osaka): a liberal non-Marxist school based at the Institute for Research in Humanities (IRH),[6] Kyoto University.

The HSS was founded in 1932 as a Marxist historians' organization, and it played a major role in historical studies in Japan, especially in Japanese history. It directed its research activities in the 1940s and 1950s against the strong influence of modernization theory in postwar Japan, which was led by Ōtsuka Hisao, professor of European economic history at the University of Tokyo. The most prominent feature of Ōtsuka's historical writings was the analytical framework of the nation-state and the national economy he used. He saw the history of the formation of English capitalism, with its base in yeomanry and the wool industry, as the model for Japanese modernization and reconstruction after the war,[7] and paid no attention to external relations such as the English trade with Europe or the Atlantic world. Asian countries completely dropped out of his analytical framework. He started what is called "comparative economic history studies" in Japan, sticking closely to the bilateral nation-state-based framework, but his excessively authoritarian influence distanced Tokyo historians from working in the perspective of world/global history.[8]

The HSS reacted strongly against this dominant academic position of the Ōtsuka school. The leading scholar of the HSS in world history was Eguchi Bokurō, who worked at the University of Tokyo. Eguchi's works covered a wide range of fields in modern and contemporary world history; an examination of his work on four topics reveals his approach. These are (1) criticism of the Eurocentric modernization theory of the Ōtuska school, (2) Asia's positive role in world history, (3) the development of nationalism in history and (4) a criticism of imperialism and an evaluation of decolonization in Asia and Africa.[9] Eguchi's original work included histories of the non-European world, especially of Asia and Africa or the so-called Third World countries. This is clearly different from the Ōtsuka school.[10] However, even though Eguchi's works on world history were heavily influenced by Marxist interpretations, his analysis remained centered on the nation-state framework. In this context, the Ōtsuka school and its fierce opponents, the HSS and Eguchi, shared an assumption about the crucial importance of nation-states.[11]

From the late 1950s onward, a collaboration of leading scholars and senior-high-school teachers engaged in world history education made an effort to arrive at new interpretations of "world history". The leader of this group was Uehara Senroku from Hitotsubashi University, Tokyo. Uehara edited *Nihon-Kokumin no Sekaishi* (World History for the Japanese People) in 1960. Originally conceived in 1958 as a senior-high-school textbook, it failed to pass the Ministry of Education's textbook screening, due to the difference of interpretations on contemporary world history, especially the Versailles System in the aftermath of the First World War. The book proposed a unique interpretation of world history, based on the concept of the geographical spheres of four civilizations: East Asian, Indian, West Asian and Western European.[12]

Uehara's group distinguished the Oriental civilizations (East Asia, India and West Asia) from Western civilization and emphasized the parallel and simultaneous development of these four major civilizations from ancient times. Their first priority was to describe East Asian civilization, which, of course, included Japan, as well as the neighboring Asian countries with which it had intimate relationships. After the late fifteenth century, an integrated world history, centered on Europe and European peoples, emerged with the modernization and the overseas expansion of Europe. However, in the twentieth century, especially after the First World War, the United States and the USSR replaced Europe's leading roles, and the peoples in Asia and Africa regained active roles in the formation of a globalized and integrated world. Uehara emphasized the distinctive and unique features of the four major civilizations and tried to present historical images or realities of each civilization rather than abstract basic principles of Marxist historical development such as development-stage theory.

Eguchi and other members of the HSS collaborated with Uehara to present their balanced pictures of world history. Through such intentional efforts to overcome the Asian stagnation theory of Marxism, they produced a more balanced interpretation of the parallel development of four major civilizations or mega-regions in the world up to the late fifteenth century. But not even Uehara could escape from the world history narrative of Europe-centered globalization starting from the late fifteenth century or the beginning of the "European Age of Commerce".

The other prominent school was centered in the Kansai region of Kyoto and Osaka and was known as the "Kyoto School" because its major scholars and historians had studied at Kyoto University and worked at the IRH. The IRH was founded in 1929 as a research center for Chinese culture and civilization and subsidized by the Japanese Foreign Ministry. After the war, the IRH started to organize a joint research system, and in the 1960s, it launched a major research project on the history of "world capitalism," at the initiative of Kawano Kenji (IRH) and Tsunoyama Sakae (Wakayama University). They continued their joint research for ten years and edited two books.[13] Their main argument was their original conception of world capitalism as a single unit of economic development. They insisted that world capitalism was a total structure consisting of heterogeneous and complex parts and regions, and that it must be comprehended in the context of the contemporary connections of various national economies. Against the core arguments of the Ōtsuka school, they saw each national economy as a part of this unified force of world capitalism that had its own historical structure and driving forces. They dealt mainly with capitalist development and the emergence of a world economy in the nineteenth century, after the Industrial Revolution of Britain.

It is worth mentioning that the publication date of this joint research project is the same as that of André Gunder Frank's dependency theory of Latin America: 1967,[14] and seven years earlier than that of the publication of the first volume of Immanuel Wallerstein's major work on the modern world system, 1974.[15] The IRH's world capitalism idea is very similar to the Wallersteinian concept of the world economy, or the modern world system as a single unit of analysis of economic development. After the translation of Wallerstein's book into Japanese in 1981, world system analysis became very popular among Japanese historians and social scientists. However, the key concepts—"connection," "relationships" and "linkages"—of various countries and regions in the world had been put forward by the IRH group in the late 1960s. The distinct difference between the IRH group and Wallerstein's interpretation lies in Wallerstein's three-layered analysis of the "world economy" (core, semiperiphery and periphery), especially the unique concept and historical role of the "semi-periphery." Also, the IRH group looked mainly at the period of the so-called long nineteenth century rather than at the "long sixteenth century."

A challenge to Eurocentric paradigms through Asian economic history from the 1980s

In the 1970s and 1980s, the Marxist-dominated and Eurocentric interpretation of world history in Japan began to lose its influence, because their modernization model became obsolete through Japan's high economic growth from the late 1950s and its transformation by the oil crises of 1973 and 1979. The focal points of world history studies gradually shifted from political and economic histories to social and cultural ones.

Under these changing modes of historiography, Tsunoyama started his studies of Japanese consular reports in the middle of the 1970s and organized a new joint research project on "comparative studies of consular reports" at the IRH from 1982 to 1984. Written by consular or commercial counselors about overseas markets and marketing strategies, consular reports had been underutilized as sources of economic information. Due to the strong tendency to consider only the nation-state or the framework of a national economy in economic history studies, Japanese economic historians had neglected transnational or intra-regional relations, and Japanese consular reports were overlooked as primary sources.[16] Tsunoyama's research group included specialists in Asian economic history like Kaoru Sugihara, Takeshi Hamashita and Heita Kawakatsu, because the main export markets for Japanese goods (cotton textiles and consumer goods like matches and glassware) were Chinese and Asian. Through the comparative studies of consular reports,[17] the seeds of further development of "global economic history" were planted by this joint research of the IRH.[18]

Kawakita Minoru, in contrast, started his wide-ranging research activities with Tsunoyama as a global historian, creating the new research field of "Toshi-Seikatsu-shi" (World history of urban everyday life). Not only did Kawakita translate Immanuel Wallerstein's four-volume work *The Modern World-System* into Japanese (1981, 1993, 1997 and 2013), in addition, he and Tsunoyama organized a small research forum in Kyoto on British urban social history. This forum was mainly concerned not with world history per se but with British socioeconomic history, especially the urban social history of ordinary life. It paid keen attention to the transformation of urban social material life in the UK from the eighteenth century onward, looking at the expansion of overseas trade and increased imports of various primary products (tea, sugar and tobacco) and Asian manufactured goods (cotton textiles and porcelain). The forum members concluded that imported goods drastically transformed the material life of British people, and that their pattern of consumption was "globalized," to a great extent, by British overseas expansion and the formation of a world economy.

Even though forum activities were confined to the fields of British socioeconomic history, the members had received a solid academic grounding in world capitalism (i.e., the modern world system) from the IRH of Kyoto. Due to the establishment of a free-trade regime and "informal empire" in the nineteenth century, British socioeconomic history was strongly connected with world history through the international and transregional transfer and exchange of goods, services, people and information.[19] In the 1980s and 1990s, Tsunoyama and Kawakita edited four books about nineteenth-century British socioeconomic or urban social life.[20] In addition, Tsunoyama wrote a best-selling book about the world history of tea drinking, and Kawakita published a popular book on the history of sugar. Both scholars successfully presented the simultaneous and related development of the mass-consumption society in Great Britain and the underdevelopment of the non-European world, especially the West Indies and British India, by utilizing the key concept of "world capitalism" or the modern world system.[21] Connections or relationships became crucial concepts in creating this research trend of world history in the Kansai region. We might call it the emergence of "relational history" studies.

The emergence of Asian economic history and the transregional approach

From the mid-1980s, there has been a new trend in the field of global history in Japan, and this trend was partly related to the weakening and subsequent demise of the Cold War regime, but mostly due to the new development of Asian economic history in the 1980s and the academic implications of the "East Asian miracle" or the resurgence of the East Asian economy. The distinctive features of the newly emerging global history studies are the shift from comparative studies to studies of relationships or linkages and the adoption of new frameworks of analysis such as wider "regions" and networks of merchants and migration. In this section, we review intra-regional or transregional approaches in the emerging Asian economic history studies, especially studies of intra-Asian trade. These approaches emphasize connections or linkages rather than comparison, and we might call them a new global "relational history." In order to create a real global history, it was essential to challenge Eurocentric structures and paradigms.

Until recently, "most of the literature on Asian economic history has been written within the intellectual framework of the Western impact and each region's response to it, and the element of intra-regional economic intercourse in Asia has not been properly assessed in a wider comparative perspective."[22] However, as already mentioned, the joint research project on consular reports at the IRH in the early 1980s gave a strong impetus to the development of new research trends in Asian economic history, the front line of the new global history studies from the mid-1980s.[23] It enables us to look at individual Asian countries in the context of an integrated Asian regional economy, and to construct the framework of an evolving economic relationship between the British Empire and an Asian regional economy during the "long nineteenth century," within a capitalist world economy. It is worth mentioning here the works of three distinguished Japanese scholars: Takeshi Hamashita, Heita Kawakatsu and Kaoru Sugihara, who share a critical viewpoint toward Eurocentric or Western-oriented historiography.

Hamashita has insisted on the importance of a Chinese-centered world system and its resilience based upon the tributary trade system. He has also emphasized the importance of silver currency circulation and the active roles of Asian merchants' networks in the promotion of intra-Asian trade in the early-modern period.[24] Kawakatsu has pointed to the two different paths of development followed by the West European and Japanese cotton textile industries and stressed the coexistence of coarse Asian cotton goods with fine cottons from Manchester.[25] Later he extended his research to cover "Asian-sea civilizations" in the early-modern period and explored global history from Asian perspectives.[26] Nevertheless, the arguments of Hamashita and Kawakatsu are oriented toward the identification of the indigenous roots of the Asian regional economies and they have not been able to incorporate the global linkages or development of a capitalist world economy.

In contrast to these two scholars, Sugihara has revealed the formation and development of intra-Asian trade from the late nineteenth century to the early 1940s by using multinational archives of trade statistics. His research offers two key insights into the pattern of modern Asian economic development, namely the emergence of "cotton-centered economic linkages" on the supply side and the effects of "final demand linkages" on the demand side.

At the end of the nineteenth and beginning of the twentieth century, a unique chain of linkages was formed between Indian raw cotton, cotton yarn exports to China from British India and Japan, the production of cotton piece goods in China based on imported yarns and a peculiar pattern of consumption of Asian cotton goods. These linkages depended on the development of the cotton industries in Japan and British India and Japanese imports of Indian raw cotton. Meanwhile, Southeast Asian countries such as Burma, the Straits Settlements and the Dutch East Indies specialized in the production and export of primary products to European countries. In return, they earned hard currency that they used to import cheap consumer goods from Japan or British India. Sugihara observes that industrialization in Japan and British India was not only generated through this "cotton-centered" linkage but was promoted by the rise in incomes as a result of the growth in exports of primary products to the West; he calls this the "final demand linkage effect."[27] Both sets of connections contributed greatly to the promotion of industrialization-based trade under the umbrella of the "Pax Britannica."

These works by prominent senior Japanese economic historians led to further research on Asian and Japanese economic history by younger scholars. Kagotani Naoto explores the interactions between intra-Asian trade and networks of Asian merchants, especially Chinese and Indian merchants, in accelerating the exports of Japanese consumer goods from the late nineteenth century up to the late 1930s.[28] Furuta Kazuko reveals the importance of the "Shanghai network" for the development of trading networks in modern East Asia, which were dominated by Chinese merchants.[29] The Japanese export of cotton goods was dependent on these indigenous networks of Asian merchants, creating intra-Asian competition in Asian markets. Through the works of Kagotani and Furuta that focus on trading linkages and the positive roles of Asian merchants, Japanese economic history studies have been integrated into a wider framework of Asian economic history,

Current projects on global history studies in Osaka

Based on the recent new turn in Asian economic history and original academic works on "world capitalism" in the Kansai region from the 1960s, global historians in Osaka are pursuing interdisciplinary global history studies from Asian perspectives.[30] They use the term "global history" to refer to a kind of transnational or mega-regional history in the context of "relational history."

The emergence of new Asian-focused studies of the modern world economy, along with developments in Asian economic history in Japan and in the Anglo-American academic world, has challenged orthodox interpretations of the modern world system.[31] The main foci of reconsideration are the early-modern world (the "long eighteenth century") and the resurgence of the contemporary East Asian economy or the "East Asian miracle." The global history project in Osaka has a special academic connection with the GEHN.[32]

The new development of Asian economic history studies also gives rise to new research on the "international order of Asia" in the twentieth century and new interpretations of the modern world system from Asian perspectives. The modern world system was sustained and stabilized by the presence of hegemonic states. Thus the rise and fall of hegemonic states and transformations or shifts in hegemony are important subjects to explore. In this historical context, British imperial history in the "long nineteenth century" can be seen as a "bridge" to global history.[33] In their second edition of *British Imperialism 1688–2000*, British imperial historians P. J. Cain and A. G. Hopkins suggest that imperialism and empires can be viewed as globalizing forces.[34] We have started to evaluate the role played by Great Britain in a capitalist world economy and its implications for economic development (industrialization) in the "long nineteenth century." We have paid particular attention to the international order of East Asia in the first half of the twentieth century, which was shaped by Britain's influence while keeping a relatively unique "autonomous" status in a capitalist world economy.

We can clearly understand unique complementary developments by reference to the Cain-Hopkins thesis that the core of British economic interests had shifted from manufacturing to finance and services, the main economic base of gentlemanly capitalism. This kind of complementarity, which in effect encouraged industrialization in East Asia, represents a special relationship. It implies not rivalry or competition but cooperation or alignment as long as individual national interests are in concert with one another. The coexistence between British economic interests and East Asian industrialization strengthened the status of the City of London as an international center of finance.[35]

In Osaka, global historians have also tried to integrate works in area studies, especially those on Asian studies, where we have the comparative advantage of multi-archival research in indigenous Asian languages. To examine the interactions or connections between the regional factors revealed through area studies and global history, we have focused on maritime history. We have organized several workshops with specialists in Asian, Japanese and European maritime history.

Momoki Shiro and his group have exposed the densely developed trade networks of Chinese, Indian and local merchants in Asian waters from the tenth century to the early-modern period, especially starting from the Ming dynasty in China in the latter half of the fourteenth century. European powers encountered these Asian trading networks and used them for their own long-distance trade between Europe and Asia in the "long sixteenth century." Due to the collaboration of Asian merchants and the acquiescence of political authorities (empires) in Asia, they made huge profits from their entry into the intra-Asian trade network. Fully utilizing local Asian historical documents as well as European sources, the Momoki group published an introductory book in 2008, the first comprehensive book on Asian maritime history.[36]

A group led by Tsukasa Mizushima and George Souza is evaluating the "long eighteenth century" from Asian perspectives by looking at Asian port cities and their hinterlands. The Mizushima group has held several workshops and focused on economic linkages between the development of long-distance/intra-regional trade in Asia and the economic development of hinterlands. They use the concept of "commodity chains"[37] to reveal wider economic linkages and connections in Asia and try to differentiate Asian patterns of commodity chains in the early-modern period from modern European/American ones.[38] The maritime history framework, coupled with the exploration of trade linkages, lets us integrate a transregional or intra-regional perspective into global history.

Osaka established close relations with many other universities, including other global history centers in East Asia. One prominent example is the IWGH at Ewha Womans University, Seoul, led by Ji-Hyung Cho.[39] The IWGH was the first academic center devoted to world/global history in Korea. The institute studies historical progress and change in terms of global networks and regional interdependence and interrelationships. Among other themes, Cho and the other members of the Institute have focused on problems of world history education in Korea, and they seek to improve its teaching and understanding.[40] They have also done excellent research on the Korean

World Map of 1402, which is the oldest extant Afro-Eurasian map showing the southernmost tip of Africa.[41]

Such transnational collaborations are possible since, nowadays, global/world history studies attract keen attention from Japanese, Korean and other Asian scholars. In May 2009, a new network for the study of global/world history, the AAWH, was formed in Osaka and more than 250 scholars and schoolteachers attended the AAWH Inaugural Congress there to discuss world/global history studies and world history education.[42] In January 2013, the AAWH launched a new academic e-journal, entitled *Asian Review of World Histories*.[43] We must continue to collaborate further with these international and transnational academic networks for the creation of a truly non-Eurocentric global history.

Notes

1. The Research Institute for World history was founded in 2004 as the NPO in Tokyo, Japan. It is intended as a cyber institution for helping and developing research and education on world history.
2. "A Brief Introduction to Series of World History in Contemporary Japan," http://www.npo-if.jp/worldhistory/wp-content/uploads/2015/10/A-Brief-Introduction-to-Series-of-World-History-in-Contemporary-Japan.pdf (accessed November 29, 2017).
3. Ara Matsuo, Horigome Youzo et al. (eds.), *Iwanami Koza Sekai-Rekishi* (*Iwanami Lectures on World History*) 31 vols. (Tokyo: Iwanami-shoten, 1969–71); Shibata Michio and Itagaki Yuzo et al. (eds.), *Sekaishi heno Toi* (*Inquiries into World History*) 10 vols. (Tokyo: Iwanami-shoten, 1989–91); Kabayama Koichi, Kawakita Minoru et al. (eds.), *Iwanami Koza Sekai-Rekishi* (*Iwanami Lectures on World History*) New Series, 29 vols., 1997–2000.
4. In this essay, the author uses the two terms "world history" and "global history" as interchangeable and synonymous, because of the unique development and wider acceptance of the "world history" curriculum and the popularity of the subject.
5. https://kenkyudb.doshisha.ac.jp/rd/html/english/researchersHtml/110009/SBT_09/110009_SBT_09_5.html (accessed November 29, 2017).
6. http://www.zinbun.kyoto-u.ac.jp/ (accessed July 7, 2017).
7. Ōtsuka Hisao, *Kindai Ōshū Keizaishi Jyosetsu* (*An Introduction to Modern European Economic History*) (Tokyo: Iwanami-shoten, 1944). Later, *Ōtsuka Hisao Chosaku-shu* (*Collected Works of Ōtsuka Hisao*) (Tokyo: Iwanami-shoten, 1969), vols. 2–5.
8. Kawakita Minoru, "Origins of Historiography of World History in Japan: Comments to Schwentker," *Creating Global History from Asian Perspectives: Proceedings of Global History Workshop, Osaka, "Cross-Regional Chains in Global History," December 2007* (Osaka: Osaka University, 2008), 60–63.
9. Wolfgang Schwentker, "Writing World History in Post-War Japan: Eguchi Bokuro and His Legacy," ibid., 41–59.
10. Eguchi Bokuro, *Sekai-shi no Gendankai to Nihon* (*The Present Stage of World History and Japan*) (Tokyo: Iwanami-shoten, 1986).

11. Rekishigaku-Kenkyukai (ed.), *Sengo-Rekishigaku Saikou: "Kokuminshi" wo koete (Reconsideration of Post-War Historiography: Beyond "National History")* (Tokyo: Aoki-shoten, 2000).
12. Uehara Senroku (ed.), *Nihon-Kokumin no Sekaishi (World History for the Japanese People)* (Tokyo: Iwanami-publisher, 1960).
13. Kawano Kenji and Iinuma Jiro (eds.), *Sekai-shihonshugi no Keisei (The Formation of the World Capitalism)* (Tokyo: Iwanami-shoten, 1967); Kawano Kenji and Iinuma Jiro (eds.), *Sekai-shihonshugi no Rekishi-kozo (The Historical Structures of the World Capitalism)* (Tokyo: Iwanami-shoten, 1970).
14. André Gunder Frank, *Capitalism and Underdevelopment in Latin America: Historical Studies in Chile and Brazil* (New York: Monthly Review Book, 1967).
15. Immanuel Wallerstein, *The Modern World-System: Capitalist Agriculture and the Origins of the European World-Economy in the Sixteenth Century* (New York: Academic Press, 1974).
16. The Japanese Foreign Ministry continued to publish several series of consular reports from 1881 to 1943, weekly or monthly or annually, in order to offer useful information about overseas markets to domestic industrialists and manufacturers.
17. Tsunoyama Sakae (ed.), *Nihon Ryōji-hōkoku no Kenkyu (Studies of Japanese Consular Reports)* (Tokyo: Dōbunkan-shuppan, 1986); Tsunoyama Sakae, *"Ttsushō-Kokka" Nihon no Jyōhō Senryaku (Information Strategy of "Commercial Nation" Japan)* (Tokyo: NHK Shuppan, 1988).
18. Tsunoyama Sakae, *"Seikatsu-shi" no Hakken: Fieldwork de miru Sekai (Discovery of "History of Everyday Life": The World Seen from Fieldwork)* (Tokyo: Chuōkōron-shinsha, 2001).
19. John Gallagher and Ronald Robinson, "The Imperialism of Free Trade," *Economic History Review* 2nd Series, 6:1(1953), 1–15; John Darwin, *The Empire Project: The Rise and Fall of the British World-System 1830–1970* (Cambridge: Cambridge University Press, 2009).
20. Tsunoyama Sakae (ed.), *Seikatsu no Sekaishi 10: Sangyo-Kakumei to Minshu (The World History of Everyday Life 10: The Industrial Revolution and the People)* (Tokyo: Kawadeshobō-shinsha, 1975); Tsunoyama Sakae and Kawakita Minoru (eds.), *Rojiura no Daieiteikoku (The British Empire Seen from a Rear-Lane)* (Tokyo: Heibon-sha, 1982); Kawakita Minoru, (ed.) *"Hi-rōudō-jikan" no Seikatsu-shi: Eikouhu Raifustairu no Tanjyo (History of Everyday Life During Non-Working Hours: The Birth of the British Life-style)* (Tokyo: Ribroport, 1987); Kawakita Minoru and Sashi Akihiro (eds.), *Shūen karano Manazashi (A Look from the Periphery)* (Tokyo: Yamakawa-shuppan, 2000).
21. Tsunoyama Sakae, *Cha no Sekaishi (World History of Tea)* (Tokyo: Chuo-Koronsha, 1980); Kawakita Minoru, *Satò no Sekaishi (World History of Sugar)* (Tokyo: Iwanami-shoten, 1996). These readable books are translated into Korean and Chinese. Cf. Sidney W. Mintz, *Sweetness and Power: The Place of Sugar in Modern History* (New York: Viking, 1985).
22. Sugihara Kaoru, *Ajia-kan Boeki no Keisei to Kozo (Patterns and Development of Intra-Asian Trade)* (Kyoto: Mineruva-Shobo, 1996), Introduction, 1–2.
23. Kyōtsū-rondai: Kindai-Ajia Bōekiken no keisei to kōzō (Proceedings of the 53rd Annual Conference of the Socio-Economic History Society, General Theme: The formation and structure of the Modern Asian trading area—from the latter half of the nineteenth-century to the First World War), *Shakai-Keizai-Shigaku (Socio- Economic History)* 51:1 (1985).
24. Hamashita Takeshi, *Kindai Chugoku no Kokusaiteki Keiki: Choko Boeki Shisutemu to Kindai Ajia (International Factors Affecting Modern China: Tributary Trade System and Modern Asia)* (Tokyo: Tokyo University Press, 1990); Hamashita Takeshi, *Choko Shisutemu to Kindai Ajia (Tributary Trade System and Modern Asia)* (Tokyo: Iwanami-shoten, 1997); Takeshi

Hamashita, *China, East Asia and the Global Economy: Regional and Historical Perspectives*, edited by Linda Grove and Mark Selden (Abingdon: Routledge, 2008).

25. Heita Kawakatsu, "International Competition in Cotton Goods in the Late Nineteenth Century: Britain Versus East Asia," in W. Fisher, R. M. McInnis, and J. Schneider (eds.), *The Emergence of a World Economy, 1500–1914* (Wiesbaden: Franz Steiner Verlag, 1986); Anthony J. H. Latham and Heita Kawakatsu (eds.), *Japanese Industrialization and Asian Economy* (London and New York, 1994).

26. Kawakatsu Heita, *Bunmei no Kaiyo-Shikan* (*Civilizations Seen from Maritime Perspectives*) (Tokyo: Chuo-Koron_shinsha, 1997).

27. Sugihara, *Ajia-kan Boeki no Keisei to Kozo* (*Patterns and Development of Intra-Asian Trade*), ch. 1; Kaoru Sugihara, "Japan as an Engine of the Asian International Economy, c. 1880–1936," *Japan Forum* 2:1 (1990), 127–45.

28. Kagotani Naoto, *Ajia Kokusai-tsūushō chitujyo to KIndai-Nihon* (*International Trading Order of Asia and Modern Japan*) (Nagoya: Nagoya University Press, 2000).

29. Furuta Kazuko, *Shanhai Network to Kindai Higashi-Ajia* (*Shanghai Networks and Modern East Asia*) (Tokyo: Tokyo University Press, 2000).

30. http://www.globalhistoryonline.com/JP/index (accessed July 12, 2014); see also Shigeru Akita, "Creating Global History from Asian Perspectives," in Patrick Manning (ed.), *Global Practice in World History: Advances Worldwide* (Princeton: Markus Wiener Publishers, 2008), ch. 4.

31. R. Bin Wong, *China Transformed: Historical Change and the Limits of European Experience* (Ithaca: Cornell University Press, 1997); Takeshi Hamashita, *Choukou Shisutemu to Kindai-Ajia* (*Tributary System and Modern Asia*); A. G. Frank, *ReOrient: Global Economy in the Asian Age* (Berkeley and London: University of California Press, 1998); Kenneth Pomeranz, *The Great Divergence: China, Europe, and the Making of the Modern World Economy* (Princeton: Princeton University Press, 2000).

32. As for the GEHN and its achievements, see the chapters by Kenneth Pomeranz and Gareth Austin in this volume.

33. Shigeru Akita, (ed.) *Gentlemanly Capitalism, Imperialism and Global History* (Basingstoke and New York: Palgrave-Macmillan, 2002), 1–16.

34. P. J. Cain and A. G. Hopkins, *British Imperialism, 1688–2000*, 2nd edition (Harlow and New York: Longman, 2001).

35. Akita Shigeru, *Igirisu-Teikoku to Ajia Kokusai Chitujo* (*The British Empire and International Order of Asia*) (Nagoya: Nagoya University Press, 2003).

36. Momoki Shiro, Fujita Kayoko, Yamauchi Shinji and Hasuda Takashi (eds.), *Kaiiki-Ajiashi Kenkyū Nyūmon* (*Introduction to Research on Maritime Asian History*) (Tokyo: Iwanami-shoten, 2008).

37. As for the concept of "commodity chains," see Steven Topik, Carlos Marichal and Zephyr Frank, eds., *From Silver to Cocaine: Latin American Commodity Chains and the Building of the World Economy, 1500–2000* (Durham and London: Duke University Press, 2006).

38. Tsukasa Mizushima, George Souza and Dennis Flynn, eds., *Hinterlands and Commodities: Place, Space, Time and the Political Economic Development of Asia over the Long Eighteenth Century* (Leiden: Brill, 2015).

39. Another prominent institution in transnational history was the Research Institute of Comparative History and Culture (RICH), led by Jie-Hyun Lim.

40. Ji-Hyung Cho and Yong Woo Kim, (eds.), *Global History Beyond Eurocentrism* (Paju: Seohaemunjib, 2010, in Korean).

41. Ji-Hyung Cho, "Dating the Ryukoku *Kangnido*, Identifying the Oldest Extant Map of the Afro-Eurasian World," *Journal of Ewha Historical Studies Institute* 42 (2010), 65–93 (in Korean).
42. http://akita4.wix.com/aawh (accessed November 29, 2017). See *The Proceedings of The First Congress of the Asian Association of World Historians: World History Studies and World History Education, May 29–31, 2009, Osaka University/Nakanoshima Center*, CD-ROM (Osaka, March 2010).
43. http://www.thearwh.org/ (accessed on November 29, 2017).

INDEX

Abdel-Malek, Anouar 218
Aboriginal history, development of 16
Aboriginal narratives 272
academic historians 56
academic historiography 217
academic journal database 63n.25
academic labor 26
academic specialization 87
academic tradition in Africa 246
Acemoglu, Daron 174
African academics, fundamental question for 242
African civilization 239
African historians 83
    anticolonial and nationalist project of 93
    generation of 93
African history/historiography 83–4, 86–90, 95–6, 235, 239, 240, 242, 245
    Atlantic slave trade and colonization 95–6
    beyond European time 243–7
    colonial frameworks 95–6
    colonial intellectual aristocracy 96
    colonialism and neocolonialism in 89
    colonial scholarship 94
    connection to world 96–8
    crisis of nationalism 95
    critical assessment of 243
    decolonization 92, 93
    detailed understanding of 86
    development of 98, 235–8
    elaboration of 91
    eurocentric conceptions of 96
    example of 98–9
    fragmentation of 84
    ghettoization of 98
    global histories of 84
    globalization 95
    global perspectives in 11
    historians of 23
    historiography, internal debate 238–43
    ideological colonization 92–3
    intellectual control 92–3
    intellectual production 94
    May 1968 99–100
    militant history 92–3
    myths and stereotypes of 94
    in other languages 92
    particularization, peripheralization and pathologization of 241
    pioneering role of foreign Africanists 90–1
    positive development for 85
    racial qualification 86–7
    recognition 85
    re-problematizing 84–6
    revival of interest in African Studies 91–2
    rewriting of 15, 95
    scholarly networks 92
    scholarship in 15, 93–4
    underdevelopment 86
    victimization 96–7
    work of generations 94–5
    writing of 241
African intellectuals 241
Africans, autonomy to 243
African slavery 70
African workers, characterization of 153
afrocentrism 88
Afro-centrist approach 244
agrarian fundamentalism 178, 179
agricultural labor 2–3
agriculture, history of 52
AHA. See American Historical Association (AHA)
Ahuja, Ravi 152
Akita, Shigeru 16
Alantic-centric approach 197
al-Bustani, Butrus 114
Allardyce, Gilbert 22
Allen, Robert 179
alternative modernities 220
American Africanist historiography 245
American Historical Association (AHA) 133
Amin, Samir 240
Anatolian civilizations 111–12
ancient library 245
Anderson, Francis 274–5
Anglo-American conspiracy 271
antagonistic complicity 15–16, 262
anti-Western Occidentalism 252
Appadurai, Arjun 31
AP world history 136
Arab historiography 120
    formation of 113
    intellectual currents within 114
    internationalization of 120
Arabization 120
Arab Middle East
    Annales on Ottoman historical scholarship 115–17
    collective memory 109

Index

concept of civilization 111–15
historiography 109, 112, 114, 117–19
issues in 110
national historiography of 111
national identity 113
source of identity and legitimacy 114
state of historiography in 109
time and space 109–11
Arab Middle East, historiography in 11
Arab nationalism 114–15
Arab renaissance 118
Arab scholarship 117–18
archive-based project 10
Argentina, canonical national historiography in 68
Arrighi, Giovanni 168, 174
Arslan, Shakib 114
Asia
  economic miracles 177
  industrious revolution in 54
  migration narratives 201
  traditional models in 53
Asian Association of World Historians (AAWH) 56, 291
Asian civilization 252, 261
Asian economic history 60, 286, 289
  development of 287
Asian maritime history 290
Asian migration 198, 200, 201, 203, 206
  comprehensive analyses of 205
Asian mobility 203, 205
Asian regional economy 288
Asian stagnation theory of Marxism 285
Asia on global stage 45–6
  comparison to study of connections 46–51
  discovering 51–5
  as opportunity and challenge 55–61
Asiatic mode of production 50, 62n.13, 256
Asiatic value-system 252
assimilation policy 259–60
Atlantic history 77
Atlantic migrations 201
Atlantic revolutions 77
Atlantic slavery, centrality of 71
Atlantic slave trade 99
Australia, global history in
  education 270–1
  globalization 271–7
  nation and globe 277–8
  view 269–70
Australia, historical scholarship in 16
Australian historians 269
Australian Historical Association 270
Australian scholars 272–3
authoritarian political culture 256
autochthonous narrative 244
autonomy, relative 75

Balfour Declaration of 1917 114
Bamako congress 244
Barkan, Omer Lutfi 115
Bauman, Zygmunt 271
Bayly, Christopher 25
Bentley, Jerry 12
beyond national history 262
Blackburn, Robin 76
black cultural identity 89
black slavery, historiography of 76
Boyd, Monica 204
Braudel, Fernand 11, 13, 27, 75
Braudelian formulation 71
Brazil, European exploration of 75
Breman, Jan 206
British economic interests 290
British imperial history 289
British Imperialism 52
The British Industrial Revolution in Global Perspective (Allen) 179
British urban social history 286
British wages 180
Broadberry, Stephen 34
Buddhism 275
Bush, George H. W. 136

Cain-Hopkins thesis 290
California school 166
  propositions 179
Cambridge University Press 87
capital accumulation 74, 170
capitalism 3, 47–9, 75, 76–7, 99, 151, 206, 221
  Braudel's definition of 174
  conceptualization of 174
  emergence of 54
  global 11
  labor under 2
  social history of 152
  three-part history of 73
capitalist development in Europe 48
capitalist economic development 196
capitalist imperialism 242
capitalist world economy 73, 75
Capital Normal University (CNU) 56, 58
Cardoso, Fernando Henrique 11
Caribbean history 67–78
  colonies 69
  slavery 70
  sugar production 70
  writing 68
Casey, Edward S. 109
centrism 195
Chakrabarty, Dipesh 31–2, 139
chattel slavery 151
chattel slaves 150
China

Index

intellectual history in 14
multilateral networks 176
nationalist anti-imperialism in 221
tribute system 176
Chinese Academy of Social Sciences (CASS) 263
Chinese anti-individualism, forms of 223
Chinese Communist Revolution 47
Chinese historical community 58
Chinese historiography/history 50, 223–4
Chinese intellectuals 117, 225
traditions 221
Chinese-Japanese Joint Committee final report 263–4
Chinese-Japanese report 264
Chinese migration 201
historical experiences of 205
Chinese modernity 223
Chinese trade 173
Christian, David 57
Christianity 275
civilization 5
development of 51–2
to historical study 56
process of 276–7
Western concept of 254
zones of 48
The Civilization of Africa: A History to 1800 (Ehret) 246
Coerced and Free Migration: Global Perspectives (Eltis) 199
coerced labor 175–6
coherence 239–40
Colley, Linda 29
colonial ideology 153
colonialism 3, 25, 70, 76, 148, 205, 219, 242–3, 257
aggressions of 45
European 11
impact of 175
colonial paradigms 89
colonial paternalism 87, 90
colonial slave mode of production 75
colonies of exploitation 175
colonies of settlement 175
colonization 99
commemoration 96–7
commercialization 177
communism 45, 49
Communist Revolution in 1949 222
communitarization 241
of historical circles 241
comparative history 3
compartmentalization 152, 236, 264
complementary trading activities 52
complex dialectic approach 236
conceptual Eurocentrism 10, 30–1
Confucian democracy 225

Confucianism 216, 222, 258
Confucian socialism 225
Connell, Raewyn 271
view of globalization 272
Conrad, Sebastian 33
constructivism 264
consumerism 52
contemporary globalization, material reality of 25
contemporary history 47
contemporary inequality 174
continuity 239–40
Cooper, Frederick 240
Crosby, Alfred W. 131
cultural chauvinism 96
cultural exchanges 59
cultural history, innovations of 217
cultural influences 170
cultural transfers 32
Curthoys, Ann 272
Curtin, Philip D. 131

Dakar school 87, 93–4, 100
work of generations 94–5
Darwin, John 30
debates on "Golden Flowers" blossom 50
decolonization 149, 163
process of 197
decompartmentalization 236
Delpechin, Jacques 239
democratic liberals 256
democratization 241
Deng, Kent 169
Deng Xiaoping 60
dependency theory 74
Deringil, Selim 117
developmentalism 219
development-stage theory 285
Diamond, Jared 60
Dink, Hrant 119
Diop, Cheikh Anta 87
Diouf, Mamadou 238–45
diversity, emergence of 237
durable hierarchy 173

early modernity 220, 225
East Asian Community 252
East Asian history/historiography
configuration of national and global 251–2
de-territorialization and re-territorialization 258–65
from enlightenment to Marxism 252–7
global 10
historical dialogues in 265
Pan-Asian history 258–61
textbook 262
writing 45

297

Index

East Asian intellectuals 258
Eastern identity, awakening of 114
Eckert, Andreas 25
ECLAC. *See* Economic Commission for Latin America (ECLAC)
Economic Commission for Latin America (ECLAC) 74
economic de-territorialization 149
economic dynamism 174
economic historians 48
economic history/historiography 25, 163–5, 167
    European 163
    scheme 255
    studies, national economy in 286
economic modernization 60
Ehret, Christophe 246
Eltis, David 199
emancipation 88
English capitalism, formation of 284
English employment law, globalization of 153
English history 251–2
ENIUGH. *See* European Network in Universal and Global History (ENIUGH)
Enlightenment concept 3
entangled histories 148
environmental history 8
equality 220–1
ethnic cleansing 97
Eurasia
    ecological crisis across 53
    real wages in 29
Eurasia Project 167
Eurocentric history/historiography
    alternatives to 139
    critique of 60
Eurocentric mobility transition 205
Eurocentric paradigms, Japan
    Asian economic history and transregional approach 287–9
    Asian economic history from 1980s 286–7
    current projects on global history studies in Osaka 289–91
    economic development and modernization in 283
    Tokyo and Kansai School 283–6
    world history in postwar Japan 283
Eurocentric world h 255
Eurocentrism 5, 9, 10, 28, 56, 60, 138, 139, 149, 195, 198, 217, 223, 254, 256
    of agency 10, 24
    of concept 24
    in global history 16
    in historiography 55
    ideology of 85
    monolithic understanding of 91

new labor history 147
    problems of 30
Europe
    capital accumulation 174
    capitalist development in 48
    civilization, dominance of 51
    colonial intervention 203
    colonialism 11, 174, 221, 258
    economic history 163
    economic space 73
    epistemic hegemony 241
    exceptionalism 24
    history/historiography 5, 30–1, 251, 254
    identity 252
    imperial authority 203
    imperialism 117, 131
    labor historians 148
    migrations 200, 201, 205
    scholars of 22
    trade of 172–3
    usurpation of universal history 242
European Absolutism 116
European Congress on Global History 1
European Enlightenment 3
European modernity 148
    challenges of 251
European Network in Universal and Global History (ENIUGH) 28
European Union 111
Europe, global history in 21–2
    debates 30–5
    definitions 22–3
    development of 54
    (re-)emergence of 24
    explorations 22–9
    growth of 21, 24
    reflections 35–6
    resurgence of 22
exploitation colonies 74
externality 75
extra-continental trade 180

fact-based research 265
Featherstone, Mike 271
feudalism 49
Five Golden Flowers 50
flying geese pattern 177
Foner, Philip 146
foreign Africanists, pioneering role of 90–1
France, historians in 8
Frank, Andre Gunder 74, 75
Frankema, Ewout 176
"free" economic choices 200
free labor 74, 151, 175
free wage laborers 151

Index

French/British slaveries 76
French Revolution 147
Fukuzawa Yukichi, 45, 253

GEHN. *See* Global Economic History Network (GEHN)
gentlemanly capitalism 52
German nationalism 275
German scholars 26
Germany, historical profession in 26–7
Gidden, Antony 271
global academic system 9
global capitalism 71, 75, 116, 148, 163
global citizen 57, 97–8
global community 277
    of scholars 5
global conceptual history 221
global economic history 138, 165, 166, 170–1, 181
    Japanese contributions to 16
Global Economic History Network (GEHN) 169, 289
global economic integration 171
global economy 77, 202–3
global historians 7
    community of 9
    in Europe 10
global historical perspectives 10, 15
global historical projects 13
global historical publications 6
global historical scholarship 8, 16
    challenges to 15
    in East Asia 10
global historical viewpoints 15–16
global history/historiography 1, 4, 5, 21, 25, 29, 30, 33, 61, 98, 100, 278. *See also* world history
    in Africa 235
    African voice in 15
    alternative visions of 16
    Anglophone contributors to 27
    Asian historians on 56
    Australian approach to 271
    branches of 3
    in Britain 22
    challenges 6
    Chinese acceptance of 58
    Chinese translation of 56
    component of writing 201
    courses 270
    critics of 37n.12, 60
    debates 13
    definition of 22
    diversity and vibrant nature of 7–8
    in East Asia 8, 10
    eloquent discussion of 72
    emergence of 1, 10
    Eurocentrism in 16
    in Europe 23 (*see* Europe, global history in))
    forms of 78
    global conversation on 269
    growth of 23
    interest in 60
    in Japan 58
    mission of 224
    movement of 71
    popularity of 1
    practices of 9
    problems of 9
    program of 90
    project of 35, 289
    pros and cons of 60
    public interest in 60
    research in 13, 59
    resurgence of 21, 34
    of slavery 1
    study of 1, 56
    surveys 271
    tradition of 11
    trajectories of 5–7
    undergraduate programs in 270
    usage of 37n.14
    varieties of 39n.36
    vs. world history 98–9
    writing of 86, 237
global integration, processes of 201–2
global intellectual history 14, 215–16, 221, 225
    in China 224
globalism 110
globality 88
globalization 6, 25, 55, 63n.24, 77, 97, 171–3, 236, 244
    of English employment law 153
    forms of 26
    history of 56
    intellectual 21
    of knowledge 84
    longevity and discontinuity of 23
    process of 243
    in Taiwan 59
global labor history 13, 146, 149, 195
    methodological problems 149–50
global migration history 3, 196, 199, 202, 205
    comparative analysis of 199
    complexities of 204
    framework of 206
    methodological formulation for 200
    rubric of 200
    theoretical-methodological discourse of 199–200
Global Migration History Program 205
global migrations

Index

comprehensive study of 198–9
critical determinant in 199
historical narrative of 198
narratives of 206
global modernization 226
global networks, asymmetrical character of 236
global perspectives in Africa 11
Global Price and Income History Project 167–8
global relevance 220
global scholarship 117
global scope of labor history 13
global trade expansion 172
global transformations 4
global village 99
Godechot, Jacques 77
Godinho, Vitorino Magalhaes 72
Goodrich, Samuel G. 252
Goody, Jack 33
Goswami, Manu 221
Grataloup, Christian 27
Green, Thomas Hill 274
Gruzinski, Serge 77
Gupta, Bishnu 34

Hall, Stuart 238
Hamashita Takeshi, 53
Harootunian, Harry 220–1
Hatton, Timothy J. 207
hierarchical order, concept of 53
hierarchy of narratives 237
historians 7
    of Africa 23
    in France 8
    in Latin America 11
historical communities, developments in 55
historical knowledge production 241
historical knowledge, production and reception of 24
historical materialism 49
historical scholarship 1, 54
historical study, civilization to 56
historical writing
    features of 128
    forms of 68
historicity 86
historicization, dimensions of 219
historiographical landscapes 215
history/historiography 45, 46, 60, 77
    of black slavery 76
    changing modes of 286
    East Asian (*see* East Asian history/historiography)
    economic 25
    Eurocentrism in 55, 60
    European 254

    global 21, 23, 25, 39n.36, 98
    Japanese 57
    Korean 251, 254, 260
    labor 150
    of Latin America 68, 78n.2
    Maoist 222
    Marxist 45–6, 49, 59, 255–6
    nationalist 61, 242
    Ottoman 116–17, 119
    Soviet 49
    Stalinist 222
    syllabus 37n.5
    Turkish 11, 12, 120
    Western models of 57
"History that Opens the Future" (HOF) 262–3
history writing
    idea, style and content of 45
    Japan 45
    nation-state focus in 59
    salient problematic in 110
    struggle in 60
    transnational framework in 60
Hobsbawm, Eric 146
Hodgson, Marshall 24
Hoffmann, Philip 179–80
homogeneity 239–40, 244
horizontal movement of history 54–5
Hourani, Albert 117–18
"human-centered" systems approach 199
human development, history of 67
human history 6
    alternative approaches to 5
    large-scale narratives of 7
    world history to 245
humanity 220–1
human migration 13–14, 196, 200
human mobility 196, 197, 200

ILO. *See* International Labour Organization (ILO)
imaginative geography 253
imperialism 47, 114–15, 148, 219
    aggressions of 45
    criticism of 284
indentured laborers 150
India
    immigrants in Malaysia 207
    intellectuals of 218–19
    political economy in 221
    workers of 153
indigenous land rights 269
indigenous modernity 225
individual biographies 217
individual subaltern workers 151
individual worker 149
Indo-European peoples 112

industrial capitalism 75
industrialization 177, 200, 255, 257
   in Japan 288
   trade 288
industrious revolution 170
Institute for African and Madagascan Curricula (IPAM) 90
Institute for Research in Humanities (IRH) 285
Institute of World and Global History (IWGH) 290
institutional influences 170
intellectual community 274
intellectual contact 72
intellectual globalization 21
intellectual historical perspectives 224
intellectual history 220
   in China 14
   of circulation and exchange 218
   debates in China 222–6
   developments in United States 216–22
   trajectories of 215–16
intellectuals 97
   interaction, cosmopolitan conception of 220
   interconnectedness 219
   tradition in Africa 246
internality 75
internal migrations 197
international academic debate 119
international cooperation 26
international division of labor 75
international history 1
International Institute of Social History in Amsterdam 29
International Journal of Business Research 245
international journals 26
international labor standards 155
International Labour Organization (ILO) 155
intra-Asian trade 288
   networks 53
intra-Asian tribute networks 53
intra-regional trade 176
IPAM. *See* Institute for African and Madagascan Curricula (IPAM)
IRH. *See* Institute for Research in Humanities (IRH)
Islamdom 130
Islamic library 245
Islamist revisionism 120
Italian intellectuals 218–19
IWGH. *See* Institute of World and Global History (IWGH)

James, C.L.R. 11, 69, 76, 148
   global perspective of 71
Japan
   capitalism 256
   development for civilizations 52
   development in Meiji 176
   economic expansion 51
   economic history 289
   economic recovery and expansion 52
   Enlightenment intellectuals 253
   European historical elements in 253
   geopolitical and cultural frame 119
   global history in 58, 283
   historiography, Western influence in 57
   imperialism 15
   intellectuals 221
   Marxists 255
   modern historiography in 251
   modernity 256
   modernization 46–7, 52, 284
   national history textbook 253
   scholarship 166
   transnational history of 260
   version of Orientalism 253
   in world history 253
Japanese-Korean Joint History Research Committee 263, 264
Jewish nationalism 114–15
Jewsiewicki, Bogumil 87
Jim Crow projection 130
Johns Hopkins University 135
Jones, Eric 25

Kake, Ibrahima Baba 88
Kang, Youwei, 5
Kant, Immanuel 5
Karl, Rebecca 221
Katsumi, Kuroita 259
Kaviraj, Sudipta 220
Kawakatsu, Heita 53
Kawakita Minoru, 286
Keizo Imperial University 261
Kemalist revolution 110–11
Kokuminka movement 260
Korea
   historiography 254, 260
   history 256, 261, 262
   intellectuals 258
   modern historiography in 251
   national history 254
   physiognomy 259
   transnational history of 260
Koselleck, Reinhart 78
Kyoto School 51

labor
   under capitalism 2
   forms of 3
   historiography 150

Index

history 149, 154
process 154
relations, formalization of 2–3
relations in Europe 152
relations in India 152
relations, transcontinental study of 149
Lake, Marilyn 272
land-intensive imports 181
Laroui, Abdallah 218
Latin American history 67–8
dependence theory of 285
global and comparative historical approaches 68
global study 73–4
history/historiography of 67–8, 76, 78n.2
languages and political concepts 78
study of 74
Leverhulme-funded Global Economic History Network 29
Liang Qichao 45
liberal policies 175
Linebaugh, Peter 147
Liu Xincheng 60
local histories, aggregation of 100
localized groups 217
Lockard, Craig A. 135
Locke, John 145
London Corresponding Society 147
London School of Economics (LSE) 25
longue-duree approach 200
LSE. *See* London School of Economics (LSE)
Ly, Abdoulaye 87

macro-invention 179
Maddison Project 166
Mafeje, Archibald 246
Manning, Patrick 196, 200, 246, 271
Maoism 223
Maoist historiography 222
March First Movement for Korean independence 259
marginality 86
maritime Asia 53, 59
Marquese, Rafael 11
Marxian universalist scheme 256
Marxism 33, 45, 46, 49, 92, 255
Asian stagnation theory of 285
Marxist historical theory 49
Eurocentric characteristic of 50
Marxist historicism 256
Marxist historiography 45–6, 255–6
dominance of 59
limits of 49
Marxist theory of social progress 49
Marx, Karl 47, 50, 145
Eurocentric bias 50

Masashi, Haneda 57, 58, 61
Master and Servant Acts 153
Maynard, John 272
Mazlish, Bruce 23
McKeown, Adam 201
Asian migration 202
Eurocentric perspectives 204
European-Atlantic and Asian migration 202
framework for global migration history 202
universalization of global migrations 205
McNeill, William 22, 60
mercantile capitalism 99
meta questions 24
metropolitan history 88
micro-inventions 179
Middell, Matthias 235
migrants' freedom 204
migration history 14, 195–7
global perspectives on 199
limitations 206–8
methodological frameworks of 207
multiple viewpoints for 197
role of empire and Indian exceptionalism 206
spatial scale of 197
transregional expanse of 198
writing 197–205
migratory movement 200
mine labor 149
mineral rights 176
Mishra, Amit 13–14
mobilization 196
history of 198
strategies of 203
modern capitalism 76
heterogeneity of 48
modernization 59–60, 255, 256
Mouhammed, Adil H. 245
Moyn, Samuel 117
multiethnic nationalism 259
Mudimbe, Valentin 238
Murdoch, Walter 276
Muslim intellectuals 113

Nabuco, Joaquim 68
Namwoon, Paik 256
national economy 285
national ethos, characteristics of 61
national history 2, 67
accommodation of 251
domain of 46
textbooks 253
nationalism 2, 3, 9, 110
studying 3
theories of 118
nationalist historiography 61, 242
national parameters 2

Index

national sovereignty 45
nation-centered histories 262
Nazis/Nazism 72
　origins of 26–7
Needham, Joseph 24
neo-Confucianism 225
neo-Marxist history 115
Newbury, David 87
Nigerian Civil War 97
non-Turkish historians 119
non-Western agency, elements of 30
North America 127–8
　contemporary world historians in 131
　educational programs 128
　English settlements in 7
　Eurocentric assumptions 133
　history movement in 128
　institutions 133–7
　paths toward world history 128–33
　political economy 132
　research and debates 137–9
　world historians 139
　world history project in 127, 129
North, Douglass 34
Northrup, David 198
Novais, Fernando 75
Nugent, Walter 197–8

objective understanding 264
O'Brien, Patrick 22–3, 169
obscurantism 88
Orientalism, Japanese version of 253
O'Rourke, Kevin 180
ostracism 87, 88
Ottoman archives 115
Ottoman Armenians, population of 119
Ottoman authority 113
Ottoman Bank 117
Ottoman Despotism 116
Ottoman economy
　history 115
　theoretical formulation of 116
Ottoman Empire
　dynamic processes of change in 118
　nationalist historiographies in 12
　scholarship of 115
Ottoman globalism 110
Ottoman history/historiography 119
　global conceptualization of 115
　global outlook of 110
　historical discourse of 109
　inherent globality of writing 110
　internationalization of 119
　modern transformations of 109
　movement in 116–17

nationalistic separations in 114
notion of global space 110
Turkish critique of 111
writing in global context 109–10
Ottoman imperialism 113
Ottoman intellectuals 110
Ottomanism 114
Ottoman legacy 120
Ottoman scholarship, Braudelian impact on 118
Ottoman/Turkish historiography, scholarship in 119
Ousmane, Sembene 240, 246
overcoming modernity 51, 261

Palmer, Robert 82n.41
Pan-African writings 244–5
Pan-Asianism 258
Pan-Islamism 113
Paris international exposition bureau 253
patriarchal dominance 47
patriotic world history 252
periodization 203
peripheral economies 173–4
Pimenta, Joao Paulo 11
plantation labor 148
plausibility 170
plausible story 171
plurality 83, 240
political democracy 255
political modernity 220
Pollock, Sheldon 220
Pomeranz, Kenneth 13, 31
population growth 170
Portugal
　European exploration of 75
　expansion of 72–3
Portus, G. V. 275–6
postcolonial emancipation 218
postcolonial theory, trajectories of 222
postwar historiography historians 263
postwar scholars, works and careers of 51
Prebisch, Raul 11, 75
precolonial institutions 175
precolonial population 175
price convergence tracks 172
professional historians 90
professional historical scholarship 137–8
property rights, theoretical issues of 116
pseudoscientific racism 96
public space 240

quasi-Malthusian 180
Quataert, Donald 116

racism 4
Randeria, Shalini 32

Index

rationalism 251
reciprocal comparison 31
recognition 88
Rediker, Marcus 147
regional histories 2
regional parameters 2
relational history 287
relative autarchy 172
relative autonomy 75
representational relativistic model 237
re-territorialization 98
Rodney, Walter 163
Rosenthal, Jean-Laurent 178
Russian Marxists 255
Russian Revolution in 1905 154–5
Russo-Japanese War 253

Sachsenmaier, Dominic 14, 33
Sanskrit cosmopolitan literary culture 220
Sartori, Andrew 14, 117, 221
scale, scope and scholarship
    central issues and recurring problem 165
    collaborations 165–6
    group research programs based on intellectual affinities 171–81
    institutional groupings 166–9
    national to global in economic history 163–5
    problems of explanation 170–1
Scandinavia, economic historians of 32
SCAP. *See* Supreme Commander of the Allied Powers (SCAP)
scholars/scholarship 24, 68
    in Africa 15
    Eurocentric tendencies in 24
    European-based 22
    historical 1
    intellectual content of 26
    opportunities for 9
second slavery 76–7
self-contained process 147
self-realization 242
semi-periphery 174
Sen, Amartya 31
settler colonies 74
sharecroppers 150
shared explanatory frameworks 170
shared histories 148
Shin, Ch'aeho 45
Shiratori, Kurakichi, 259
Silences in African History: Between the Syndromes of Discovery and Abolition (Delpechin) 239
Sima Qian 128
Sino-centrism 254
Sino-Japanese joint history 264
Sino-Japanese War 253

slaves/slavery 1, 3, 75, 76–7, 79n.8, 151
    rebellions in Barbados 70
    system 71
    trade 70
social development, Marxist scheme of 54
social history 167
socialism 49
social networks 204
social progress, Marxist model of 50
social theory, category in 145
southern theory 272
South Korea 177
    history textbooks of 261–2
Soviet historiography 49
Soviet intellectuals 218–19
Soviet world history 49
spatialization 196
Stalinist historiography 222
Stanner, Bill 269
stereotypes 85
Stern, Steve 76
strikes 148
The Struggle for Freedom (Murdoch) 276
subaltern class 32
subaltern workers 151, 154
Subrahmanyam, Sanjay 219
Sugihara Kaoru 53–4
Supreme Commander of the Allied Powers (SCAP) 46

Taiwan 177
    academic journal database 63n.25
    globalization in 59
tea, history of 52
technology transfers, importance of 2
teleology 165
territorialization 196
Thompson's writing 147
time periods 6
Toprak, Zafer 117
trade
    liberalization 173
    unions 148
trading networks, development of 289
traditional authorities 175
traditionalism 117
traditional law 175
traditional teachings 222
traditions 11
transatlantic slave trade 70
transatlantic trade 173, 180
transborder migrations 197
transcultural comparative approach 199
transnational history 28, 29, 33, 35, 57, 258, 273
    in Australia 273–4

www.ingramcontent.com/pod-product-compliance
Ingram Content Group UK Ltd.
Pitfield, Milton Keynes, MK11 3LW, UK
UKHW021904220326
469204UK00008B/181